The Bible for Everyday Life

The Bible for Everyday Life

Consulting Editor

GEORGE CAREY
Archbishop of Canterbury

Organizing Editor

ROBIN KEELEY

WILLIAM B. EERDMANS PUBLISHING COMPANY
GRAND RAPIDS, MICHIGAN

First published 1988 by Lion under the title
The Message of the Bible
This edition published 1994 by Lion

This edition published 1996 in the United States of America
through special arrangement with Lion Publishing by
Wm. B. Eerdmans Publishing Co.
255 Jefferson Ave. S.E., Grand Rapids, Michigan 49503

Printed in the United States of America

02 01 00 99 98 97 96   7 6 5 4 3 2 1

Library of Congress Cataloging-in-Publication Data

The Bible for Everyday Life
  The Bible for everyday life / consulting editor, George Carey :
  organizing editor Robin Keeley.
    p.   cm.
  Originally published: The message of the Bible. Tring, Herts., England ;
  Batavia, Ill. : Lion Library, c1988.
  ISBN 0-8028-4157-0 (pbk.)
  1. Bible — Introductions. I. Carey, George. II. Keeley, Robin. III. Title.
  [BS475.2.M43 1996]
  220.6'1 — dc20   96-2478
                          CIP

Contributors

Dr Daniel Berkovic, Lecturer, Biblical Theology Institute, Zagreb, Yugoslavia; *Daniel*

Dr John J. Bimson, Lecturer in Old Testament and Hebrew, Trinity Theological College, Bristol, England; *Job, Song of Songs*

The Rev. Paul Burgess, Formerly Warden, Church of Scotland Education Centre, Musselburgh, Scotland; *Acts*

The Rev. Dr. Michael Butterworth, Lecturer in Old Testament, Oak Hill Theological College, London, England; *1 and 2 Samuel, 1 and 2 Kings, Haggai, Zechariah, Malachi*

The Right Rev. Dr George Carey, Archbishop of Canterbury; *Belief features, How to Understand the Bible, The Book of Books, Philippians, Colossians, 1 and 2 Thessalonians, Philemon, 2 Peter, Jude*

Dr David Clines, Professor of Biblical Studies, University of Sheffield, England; *Proverbs, Ecclesiastes*

David V. Day, Principal, St John's College, University of Durham, England; *Belief features*

The Rev. Dr John Drane, Lecturer in Department of Religious Studies, University of Stirling, Scotland; *Tracing Bible Origins* (adapted from *Lion Encyclopedia of the Bible)*

Mary J. Evans, Lecturer in Old Testament, London Bible College, England; *Deuteronomy, Joshua, Judges, Ruth*

The Rev. Thomas W. Franxman SJ., Lecturer in Sacred Scripture, Heythrop College, University of London, England; *The Deuterocanonical books*

The Rev. Dr John Goldingay, Principal, St John's College, Nottingham, England; *Psalms*

The Rev. Dr Richard A. Hines, Lecturer in Liturgical Studies, Oak Hill Theological College, England; *Obadiah, Jonah, Nahum*

Dr Andrew O. Igenoza, Lecturer, Department of Religious Studies, University of Ife, Nigeria; *Jeremiah, Lamentations*

Geoffrey F. Kimber, Formerly Director, Theological Education by Extension, Church of Christ, Nigeria; *Numbers, Ezekiel, Joel, Habakkuk, Zephaniah*

The Rev. Dr Kai Kjaer-Hansen, Author, Formerly Lecturer, Free Faculty of Theology, Lystrup, Denmark; *Matthew*

The Rev. Dr Christopher Lamb, Secretary, Inter-Faith Consultative Group, Board of Mission, Church of England; *Ephesians, 1, 2, 3 John*

The Rev. Gordon McConville, Lecturer in Old Testament Studies, Wycliffe Hall, Oxford, England; *Genesis, Esther*

Melba Maggay, General Director, Institute for Studies in Asian Church and Culture, Philippines; *Galatians*

Dr Enio Mueller, Researcher in Bible interpretation within grassroots communities, Brazil; *1 Peter, James*

The Rev. Dr R. Wade Paschal Jr, Associate Minister, First United Methodist Church, Tulsa, United States; *John, 1 and 2 Timothy, Titus*

The Rev. Canon Graeme Rutherford, Vicar, St John's Anglican Church, Camberwell, Australia; *Luke*

The Rev. Joy Tetley, Examining Chaplain to Bishop of Rochester, England; *Hebrews*

Dr Stephen H. Travis, Director of Academic Studies, St John's College, Nottingham, England; *Revelation*

The Rev. Dr Graham H. Twelftree, Minister, Hope Valley Uniting Church, South Australia; *Mark, Corinthians*

The Rev. Dr Dwight W. Van Winkle, Associate Professor of Religion, Seattle Pacific University, United States; *Isaiah*

Professor Hugh Williamson, Regius Professor of Hebrew, Christ Church College, University of Oxford, England; *1 and 2 Chronicles, Ezra, Nehemiah*

The Rev. Dr Christopher J.H. Wright, Principal of All Nations Christian College, Easneye, Ware, England; *Exodus, Leviticus*

Professor Julio P.T. Zabatiero, Coordinator of Latin America Theological Fraternity in Brazil; *Amos, Micah, Hosea*

The Rev. Paul F.M. Zahl, Rector, St Mary's Church, Scarborough, New York, United States; *Romans*

Contents

Key Beliefs

Charts

Maps

Preface

Millions of people read the Bible; some occasionally, many regularly. Millions more want to know how to read it. There is an endless interest in this ancient collection of books which can speak powerfully to the modern world.

Why read it? If our sole reason is to gain knowledge of Bible times and peoples—to become a kind of Bible quiz expert—then we may miss the point. Its writers intended more than to deepen their readers' knowledge: they aimed to change lives. So to learn what is in the Bible is a vital first step, which is meant to lead on to applying its message to our lives. Only then can the Bible mean something to us personally. We need, in the words of James' letter, to become 'doers of the word, not hearers only'.

The Bible for Everyday Life has been written to help people understand how the Bible is relevant in our own times, and how living by its teaching can make a difference to us. Who is my neighbour, for example, in today's global village?

The contributors have laid the foundation by describing the setting of the sixty-six Bible books, and show how the different books link up with each other. But the emphasis throughout is on relevance. How can the Bible's teaching, written in the ancient world, be validly interpreted so that it teaches us God's principles for living in the varied societies of our own world? This is a crucial question if the Bible is to be fully understood.

It is also a lifetime's task: there is not space here to comment on every verse in the Bible. So the aim is to get the reader started, by giving an overview, with plenty of examples.

The overview is given through the introductions to each Bible book (for example, 'The Message of Genesis'). These explain what each book says and show its general relevance. The outlines serve the same purpose. The features on central Bible beliefs (such as 'God the Creator') take us to the heart of Bible teaching.

The examples are the key passages, about 200 of which have been selected from the whole Bible. These show how to understand and apply the Bible's message today.

This book is offered as an introduction to understanding the Bible today. It is hoped that it will open up the relevance of the Bible's message to a wide readership all over the world, and that as a result many will be shown how to apply their own reading of the Bible to their everyday lives—and be stimulated and excited to do so.

Putting This Book to Use

The Message of . . . Each book of the Bible is explained to show its setting and to give some hints on how to apply its message today. Read this first, before going on to key passages in that book.

Key Passages For all but the smallest books, passages have been selected which are key both to understanding that Bible book and to seeing how it works out in the modern world. Study these with your Bible open at that passage. Then you may want to go on and use the same principles for other passages in the same book.

Key Beliefs 48 of the most important beliefs in the Bible are explained and applied for today.

Outline These are included for nearly all Bible books. They give a bird's-eye view of each Bible book as a whole. The key passages, and other passages, can be put into their contexts using these outlines.

How to Understand the Bible

George Carey

'The Bible is like a wide river in which lambs may splash in the shallows and elephants may swim to their hearts' content.' So said Pope Gregory the Great long ago, and he was quite right. The Bible does indeed have the resources to feed the most junior disciple and nourish the greatest saint.

But the Bible, like a great river, is rather forbidding at first glance. We find ourselves asking: How do I get into it?

How may I understand the different parts of this vast book? Are there basic principles to guide me?

WHAT KIND OF WRITING?

The Bible has a very complex history that arches over more than a thousand years, culminating in the story of the growing Christian church. It is more a library than one single book. In fact, it

Getting the Message

People who read the Bible regularly should find it makes a practical difference to their lives in the world. And yet the books of the Bible were written many centuries ago, in very different times.

What was the original meaning?

The Bible writers were not shut off from the world they lived in. They were part of their culture, and they often wrote about the historical events of their time. To understand thenm, we need to find out about this background. Most of the information can be quarried from the Bible itself—Kings and Chronicles for the prophets, Acts for Paul's letters, for example. The articles in this book will be helpful in setting the scene and summarizing information.

Can I apply this meaning today?

Some things have not changed. Teaching on prayer, for instance, can be understood exactly as it stands. And God does not change. But what of justice in a world of international trade agreements? And how, in today's global village, would Jesus answer the question, 'Who is my neighbour?' The principles we find in the Bible must be applied carefully to the societies we live in. We need to know the Bible and know our own world—and love both.

How can I put it into practice?

Steps one and two can be done in our heads. But we need more than a change in our thinking—we need changed lives. This happens in our hearts, as we accept God's grace to help us and in our wills, as we obey the teaching we have understood. The Bible writers were God's messengers; to obey their teaching is to obey God.

consists of sixty-six books containing many different types of literature.

Clearly, then, our understanding of what we read will depend on what type of book or writing it is. For example, when we are reading a psalm, we should bear in mind that the Psalms are a body of spiritual literature with human emotions of anger, despair, hope and faith expressing the honest feelings of the people of God. It is not surprising that millions of people have found the Psalms a wonderful vehicle for worship and faith. Many depressed people have found the words of Psalm 38 fitting their own feelings exactly, and without having to find words of their own have used its language to speak to God: 'I am worn out and utterly crushed; my heart is troubled, and I groan with pain. O Lord, you know what I long for; you hear all my groans.' Or if you are bursting with joy and happiness, try the splendid words of Psalm 98: 'Sing a new song to the Lord, all the earth!' But it would be a mistake to build up carefully constructed doctrines from the Psalms, because that is not their purpose.

Similarly, the history books and stories should be interpreted according to their own categories and not pushed beyond the obvious

Understanding a Bible Passage

How can we take this teaching about understanding the Bible and apply it to a particular passage? Are there general principles that may help us become better students of the Bible? The passage chosen is Luke chapter 10 verses 38 to 42; it is about Jesus' friends Martha and Mary.

As Jesus and his disciples went on their way, he came to a village where a woman named Martha welcomed him in her home. She had a sister named Mary, who sat down at the feet of the Lord and listened to his teaching. Martha was upset at all the work she had to do, so she came and said, 'Lord, don't you care that my sister has left me to do all the work by myself? Tell her to come and help me!'

The Lord answered her, 'Martha, Martha! You are worried and troubled over so many things, but just one thing is needed. Mary has chosen the right thing, and it will not be taken away from her.'

At first sight the meaning of this little story seems very plain. Many preachers speak of it as though it is about two types of woman, one very spiritual and the other very practical and down-to-earth. But there is more to it than meets the eye, as we shall see.

First, we must put these verses in context. Are there any other Bible passages which bear on this one? Either our existing Bible knowledge, or a commentary, or a cross-reference in our Bible will point us to another story about this family, in John chapter 11. The place was Bethany, a few miles from Jerusalem, and these two women had a brother called Lazarus, whom Jesus was to raise from the dead. From the sound of it, Martha and Mary were close friends of Jesus, and perhaps he and his disciples called on them frequently and received generous hospitality.

Now, to our second question: What is the story about? There are two central characters involved, Martha and Mary. Let's deal with Martha first. What kind of meaning they convey. So before we attempt to find spiritual meanings in the text we will first want to know what would have been the original meaning had we been living at the time. The same will be true of the prophetic books; it helps a lot to know the background, and where each prophet fits in the history told in Kings and Chronicles.

The Gospels are a particular kind of history, focussed entirely on understanding the meaning of Jesus' life, teaching, death and resurrection. And the letters, again, will become much more meaningful to us if we can see how

they fit into the story of the early Christians, part of which we can read in the Acts of the Apostles.

A brief account of this kind of historical background can be found in this book, in such pieces as *The Message of Isaiah.*

UNDERSTANDING THE MEANING

Look at the boxed feature, *Understanding a Bible Passage.* What are the steps we must take to get from a first reading of those verses to making them practically helpful in our daily lives?

---

impression do we get from the story? She was probably the elder sister because she is mentioned first and the house is said to be hers. She may have been a fairly blunt and direct sort of person. She was getting fed up catering for twelve hungry men on her own—and she was going to sort her sister out! But there is one curious feature. Why doesn't Martha say to her sister: 'Eh, Mary. It isn't fair that you spend all your time listening to Jesus. Give me a hand, will you?' She does not say this, but brings her complaint to Jesus, which suggests that the story is about something more than a dispute between two sisters.

So let us look at Mary. Perhaps she is the less practical of the two women. But that is not the key factor here. Look at the phrase, 'Mary, who sat down at the feet of the Lord and listened to his teaching'. There she was, with the disciples, at Jesus' feet. Now the phrase 'at the feet' means to be a disciple. It indicates obedience to one you acknowledge as Lord. So the passage takes on a deeper significance: it is not about two different types of woman at all but about following Jesus. Mary was a follower of

Jesus and was taking advantage of this opportunity to drink in her Master's words. It would have been no use for Martha to say to Mary, 'Oh, for goodness sake, give me a hand with the dishes!' because Mary would have responded, 'Of course, Martha, but first of all let's listen to the Lord's teaching and then we'll do it together.'

What, then, is Martha really signalling? 'Jesus, I am afraid that through your ministry I am losing my sister. You are closer to her now than I am. I don't want to lose her because she is precious to me. Will you please let her go?' And Jesus responds gently: 'Martha, Martha,' (twice for emphasis and expressing tenderness) 'your life is crowded by too many things. There is only one necessary thing, which Mary has chosen, and that is following me. I am certainly not going to deprive her of the most wonderful thing of all.'

If you look on to John chapter 11, you will see that Martha herself has moved on a long way in her discipleship and seems to make her own acknowledgment that Jesus is the Lord. In verse 27 she says: 'I believe that you are the Christ, the son of God.'

■ **First, put the passage in its context.** What happens before and after these verses? (The whole of this part of Luke is about what it means to be a disciple.) What else does the Bible tell us about these people, or about this particular belief? (See the 'Key Beliefs' section, for example *God the Creator.*)

■ **Next, look at the main characters and the significance of what they are saying.** Martha and Mary each had important words to say. So did Jesus.

■ **Then try to draw out the central teaching of the passage.** We saw that it was all about discipleship and following Jesus.

■ **Finally, we need to go on and apply the story to our particular situation.** To this we now turn.

APPLYING THE BIBLE TO OUR LIVES

The Bible is God's message to us, intended to shape our living and thinking. How many of us have said after a difficult or painful situation, 'I have to admit that I did not call upon the resources of the Bible then'? There are three things that will make us better at applying the Bible practically:

■ **We need to carry out daily Bible reading into our daily life.** Take the Mary and Martha story as an example. We saw that it was about a follower of Jesus and 'sitting at his feet'. So, in whatever situation today—at home, at school, at work, wherever—I must constantly ask

what it means to be a disciple of Jesus there. Does it show in my thoughtfulness towards others; my speech and attitudes; the character of my life?

■ **We can draw strength from the Bible in the problems and situations we enter.** How do we face unemployment, severe illness, the prospect of dying, anxiety about members of our own families? At such times the Bible is a wonderful comfort, support and strength because it brings to us all the resource of God himself.

A very good friend of mine, Joan, died of cancer a few years ago. Her attitude towards her own death was an inspiration to us all. Her secret was that she took the Bible at its word. She trusted in Jesus, applied the rich message of the Bible to her daily life and was not found wanting when she had to face up to her own death.

Another friend, John, had been a Christian for only four years when he was made redundant. He had no job to go to and he experienced the soul-destroying experience of searching for work without success. But from the first he said, 'God is my heavenly Father. He will not fail me. I will continue to trust him and I know that something will turn up.' But for months nothing did turn up and when it did the job was not as well paid as his previous one. A particular passage that helped John was Matthew chapter 6 verses 31 to 33. 'Jesus said, "Do not worry, saying, 'What shall we eat?' or 'What shall we drink?' ... your heavenly Father knows that you need them. But seek first his kingdom and his righteousness, and all these things will be given to you as well." ' John made this passage his armour and clung to it when things were tough and he and his wife got discouraged. His testimony today is that God carried him through, and his faith grew strong and more confident.

■ **It helps if we listen to what God is saying through others.** We cannot live the Christian life on our own: we need Christian fellowship, which is where the church comes in. It often helps to read a Bible passage with Christian friends, who can each bring their own encouragement, experience and insights to one another. God often uses the sermon in church, too, to encourage and challenge. So listen carefully, asking in prayer beforehand, 'Is there a special word for me in this address?'

There are some practical tips which help us grow in understanding and applying the Bible. A good translation with clear print is essential. There are many excellent versions on the market these days and it may be advisable to ask someone from church before buying a Bible. Once you have decided on a certain version, it is worth sticking with it. Also, it is important to be regular in our reading. Better a little study regularly than an enormous and impressive onslaught once a month.

The message of the Bible is as vital today as when it was first written. It is worth becoming practised and skilled at understanding what the Bible means.

The Book of Books

George Carey

Christians regard the Bible as uniquely inspired by God. But others, not Christian, also set a high value on this book. Thomas Huxley, a nineteenth-century agnostic and evolutionary pioneer, said of the Bible: 'This book has been woven into the life of all that is best and noblest in Western civilization.' Of course the language of the Bible has penetrated Western culture, but Huxley meant more than that. The Bible has changed the lives of countless individuals, and through them has had a profound influence for good on our moral and cultural life. This influence now spreads out far beyond the West.

Where has this unique power come from? Christian churches agree that the Bible is inspired by God and authoritative for life and belief. Why?

We must begin with the book itself. The Bible we hold in our hands is really a library of books—thirty-nine in the Old Testament and twenty-seven in the New. (Strictly speaking we should be calling them Old and New Covenants rather than Testaments.) The first part—the covenant, or agreement, God made with the Israelites—is the Bible of the Jews. Only the second part can be called 'Christian' in the fullest sense, because these books were written by convinced Christians.

It is a matter of resentment among many Jews that the Christian church has taken over their sacred writings and made them part of our 'canon', or list of inspired books. But the remarkable process by which this took place began entirely through the impact of Jesus Christ. The whole Bible clusters around him and we must go back to his life, death and resurrection to trace those steps which led to the Bible acquiring the authority it has today.

JESUS AND THE BIBLE

Jesus was a Jew, of the tribe of Benjamin and of the house of David. He grew up in Nazareth as a devout Jew and was apprenticed to his father's trade. He drew no attention until in his early thirties he left his work, announced the coming of God's kingdom, gathered followers around him, spoke with exceptional fire and force and performed miracles of healing. After a mere three years his career finished brutally on a cross. Yet within a very short time his followers were everywhere saying he had risen from death, and broadcasting the coming of his kingdom. A century after Jesus' birth, the Christian faith had penetrated every level of society.

How does all this about Jesus link in with the Bible?

■ **Jesus loved the Old Testament.** For him the Old Testament was the holy word of God and the centre of his faith. He was brought up to love it and read it daily. But even here Jesus' remarkable authority can be seen. He did not simply accept it and submit to it like any other ordinary believer; he handled it as if he were its author and creator. 'You have heard that it was said . . . but I tell you . . .' is a familiar refrain in the Sermon on the Mount. This attitude to the Law played no small part in his ultimate condemnation: according to the temple officials he had cotmmitted blasphemy by his arrogance, acting with an authority as if he were an equal to the sacred writings.

■ **The first Christians used the Old Testament.** After Jesus' resurrection the first Christians continued to worship with other Jews and during this period they tried to explain how the Old Testament writings pointed ahead to him. Most probably relevant passages of the Old Testament were drawn together and began to be circulated as a separate document which the Christians used as a tool to convince fellow-Jews.

■ **Stories about Jesus were collected.** Alongside the use of the Old Testament as witness to the claims of Jesus, stories about him were written down and circulated. People were anxious to know about his teaching and his miracles. Eventually many of these accounts found their way into the Gospels which bear the names of Matthew, Mark, Luke and John, acquiring an authority equal to that of the Old Testament.

■ **Apostles wrote letters,** and a final development took place when these letters, from such Christian leaders as John, James, Peter and Paul, were accepted by the second generation of Christians as inspired by God. This was only to be expected. The fast-growing churches needed authoritative guidance and it seemed quite natural to give to the apostles of Jesus an obedience they would have given him.

Thus by the end of the first century the shape of the New Testament was more or less what we have now. Although it was not until AD363 that the church gave final and official approval to a canon, to all intents and purposes the form was already fixed.

So within a few decades of the start of the Christian church an important position had been reached. Both Old and New Testaments were regarded as the word of God. This whole collection of books was **inspired** by God, **revealed** God's full salvation and was the church's **authority** for true Christian faith and practice.

THE INSPIRATION OF THE BIBLE

The word 'inspiration' means 'God-breathed'. It comes from the belief that every human being has his or her lungs inflated by God's breath at birth, and that at death one's breath is given back to him. Heroic figures like the prophets were thought to have been inspired with a fuller burst of divine breath than ordinary mortals. Logically then, the sacred writings must have received a special inspiration, because they came from men specially inspired by the breath of God. So Paul reminds Timothy that the Old Testament was inspired by God and is 'useful for teaching the truth, rebuking error, correcting faults, and

giving instruction for right living'
(2 Timothy 3:16).

Inspiration, then, was the means by
which the Bible gained God's authority.
But what is the meaning of the rather
different idea of 'revelation'? Here we
are thinking of *what* God communicates
to us rather than simply how he did it.
God in his revelation made certain
things known to us through the inspired
writers.

This distinction is crucial to get hold
of, for the following reason. The
Christian believes that everything in the
Bible is inspired, but not everything has
the same importance as revelation.
Some parts of the Bible reveal God more
fully and more clearly than others. Take
two books, Leviticus and the Gospel of
John. Both are inspired. But it is quite
obvious that from the viewpoint of
Christian truth John's Gospel is far more
important as revelation than Leviticus.
Yet both are crucial to the unfolding
drama of salvation. The story grows
from somewhat undeveloped ideas of
God and his ways in the early parts of the
Old Testament, on to the clearer
teaching of the prophets and into the full
light of the New Testament.

The point of **revelation** is that the
Bible witnesses to God's salvation in
Christ. The whole purpose of
inspiration is that this process should
be effective. The Holy Spirit inspired the
writers of the different books, and he
continues to use them as tools through
which he makes Jesus Christ known and
builds up the Christian family. The Bible
is not the only tool by any means. God
ueses preaching, fellowship, the
sacraments and other means of grace to
bring people to himself. But the Bible is
the main artery of inspiration which

links us today with God's word first
spoken. We can be sure that his
revelation in the Bible can be relied on
because the Holy Spirit inspired the
human writers to record a reliable
account of what God did in history and
what his will is.

As intelligent people we are bound
sometimes to wonder, 'Are all the Bible's
words inspired? Does its inspiration
include issues such as human history
and how the world began?' A full answer
to these questions would take us beyond
the scope of this book. But we need to
keep the following guidelines in mind:

■ **Remember what the Bible is about.**
It is not a comprehensive
Encyclopedia of Life but a book about
God and his great offer of salvation. It
is such a remarkable book that we are
tempted to use it to explain
everything in life or even as a kind of
'railway timetable', but this is false to
what it is. For example, the Bible is
supremely indifferent to the
question, 'How was the universe
formed and made scientifically?' Its
attention is on the fact that God
created it for his glory.

■ **Remember the divine and human
elements in the Bible.** They jostle
side by side. The Holy Spirit used
human beings, and he did not
suppress their humanity as he did so.
So not surprisingly we find evidence
in their writings that these were
people of their own times, and we
shall need to take such cultural
factors into account when we read
the Bible. This does not in any way
undermine their value for us, but
reminds us again that the Bible is a
historical book. The Holy Spirit of

God used ordinary people in particular times and places to be channels of his marvellous revelation.

AUTHORITY

The authority of the Bible stems not from itself but from its author. It has authority because it is God-inspired. But what kind of authority does the Bible possess?

It helps to distinguish **external** and **internal** authority.

■ **External authority** is possessed by a person because a recognized group in society has given him or her power. So our friendly neighbour may don his uniform and become our friendly police officer—with an authority which is official and external.

■ **Internal authority** rests in the quality either of an impressive life or of acquired knowledge. For example, millions of Indians during Gandhi's lifetime regarded him as their guru and 'authority'. They paid attention to his words and example. But for most of his life he possessed no external authority at all. Within the Christian church we could say that the authority of a bishop is external whereas that of a saint is internal.

Transferring this distinction to the Bible, it is clear that the authority of the Bible is almost totally internal. Of course, the church regards the Bible as authoritative, yields to it and wants its members to believe it. But this cannot be imposed—it has to be accepted. The enquirer has to be convinced that this book is what Christians claim. If it does not bear the seal of God's signature there is no reason why you or I should accept it or give it our allegiance. Yet down the centuries millions of people who have read the Bible, anxious to find the living God of whom it speaks, have found him. And this has led them to recognize that in this book lies the authority not of human beings but of God. The Bible has an authority which consists not in learned words but in transformed lives—a 'gospel-authority', which is 'God's power to save all who believe'.

Tracing Bible Origins

John Drane

What does the Bible say—and what does it mean?

To understand the Bible fully we must answer these two questions—and the process of doing so is called 'biblical criticism'.

In this context, criticism does not mean fault-finding, but, as in literary studies, it refers to thorough analysis of a particular piece of writing, examining its language, thought patterns and concepts. Biblical critics, far from trying to undermine the Bible's message, are actually trying to understand and explain it in all its possible ramifications.

WHAT DOES THE BIBLE SAY?

This may seem an odd question, for with the Bible in front of us it seems perfectly obvious what it says. Yet the very fact that we can read a Bible that makes sense in our own language is itself a tribute to the endeavours of past generations of biblical critics.

The New Testament was written in Greek, and the Old Testament mainly in Hebrew, with a few pages in Aramaic. To understand what the Bible says, we need to have a good grasp of these languages. Nobody today speaks any of the Bible languages. The modern languages called Hebrew and Greek both differ significantly from their predecessors in Bible times. New Testament Greek is different even from that used by classical thinkers like Plato, writing only a few centuries before the time of Jesus. Discovering the exact meaning of the Bible languages includes the study of history and culture as well as strictly linguistic considerations.

There is another piece of detective work to be done, too. Our most ancient Greek and Hebrew texts are copies of yet older copies, and all the oldest copies were made long before the invention of printing. Scribes wrote them by hand, often in difficult conditions—and they occasionally made mistakes. They often wrote from dictation, and sometimes heard the words wrongly. Even when copying from other written manuscripts, an ancient scribe would occasionally miss out whole sections of text. Or if a previous reader had made comments in the margin, they might sometimes be copied into the text as if they were a part of it. Then, on top of that, groups of people with a particular message to put over might occasionally introduce deliberate changes in order to provide 'biblical' evidence in support of their point of view.

■ **Textual changes.** The first part of the job of the biblical critic is to discover as accurately as possible what the Bible writers actually wrote. This form of investigation is often called 'textual criticism', because it is concerned with establishing the text of the Bible as accurately as possible. It is also occasionally called 'lower criticism', because it forms a foundation from which we can go to ask other questions about the Bible's origins and meaning ('higher criticism').

There are literally thousands of Bible manuscripts, some of them written within a generation or two of the original authors. They are written on all sorts of materials, and vary from virtually complete Bibles to mere scraps. When we put these alongside ancient translations of the Bible into languages like Coptic or Syriac, and then take account of the many quotations in the writings of the early Christians, our knowledge of the Bible text is really enormous and far more extensive than what is known of any other book from the ancient world.

Konstantin von Tischendorf (1815–74) was one of the first to realize the importance of such textual study. In a monastry at the foot of Mt Sinai, he discovered what is still one of the most accurate ancient manuscripts: Codex Sinaiticus, written in Greek about AD350, and containing the whole New Testament as well as much of the Old. Following this, he and other scholars—notably B.F. Westcott (1825–1901) and F.J.A. Hort (1828–92)—established rules for assessing this mass of documentary material, and ensured that our modern versions of the Bible are based on the most reliable texts possible.

■ **Bible languages.** Other important discoveries are helping us to understand the exact meaning of the Bible languages. Our knowledge of the Hebrew Old Testament has been immeasurably enriched by the discovery of the Dead Sea Scrolls, with examples of Hebrew texts several centuries older than any previously known. Inscriptions found in Jerusalem have also cast light on the way the language was used during the Old Testament period.

The Ras Shamra texts, written in Ugaritic, a related language, have shed a new light on many obscure Hebrew expressions. Since these texts concern religious topics, much of their imagery has had a direct bearing on our knowledge of Old Testament Hebrew.

Texts written in Hellenistic Greek also shed new light on the New Testament books. We now know, for instance, that Paul's letters were not literary 'epistles', but personal letters written between friends. In both language and structure, Paul's letters are strikingly similar to many letters written on papyrus sheets by ordinary people at about the same time.

All these things have expanded our understanding of the actual words of the Bible, and thanks to the work of biblical critics we now have a much better idea of what the Bible says.

WHAT DOES THE BIBLE MEAN?

Here the answers are far less certain—partly because of the nature of the question. For it is really two questions: What did it mean—then? and, What does it mean—now? In theory, biblical critics have tried to keep them separate. But it is not so easy, and quite often what particular people think the Bible means *now* will affect the way they view its meaning in its original context. This so-called 'higher criticism' inevitably must be a good deal more subjective than 'lower criticism'.

Every part of the Bible comes to us today as part of an alien culture. We are not the same even as ancient Greeks or Romans—let alone ancient Canaanites or Egyptians! The way they thought and wrote needs to be interpreted and re-formulated if it is to have the same impact on us today.

Also, the Bible is not just one book. It is a whole library. Moreover, the Old Testament is a national archive, and its assorted parts were variously used at different periods.

The book of Psalms has many references to the king who ruled as God's agent in Jerusalem. Before the exile, these were hymns of celebration in the worship of the temple. But later, when the monarchy had disappeared, they were understood in a different way, and even in the Bible itself we can see signs of a reinterpretation of them.

The same phenomenon is present in the New Testament, though on a shorter time-scale. The Gospels inform us about the teaching and life of Jesus. But they were also part of the preaching of the earliest Christian churches—and what their teaching meant in the church was not necessarily exactly the same as it meant in Galilee at the time of Jesus.

The story Jesus told about the lost sheep, for example, has two meanings given to it: referring to the work of the evangelist who goes to those who do not know God (Luke 15:1–7), and also to the work of the pastor caring for those who are already followers of Jesus (Matthew 18:10–14).

■ **Sources.** Biblical critics have come to see that part of understanding the Bible is asking where it has come from. How were these books written? Who wrote them—and why? Knowing what an author is doing is not of course the same thing as understanding what is being said. But if you know how the material is tackled, then you have a better chance of appreciating what the author is getting at.

A modern author—especially of history or biography—may use several sources, which will be reinterpreted and incorporated into the work. The Bible writers were just the same. Luke categorically tells us this is how he wrote his Gospel (Luke 1:1–4). And the Old Testament also has many references to sources that are either consulted or quoted (Joshua 10:13; 1 Kings 11:41; 1 Kings 14:19, and so on).

It has been the work of *source critics* to try to identify some of these materials. In 1924, B.H. Streeter expounded a view of how the first three Gospels were written that is still widely held today. Matthew and Luke, he said, copied Mark's Gospel almost word for word, supplemented with selections from another document containing Jesus' teachings (called Q), together with various other materials. His theory has stood the test of time largely because we still have Mark's Gospel, and we can check whether and how Matthew and Luke used it.

The work of other source critics has been less durable, like that of Julius Wellhausen (1844–1918), who argued that the first five books of the Old Testament were composed out of four different sources, each one more advanced in theology and morals than its predecessor: J (950–850BC), E (850–750BC), D (621BC) and P (450 BC). He believed that the author of the books of Genesis to Deuteronomy operated with scissors and paste to join together various bits of these documents to make a coherent whole.

Further knowledge about ancient methods of writing, and a general discrediting of the idea that human history has moved from savagery to sophistication, have put serious question-marks against Wellhausen's reconstruction of Old Testament history. But most biblical critics would still accept that the search for sources of many of the Bible books is a valuable way of getting at its message.

■ **Contexts.** Some of the Bible books existed in spoken form long before they were written down, and other critics have tried to explore these oral forms.

Form critics base their findings on the fact that in the ancient world the actual literary form of a piece can often indicate the way in which it was used. Careful application of this insight by Hermann Gunkel and others shed valuable light on the way the Psalms were used in Israel's worship; while people like Rudolf Bultmann and Martin Dibelius have helped us to see how the Gospel stories were used in the life of the early Christian communities.

This approach has often been associated with extreme scepticism about the historical value of some parts of the Bible. But that is not an inevitable outcome of form criticism itself: it is rather a by-product of the theological position of some of its practitioners.

■ **Authors.** None of the Bible writers was a mere recorder of materials handed on from others. They all interpreted their materials, explaining their significance for their own readership. Like any other authors, the Bible writers had their own perspective, and the way they tell a story can often show us what that perspective was. The modern search for it is called *redaction criticism.*

In the study of the Gospels, for instance, we can often learn a good deal about the diversity of life and thinking in the early churches by comparing the different ways the four Gospel writers recorded the life and teaching of Jesus. And the same is true in the Old Testament, especially the history books and the messages of the prophets.

Biblical criticism has been with us now for a couple of centuries, and there can be no doubt that it has made a valuable contribution to our understanding of the Bible and its message. Much of it is painstaking— even tedious—and there have been many false trails and blind alleys. But it is an essential tool in biblical exposition. Whether or not we agree with the ever-changing theories of the experts, every modern reader has much to learn from them. Finding intelligible answers to the questions which biblical criticism raises will help to apply the Bible's message more fully to our own life experience.

The Old Testament

The Old Testament Library

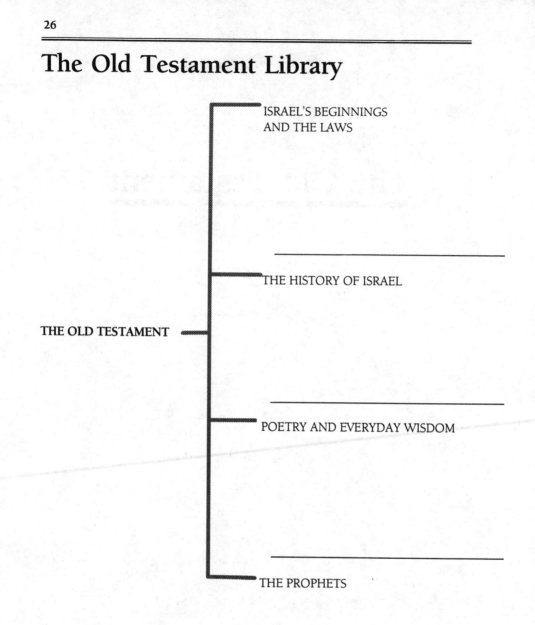

THE OLD TESTAMENT

ISRAEL'S BEGINNINGS
AND THE LAWS

THE HISTORY OF ISRAEL

POETRY AND EVERYDAY WISDOM

THE PROPHETS

The Deuterocanonical Books

Great stories of God creating the world and rescuing humanity are interlaced with basic laws. Laws of creation, in early Genesis, give unshakeable principles of how things were made to be—marriage, humanity in creation, work and rest... The Ten Commandments are a timeless foundation for morality. But what of the many priestly laws, civil laws, laws for family and society? Though reflecting a very different world, they embody principles about God and human life which we can apply in our own times.

Genesis
Exodus
Leviticus
Numbers
Deuteronomy

This is a special kind of history, with God as the central figure. In Deuteronomy, blessing was promised for people who obeyed his laws and judgment for those who did not. The history books often show this happening—for kings, often for whole nations. Can we apply these stories of God's special people to our own personal, national and church lives? Yes. It always leads to disaster when people disobey God.

Joshua
Judges
Ruth
1 & 2 Samuel
1 & 2 Kings
1 & 2 Chronicles
Ezra/Nehemiah
Esther

Psalms are poems, full of beautiful imagery. Their themes are God, worship and people's joys and griefs. We can identify with the writers and often read from their world to ours. Job, Ecclesiastes and Song of Songs are about perennial issues: suffering, the meaning of life and sexual love. Proverbs applies God-based common sense to everyday life—family, friendship, society. Unpack the cultural covering and human nature emerges unchanged.

Job
Psalms
Proverbs
Ecclesiastes
Song of Songs

A prophet's main task was to bring God's message to the people of his time; foretelling the future was secondary. Prophets called their contemporaries back to God and his ways. So to understand their message we must know something of their historical background, which we can find in the books of Kings and Chronicles. Then we can grasp their central concerns—as, for instance, justice for the downtrodden—and see how they can work out in our own world.

Isaiah
Jeremiah
Lamentations
Ezekiel
Daniel
Hosea
Joel
Amos
Obadiah

Jonah
Micah
Nahum
Habakkuk
Zephaniah
Haggai
Zechariah
Malachi

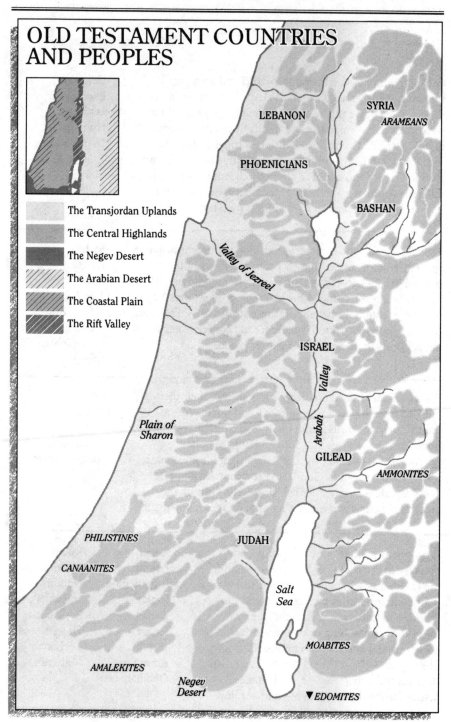

OLD TESTAMENT COUNTRIES AND PEOPLES

The Transjordan Uplands
The Central Highlands
The Negev Desert
The Arabian Desert
The Coastal Plain
The Rift Valley

LEBANON

SYRIA
ARAMEANS

PHOENICIANS

BASHAN

Valley of Jezreel

ISRAEL

Valley

Plain of
Sharon

Arabah

GILEAD

AMMONITES

PHILISTINES

JUDAH

CANAANITES

Salt
Sea

MOABITES

AMALEKITES

Negev
Desert

▼EDOMITES

OLD TESTAMENT TOWNS

Sidon

Zarephath

Tyre

Damascus

△ Mt Hermon

Dan

Hazor

Lake of Chinnereth

△ Mt Carmel

Mt Tabor △

Shunem ● Endor

Megiddo

Ramoth-gilead

△ Beth-shan

Mt Gilboa

Dothan ● Jabesh-gilead

Great Sea

Tirzah

Samaria ● Penuel

△ ● Shechem Mahanaim

Mt Ebal △

Mt Gerizim

River Jordan

● Joppa

Shiloh

Bethel Rabbah

Mizpah ● Ai Gilgal

Gibeon ● Jericho

Kiriath-jearim ● Michmash

Ekron ● Gibeah Shittim

Ashdod ● Jerusalem

Beth-shemesh △ Mt Nebo

Libnah Makkedah ● Bethlehem

Ashkelon

Lachish ● Mamre

Gaza ● Engedi

Hebron Salt Sea

Gath River Arnon

● Ziklag

Beersheba

Ar

Kadesh-barnea ● Ziph

River Jabbok

The Message of Genesis

Gordon McConville

There are certain important questions which every nation and civilization has asked. How did the world begin, and does it have a purpose? Is there a God, and is he interested in *me*? It is because Genesis gives answers to questions like these that it has become so deeply influential in the understanding of both Jews and Christians. It lays the foundations for the Bible's answers to these universal human concerns.

And so it begins at the beginning, with creation. There is a beautiful simplicity about Genesis chapter 1.

It tells of God making and then ordering the various parts of creation. Its message in brief is threefold:

- The world as God has made it is good.

- There is a very special place in this world for humankind. God appears to take special thought before making people. Male and female, humanity is in God's 'image'. In some important way we are like God, and specially called into a relationship with him.

- Humanity has a special duty to exercise responsibility over the rest of the created order. This seems to be part of what it means to be in God's image.

This view of creation has more impact than many realize on the way in which modern people think. The goodness of the world explains why we can feel that many of life's most natural pleasures—human love, good food, absorbing hobbies—are wholesome and right, when not abused. Humanity's creation in God's image underlies the belief, usually unquestioned, that people have an inborn dignity which is somehow sacred, and it explains the outrage which is so widely expressed whenever there are serious breaches of human rights.

The commission to be stewards of the creation is the origin of another modern belief which all would think natural, namely that the world is open to scientific enquiry. It is ironic that so many today think science is in conflict with Genesis, when it is Genesis itself which gives us a mandate to explore the world God made, in order to know and enjoy fully the blessings which he intended for humanity.

But the creation is fallen. The nature of our world is only half explained with this first chapter. There is another set of questions still unanswered. Why are human relationships so often characterized by tension and distrust, even cruelty? Why is life hard and painful for so many? Why do children, and the innocent, suffer and die? Why must *anyone* die? Chapters 2 and 3 narrate a powerful story which points to the answers.

The story is well known. We now have a particular man and a particular woman, who apparently have it within their grasp to live in harmony with God indefinitely, but lose that opportunity because they are induced to do the very thing which God has forbidden. The result is a disruption in all those relationships which were brought into being in humanity's creation. The man and the woman are at odds (3:12). They together are at odds with the rest of the created order, as shown by their enmity with the serpent and the difficulty with which they will henceforth have their living from the soil (3:17–19). Above all they lose the immediate relationship with God which they had evidently enjoyed. They go out from the garden into a hostile world.

The story of humanity's fall, therefore, not only explains the presence of human sin in the world, but also accounts for every kind of disharmony, disease and trouble. In the world that was good, everything held together; in the world which sin has entered, everything has fallen apart.

The rest of Genesis is the beginning of the story of the mending of the broken world. It brings bad news and good news, stories of judgment and of salvation.

- There is judgment because that first experience was extremely serious in its effects. Sin does not stop with Adam and Eve. Rather it gets worse. Their firstborn, Cain, introduces murder to the world and his descendant Lamech makes of it both a habit and a boast (4:23–24). God looks down on the evil on the earth and resolves to make an end of all that he has made (6:5–7). The consequence is the flood story (6:9—8:12), in which that ordered act of creation in chapter 1 is put into reverse, and the earth with its creatures sinks below the waters from which it had first emerged. The flood shows that a sinful world is under the judgment of God, and that theme of judgment remains a basic part of the message of the Bible until its last page.

- But there is salvation too. For Noah sails above the flood, and the world goes on. And this is God's decision. Along with judgment goes his will to save, to make something yet of his world, and to enjoy at last and at whatever cost that relationship with humanity for which he created us at first. After the flood, all those parts of creation which had drowned appear again in their old places. So there is to be a new start. The rhythm of the seasons will continue into unseen generations (8:22). There will not again be a universal flood. God has decided to persevere with the world, and the humanity, he has created. Indeed he makes a 'covenant', a kind of solemn undertaking, that this will be so (9:11).

Yet the first part of Genesis ends at chapter 11 on a low note. The events at Babel leave humanity in fragments, scattered over the earth, dividing into nations speaking different languages, which will become marks of distinction and then hostility. The world goes on, but it does so under a shadow.

Yet now God does something entirely new. He makes a promise.

A family sets out from the 'deep South' of Mesopotamia, near the Persian Gulf, and settles at Haran in the north. One of its sons is Abram. There is nothing special about him yet. Like the rest of his family he worships many gods, the gods of the region from which he has come.

Suddenly he is confronted by the God of all creation, with the command to leave his extended family; and he is given a promise (12:1–3). He will become the father of a great nation, which will have a special relationship with God. Because of that nation, all the nations of the world will be blessed. This, then, is how God has chosen to save his chaotic world. Abram, and in him the nation of Israel yet to come, is chosen, not to keep God's blessings to himself, but to restore the lost harmony of the first creation for all humanity.

The promise now becomes the theme of the remainder of Genesis. After Abram it comes to his son Isaac (26:2–4), then to Isaac's son Jacob (28:13–14; 35:11–12), and finally to the next generation, the fathers of the twelve tribes of Israel themselves (48:3–6). The story of 'the patriarchs', as these forefathers of Israel are called, is really the story of this promise. By the end of Genesis it is on its way to fulfilment, for when Jacob takes his sons to Egypt to join Joseph there, he already has seventy descendants. The story, then, speaks of God's faithfulness. Humanity, however, is proving hard material to work with, and the progress is slow and painful.

Abraham (as he became) and his descendants stand at the beginning of God's work of re-making humanity. It is hard for us to picture what their understanding of God was like. In some ways they seem intimate with God, talking to him as if he stood beside them (see 18:1). On the other hand, they do not have much information about who he is.

Typically, God is named by association with the patriarchs themselves (the God of Abraham, Isaac or Jacob). When he later makes himself known to Moses by name as Yahweh (Exodus 6:3), he says expressly that he did not reveal this to the forefathers. Certainly there are as yet no regular institutions devoted to his worship, nor is there a revealed law. God is still slightly aloof. This may explain why there are a number of decidedly curious encounters between God and the human actors—such as Jacob's struggle with 'a man' at the river Jabbok (32:24).

Abraham's faith, in these circumstances, is all the more remarkable. Later generations could point back to so much that God had done for them in their past. But when Abraham was told to leave Haran he had no guarantees based on past experience. When he lifted the knife over his own son—the one by whom the promise of descendants was at last to be fulfilled—he showed an astonishing faith in God's good purposes for him (chapter 22). So often, indeed, it looked as if the promise simply could not be fulfilled. Yet Abraham believed, and because of his faith, God accepted him as 'righteous' (15:6).

Genesis, therefore, poses the vast problem of human sin and failure, and begins to unfold God's response to it. It leaves many questions yet to be answered. But it introduces themes which will become familiar as we turn the pages of the Bible:

- The love of God, outraged but undeterred when people fail.

- Human sin, always finding new expressions, whether in the twistiness of Jacob or the conceit of Joseph.

- But faith too, that essential element in the developing relationship between God and human beings.

THE CREATOR
Genesis 1:1—2:3

This beautiful chapter quite simply introduces us to God. The words 'In the beginning...' tell us nothing about the when or the how of creation. It is the beginning of God's activity in the universe, and the words show at the same time that God himself had *no* beginning. It is taken for granted that he was just there.

Certain other things are taken for granted also. God is personal; he thinks and speaks. Regularly we read here: 'And God said...' Because for many readers these words are so familiar, it is easy to miss their real impact. The basis is laid here for the belief throughout the Bible that God can communicate with his creatures about himself, the world and them. This has not been obvious to all people in every generation, to people in the twentieth century perhaps least of all. But the God of the Bible seeks above all to make himself known to his creatures. The rest of the Bible is the story of how he does so, despite the reluctance of those creatures to hear him.

The account is concerned with the orderliness of the creation. Everything has its place: light is separate from darkness, waters from land, the creatures from each other. There are creatures that belong in the sea, and others on land. Everything is 'according to its kind'. God is not removed from the world, nor has he any rivals in it. All the creation, animate and inanimate, is fully under his control. And there is purpose in it, because God is purposeful.

This chapter, then, is probably more important than any other in the Bible for giving us our basic understanding of who God is. He has made a good world (even if we have impaired that goodness). And he has made humankind in his 'image', with the intention of blessing us. How right it is to worship the Creator, to pray to him and to put our trust in him.

(For other important lessons in this chapter, see *The Message of Genesis*.)

FREEDOM TO CHOOSE
Genesis 2:4–17

After the first passage has spread before us the orderliness and grandeur of creation, we come 'down to earth', as it were, with a man in a garden. Shortly he will have a woman to keep him company, but there are matters to be settled before that.

The garden has the stamp of that goodness of creation of which the previous chapter spoke. The description of Eden is one of plenty and delight. We should not press the geographical details too far, in fact history and geography do not enter into it; it is not that kind of story. The point rather is to picture the man in his created innocence.

His innocence, indeed, is the great issue. There are two trees in the garden: the first is the Tree of Life, which somehow stands for the immortality to which the man has been born; the second is the Tree of the Knowledge of Good and Evil. With these comes a test. The good life of Eden has a condition attached, namely that the fruit of the Tree of the Knowledge of Good and Evil should not be eaten. Why did God put it there then?

God apparently intended that the man should have a real choice about whether he ate the fruit or not. God wanted him to choose to live in dependence on him. Only in this way could the man remain innocent. This required a certain childlike obedience of him. There was a kind of knowledge which only God should have, and the man must be content not to seek it. He is asked, too, to believe that somehow this is for his good. Indeed, if he chooses to eat he will die (verse 17).

We know, of course, that the man, and the woman, did eat the fruit of the tree. God's verdict is that they have now become 'like one of us', like God, and he puts them out of the garden, so that they should not 'live for ever' (3:22).

In an age when the many perversions of human life are daily borne in upon us, and which lives in dread of a holocaust devised by human ingenuity, it is not difficult to accept that there is a kind of knowledge which it would be better for human beings to be without. Perhaps we can accept too that the limit set on the span of our life in this world is actually an act of God's mercy, preparing the way for a better life to come.

THE CURSE
Genesis 3:14–21

These verses contain God's 'curse' on humanity, on the creatures and on the earth itself. The curse is not God finally casting humanity off—he has never done that. It is rather his response to the man and the woman's abuse of the world which it was their responsibility to respect and cultivate. The sin and its consequences are recorded in the first part of the chapter, where we see that all the harmonies built into the creation have now been dashed. The relationships of men and women with each other, with God and with their world, have all come adrift. And so God now addresses the serpent, the woman and the man in turn.

The serpent appears in the story simply as one of the creatures. When he tempts Eve we are not told why it was that he already had a vested interest in opposing God. Here he is just a creature which has committed evil; as such, he will suffer, and indeed at the hands of the offspring of the human pair. The ferocity of the animal world, and humanity's exposure to it, is thus introduced. The woman will suffer in childbirth, which should have been only joyful, and also in her relationship with her husband. He for his part will now get a hard living from the earth which should have yielded up its produce without resistance. The pleasant garden is exchanged for a hostile earth.

The picture left us by these verses is true to much human experience. There is a hardness in earthly existence known in toil, want, pain and grief. This is not the whole story. Immediately after the 'curse' it is clear that life will continue:

Eve becomes 'the mother of all living', and God himself enters the situation to make it more bearable (3:20–21). Life is not *all* hard; we do know joys as well as sorrows. The picture is of something good that has been spoiled, but still has marks of its goodness upon it.

Genesis chapters 2 and 3 contain the Bible's answer to the question, why is there evil in the world? Humanity's suffering should not be explained away as if it was unreal. But nor is it an irremovable block to experiencing the goodness of God. For the Bible story does not stop with a curse. The God who sees his world fall into disobedience and pain also takes it on to a glorious restoration.

AFTER THE FLOOD
Genesis 8:20—9:17

In the days before the flood, God had found that the thoughts of people's hearts were evil through and through (6:5). It was for that reason that he had resolved to make an end of the thing that he had begun. The flood has now subsided, Noah and his family have found dry land again, and give thanks to God for their rescue (8:20). They do so by means of a sacrifice, and we are told in picturesque language that God is pleased. God will never again curse the ground because of humanity, and the reason is surprising—because people are evil! Yet this was the reason why he had set out to destroy humanity in the first place.

There is something odd about the result of the flood, therefore. Noah may have 'found favour' with God (6:8), but that does not mean that God set out to rescue only good people. In fact after the flood people seem to be just as bad as ever. It is not long before Noah himself goes and gets drunk (9:21). So what does it mean that 'Noah found favour in the eyes of the Lord'? Surely that even in deciding on the flood God was resolving to save some people from it. This would be purely out of his love for them, because they had shown that they could not deserve to be saved.

In our passage, therefore, the flood is behind, once and for all. Soon the rainbow will come as a guarantee that there will be no such thing again (9:12–17). For us this means that God will never simply give up his declared aim to save humankind. It means too that God is in control of all the power that is within his creation. There can be no 'accidental' end to the world. It will come in God's good time.

A FAILURE OF FAITH
Genesis 12:4–20

Abram has now received the promise of God that his descendants will possess the land of Canaan. The story goes on as he arrives in the land, sees it for himself and hears the promise repeated. Shechem and Bethel are places which will become very important in Israel's later history, and it is as if Abram stakes a claim for his descendants by building altars and spending some time there.

There follows one of the unhappier incidents in Abram's life. There is a famine in the land of Canaan, and Abram goes down into Egypt—just as Jacob would later do. There, fearing that his own life might be in danger from Pharaoh on account of his beautiful wife

Sarah (here called Sarai), he claims that Sarah is his sister. There is truth in this; Abraham later points out to a different king that Sarah is in fact his half-sister (20:12). However, it is apparent that Abram intends to deceive Pharaoh, and that his motives are less than noble. Pharaoh evidently makes the most of the situation, as Abram knew he would. Yet in a way he comes out of the encounter with more honour than his visitor, when he declares that he would have respected Sarah's true position had he known what it was, and indeed when he sends Abram off without any reprisal.

Abram's great flight of faith in the first part of the chapter is followed, then, by a serious failure to believe God. If God had promised that he would be the father of a great nation, how could Abram doubt that God would protect him, as well as the mother of that nation? Faith has given way to fear, as it will when the person who believes ceases to look to God for reassurance and guidance.

The story of Abram will continue to be a struggle between faith and doubt. (See again the similar incident, involving a different king, in chapter 20.) In Abram's life, faith gained the upper hand in the end. But this did not come without discipline and false starts. The giant of faith is an encouragement to us perhaps as much in his weakness as in his strength.

THE CALL TO SACRIFICE
Genesis 22:1–24

The promise that Abram would have many descendants came down in the end to one vital question—could Abram (now Abraham) and Sarah have even one son? After many trials of the old couple's faith, Sarah at last bore Abraham the boy they so much desired (21:2). Through Isaac the promise would be fulfilled after all.

Imagine, therefore, Abraham's dismay when the call of God comes again, this time to sacrifice Isaac! Abraham responds without question. There is something unbearable about verses 3 to 7 which relate the journey to Mount Moriah. The climax is Isaac's question: where is the lamb for the offering? And his father's reply: God will provide.

We should not try to reduce the pain by imagining that Abraham knew God would not let him go through with it. There are two things to observe about his faith here:

■ **He believed that God is powerful enough to fulfil his promises.** He had given Abraham a son once; perhaps he would do it again. According to Hebrews chapter 11 verse 19, Abraham saw that God could raise Isaac from the dead if necessary. Almost certainly, Abraham was very perplexed by the whole thing, and had no idea what God was doing in it. Yet this man's faith is such that he goes on believing even when the most perplexing things happen. He knew that the road to Moriah was the way of faith, even though he did not see how it could be. To have refused to go would have meant jeopardizing the fulfilment of the promise.

■ **Also, Abraham's faith gave him a simple readiness to give up what was most dear to him,** just because it was God's command that he should.

From the other side of his great act of self-sacrifice, he could see that God's intention all along was to bless him more and to deepen his faith. And he could say with all the more understanding and conviction, 'The Lord will provide' (verse 14).

THE BROTHERS
Genesis 27:1–45

Isaac occupies the stage of Genesis far less than either his father Abraham or his son Jacob. The scene before us is an important one because it concerns the passing of the 'blessing' to the third generation, and thus shows the way in which God's promise to Abraham is to be carried forward towards fulfilment. The stage was already set for this scene when, at the birth of her twins, God showed Rebekah that his favour lay not with Esau but with the younger brother, Jacob (25:23). In that same chapter Esau, grown up, sells Jacob his 'birthright' for some soup (verses 29–34). He is thus depicted as a man of sensual appetite, thinking of immediate satisfaction.

If the birthright gives to Jacob all the rights of the elder brother, the blessing is Isaac's express commission to his son to inherit and carry on the promises made to Abraham. Jacob thus becomes, in this chapter, the next forefather of the great nation which will one day occupy the Promised Land. In doing so he brings God's word to Rebekah to fruition, apparently in spite of Isaac's attempt to win the honour for his preferred son, Esau. Isaac is, therefore, not without blame in the affair, and indeed his reasons for favouring Esau stand little scrutiny (verses 3–4).

However, the manner of Jacob's victory is not edifying. Esau is, in God's eyes, unworthy to become the heir to the promise. But how is Jacob any better? He takes matters into his own hands rather than waiting for God, and his calculated deception of his father shows him to be a natural crook.

In Jacob, more than the other forebears of Israel, is evident the rawness of the material with which God was prepared to work. But God has insights into character and potential which are barred to us. And this is just one of many instances where God's favour comes purely from grace, to the undeserving.

WRESTLING WITH GOD
Genesis 32:22–32

This passage records a strange little incident. Jacob is preparing for a somewhat dreaded encounter with Esau, years after they parted in anger. At the River Jabbok he meets a man who wrestles with him all night. Though the man apparently initiated the struggle, Jacob refuses to let him go. As we read on it becomes clear that this is no ordinary man, but in some strange way, God himself.

Such an appearance of God is unusual even in the Old Testament! The patriarchs lived in a time before more regular ways of meeting with God had been revealed, as they later were through Moses; this encounter belongs to their time. Jacob's cry in verse 30 is due to the belief, widespread in Old Testament times, that anyone who saw God face to face would die.

Yet Jacob had held on to 'the man', and this becomes an important turning-point in his life. He is given a new name, no longer one that hints at his twisty character, but one that records that he has 'striven with God and with men, and won'.

The statement is as curious as the rest of the story. But the essential meaning is that Jacob has obtained from his struggle a new standing with God. He has now fully become the man through whom God will carry forward his plans for the nation. And this nation will bear the new name of its father: not Jacob but Israel.

The change in Jacob can be observed, even though this is not the first time he has met God for himself. Already, in his conversations with Laban, he has acknowledged a real dependence on the God of Abraham and of Isaac for his security (31:42). This struggle, however, seems to be a deeper expression of his need of God.

And in the story as it unfolds further, Jacob appears less as the cheat, manipulating situations, and more as a man trying to follow a course through the fortunes and misfortunes of life.

THE PRICE OF INTEGRITY
Genesis 39:1–23

Joseph, the last but one of Jacob's sons, finds himself in Egypt, sold into slavery by his brothers. Yet he has not found servitude but has risen to a place of honour in the household of an eminent Egyptian. Then comes a test, in the form of temptation to immorality. The story is told to show us what kind of person Joseph is.

He had been a conceited youngster. That was why his brothers came to hate him. Perhaps time has mellowed him, for he is different here.

When Potiphar's wife frames him, his situation is alarming. Once fallen from grace, there would be no limits to the unpleasantness which might follow—as Joseph's fellow-prisoner, the baker, was soon to discover (40:22). The temptation facing him, therefore, is more than the run-of-the-mill lust of the flesh. He may give in to Potiphar's wife just to save himself from the consequences of her displeasure. The stakes are very high, then, when Joseph decides to insist on doing what he knows to be right.

Joseph is, in this story, the model of a righteous man. His chief concern is not to sin against God, though there is also a strong element of loyalty towards the master who has treated him well (verse 9). He is prepared to pay the price for his integrity.

It seems that his fate is sealed, as he joins the other wretches in an Egyptian prison. But the other side of Joseph's faithfulness to God is God's faithfulness to him. Because God is with him even in prison Joseph's qualities earn him respect and a kind of eminence even there. His godliness is of the kind which gains the respect even of those who have no time for God.

This, indeed will become a habit with Joseph, and he will emerge as Prime Minister of Egypt. So a son of Abraham, who was promised that his descendants would be a blessing to the nations, becomes a blessing to this nation at least. And all this stems from the gifts God has given him, and from a resolute integrity.

A FAMILY RECONCILED
Genesis 45:1–15

The tables have turned dramatically on Joseph's brothers. Once they held him in their power, and they made a slave of him. Now he holds them in his, and they must fear for their lives; but he rewards evil with good. His acceptance of them is one of the Bible's great stories of reconciliation and forgiveness.

Joseph, of course, was not seeing the situation only in family terms— even if a reunion with his father cannot have been far from his thoughts. In accepting his brothers he is also concerned that God's greater purpose, for the fulfilment of a promise that would benefit all humanity, should go forward. As one who has stood close to God, he can see the real meaning of the events in which he is participating. He had suffered at the hands of those who wished him ill. Yet the brothers' hatred was only part of the story, for above their sordid dealing, it was God who had brought Joseph to Egypt (verse 8). A little later he could say to them: 'You plotted evil against me, but God turned it into good' (50:20).

In seeing this, Joseph shows himself a worthy successor to his fathers in the faith. His interest in God's dealings with him and his family is not selfish. His point is not just that God has made him rich and famous, nor even only that his family will now be spared the effects of famine in Canaan, though that is part of it. The real point is that in his mysterious way God has ensured through these events that this generation too will enjoy the benefits of the promise to Abraham, and be able in

turn to pass it on to the next.
Interestingly, the promise is fulfilled in
this story not only for the forefathers of
Israel, but also for Egypt. Abraham's
descendants were chosen to be 'a
blessing for the nations' (12:3). In
Egypt's deliverance from famine
through Joseph, that side of the
promise gains a first fulfilment too. But
its real climax must wait many
centuries until the gospel comes at last
to the Gentiles.

The Message of Exodus

Christopher Wright

From Genesis we know that in spite of the mess we have made of ourselves and our world, God intends to do something about both. His promise to Abraham that he would bring blessing to all nations is what gives a purpose to the rest of the Bible's story. That promise had three main points:

- There would be a people—the descendants of Abraham;

- There would be a special relationship between God and that people;

- God would give them a land.

Exodus opens with the first part of that promise fulfilled. The family of Abraham, after all their problems, have at last multiplied into a great nation. But the other two parts are still unfulfilled. Indeed, an enormous barrier stands in the way, for the descendants of Abraham are slaves in the land of Egypt. Having gone there as guests of a friendly Pharaoh, they are now the victims of a tyrant. They have no close relationship with God and certainly no land of their own. So, before God's plan for his people and the rest of the world can move forward, this great obstacle has to be removed.

The first great theme of the book of Exodus is rescue: the liberation of the Israelites from their slavery in Egypt. This is what gives the book its name. 'Exodus' means 'way out', and the first half of the

Exodus OUTLINE

book describes the great escape of the Israelites from Egypt under the leadership of Moses. This remarkable historical event made a terrific impression on Israel. In fact they looked back to it as the foundation of their nation, and Jews celebrate it still today in the Passover. In the rest of the Old Testament, the exodus is regarded as God's greatest act. God, they said, had 'redeemed' them. 'Redemption' sounds religious to us, but it originally meant achieving freedom for someone else at one's own personal cost. In the exodus God did exactly that for his people.

The book of Exodus, therefore, reveals to us the character of the God of the Bible. Not only is he the Creator, as shown in Genesis, but also the powerful, liberating God who breaks into human affairs to establish justice. Today, the cry for liberation and justice is heard on all sides in our suffering world. We can see in the exodus a model of God's passionate concern for the suffering and oppressed, and of his desire that they should be liberated.

The exodus shows us the breadth of God's concern for people. The people of Israel were set free in four different ways:

- Politically—from oppression as an immigrant minority, giving them rights as a free people;

- Economically—from exploitation as cheap labour, giving them 'a land of their own';

- Socially—from state interference in their family and cultural life;

- Spiritually—from bondage to Pharaoh's gods, bringing them to know and worship him as their true and living God.

The exodus was thus not merely liberation *out of* slavery, but *into* a new relationship with God. This new relationship becomes the dominant theme of the second half of the book.

After the exodus and three months' travelling, the Israelites reached Mt Sinai. There, God had his people all to himself at last. So he set about teaching them who they really were and what their role and mission in the world was to be, as his people. (See key passage *God's Purpose for Israel*.) This relationship between God and his people is seen in three ways in the rest of Exodus:

- The covenant. Through a sacrificial ceremony, God bound the people to himself and to each other (chapter 24). God had taken the initiative and redeemed them—by his grace. In gratitude, they were to respond to him in loyalty and obedience.

- The Law. Obedience was to be expressed through keeping the Law, including especially the Ten Commandments (chapters 20—23). The point of the Law was not so that Israel could earn God's favour. Rather it was based on who God was and what he had done for them: 'I am the Lord your God, who brought you up out of . . . bondage.' And then it gave them a practical framework for the way God wanted them now to live.

- Worship. Most of the second half of Exodus is concerned with the construction of the sacred tent and its furnishings. The amount of space it gets shows how important it was for Israel. It was called God's 'dwelling-place', because it was the focus of God's presence among his people at all times. And also, as the place of sacrifice it was where people could meet God, receive his forgiveness, and hear his word as it was taught by the priests.

Exodus, therefore, also reveals to us God actively and eagerly wanting to relate to us as his people. He commits himself to us in covenant promise. He demands our wholehearted obedience. And he meets us in worship. For Christians, all these are facets of our relationship to God through Jesus Christ. His cross is both our liberation and our gateway into the dwelling-place of God.

THE CALL OF MOSES
Exodus 2:23—3:17

The first two chapters set the scene, but the action really begins in chapter 3. The people of Israel are in acute need, suffering from exploitation and persecution, crying and groaning under their bondage. The Bible does not avoid the harsh realities of human life. In fact, it clearly exposes the major cause of such suffering—our own inhumanity to our fellow human beings through deliberate oppression.

But these people are not forgotten. God has a concern for them. He now enters the drama and his character is very clearly drawn. Notice the list of words linked with God: 'God heard... remembered... looked... was concerned'; 'I have seen... I have heard... I have come down to rescue.' This is the primary identity of the God of the Bible, for all this is linked to the revelation of his *name* in this chapter (verses 13–15). So whenever the people of Israel used the name of God, these were the qualities they associated with him—a God who knows and cares about human need. Indeed, all God's dynamic action in the following chapters is triggered off by this concern. And also by his faithfulness to his promise. Centuries earlier, God had made his promise to Abraham (see Genesis 15:12–16). Now he will carry it out fully, for that too is characteristic of him.

In chapter 2 we see that Moses was a man who shared God's concern to protect the weak and exploited from the strong and the cruel. But at first he went about it in the wrong way, and ended up in the desert for many years. Perhaps he spent those years wondering if God had after all forgotten his people in Egypt. His fiery encounter with God at the bush showed him that, on the contrary, God was more aware of their need than even Moses himself, and even more prepared to do something about it. But verse 10 transforms God's concern into Moses' mission. God expresses *his* purpose ('I have come down...'), and then commissions Moses to carry it out ('I am sending you').

This is the way that God calls people to work for him. It is not what we volunteer to do for God (Moses was very reluctant). It is what God is doing and plans to do in his world and how he then invites and fits us into a share in his work.

GOD'S MANIFESTO
Exodus 5:22—6:8

Moses' first attempt to strike a blow for freedom had ended in disaster (chapter 3). Now his second attempt

FROM EGYPT TO THE PROMISED LAND

Escape from slavery in Egypt, a journey through the wilderness, moving into the Promised Land – the story is a great picture of salvation. God rescued his people from soul-destroying bondage and brought them to where they could begin to live out their destiny. The exodus set the pattern for his dealings with people everywhere.

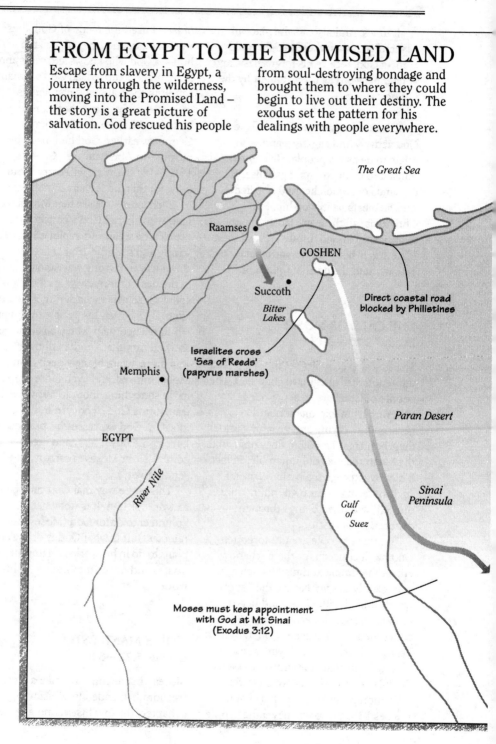

The Great Sea

Raamses

GOSHEN

Succoth

Bitter Lakes

Direct coastal road blocked by Philistines

Memphis

Israelites cross 'Sea of Reeds' (papyrus marshes)

Paran Desert

EGYPT

River Nile

Gulf of Suez

Sinai Peninsula

Moses must keep appointment with God at Mt Sinai (Exodus 3:12)

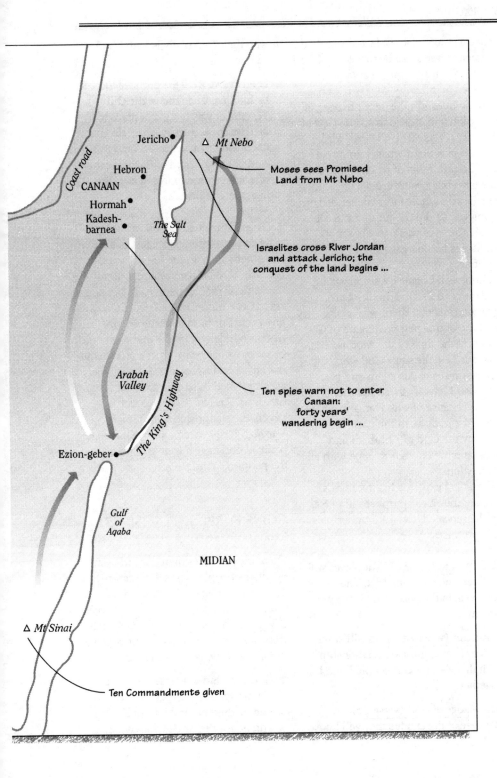

Jericho

△ Mt Nebo

Moses sees Promised
Land from Mt Nebo

Hebron

CANAAN

Coast road

Hormah

Kadesh-
barnea

The Salt
Sea

Israelites cross River Jordan
and attack Jericho; the
conquest of the land begins ...

Arabah
Valley

The King's Highway

Ten spies warn not to enter
Canaan:
forty years'
wandering begin ...

Ezion-geber

Gulf
of
Aqaba

MIDIAN

△ Mt Sinai

Ten Commandments given

seemed a failure also. In fact, things had got much worse since he turned up (see 5:6–21). Typical of most servants of God when in difficulty, Moses runs back to God to question the very purpose of his mission and indeed to accuse God of failure also (verse 22). 'O Lord, why . . .? God, please explain what is going on.' It's a question most of us have asked at some time, but it was a crucial one at this point. Israel's whole future depended on the answer, as did the future of us all.

God's answer was probably more than Moses had bargained for. Responding to the importance of the question, God begins by emphasizing his identity (6:2–5): 'I am the Lord.' Verse 3 means that there was a new revelation of this personal name of God *Yahweh*, at the time of the exodus. 'But,' says God, 'I am the same God who made those promises to Abraham and his family and I haven't forgotten them. So trust me because of who I am and what I have said and done in the past.' God is still today the God of Abraham and Moses, and big enough to cope with all our questions.

Then God explains his intentions. There are four clear purposes in verses 6–8; the repeated 'I will . . .' underlines God's promises:

- **Redemption (verse 6). The slaves will be freed and God will do it. This is the key event in the book. God is the great liberator.**

- **Covenant (verse 7a). God will enter into a special, intimate relationship with them—God and people bound together.**

- **Knowledge of God (verse 7b). Because of the exodus they will know** who their God really is and what he can do.

- **Land (verse 8). This promise too will be fulfilled. The land in the Old Testament was not just a place to live in. It was a place to live a certain *kind* of life in God's presence—a land in contrast to the land of Egypt, a land where they were to live in equality, freedom and justice.**

These four great intentions of God can be traced through the rest of the Old Testament story in the life of Israel. But they can also be seen as a manifesto of God's desire for all people. The exodus stands as a model or pattern of God's answer to our human predicament. God desires our deliverance—that we should be saved from sin and all its effects in our own lives and in society. He has finally accomplished this through what Jesus has done. And he invites us into a covenant relationship with himself. Through Jesus we can know God as he really is, and have our own place among the people of God.

GOD'S PURPOSE FOR ISRAEL
Exodus 19:1–6

Three months after their escape from Egypt, the people of Israel are camped at the foot of Mt Sinai, just as God had promised Moses in verse 12 of chapter 3. What God now says to them sets the scene for the law and covenant which is about to follow. Four points stand out.

- **God's initiative (verse 4).** 'You yourselves have seen what I did . . .' There could be no mistake about it. Three months earlier they were slaves in Egypt; now they were free. God had acted first. Everything that followed was based on that fact.

■ **God's universal interest (verse 5).** God tells Israel that they have a very special place in his purpose, but he still has his eye on the rest of the earth because 'the whole earth is mine'. This is a reminder that the covenant God made with Abraham and his descendants was ultimately for the blessing of all nations. Here and elsewhere, all God's actions in Israel have the rest of the world in mind.

■ **God's intention for Israel (verse 6).** Two phrases express what God wants Israel to be—phrases which are also applied to the church in the New Testament: 'a priestly kingdom and a holy nation'.

A priest was someone who stood between God and the rest of the people. On the one hand he represented God to the people by his life and example, and by teaching the Law of God. Through the priest, people would *know* God. On the other hand, the priest represented the people before God by bringing their sacrifices to the altar. Through the priest, people would *come* to God. So God says to the whole community of Israel: 'You will represent me, my character and my salvation, to the rest of the world. And through you I will bring all people to myself.' That is true priesthood. It is still the job of the people of God in the world today.

Holiness means 'set apart' or, simply, being *different*. Israel's holiness among the nations did not mean they should shut themselves away, but that they should be a different kind of people—in every practical way reflecting the character of God. Leviticus 19, for example, shows that holiness included every aspect of life—social, family, economic, political, judicial, racial and so on. God's people are called to be visibly different from the rest of the world. 'Priestly' and 'holy' sound very pious, but in fact they are practical and down-to-earth because they describe the identity and function of God's people in the world.

■ **God's condition (verse 5).** How were the people of Israel to live up to such a high calling? Only if they would live in loyalty to the covenant and in obedience to God's Law. Keeping the Law was not so that God would save them, for he had already done that! It was so that they could now go on to be what he wanted them to be in the midst of the nations.

THE TEN COMMANDMENTS
Exodus 20:1–17

The Ten Commandments are like a policy statement setting out basic areas of behaviour for God's people. The statement begins with a statement, not a command. God reminds Israel of what he has done. These ten commands are not just general moral principles, but specific instructions for the people whom God has redeemed and who know him as their God. They, above all, are to live in this way.

The first four commandments set out our duty towards God and the last six relate to relationships with our fellow human beings. Each is essential to the other.

If we look at the commandments in the context of what Israel had just experienced, it helps us see their very practical relevance.

■ **Only one God.** Now that their living God had proved his reality in the exodus, Israel must have no other gods.

■ **No idols.** Since God is living, active and speaking, he is not to be compared to or represented by any lifeless, dumb image.

■ **God's name is precious.** Now they know the power of his name; they must not misuse or squander it. It stands for the person of God, so to dishonour it by word or life is to dishonour him.

■ **The sabbath.** Released from slave labour, they must protect a day of rest. This is specifically given for the benefit of workers—the Old Testament has great concern for conditions of employment. It is still a valid principle.

■ **The family.** Freed from the bad effects on their family life of Egypt, they must respect the authority of the family structure.

■ **The sanctity of human life,** so ruthlessly violated in Egypt, is to be upheld.

■ **Marriage.** Human sexuality is part of the image of God in us, and infinitely precious. Marriage—the basis of the family—must be protected, both for the stability of the family and the whole of society.

■ **No stealing.** Theft was forbidden, not because property is 'sacred' in itself, but because it is part of the world God gave us to share in honesty and integrity.

■ **Total honesty.** Freed from injustice, they must protect truth, especially in legal cases, because without it, the whole community and its values would collapse.

■ **Contentment.** The inner motives of the heart matter too, for that is what leads to success or failure in all the other commands.

SIN AND FORGIVENESS
Exodus 33:1–6, 12–23

All seemed to be going well now. The Israelites had been rescued from Egypt. They were physically safe and adequately fed. God had given them the Law and they had willingly agreed to obey it and keep their side of the covenant (chapters 20—24). Now Moses was up Mt Sinai receiving plans for the tent which would embody the relationship between God and his people (chapters 25—31). At that point, disaster struck.

The people conclude that Moses and his God have abandoned them, and they fall straight into idolatry and revelry (32:1–6). They make a golden calf and worship it instead of worshipping God. They break the commandments they had promised to keep.

God's first reaction is recorded in chapter 32 verses 7–10. Understandably, he gives vent to his anger against a people who can promise one thing and break it within a month. He proposes to destroy them, and to start again with Moses himself.

In the following verses, Moses does not try to excuse the people. Rather, he reminds God yet again of his promise to Abraham. What would happen to that if he destroyed Abraham's descendants? Moses' prayer shows that he knew what was closest to the heart of God. God's promise to Abraham had the whole world in view. That was the mission of Israel. Moses would not envisage God aborting his own mission in such a way.

In chapter 33 verses 1–3, God responds to Moses' prayer by agreeing to fulfil his promise to Abraham. The people will be spared (though after punishment), and they may go up and take the land he had promised. But God *himself* would not go with them. Most of us would have been satisfied with the 'let off' and rejoiced at such an 'answer to prayer'. But not Moses.

With incredible boldness, Moses tells God that such a partial answer is not good enough (verses 12–16). Just as he had 'reminded' God of the Abraham covenant, now he also reminds him of the Sinai covenant, established only a month before. Israel would be God's special people and he, their God, would always be with them. So Moses throws the responsibility back to God— 'Remember that this nation is your people.' As a result, not only did Moses have a fresh experience of God's glory and presence, but God wholly restored the covenant (chapter 34), and the story could move on.

These chapters teach us two fundamental truths. First, our relationship with God is not only started from his side, but it is sustained only by his forgiving grace and faithfulness to his own promises. Second, we can be bold in prayer when we appeal to God's own promises and intentions.

The Message of Leviticus

Christopher Wright

Leviticus gets its name from the fact that it consists mostly of laws and regulations that concerned the priests, who were from the Levite tribe. But although it is a book of laws, we should look at it in the context of the Pentateuch—the first five books of the Bible.

It comes while God's people were camped at Mt Sinai, after the exodus and before they moved on to the conquest of the promised land. This 'view both ways' puts these laws in perspective.

- They were based on what God had already done—by rescuing them from Egypt.

- They will enable the people to live in a way pleasing to God when they move into the promised land.

Exodus 19 tells us that God calls his people to be a *priestly* and a *holy* people—features which are found in the two main divisions of Leviticus. Chapters 1—16 are mainly concerned with the priests—their sacrifices, ordination, practical health, duties, and so on. Chapters 17—26 are mainly concerned with the holiness of the people in every aspect of life. When we remember that Israel was a priestly and holy people in order to fulfil their mission as God's own people in the midst of the nations, we can see that Leviticus, for all its rules and rituals, fits into that purpose.

The people of Israel needed to stay in close contact with their God. But how

could they do so if sin got in the way?

The Levitical system of priesthood and sacrifices provided a way of restoring and maintaining the relationship between the people, or an individual, and

Leviticus OUTLINE

1:1–16:34   A priestly people

1:1–7:38   Regulations for sacrifices and offerings

8:1–9:24   The ordination of Aaron and sons to the priesthood

10:1–20   The death of Nadab and Abihu

11:1–47   Clean and unclean food

12:1–15:33   Laws of cleansing: women after childbirth; people, houses or objects in cases of infection or pollution

16:1–34   The Day of Atonement

17:1–27:34   A holy people

17:1–16   The sacredness of blood

18:1–30   Unlawful sexual relationships

19:1–37   Practical holiness in the social community

20:1–27   Laws against idolatrous and sexual practices

21:1–22:33   Special rules for priests and their families

23:1–44   Special feasts and festivals

24:1–9   Lamps and loaves in the presence of God

24:10–23   The stoning of a blasphemer underlines the holiness of God's name

25:1–7   The sabbatical year on the land

25:8–22   The jubilee year

25:23–55   Economic justice

26:1–46   Blessings and curses

27:1–34   Rules about dedication of people or objects

God. Through the blood of sacrifice, the guilt and uncleanness of sin could be covered over (the literal meaning of 'atoned for'). A blood sacrifice was a costly and painful thing, which pictured for Israel the seriousness of sin in the sight of God. The New Testament, especially Hebrews, sees in this a picture of the final sacrifice of Jesus, 'the Lamb of God', on the cross. The shedding of his blood achieved atonement of eternal and universal value.

The second part of the book is concerned with practical holiness of the people. The keynote is 'You shall be holy, because I, the Lord your God, am holy' (19:2), with the explanatory addition, 'I have set you apart from the nations to be my own' (20:26). Holiness certainly included a variety of 'religious' regulations—such as rules for priests' families (chapter 21), and various popular festivals (chapter 23). But it was also very practical and down-to-earth, applying to family life and sexual morality (chapters 18 and 20), social and community living (chapter 19), and national economic affairs (chapter 25).

The message of Leviticus is that no area of life—from secrets of the heart to public and social actions and policies—stands outside God's concern or can be considered irrelevant to our commitment to him as our covenant God.

THE COMMUNITY LAWS
Leviticus 19:1–37

This chapter is an excellent example of the Old Testament's concern for the whole of life. It mixes 'sacred and secular' in a way which shows that there was no basic distinction between them

in the way the Israelites thought. All life was lived before God. This had a powerful impact on the New Testament. The 'second greatest commandment in the law' according to Jesus, was quoted from this chapter (verse 18), and his teaching echoes the force of verse 17 onwards.

In the verses below it is worth comparing the same laws in Deuteronomy which are fuller in giving reasons.

■ **Remember the poor** (verses 9–10; see Deuteronomy 24:19–22). Put the rights of the poor above the right of private ownership. It may legitimately be *my* land, *my* property. But ultimately it is God's.

■ **Pay wages promptly** (verse 13; see Deuteronomy 24:14–15). Uphold the rights of workers. Untold misery could be spared for millions in our world if they were paid justly.

■ **Uphold justice** (verse 15; see Deuteronomy 16:18–20). Justice is basic to the health of any human society. Once that is corrupted, there is little hope for fairness in any other part of life.

■ **Be responsible towards other people** (verses 16–18; see Deuteronomy 19:15–20; 22:8). Care for the interests of others. In India, a steady toll of human lives is the price of faulty construction work and neglect of safety regulations (both tolerated by bribed officials).

■ **Treat everybody equally** (verses 33–34; see Deuteronomy 24:17–22). Uphold the right of aliens, immigrants and ethnic minorities.

Equal rights according to the law of the land apply to all. 'Love him as yourself' calls for even more.

■ **No cheating** (verses 35–36; see Deuteronomy 25:13–16). Total honesty in the market-place. No false measures. This can be applied to both the shopping basket and international economic trade.

Many Christians say they are inspired by the teaching of the Sermon on the Mount. Few of us have yet begun to live by the values of this 'sermon' on Mount Sinai, when we seriously reflect on the implications of this chapter.

THE JUBILEE
Leviticus 25:8–55

The land was God's greatest material gift to Israel and proof of his faithfulness to his promise to Abraham. But it was still his land (verse 23). The Israelites, like tenants, had no absolute ownership of it, but were accountable to God as 'landlord', to share it fairly and use it justly. Their responsibility to God for their land is similar to our responsibility to God for the earth itself. So the principles which underlie the jubilee laws can be applied more widely.

■ **Social concern.** Israelite society was based on its system of extended families or households, every household having a share in the land as 'tenants'. If a family became poor and lost its land, or its members became slaves to pay off their debts, the jubilee in the fiftieth year was to release and restore them to their original inheritance (verses 35–43).

The jubilee encourages us, in any community, to work towards the goal of social freedom and economic independence for family units (which will vary in size and nature in different cultures). The questions we should ask about the laws and policies in our own societies is: do they promote the *whole* welfare of families, in economic as well as 'moral' terms?

■ **Economic concern.** The jubilee aimed to ensure that as many families as possible had land, by preventing the wealthy few from building up large estates. As well as the regular restoration of land, it also required financial support and employment for poor people in the years in between (verses 35–40). The majority of revolutionary conflicts in today's world seem to be fought over land-reform and the unjust distribution of resources. The jubilee in no way encourages violence, but it does major on the fair sharing of land. Ownership by a privileged few and agricultural bondage for the rest is no part of God's intention for human life in his earth.

■ **Spiritual concern.** The jubilee was mainly concerned with the economy, but it also contained spiritual values— trust in God's ability to provide (verses 18–22); the remembrance of their escape from Egypt (verses 38, 42, 55). It began with national confession and forgiveness on the Day of Atonement (verse 9). And it gave the people hope, as a symbol of the release and restoration that God has promised to bring to both humankind and his earth.

The Message of Numbers

Geoffrey Kimber

Dry statistics (from which this book gets its name), weird worship regulations, ancient stories of the meanderings of desert folk. Are these your immediate impressions as a modern reader of Numbers? Yet each of these three ingredients—statistics, regulations and stories—can teach us a great deal.

Numbers is the third part of a close-knit sequence starting in Exodus with God's liberating Israel from slavery in Egypt, going on through Leviticus, and bringing the Israelites by the end of Numbers to the borders of the Promised Land.

For the Israelites of later years, the statistics were the equivalent of the family photograph album. They were also a constant reminder that God had kept his promise to Abraham to make his descendants into a mighty nation. The regulations told them how God, who had liberated their ancestors, wanted them to behave towards each other and towards him. The stories both reminded them what God is like in action, and warned them what they themselves could become if they did not heed God.

We look back on all this across a gap of some three thousand years. We will only make sense of it if we realize that in all that time God's essential character has not changed at all. Human nature has not changed that much either! The Israelite problems with pride, envy and lust are still ours today.

For us, the regulations demonstrate

Numbers OUTLINE

1:1–12:16 The Israelites at Sinai

1:1–2:34 Population statistics and camp layout

3:1–4:49 Levite statistics and their duties

5:1–6:27 Regulations about purity and justice

7:1–89 Statistics of dedication offerings

8:1–10:10 Setting up the worship centre

10:11–12:16 Journey narrative: three sins of grumbling

13:1–21:35 The Israelites at Kadesh

13:1–14:45 Narrative: the Israelites fear to enter Canaan

15:1–41 Regulations about offerings

16:1–17:13 Narrative: Dathan's rebellion

18:1–19:22 Regulations about priestly duties and cleansing

20:1–21:35 Journey narrative: more grumbling; some enemies defeated

22:1–31:54 The Israelites on the plains of Moab

22:1–24:25 Narrative: Balaam and his four prophecies

25:1–18 Narrative: Israelites seduced into pagan worship

26:1–65 Statistics of second census, forty years on

27:1–23 Narrative: Joshua chosen to succeed Moses

28:1–30:16 Regulations about offerings, feasts and vows

31:1–54 Narrative: Israel's vengeance on Balaam and the Midianites

32:1–36:13 About the Promised Land

32:1–42 The land east of the Jordan

33:1–56 Recap of the journey so far

34:1–35:34 Boundaries, Levite cities, cities of refuge

36:1–13 Female inheritance regulations

above all that God is holy. For us, holiness is a very difficult idea to grasp. God's holiness is a little bit like the heart of a nuclear reactor. If you approach it unprepared, you will die. The Israelites, like us, were unprepared both in their characters and in their actions. They were unsuited to approach a holy God.

God's kindness is shown in that he provided special people, made holy through ceremonies he laid down, to approach him on behalf of the whole nation. These were the priests and their associates, the Levites. Their tents physically surrounded the tent of meeting to prevent unauthorized entry. They mediated with God for the people, presenting their gratitude and repentance to him through sacrifices. They also intervened with God when he was angry with his people, re-establishing good relationships (this is known as 'atonement'). The New Testament has done away with the need for these regulations of Numbers. God is still holy. But Jesus Christ has gloriously fulfilled the roles both of priest and of sacrifice. He died like the sacrificial bulls in our place, gaining forgiveness for our sins. Like a priest, he mediates between us and God, so that in his name and through his sacrifice we can approach God, and find peace with him.

We see in Numbers that God is angry with those who approach him arrogantly, those who are envious, rebellious, immoral or who do not trust him. The New Testament points out that these stories are written as warnings for us, too. Yet through it all, God who began their liberation had a continuing, loving purpose to bring them to the Promised Land.

For us also today, he has plans to liberate us from the oppression of sin and to make us a people who can fulfil his purposes.

THE REWARD OF UNBELIEF
Numbers 13:1—14:45

Why did the Israelites spend forty years wandering through a desert which even in their days traders could cross in a week or so? The answer lies in this passage.

God had brought his people to the edge of the Promised Land and now told Moses to send twelve spies to check out the benefits and obstacles that lay ahead. All twelve brought back a true report—great benefits but also formidable obstacles. The dispute arose over the conclusion. The majority considered the task impossible. Only Caleb and Joshua applied their past experience of God to this new situation and presented their minority report: we can do it—with God.

What is the opposite of faith? It is fear. This fear spread through the camp, wiping from their memory all God had done in the exodus, producing complaints, anger and rebellion.

Moses had once more to stand before an angry God on behalf of an angry people—a sort of religious barrister—pleading guilty but arguing for clemency, not because Israel deserved it but because of God's glory and reputation. God heard his prayer and reduced the sentence from capital to custodial—forty years in the desert. They were not ready for their own land yet: they had so much still to learn.

Like them, we need to learn how to trust God, so that our faith may grow large enough for tomorrow's obstacles. Faith is a dynamic, effective thing: a vehicle for progress, not a monument to rest beside. If we have no ambition to move on, and nothing to be fearful about, then in many ways we have no need of faith.

We learn, too, about prayer for ourselves and for others. It is hard work, perhaps thankless, yet it is crucial. Moses did not achieve all he asked for but God gave him enormous concessions through his prayer.

The ending of the story, as the people tried too late to enter the land, illustrates the dangers of half listening to God, and half obeying him. The Israelites thought that they could do today on their own what God had wanted to do with them yesterday. It was the first day of their forty-year training course, and already they were in trouble again.

THE REWARD OF FAITH
Numbers 21:4–9

I wonder how many Israelites would have had the courage to follow Moses out of Egypt if they had known what lay ahead. It is a question we can ask ourselves about our own journey of faith.

It is easy to criticize the Israelites in the desert as a whining bunch of children. We need to remember that they seem to have obeyed Moses quite thoroughly over all the regulations in Numbers and to have moved camp faithfully when God called them without prior warning.

We often fail God, not in the major decisions of life, but in the day-to-day minor events. The Israelites reached this crisis-point in reaction to their daily diet. The pattern of grumbling, plague, intercession, relief—which comes so often in Numbers—was once more acted out.

But this time there was a difference. God sent snakes. Snakes mean little to people living in temperate climates, but in many parts of the world the word 'snakes' has the same kind of heart-freezing effect as 'AIDS' or 'cancer'. There must have been panic in the camp.

There was another difference, too. When Moses prayed to God for the people, God did not take the snakes away, nor provide miraculous cures. His answer helped only those with faith. Moses was told to make a bronze snake and raise it on a pole and everybody who looked at this snake would be healed. Easy! No sacrifices, no effort, just look. I used to assume that everybody looked and got healed. Now I am not so sure. In the general panic of being bitten, I wonder how many doubted whether just looking at a bronze snake would really help in such an extremity. After all, snakes were the source of the trouble. How could another snake be the cure?

John's Gospel looks back on this incident to help explain Jesus' death. Jesus on his cross became like that snake—a reminder of something awful that we shudder at. Our problem is sin; the result is fatal at a spiritual level. Jesus bore God's curse on sin so that we might be free from that curse.

The Israelites had to look at a snake to be free from snake poison. We have

to trust a man who died to be free of
death. Easy at one level, and yet many
have found it profoundly difficult and
humbling. They have hesitated and
agonized long before taking that step
of faith.

In this story all who looked at the
snake lived. But how many looked?

The Message of Deuteronomy

Mary Evans

Most countries and most organizations have a constitution, whether written or unwritten, setting out the principles on which they run. Deuteronomy, set out in the form of speeches given by Moses not long before Israel entered Canaan, the Promised Land, is the nearest the people of Israel had to a constitution. It is similar to the kind of international treaty document used in the ancient Near East when treaties were made between powerful nations and weaker, usually conquered, neighbours. Protection was given in exchange for agreement to certain demands. This document introduced the partners to the covenant,

Deuteronomy OUTLINE

1:1–3:29 Historical introduction

1:1–18 Moses' first speech begins and leaders are appointed

1:19–46 The Israelites rejected the spies' message; God refused them entry to the land for forty years

2:1–3:11 Desert wanderings: encounters with various local nations

3:12–29 The land east of the Jordan is divided: the end of Moses' mission

4:1–8:20 First summary of the Law

4:1–49 God, the only sovereign Lord, chose Israel: the Law comes from him

5:1–33 The Ten Commandments

6:1–25 The Law is for real life. It cannot be kept unless everybody knows it

7:1–26 The Law cannot be kept alongside other traditions

8:1–20 Obeying God brings blessings, but do not forget they come from God

9:1–11:32 God's choice of Israel

9:1–6 Chosen, but not because they were righteous

9:7–10:11 They were always rebellious

10:12–11:32 What it means to belong to God: the reasons for loving and obeying him

12:1–26:15 Laws for life and worship

12:1–13:18 Worship God alone, in the place he appoints

14:1–29 Food for a holy people; God's share of the harvest

15:1–23 A generous lifestyle

16:1–17 The three annual feasts

16:18–18:22 Rules for judges, kings, Levites and prophets

19:1–21:23 Matters of life and death, murder and war

22:1–25:19 Miscellaneous laws, family and business life

26:1–15 Giving to God, the Levites, and the poor

26:16–31:29 Covenant commitment

26:16–19 A two-way relationship

27:1–28:68 Blessings and curses

29:1–30:20 Commitment is serious, but worthwhile and possible

31:1–29 Moses hands over to Joshua; the Law is read, Israel's rebellion predicted

31:30–34:12 Moses' final messages

31:30–32:43 A song for Israel

32:44–47 A solemn declaration and a plea

32:48–52 Final preparations

33:1–29 Final blessings

34:1–12 The end of an era

described what had happened so far, listed the demands, outlined the benefits of keeping the covenant, the punishment for breaking it and instructions for keeping a copy and explaining to future generations what it was all about. The covenant—the special relationship—between God and his people described in Deuteronomy uses this pattern, though it is adapted to take account of a unique understanding of God.

The key to this particular covenant is relationship. The book of Deuteronomy shows how much God wanted people to relate to him. The covenant makes such a relationship possible and shows how it can be worked out. Israel's covenant Lord is the great Creator God, King of the whole universe, who is holy, pure, just, loving and awesome. He chose Israel to be his people, to relate to him and also to represent him in the world. He loved them as a father loves his child, giving them tremendous compassion and care and also discipline.

He wanted them to respond to him, not slavishly keeping the Law out of fear, but turning to him in love and gratitude.

At the beginning of the book, Moses reminds the people what God has done for Israel. God is fully involved with them, actively at work to free them and bring them out of Egypt, and protecting them in their desert wanderings. This provides clear evidence that God keeps his promises and will continue to take care of them. The rest of the book looks forward to the working out of their future relationship.

God is holy, and so Israel as his people also had to be holy, otherwise the rest of the world would get the wrong idea about what God was like, thinking it did not matter to him how people behaved.

The covenant requirements, given in the Law, explained what it meant to be God's people and showed how they could be holy. The blessing and prosperity given to those who kept the covenant was not simply a reward for keeping the Law but the inevitable result of living as God's people; the greatest blessing was being in relationship with him. The judgment and disaster which would come to those who broke the covenant was not vindictive retribution, but the inevitable result of turning away from God.

The requirements of the Law involved every part of life. The regulations cover anything from dealing with serious criminal offences like murder or rape, to apparently trivial points like allowing a passing walker to eat grapes from a vineyard but not to take any away. There are rules about relations between bosses and workers, the correct way to worship, money management, and the right kind of diet. These rules involve both individuals and the nation as a whole. There is no distinction between religious and secular regulations. If his people were to represent God and show the world what he was like, they had to do so all the time in every area. The concept of the church—God's people today—keeping its nose out of business or politics and sticking to religion is nonsense as far as Deuteronomy is concerned.

Being in a relationship with God today may not mean keeping the Israelite Law, but it still involves living in a way that reflects God, showing the rest of the world what God is like and doing so wholeheartedly, because we love him.

COVENANT COMMITMENT
Deuteronomy 6:1–25

In chapter 5, the Israelites are
presented with a neat summary of the
Law, usually known as the Ten
Commandments. But Moses' speech
goes on to insist that these were for
keeping, not just quoting. The Law was
not only for specially religious days or
for specially religious people; it was for
real life, for every day and for
everybody. But the Law could not be
kept unless everybody knew what it
was. And it was unlikely to be kept
unless the ordinary people understood
why they should keep it and what
benefit they would get out of it.
Chapter 6 uses a pattern of reverse
repetition to make sure that these
points are driven home:

A. Reasons for keeping the Law
(verses 1–4)

B. What is involved in keeping the
Law (verse 5)

C. Make sure you remember
(verses 6–12)

B. What is involved in keeping the
Law (verses 13–17)

A. Reasons for keeping the Law
(verses 18–25)

A. The Law is to be kept because God has
commanded it, and he, the unique Lord,
who rescued their ancestors and has
promised to look after their descendants, is
worth serving. Keeping the Law will bring
them long life, prosperity and victory over
their enemies.

B. To keep the Law means total
commitment. All their energy is to be put
into loving, honouring, trusting and
obeying God alone.

C. To remember the commandments,
and the God who gave them, God's people
are to recite them, debate them, teach them
and generally soak themselves in them.

Relating to God is not a hobby, like
taking up stamp-collecting or jogging; it
is a total lifestyle. It means giving him
wholehearted and unswerving loyalty
all the time, putting time and effort into
finding out what he wants and letting
what he wants be the priority in family,
business and social life.

THE COVENANT GOD
Deuteronomy 10:12–22

It mattered that the people of God
understood that the covenant was not just
a business arrangement. It meant both
relating to God and representing him, and
it involved family ties. This chapter
reminds them again of who God is.

God is supreme, greater than anyone
could possibly imagine. The whole
universe belongs to him; in comparison
to his power, human rulers are nothing
(verses 14, 17). But this great God loves
Israel and has committed himself to
them. They are to belong to him as his
special people (verse 15).

God is not only great, he is also just,
absolutely fair. He cares about people,
especially those who have no one else to
look after their interests. His love is not
limited to Israel, for he also cares about
the foreigners who live with them
(verses 17 to 18).

If God is so great, no wonder his people, Israel, were encouraged to stand tall and take pride in belonging to him. If God is like this, and has chosen Israel, surely he is worth all the worship, love, service and loyalty they can possibly give him. And if God cares so much about justice and about making sure that immigrants and one-parent families are properly looked after, his people must do the same.

God has not changed! Do we really appreciate how great God is and take pride in proclaiming our allegiance to him? Do we put our heart and soul into serving him? Do we demonstrate his concern for justice and especially for the deprived? If not—why not?

COVENANT LIFE
Deuteronomy 30:11–20

The Old Testament is always realistic about people's reactions. There was a likelihood that Israel would see the covenant, putting them in relationship with almighty God, as a nice ideal but totally unreachable as far as they were concerned:

■ **The possibility (verses 11–14).** These verses undermine this argument before it has even been voiced. God is not expecting his people to achieve things that are as impossible for the ordinary person as a trip to the moon or even to the other side of the world! Nor is he expecting them to obey laws that are impossible to understand. God's requirements are quite clear and each command is capable of being kept by everybody. The covenant is a very real possibility.

■ **The choice (verses 15, 19–20).** The covenant was not something which was forced upon his people. God deeply wants to relate to us, but he never compels anyone. Of course it was not a contract between equal partners: the terms were set down by God. But nevertheless, Israel had to confirm their agreement and acknowledge their acceptance. They knew the terms; the choice to accept or reject those terms was theirs.

■ **The consequences (verses 16–18, 20).** The result of their choice ought to be a foregone conclusion. It was like choosing between life and death. Accepting the terms and keeping the covenant meant long life and prosperity. Turning from God and breaking the covenant rules meant disaster and ultimately the end of the nation. The Bible knows only too well that sometimes good people do suffer, and really evil people thrive (see, for example, Job 21; Psalm 37); God's blessing isn't always seen in material terms. But Deuteronomy wants them to understand the principle that obedience will bring God's blessing while disobedience will bring judgment and disaster.

The Message of Joshua

Mary Evans

Moving to a new area or starting a new job often involves risk. Perhaps the long-awaited move is rewarded by success; sometimes, however, disappointment comes when things do not turn out as planned. It was no different for God's people, Israel, when they entered the Promised Land. As the covenant relationship described in Deuteronomy began to work out, there were both encouragements and disappointments. We read of the continuation of God's mighty work, begun in the exodus, of protecting and helping Israel. But also Israel was already disobeying and deserting God. These two emphases, the failure of God's people and his faithfulness to them, explained for later readers why Israel was punished and her hopes not fulfilled, but it also gave new hope to those who were faithfully following God.

- God keeps his promises. As the people moved across the Jordan, taking over city after city, there was no doubt that God's promises were being fulfilled. Having made the covenant with his people, God did not leave them in the lurch, but gave continued provision and support. Not everything was completed immediately; there remained still more to be achieved. And God's activity did not mean that Israel could sit back and do nothing. They had to play their part in fighting for the land, in continuing to serve God and in keeping the Law. If they disobeyed, God's promises of judgment would be fulfilled.

- The new land. In the book of Joshua we see why Israel always put so much importance on the land. It was *theirs*, given by God; a symbol of his

Joshua OUTLINE

blessing on and relationship with them. It seems unfair that the previous inhabitants were so cruelly destroyed. But this was not done simply to make room for Israel. God was punishing them for their own cruelty and corruption (see Leviticus 18:24–28) and it is made very clear that Israel would lose the land if they behaved in the same way (23:15–16; 24:20).

- Good leadership. Joshua was a first-class replacement for Moses. He was not only a good administrator and an excellent military tactician, but, more important, he was totally committed to obeying and serving God. He is presented as a model of good leadership.

The call for good leadership, justice in the land and trust in God who keeps his promises goes out to God's people throughout the ages.

THE FINAL MESSAGE
Joshua 23:1—24:23

The campaign to conquer the Promised Land took many years, and as Joshua's death approached there was still much to do to establish Israel as a smooth-running nation. Joshua knew the people's weaknesses and he was afraid that they would never make it. Before he died he gathered them together and, with a series of reminders and warnings, did his best to keep them on the right lines, ensuring that they knew exactly what was involved in being God's people.

■ **A reminder of what God had done.** It was God who rescued them from Egypt and brought them into the new land. Because God was with them, they had been able to survive and progress, against apparently impossible odds.

■ **A call to commitment.** God expected obedience and loyalty from his people. But this would not happen automatically; it took a conscious decision and much effort. Joshua knew how easily they could get sucked in by the pressures and temptations of the surrounding society, and warned them to be particularly careful to avoid this.

■ **A reminder of what God would do.** While they remained faithful, their future was secure. The nation would become firmly established and able to stand against any enemy. But once committed to serving God, any violation of the covenant, especially giving allegiance to other gods, would bring disaster.

■ **A warning against complacency.** They must not persuade themselves that God would tolerate rivals. He was not that sort of God. Loyalty had to be total and they ought to be aware of this and of their own weakness before they committed themselves.

Belonging to God still involves total commitment. If we choose to serve him, we must do so with our eyes open. Neither money, status, power or any other modern god must ever take God's place.

The Message of Judges

Mary Evans

Stories of the heroic exploits of ancient leaders have often been a challenge and inspiration to later times. But the book of Judges is somewhat less than inspiring. It is a collection of stories about a very mixed bunch of men and women whom God chose to use to hold Israel together and to prevent them being totally absorbed by the pagan nations surrounding them. These leaders, known as 'judges' though they worked in a variety of ways, are portrayed very honestly. There is no whitewash to hide the marked decline in standards since Moses and Joshua—a decline not limited to leadership, but including the moral, religious and political life of the whole nation.

In chapter 2 verses 10 to 20 we read of the sad pattern which developed. Israel deserted God and started worshipping Canaanite Baals; they began to suffer defeats; they were in a state of collapse; God sent a leader who solved the immediate crisis and reminded them of the loyalty they owed to God; the leader died; Israel again turned to the Baals. However, in the midst of this account of disloyalty, disobedience and decline, there are high spots and positive lessons to learn.

- God is righteous. He cannot and will not allow sin to go unpunished. All nations, including Israel, are dealt with according to how much regard they have for the moral law.

- God is in control. He can transform situations even when there appears to be no hope.

- God is patient. He does not give up easily. Time and again he gave Israel another chance, calling another leader to challenge and rescue them.

Judges OUTLINE

1:1–3:6 Introduction
1:1–2:5   An uncompleted take-over
2:6–3:6   A bad start to life in the land

3:7–16:31 The Judges
3:7–11   Othniel
3:12–31   Ehud and Shamgar
4:1–5:31   Deborah the prophetess; Deborah's song
6:1–8:35   Gideon defeats the Midianites
9:1–10:5   Abimelech (Gideon's son), Tola and Jair
10:6–12:7   Jephthah of Gilead—a great soldier, a thoughtless vow
12:8–15   Ibzan from Bethlehem; Elon from Zebulun; Abdon from Pirathon
13:1–25   The birth of Samson, a man of remarkable strength
14:1–15:20   Samson makes an unsuccessful marriage and takes revenge
16:1-31   Samson and Delilah; Samson's final act of defiance

17:1—21:25 Other events of the time of the Judges
17:1–18:31   Micah and the men from Dan
19:1–30   A Levite and his concubine
20:1–21:23   In-fighting with the Benjaminites
21:24–25   The end of the beginning

- God starts from where we are. God responded to the slightest hint of Israel turning to him, even when their cries arose from despair rather than from trust. He did not wait for them to sort themselves out before he reached out to help them.

- God uses all kinds of people. The judges really were a motley crew. Though Deborah seems to have been a remarkably gifted woman, Barak was unwilling to take responsibility; Gideon began as a coward and ended up encouraging the people to worship an idol; Jephthah was a brave soldier but did not always think before he spoke—and the less said about Samson's moral life the better. Yet, as the book of Hebrews reminds us (see Hebrews 11:32), each one did have some faith in God. God makes use not only of outstanding men like Moses and Joshua. Even a little faith with very little understanding enables God to work.

Judges' picture of life in Israel is not glorious, but it encourages us not to write off any situation as being beyond God's help or anyone, including ourselves, as being too cowardly or too stupid or too lacking in faith to be of use to God.

VICTORY AGAINST THE ODDS
Judges 7:1–25

Gideon's defeat of the Midianites showed what could be done when God was allowed to take control in Israel. Nobody could be left in any doubt that this battle was not won by force of numbers, or that the credit should not

go to Israel. The army were given the opportunity to go home if they were afraid and two-thirds of them went. Low morale was understandable when Midian had been in total control for the last seven years. But to reduce the army still further to a mere 300 men seemed little short of ridiculous (see verses 1–8).

It is not surprising that Gideon needed the reassurance that came from overhearing the dream of the Midianite soldier. Often, even after a step that took real faith has been taken, doubts begin to creep in. It is interesting to see how often in the Old Testament doubt is recognized and reassurance given. Doubt or fear is not failure, nor is it a barrier to continued service of God. Confidence is catching, and Gideon returned to reassure his followers with his own renewed faith that God, who was sovereign, was acting for them (verses 9–15).

The battle was won without a fight. The unexpected noise in the middle of the night caused panic and pandemonium in the Midianite camp. They virtually defeated themselves and all that was left was a mopping up operation (verses 16–25).

It is rather sad that after such a demonstration of God's power, the very next chapter returns to an account of resentment, in-fighting, treachery and idolatry.

ISRAEL'S CLOSEST ENEMIES

The Israelites had settled in the Promised Land, but they were still under threat from hostile tribes and peoples. These battles lasted well into King David's time. In a similar way, the Christian life is more than a first step of faith: it involves constant struggle against all that denies God.

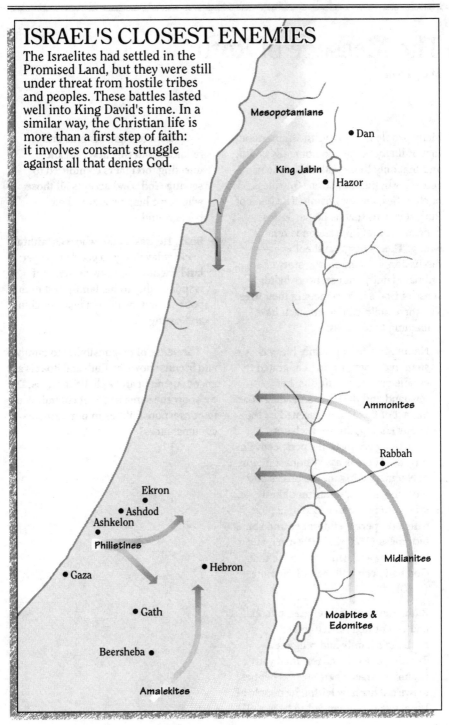

Mesopotamians

● Dan

King Jabin

● Hazor

Ammonites

● Rabbah

Ekron
●

● Ashdod

Ashkelon
●

Philistines

● Hebron

Midianites

● Gaza

● Gath

Moabites &
Edomites

Beersheba ●

Amalekites

The Message of Ruth

Mary Evans

Many people today have the impression that ordinary people do not really count; and that only those with influence or control, whether in nations, businesses or churches, are significant. The book of Ruth shows us that as far as God is concerned, that impression is totally wrong. This is no great theological discussion, it is simply the story of an ordinary family with an overwhelming sense of God's involvement in their lives. The three main characters each have something to teach us:

- Naomi. Her happy family life was shattered when, having emigrated to escape famine conditions, her husband and both her sons died. The impact of this is not lessened by the happy ending, but we do learn something about God's perspective in tragedy. There is a very honest picture of Naomi picking up the pieces and returning home, not triumphantly, or even with peaceful acceptance, but with a desperate endurance and some bitterness (1:20–21). However, she kept going and came to realize that God had been with her all the time (2:20).

- Ruth. She, too, had suffered but she had committed herself to her husband's family and religion. Trusting in God, she returned with Naomi to Israel where she did her best to live out her new faith. The people of Israel were commanded to keep well away from foreign customs and religions, but this never meant rejecting foreigners committed to serving God. God accepts all those who serve him, whatever their background.

- Boaz. He was a man who was faithful in everyday things: a good employer; a kind friend with a strong sense of responsibility to his family and to the poor; a man aware of a just, watchful and caring God.

The sense of responsibility to family and friends shown by Ruth and Boaz is an encouragement and a challenge to us. Do we show the same sense of commitment to our responsibilities in our particular circumstances?

The Message of 1 & 2 Samuel

Michael Butterworth

The history of the twentieth century is full of political upheavals—the partition of India, for instance, and the turmoil produced as people transferred from India to Pakistan or the other way round; the independence of various countries:

Bangladesh, Zimbabwe; the formation of the modern state of Israel and the ending of apartheid in South Africa. We know something of the difficulties that a state faces in establishing law and order, a fair deal for all, and stable government.

The books of Samuel describe the transition of Israel from an alliance of tribes to a monarchy; from being an oppressed, backward people to a powerful people ruling over a small empire. This is described, not as dry political history, but by marvellously vivid personal stories. We see God's chosen leaders, frail and imperfect, taking three steps forward and two (or sometimes four) back. But God sticks with them.

The stories are allowed to speak for themselves. Characters are never all good or all bad. We are not told what to think about them, but are left to draw our own conclusions.

The following themes come out strongly:

- God's providence. Most of the time God does not intervene in startling ways. He works through human instruments and remains hidden. God uses Nathan the prophet to confront King David with his own sins of adultery and murder, which he had hoped to hide. Nathan prophesies that 'the sword will never depart' from David's house.

In the next few chapters David's son Absalom kills his half-brother, then ousts his father from power before being killed himself. Another son, Solomon, kills his half-brother Adonijah, recorded in 1 Kings. God does not act directly but it is clear that he is the one in control.

- Kingship, children and succession. The Israelites' request for a 'king like the nations' is seen as a bad move. Nevertheless God allows them their king and is able to use this unpromising institution as a way of teaching about the nature of kingship, and looking forward to Christ the King. (See key passages *Give Us a King* and *An Everlasting Covenant*.) God makes a covenant with David that will never be broken despite human disobedience (2 Samuel 7:14–16).

Several times in these books a good man's children fail to live up to expectations. We are surely meant to take note. Eli the priest's sons treated the temple offerings with contempt; Samuel's sons took bribes. We are invited to enter the lives of these men of God and ask where they went wrong. (See 1 Samuel 3:13 and 1 Kings 1:6.)

There is something else to puzzle over. Children often do not prove worthy successors, yet the Lord makes a covenant—a promise of a special relationship—with David's descendants. 'Your house and your kingdom shall endure for ever before me.' It seems a dangerous plan, but then, with human beings, everything is dangerous. It is as if God says to the people: 'This is what I have decided. They may be horrible but you'll have to accept them. They are my choice and I can handle them.'

There is something to learn about the importance of timing, too. Twice David had the opportunity to get his revenge on Saul. Each time he resisted. (Look up these dramatic stories in 1 Samuel 24:8–10; 26:22–24; 2 Samuel 1:14–16.) A hasty action, ill-feeling and underhand tactics or, worse, unnecessary destruction or bloodshed can so easily arise out of impulsive behaviour.

I well remember a Diocesan Council meeting in India at which hired thugs attempted to enter the room and disrupt proceedings because the elections were not going the way some had planned. This abortive attempt was followed by months of legal wrangling.

We all need to learn the lesson David learned so well—never to try to force the hand of God.

'GIVE US A KING'
1 Samuel 8:1–22

It is quite hard for us to follow a leader we can't see. And most institutions find it difficult to manage their affairs without at least a standing committee.

When they first settled in Canaan, the 'promised land', the Israelites committed themselves to God, who was in effect their king. In the covenant made with Abraham, Isaac, Jacob, and finally Moses, they promised obedience to God's commandments. This also implied commitment to each other. If one tribe was attacked, the others were to come to their aid. But this didn't always happen. The people *should* have remained faithful to God, ready to heed his warnings and to receive his help. But they couldn't keep it up. Their leaders let them down. And even good leaders seemed to have poor successors.

When the people asked God for leaders, he gave them 'judges' (local rulers) to rescue them. (See the book of Judges.) But it often took a long time. Many times the people had strayed far away from God and were not geared up to responding to a call from such a judge. 'Who says the Lord has raised him up?' 'How do we know we'll win?' they asked. They felt they needed someone permanently in charge, and they wanted continuity in the leadership.

This led to their request for a king. Samuel does not like the idea. God is their king—are they rejecting him? No doubt Samuel was horrified at the thought of being 'like the nations'. After all, they were God's people—different and special. In spite of this, God granted their request, with a strong warning about the consequences and the dangers.

The books of Samuel show us that leaders cannot always live up to God's ideals. Fortunately, he remains the same gentle, long-suffering God.

JUDGING BY APPEARANCE
1 Samuel 16:1–13

Sometimes God chooses the most unlikely people. His choice of David, a young shepherd-boy, would have surprised anybody. But while 'man looks at the outward appearance, the Lord looks at the heart.'

It takes great courage to speak against a man who has the power to liquidate you. Samuel did this when he told King Saul that God rejected him (chapter 15). But then Samuel was a public figure who inspired awe in all the people. Time passed; Saul carried on as king, Samuel withdrew from public office. This was a much more dangerous time to carry out the next commission: to anoint a rival king! 'How can I go?' asks Samuel. 'If Saul hears of it he will kill me.'

So, as God directed him, Samuel went to Bethlehem and organized a small sacrificial meal with the elders. They were apprehensive—Samuel was out of favour with the king; and, besides, he was a man of God and you never knew quite what to expect.

The elders fade from view as the story continues. Perhaps they were present but sworn to secrecy. Samuel tries to assess which of Jesse's sons is the chosen one. After all seven apparently eligible sons are rejected, David has to be brought from tending the sheep. God whispers to Samuel that he 'does not look at the things man looks at'. This is the one.

Well, we *try* not to look on the outside. We do not ask candidates for a job to parade in swimming costumes. We take character references and conduct psychological interviews. But we remain human beings who do not see as God sees.

It was not that David lacked looks—he is described as handsome, with beautiful eyes! He also played the lyre well and had even wrestled with lions. Later he defeated Goliath. But most importantly, he was God's choice, chosen through Samuel's steadfast, even courageous obedience to God's voice.

AN EVERLASTING COVENANT
2 Samuel 7:1–29

Even prophets make mistakes. Nathan immediately felt that David showed insight: it didn't seem right that the king should live in a fine house while the 'Lord's house' was a tent. Still, Nathan's approval was too hasty and too general.

Fortunately, Nathan was also open to correction and received a message in the night for David: 'You want to build *me* a house? No, I will build *you* a house!' says God. God's promise in this passage was of tremendous significance for David, for Israel, and for us all.

David is promised that his descendants are to be the rightful kings of Israel. Hereditary kingship is given divine sanction—even when kings do not come up to the mark—'My love will never be taken away from him.' This gave political stability to the administration, particularly when a king died (once David's sons sorted themselves out, that is! See 2 Samuel 15—19; 1 Kings 1—2).

But, more than that, this unconditional covenant that God makes with his people is central to Christianity: we come into God's favour and blessing solely through his grace. We do not and cannot earn it.

David's marvellous prayer in verses 18 to 29 acknowledges his unworthiness in amazed thankfulness. Indeed, what more can he say?

Later, when David's son Solomon died, ten of the twelve tribes rebelled against his son Rehoboam. Still the covenant with David stood. Even when Jerusalem fell 350 years later and King Jehoiachin was exiled to Babylon, the people still looked to God to send another anointed one ('Messiah') in David's line. He came, and his name was Jesus.

'You have established your people Israel as your very own for ever and you, O Lord, have become their God.' This promise reaffirms God's purpose for his people, and looks forward to the new relationship God offers to us through Jesus.

JOAB SAVES DAVID FROM HIMSELF
2 Samuel 18:31—19:8

This little passage is surely one of the most moving in the Bible. If you've only skimmed it it's worth stopping here and going back to read it properly—out loud, if possible.

What, I wonder, did David's tears express? Love for a lost son, of course. But probably also remorse for the way he had failed this son—and the others. The hopes he had once had for this handsome, likeable and enterprising son lay dashed. (Look up 13:28; 14:25; 14:29–31; 15:3–6.)

Absalom had forced his father to flee for his life, and had taken over his concubines 'on the roof', probably reminding David of his own sin which started with a woman 'from the roof'. If David had not seen Bathsheba, and then committed adultery, Solomon would never have been born, and perhaps Absalom would have remained a loyal son content to wait for the throne until his father's death. 'If only' probably played a large part in David's paralyzing remorse.

However, David was fortunate to have a tough man close to him. While David mourned for the death of Absalom, Joab, his nephew and commander-in-chief, charged him with insulting his many loyal servants who had risked their lives to save him. He warned that David would lose the kingdom altogether unless he pulled himself together.

However bad our mistakes, God does not require remorse and despair. He asks for repentance, which literally means 'turning'. It is a movement word.

We change direction: from ourselves to God. From sin to right action.

David had learned, after his sin against Uriah, recorded in chapter 11, that God can pull us out of the very deepest pit. That was an amazing demonstration of God's steadfast love. But David needed to learn the lesson again. Because of what Jesus has done on the cross, we have stronger grounds for believing this. John writes in his first letter, 'If we confess our sins, he is faithful and just and will forgive us our sins and purify us from all unrighteousness.'

David's experiences help us to see our own particular situation as one which God may use for his glory and for our blessing. We may have to learn the lesson again and again.

ISRAEL'S WIDEST BORDERS

King David's conquests put
Israel in control of most of
the land between the Great
Sea and the Arabian Desert.
These were the widest borders
Israel ever had.

For ever after, the Jews looked
back to David's kingdom as
their time of true greatness.
But Jesus was to speak of a
'kingdom of God' not marked
out by physical frontiers.

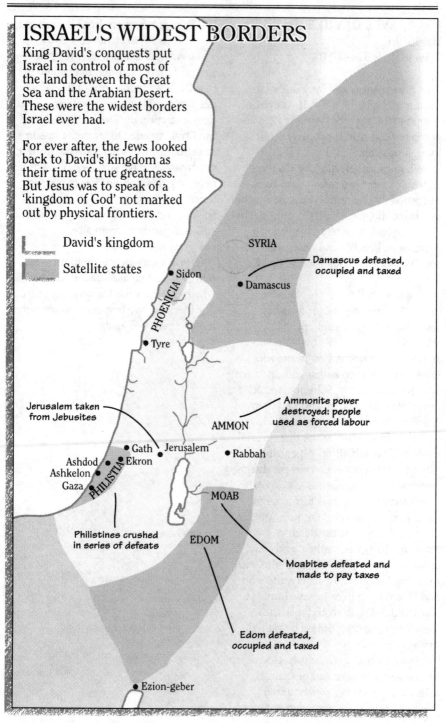

David's kingdom

Satellite states

SYRIA

Damascus defeated,
occupied and taxed

Sidon

PHOENICIA

Damascus

Tyre

Jerusalem taken
from Jebusites

Ammonite power
destroyed: people
used as forced labour

AMMON

Gath • Jerusalem

Ashdod • Ekron

Ashkelon •

Gaza

PHILISTIA

Rabbah

MOAB

Philistines crushed
in series of defeats

EDOM

Moabites defeated and
made to pay taxes

Edom defeated,
occupied and taxed

Ezion-geber

The Message of 1 & 2 Kings

Michael Butterworth

The story of Solomon's reign is a terrible warning to highly successful people who overreach themselves. But Solomon's is a success story compared to most of the kings of Judah and Israel who followed after him.

The books of Kings tell about the history of Israel in three phases:

- The united kingdom of Israel under Solomon

- The divided kingdom: Israel (north) and Judah (south)

- Judah alone to the fall of Jerusalem

The opening eleven chapters of Kings

---

1 and 2 Kings OUTLINE

describe how Solomon established the kingdom, built the temple and carried out various other grand projects. The story tells of his wisdom and ultimately of his foolishness: in oppressing the people and marrying many wives, including some with pagan beliefs. It is a story with great heights (see key passage *The Dedication of the Temple*) and a sorry end. But even here there is encouragement because God still honours his promises—entirely in keeping with his character.

Following the succession of Rehoboam, Solomon's son, ten of the twelve tribes of Israel broke away to form Israel in the north, under the kingship of Jeroboam. The book of Kings is just what it says—a history, giving accounts of the reigns of each king of Israel and Judah. The writer also makes a brief evaluation of each king's reign, and clearly regards both kingdoms as God's people, alternating between them as the story unfolds.

The kings of the northern kingdom are virtually all bad. They got off to a disastrous start with Jeroboam. Despite being offered a covenant similar to David's—the words in 1 Kings 11:37 echo closely the covenant with David in 2 Samuel 7 and with Moses in Deuteronomy—he turned away from God and set up two golden calves at Bethel and Dan, the rival sanctuaries to Jerusalem. Many kings followed 'in the sins of Jeroboam', worshipping idols and indulging in pagan practices, until God's patience was exhausted. (See key passage *Samaria's Sins Bring Destruction*.)

Judah's kings mostly 'did what was right in the eyes of the Lord'. Nevertheless the writer records that, with the exception of Hezekiah and Josiah (2 Kings 18:4; 23:8), they did not destroy the 'high

places'. These were hill sanctuaries at which, in the first place, orthodox worship took place. In 1 Kings we are told that Solomon sacrificed at the great high place in Gibeon, but this is excused because the temple was not yet built. But the 'high places' were liable to corruption—and often used for idolatrous pagan worship, an offence to God.

When the 'book of the Law' was discovered (2 Kings 22—23) they had to go. The writer of Kings says in effect: 'A kingdom must be built on careful obedience to what God has commanded. We have this in the Book which he has given. The temple at Jerusalem is the place where God has chosen to put his name. This is the place for sacrifice and a defence against the dangers of corruption from Canaanite religion.' (See key passage *The Dedication of the Temple*.)

Into this history of the kings of Israel and Judah comes God's 'word', brought by prophets, men of God who speak out God's thoughts—his intentions, his warnings—in a particular situation. The writer of Kings notes carefully the fulfilment of prophecy. But prophecy is not just a matter of prediction.

- The word of a God-sent prophet brings about change. For example, Elijah is told to anoint not only his own successor, but a rival king for Israel, and also one for Syria!

- A prophet's predictions of judgment can be avoided if the people change their ways. Turning away from sin and repenting may avert punishment, though the 'word' still hangs over the people.

These books tell of a massive failure of God's people. Some see that as the end of the story. By the end of 2 Kings the king of Judah, Jehoiachin, is in exile in Babylon. But he is still king. He is 'graciously freed' (2 Kings 25:27, 28) and given a seat above other exiled kings. God had not abandoned his people. King David himself had said: 'You spread a table before me in the presence of my enemies.' This came true for King Jehoiachin. He was humbled but he received mercy.

Solomon's prayer in 1 Kings 8 had shown that God hears his people's prayers, even far away in a foreign land. His promise to David and his descendants did not fail.

The world of the books of Kings is not so far away from us as we imagine. Many today face, or will face, great difficulties: depression, persecution, failure. The message of Kings assures us that God will stick with his people, those who are in covenant relationship with him, through them all.

THE DEDICATION OF THE TEMPLE
1 Kings 8:22–61

The human mind finds it difficult to grasp the idea of 'grace'. A Hindu gains merit (a good *karma*) by living according to duty (*dharma*); the first responsibility of a Jew is to keep the Law (*torah*); most church people also seem to feel that they must in some way earn their acceptance with God.

But Solomon's prayer speaks of the good news of the gospel: 'if they turn from their sin . . . and acknowledge your name . . . then hear and forgive.' This pattern is outlined for several situations: defeat in battle; drought; famine or pestilence.

By this dedication prayer the temple becomes a reminder that God is faithful, generous and forgiving. The sacrifices which will be offered there must never suggest that God's acceptance can be earned. Verses 41–42 speak of how people of other faiths may understand and call upon God's name.

Solomon knows that the temple is a useful symbol. But also it might be misunderstood. So Solomon emphasizes that the temple is not literally God's house—the whole earth is too small to contain him! Nevertheless God has chosen to 'put his name there'. In Hebrew thought the 'name' stands for the person. So God says, 'I'll certainly be there—but not only there.' We learn, from verse 41 onwards, that God hears prayer outside the temple, on the battle field, even in a foreign land.

God's presence in the temple is confirmed by the cloud (verse 10). This reminds us of the cloud that went before the Israelites when they came out of Egypt. The expression 'the glory of the Lord' (verse 11) is used in a similar way to 'the name'. It signifies God's presence. The prophet Ezekiel speaks of a vision where the glory departs from the temple—this means that the Lord has forsaken his house. They may no longer meet him there.

As the Israelites turned towards the temple with the assurance that God would hear their prayers, Christians look to the cross of Christ.

SAMARIA DESTROYED
2 Kings 17:1–41

'God did that' is not something we say very easily today—whether it is an

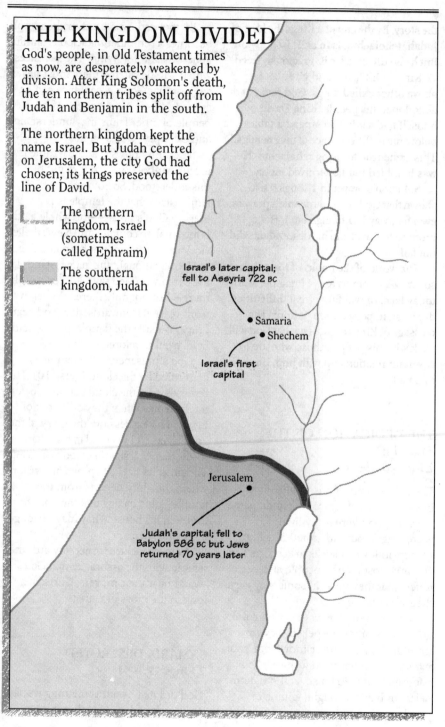

THE KINGDOM DIVIDED

God's people, in Old Testament times as now, are desperately weakened by division. After King Solomon's death, the ten northern tribes split off from Judah and Benjamin in the south.

The northern kingdom kept the name Israel. But Judah centred on Jerusalem, the city God had chosen; its kings preserved the line of David.

The northern kingdom, Israel (sometimes called Ephraim)

The southern kingdom, Judah

Israel's later capital; fell to Assyria 722 BC

● Samaria
● Shechem

Israel's first capital

Jerusalem ●

Judah's capital; fell to Babylon 586 BC but Jews returned 70 years later earthquake, prolonged drought, or personal disaster. Most Christians agree that God is active in the world but it is difficult to agree on precisely what he does.

The writer of Kings makes a plain statement: Samaria, the capital of the northern kingdom, fell to the invading Assyrians because the people sinned against God (verse 7). He makes the point that throughout the history of Israel God responded to the righteousness or evil of the kings by sending blessing or judgment.

God's intervention was very seldom direct, and judgment usually came through a foreign power. In 721BC the Assyrians conquered Samaria, destroying the unity of the country by capturing 27,000 Israelites, taking them into exile and bringing in thousands of foreigners. With them they brought a strange mixture of religions.

The books of Kings are different from Samuel. While Samuel merely tells us what happened, in Kings the writer states clearly the lessons he wants us to learn.

Many people today find the message of Kings simplistic and crude. But there must always be some degree of simplification, and when the writer says, 'This was because . . .' this is not necessarily the only reason. He draws attention to important connexions between God's requirements and policies, and earthly events.

The northern kingdom, the 'ten tribes' taken from David's descendants, consistently refused to follow God's teaching and commandments. They survived for about 200 years after this time but finally they were destroyed. They reached the point of no return.

CONTEST ON MOUNT CARMEL
1 Kings 18:20–46

People give all sorts of explanations for things that happen to them. Superstitions are found all over the world. Often only faith can see the connection between something that happens in the world and God's action.

The Israelites, ruled by King Ahab (himself ruled by the dreaded Queen Jezebel, who did everything possible to make people stop worshipping God), fell into worshipping the Baals. These localized pagan gods were connected with a mythical figure in Canaanite religion: Baal. The people believed that the Baals had power to send or withhold rain, so they prayed and sacrificed to them. Some of the practices were horrific, including sacred orgies and child sacrifice. Even today we see evidence of such things—witchcraft is widespread. In India there are stories of children being stolen, sacrificed and buried in the foundations of large buildings.

At this point in Israel's history, it must have seemed to faithful people that true worship had gone for ever. The prophet Elijah was on the run, fearing for his life; Jezebel was determined to wipe him out. She had already killed many prophets. But Elijah was the one most responsible for turning Israel back to God. His most significant act was his contest with the prophets of Baal on Mount Carmel. With a faith that must have seemed sheer foolishness, he challenged the prophets to call on Baal to send fire to consume their sacrifice. And with *real* foolishness, they accepted. The end of the story is well known (verse 38).

How and when should we expect God to demonstrate his power in response to our prayer? How do we *know* what to pray—what is unbelief, faith, presuming on God? Elijah was unique, and faced a unique crisis for the whole nation. Nevertheless, he encourages us to think bigger. God does not limit himself to boosting our feeble efforts. He is much more powerful and surprising than we can think or imagine.

But Elijah did not escape human weakness, danger and depression (see 1 Kings 19). Even in the depths of despair, God met Elijah's needs.

The Message of 1 & 2 Chronicles

Hugh Williamson

The Bible includes many books which have been labelled 'history'. Apart from those passages which tell of vital events in the formation of our faith, such as the death and resurrection of Jesus Christ, people often find it very difficult to know how to draw lessons from these books for life in the twentieth century. After all, not every action recorded in the Bible provides us with a good example to follow.

1 and 2 Chronicles OUTLINE

The author of 1 and 2 Chronicles faced a similar problem. By his day the history of the kings of Israel and Judah had already been recorded in the books of Samuel and Kings. The Chronicler wanted to make that old story relevant to his readers who lived a long time after. So as he retold the narrative, he did what many preachers still do today: he described the events as if they were taking place in his 'modern' world, rather than being concerned with all the historical details of earlier centuries.

In addition, he looked in the stories for patterns which point to the hand of an unchanging God behind the variety of life. Sometimes, as we shall see in our first key passage, he actually interrupts the account to comment on these important lessons from the past. In this way, he showed his readers—and us—how to learn from Bible history.

The main pattern which the Chronicler sees is that his people could be living through one of two different kinds of period:

● It might be a period of 'exile'. This would remind them particularly of the Jews' exile in Babylon. Literally speaking, when the people of Israel persisted in sin, God allowed a foreign power to defeat them in battle and to take many of the people away captive into exile. But the Chronicler saw that in a lesser way this 'exile' experience could be a picture for the people. It could show them what happens to any group or nation which turns its back on God and does not approach him in faith, worship and service. They may not go into a literal exile, but they can be cut off from God's blessing with the result that all sorts of things go disastrously wrong.

● Or it might be a period of 'restoration from exile' when the people repent. As soon as this happens, the Chronicler shows how God's blessing follows. In the way things were generally understood at that time, blessing is demonstrated by, for instance, a large family, success in building projects and victory in battle.

The Chronicler believed that his readers were living in a period like the exile. He wanted first of all to encourage them to believe that God was able to change their situation, and then to show them what God required from them before that change could happen. So he gives plenty of examples of God producing such a change in the past. At the same time he includes a number of short sermons by prophets or Levites which spell out the timeless truth of God's requirement that people should humble themselves before him. When the warning of God's word was ignored, exile-like disaster usually followed soon after; when it was heeded, God stepped in to restore the good times.

As you read the books of Chronicles, bear this pattern in mind:

● Watch out for these changes of fortune, either between one king and another or between different parts of a single king's reign.

● Then look to see what explanation is given in a speech or other comment by the author.

● Finally, allow the narrative to challenge your own faith and commitment as you see similar patterns in your own life or that of your community.

ISRAEL IN DEFEAT
1 Chronicles 10:1–14

This chapter marks the beginning of the Chronicler's narrative proper, and it tells of King Saul's defeat and death in battle. Most of the material is taken straight from 1 Samuel 31 and knowledge of the background to the account is obviously presupposed.

If we put the two accounts alongside each other, we shall discover that the Chronicler has made a couple of significant changes:

■ **First, he has made verse 6 ring with the ominous-sounding word 'died'.** He says not just that Saul's men died, as Samuel does but that Saul's whole royal house was wiped out. Actually, the Chronicler knew, as the genealogy shows, that some of Saul's family survived, but theologically that was irrelevant; in God's purposes there was no future for Israel under this faithless king. Often we get so caught up in day-to-day details that we fail to see the broad scope of God's work in this world. The Chronicler teaches us how to step back and distinguish the significant from the trivial.

■ **Then he adds verses 13 and 14 as his personal comment on the story he has just told.** The words he uses to explain why Saul failed crop up time and again in the rest of the books. To be 'unfaithful', for instance, means to offend against the ark or the Jerusalem temple and the purity of its service, sometimes bringing in the worship of foreign gods. The result is always military defeat and eventually the final exile both of Israel and of Judah.

Clearly, this is intended as a warning to the Chronicler's readers not to go down that same fatal path. The answer in Saul's day lay in God 'turning the kingdom over to David' as a king who would put right many of Saul's abuses (for instance, by bringing the ark back from neglect). The way in which we today must 'consult the Lord' may be different from Saul or David, but the underlying principle remains unchanged.

THE WAY OF REPENTANCE
2 Chronicles 12:1–12

Although Rehoboam reigned over the southern kingdom of Judah a full two generations after Saul, his story in this chapter begins in a similar situation to that at which Saul's left off. Having turned his back on God's Law (verse 1), he was immediately threatened by foreign invasion (verse 2), 'because', the Chronicler explains, using the same language as in Saul's case, 'they had been unfaithful to the Lord.'

On this occasion, however, a prophet, Shemaiah, gives a brief explanation in God's name of what has gone wrong (verse 5). The response is immediate: three times in verses 6 and 7 (and once in verse 12) it is recorded that the king and his people 'humbled themselves'. This is one of several key words in the Chronicler's vocabulary of repentance. We know this is so because it is at the heart of the famous verse, 2 Chronicles 7:14. In that verse, God sets out the conditions under which he will forgive and restore his people if they have turned away from him and so fallen under various kinds of judgment. They must 'humble

ISRAEL AND THE GREAT EMPIRES

Israel and Judah were small nations in a region dominated
by four great powers, each succeeding the other by conquest.
Yet theirs is the faith that has survived.

What matters longterm – the strength of the superpowers
or the spiritual qualities of faith, hope and love? Does God
measure current events by a different yardstick from the
political commentator?

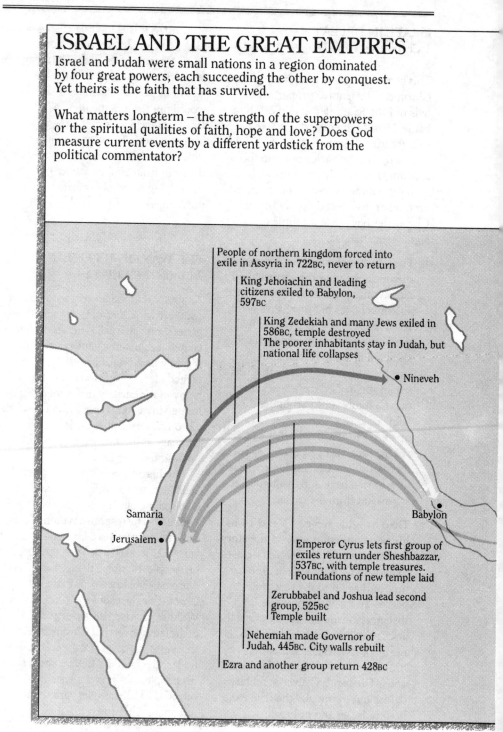

People of northern kingdom forced into
exile in Assyria in 722BC, never to return

King Jehoiachin and leading
citizens exiled to Babylon,
597BC

King Zedekiah and many Jews exiled in
586BC, temple destroyed
The poorer inhabitants stay in Judah, but
national life collapses

Nineveh

Samaria

Babylon

Jerusalem

Emperor Cyrus lets first group of
exiles return under Sheshbazzar,
537BC, with temple treasures.
Foundations of new temple laid

Zerubbabel and Joshua lead second
group, 525BC
Temple built

Nehemiah made Governor of
Judah, 445BC. City walls rebuilt

Ezra and another group return 428BC

1. **Assyria** was the power from the north. Defeated Samaria. Besieged Jerusalem but withdrew.

2. **Babylon** defeated Assyria 612BC. Sacked Jerusalem, took its people into exile.

3. **Persia** defeated Babylon 539BC. Permitted exiles to return home.

4. The **Greek Empire** dominated between the testaments.

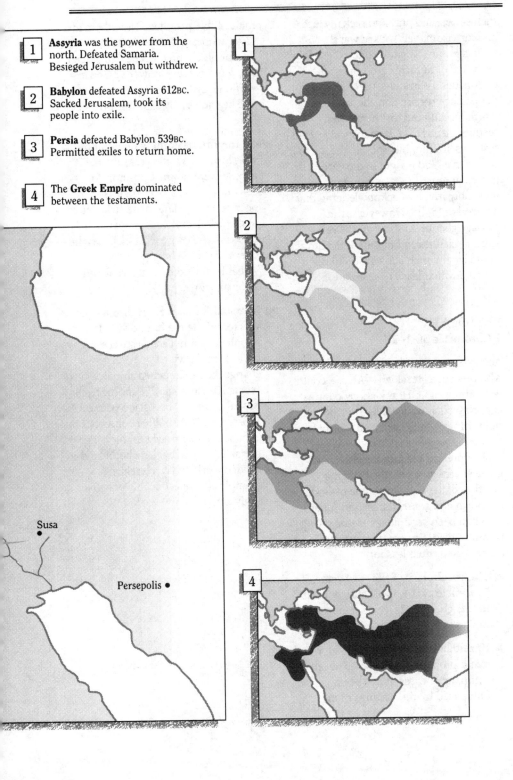

Susa

Persepolis

themselves, and pray and seek my face, and turn from their wicked ways'.

It is astonishing how often these four verbs occur at turning-points in the Chronicler's narrative, just as they do in the passage we are considering. It is worth looking out for them when reading through 2 Chronicles. As verse 6 shows, to 'humble oneself' means to accept that God is right in the verdict he passes on our sin, even though that inevitably involves acknowledging that we are not 'right'. However, as the passage goes on to show and as verse 12 summarizes, that admission is the lifting of the latch which allows God to open the gate which leads to restoration.

RESTORATION
2 Chronicles 30:1–27

According to the Chronicler, the king who preceded Hezekiah—Ahaz—could do nothing right. Hezekiah, by contrast, is portrayed as an ideal figure who put right things which had been wrong for centuries.

The present chapter describes his greatest achievement, the bringing together of the divided people of God in the north and south (Israel and Judah), who had been separate ever since King Solomon died. Several points bring home the spiritual lesson:

■ **The vocabulary of that key verse, 2 Chronicles 7:14, is all clearly used in this chapter.** Trace its importance in verses 6, 9, 11, 18, 19 and 20.

■ **Hezekiah's letter (verses 6–9) is like a prophetic speech.** As in other comparable cases, it has been influenced by the writings of the major Bible prophets. Here there are clear echoes of Jeremiah and of Zechariah chapter 1. The Chronicler knew the creative power of God's written word in the life of any nation, and he shows it by using the prophets here.

■ **An important point is made about worship.** For various reasons the people were not in a position to celebrate the Passover on this occasion according to the strict letter of the law. Hezekiah's prayer (verses 18–20) shows that the right intention of the heart is more valuable to God than external and legalistic correctness.

■ **Hezekiah's major effort throughout was to reunite the long-divided people.** It was not a total success, because many were too proud to change their entrenched attitudes (verse 10). But some did, and the result was emphatically one of joy (verse 23 and verses 25–26). What is more, God then heard their prayer for blessing (verse 27). To a divided church and a divided world today, Hezekiah's example is unquestionably one to study and to follow.

The Message of Ezra & Nehemiah

Hugh Williamson

How should a religious minority relate to civil powers and suspicious neighbours while at the same time preserving a strong sense of identity and loyalty to its past traditions? These questions are faced by Christians in many parts of the world today, and they are not unlike those which the authors of Ezra and Nehemiah confronted. The Jewish community of which they tell had been in exile in Babylon. Under the Persian rulers they were allowed to return home, but not as an independent nation.

We can see how they worked out these problems, by looking at the three communities involved:

- Their own Jewish community. They characterized themselves as the true heirs of Israel before the exile. The return from exile is described in a way which makes it look like a second exodus; the building of the temple recalls the building under Solomon, and so on. Most of all, the 'book of the Law' ensures that the life of the community was informed by the same values as its predecessors.

- The foreign power. Persia. This is generally represented as sympathetic to the Jewish cause. Prompted by God, its kings authorize the various journeys back from Babylon and give financial support for the rebuilding and maintenance of the temple. A clear message which comes through these books is that, even if present

Ezra/Nehemiah OUTLINE

(It helps to see these two books as one)

EZRA

1:1–6:22 The exiles return and rebuild the temple

1:1–11 Cyrus permits the Jews to return from Babylon to Jerusalem with their temple vessels

2:1–70 A list of those who returned (not necessarily all at once)

3:1–4:5 Worship at the temple site is restored, but the building is held up

4:6–24 Opposition

5:1–6:22 Despite intimidation, the temple is rebuilt and dedicated

7:1–10:44 Ezra (and see Nehemiah chapter 8)

7:1–28 Introduction to Ezra and his commission

8:1–36 His journey to Jerusalem

9:1–10:44 The problem of mixed marriages

NEHEMIAH

1:1–7:73 Nehemiah

1:1–2:10 Nehemiah secures permission to travel to Jerusalem

2:11–3:32 The ground prepared and the walls rebuilt

4:1–23 Opposition and countermeasures

5:1–19 Internal difficulties and solutions

6:1–19 The walls completed despite intimidation

7:1–73 The need to repopulate Jerusalem

8:1–13:31 Climax and conclusion

8:1–10:39 Covenant renewal: the reading of the Law, confession and pledge

11:1–12:26 The population of Jerusalem and other lists

12:27–43 The dedication of the walls

12:44–13:31 Concluding reforms, pointing to the need for continued vigilance conditions are not all that might be wished for (as, for instance, in Nehemiah 9:32–37), still it is best, as far as possible, not to rock the boat with the authorities. Quite often, as in this story, God uses them as an instrument to help his people.

- **The neighbouring population.** They were quite a different matter. They were all the more dangerous because in many respects they were close to the Jews in their history, religion and culture. But the Jewish leaders realized that if they allowed relations to develop unchecked, the distinctive aspects of their own beliefs and practices would become so watered down that they would lose their cutting edge altogether. Sometimes the measures they adopted in consequence, such as splitting up mixed marriages, seem harsh to us, but we need to recognize that survival was at stake. Tolerance demands a greater measure of security than was available to them.

The books of Ezra and Nehemiah serve as reminders for us to hold in balance our differences from, as well as our similarities with, our culture. The church must never become indistinguishable from the world, or it will lose its capacity to serve that world as salt and as light.

CONTINUITY AND CHANGE
Ezra 1:1–11

We live in days of rapid and sometimes momentous change. This affects each of us individually, but even more it affects nations and states in which constitutional developments are often fast and radical. Generally at such times people need symbols or traditions which are familiar to them; these give necessary stability as well as a framework of thought within which to come to terms with new developments. This passage shows sensitivity to these needs as its author describes the background of the Jewish exiles' return from Babylon to Jerusalem.

- **The motivating force is not the Persian Emperor Cyrus but the God of Israel,** who had spoken to the people previously through the prophets.

- **The story of the return recalls the exodus from Egypt.** A number of details show that the link is intentional, such as the references to collecting the necessary equipment from their non-Jewish neighbours and carrying the holy vessels on the journey.

- **The temple vessels themselves came from the first temple which had been destroyed (verse 7).** They thus gave to the worshipping community a sense of physical continuity.

This way of presenting history— moulding the new according to an older, familiar model—is called typology. It affirms that the God who is known from the past is still active today. The circumstances may be vastly different, but he acts according to consistent principles which he has made known and which can be relied on. If Christians today are to speak with real authority about contemporary and global issues, we must learn to read current events with such eyes of faith.

THE PRESENTATION OF THE LAW
Nehemiah 8:1–18

At the centre of all the reforms described in the books of Ezra and Nehemiah there stands this chapter, which tells how Ezra presented God's Law to regulate the life of the people. It is full of pointers for us too as we approach the Bible.

■ **The people came eagerly, expectantly and reverently** to listen to the reading. This was no optional extra in a church service; it was at the heart of all the people wanted. What is more, they were responsive to what they heard.

■ **Ezra and the Levites were willing teachers,** concerned to ensure that the people understood what was read. It is unlikely that the Law was completely new, but as circumstances had changed with the shift from Israel as a nation to the Jews as a religious community, much of it had fallen into neglect and disuse. As we know from elsewhere, part of Ezra's work was to demonstrate how the principles of the Law could be applied even if its letter could not. It was this which came across in so fresh and challenging a way to the people. True, the Bible is an ancient book from a culture remote from our own; but with careful study its underlying teachings can be teased out and applied to the modern world.

■ **As the people heard the Law explained, their first reaction was of sadness that they had neglected it so (verse 9).** There is a place for this, as the confession in chapter 9 shows. But Ezra was clear that this should not be the main impact of God's word. 'Go home and have a feast,' he said. The Bible is meant to bring joy in the God of salvation.

We can see from this that the Bible is the main source of authority for the people of God, but we still need to think hard how to understand and interpret it. Tradition is also necessary; we need guidance from past experience to point us down the right lines in applying the Bible's teaching.

Finally, the Law was given to a community which had already made giant strides in reforming itself. The Bible triggers reform, reform leads to fuller understanding of the Bible, and so on in a never-ending upward spiral. This is a vital principle; to neglect it is to drift into a stultifying backwater where we fail to grow towards maturity and where our lives are ignored by society at large.

The Message of Esther

Gordon McConville

The story of Esther is set in Persia. The time is not long after Persia has succeeded Babylon as the dominant power in the Near East, and the events concern Jews who, following the Babylonian exile, have chosen not to return to Judah, though permitted to do so by their new Persian overlords. King Ahasuerus is better known to history as Xerxes, which means that the period in question is 486–65BC.

Esther, not through choice but more by the turn of events, becomes wife to Ahasuerus. Meanwhile, the ambitious Haman seeks the destruction of the entire Jewish people, because of his personal hatred for Esther's cousin Mordecai, and obtains a decree to this effect from the King (who, of course, does not know that Esther is Jewish). By a combination of circumstances and the courage of Esther the threatened disaster is averted, the Jewish people saved, and the tables turned on all who had sought their downfall.

Strikingly, the name of God is not mentioned in the book. Yet the story has everything to do with the way in which he works, unseen, in events. What appears to be coincidence plays a decisive role in the book:

- It happens that Queen Vashti falls from grace, and is succeeded by the Jewish Esther.

- It happens that Mordecai does the king a favour before Haman hatches the plot against him (2:21–23).

- It happens that this, by a pure chance, is brought to the king's memory just at the moment which will ensure Haman's downfall and the Jews' salvation (6:1–11).

Coincidence, it seems. But the real message is that God is behind events, directing them to an outcome favourable to his people.

The main characters also play a part in the course of events. Mordecai's exhortation to Esther in chapter 4 verse 14 is the centre of the piece: 'Who knows but that you have come to royal position for such a time as this?' Esther is in a unique position to plead for her people. To do so, she must risk her own life. But, argues Mordecai, perhaps it is just for this that she has become queen. Esther's assent, an act of courage and faith, is vital to the triumph that follows.

A secondary theme is that people can be loyal both to God and to a secular power. This is a hard balance to achieve, especially when, as so often today, the state and its laws are hostile to Christian faith.

The Message of Job

John J. Bimson

The book of Job is one of the great poetic masterpieces of the Bible. We know nothing about its author, but this does not stop us appreciating his magnificent creation. Nor does it matter whether the work has any basis in history.

Plainly the book is concerned with 'the problem of suffering'. However, if we come to it with the question 'Why does suffering happen?', the book of Job will disappoint us. It offers no solution to that problem. The author is concerned instead with a different question: Do *innocent* people suffer? To many today, the answer may seem obvious: surely plenty of suffering takes place which is not deserved.

But the question is far fron irrelevant. There *are* religious philosophies in existence which view *all* suffering as deserved, if not by actions done in this life, then by actions done in a previous existence. Such is the Hindu and Buddhist system of *karma*, now enjoying wide popularity in Western society as well as in the East. Even within Christian-influenced culture, the idea runs deep that all suffering *ought* to be explicable in terms of punishment. 'What have I done to deserve this?' is a common cry from the modern sufferer, filled with a sense of injustice. Such gut reactions make us close relatives of Job, who knew that his suffering was undeserved and raged against it. 'I've been wronged! ... There's no justice!' (19:7) are cries which find many echoes today.

Job OUTLINE

1:1–2:13 Prologue: the affliction of Job. Satan is allowed by God to put Job's integrity to the test. A series of calamities befall Job

3:1–26 Job's outburst Job wishes he had died at birth. Why must life go on?

4:1–27:23 Job defends himself against his three 'comforters' Three friends—Eliphaz, Bildad and Zophar—make statements trying to explain Job's suffering. They all amount to saying that he is being punished by God. Job responds to each statement, protesting his innocence. He longs to be allowed to plead his case direct to God

28:1–28 A poem on wisdom Only God has full wisdom. For mankind can only 'fear God and depart from evil'

29:1–31:40 Job's final defence He defends himself before an imaginary divine court. He contrasts his earlier friendship with God and his present agonies, then challenges God to charge him and hear his defence

32:1–37:24 Elihu's view of suffering An angry young man, Elihu explains suffering as God's discipline in advance, turning us away from sin. He is sure God will not appear before Job

38:1–42:6 God appears to Job God unfolds the order of his created world, and shows Job how limited is human understanding. God's cosmic design does not depend on laws of reward and punishment to hold it together. Job repents of his foolish challenge

42:7–17 Job's restoration God restores Job's fortunes and vindicates him in the eyes of his community

The assumption of Job's three friends, and of Job himself at the beginning, is that all suffering can be explained as punishment for sin. This was presumably the common belief of the author's day. Divine justice was thought to be woven into the whole fabric of life, so that righteousness was always rewarded and evil always punished. The story deals the death-blow to both aspects of this equation, by showing both that Job was righteous and that he suffered. Hence it has been wisely said that the book of Job does not so much answer a question (Why is there suffering?) as question an answer (that suffering is always God's punishment).

So the story of Job shows us that innocent suffering does happen. But this raises new questions: If there is no obvious divine justice in the pattern of things, in what sense is God sovereign? How can we be sure that God is just? Wouldn't a just God intervene to help the suffering masses? These are some of the questions Job asks. They are also asked today, in a world where war and famine produce staggering numbers of innocent victims. Indeed, Job's description of the starving and oppressed, whose cry for justice goes unheeded (24:12), is disturbingly close to the too frequent pictures on our television screens.

So, at its deepest level, the book asks how we can possibly relate to God when the world he has made does not seem to make sense. Its answer is that God is to be trusted, because he made and governs the world according to his wisdom. Even though we cannot neatly pigeon-hole his purposes in terms of reward and punishment, there is still a basic order of integrity about the way he governs his universe. Although we cannot know why suffering happens, God is still the great Creator, worthy of our faith and worship.

The outline provides a brief guided reading of the book, and shows how it goes about suggesting this answer.

INTEGRITY ON TRIAL
Job 1:1–12

The setting of the story is vague and mysterious. The 'land of Uz' lay somewhere in 'the east' (east of the Jordan Valley), a region renowned for its ancient wisdom. The nature of Job's wealth (verse 3) and his long lifespan (42:16) suggest a time in the dim and distant past, around or before the days of Abraham. By showing that his hero belongs outside the geography and history of Israel, the writer makes the story relevant to people from all times and places.

Three times we learn that Job is righteous; twice God himself tells us so. This is important for all that follows. To make his case for innocent suffering, the writer has to establish Job's innocence at the outset. The four terms used to describe Job (blameless, upright, fearing God, shunning evil) do not imply sinless perfection, nor does Job ever claim that for himself. But his integrity is beyond reproach. There is nothing false about Job; his outer actions and inner thoughts are all of a piece.

We are then introduced to a meeting of the heavenly court. The 'sons of God' or heavenly beings (verse 6) are his angelic courtiers. Among them comes 'the Satan', which means the adversary. We should not expect Satan to be portrayed here in exactly the same way as in the New Testament; the picture of

Satan came into focus only gradually during the Old Testament period. His role here is that of an accuser, but he is more than just a spying angel whose job is to detect failings. There is hostility to God and his servants in his attack on Job's integrity, and by questioning God's own claims about Job, he is calling God a liar, as the serpent did in the Adam and Eve story. In verse 9 he casts doubts on Job's inner motives. Job, he says, serves God only for the gain it brings him; strip away all Job's security, and it will be a different story! One of the book's most profound challenges is whether service for God can be truly disinterested.

The author does not mean to shift the responsibility for Job's suffering away from God onto Satan (see 42:11). God himself initiates the conversation with Satan (verse 7) and his sovereignty is affirmed throughout the book. At the end, Job's questions are resolved without his ever knowing of Satan's role in events.

GOD WILL STAND ON THE EARTH
Job 19:23–29

Job is certain that he is an innocent sufferer. But this places him in awful tension. To a world which understood God as Job's friends did, Job's sufferings proved beyond doubt that he was guilty. Against this background, Job longs for vindication, a public demonstration of his innocence. But to whom can he appeal? To God? Before catastrophe overwhelmed him, Job shared the common belief that God punished evil and rewarded goodness (1:5). Now, the

facts suggest otherwise. God is afflicting him, but he is innocent. So how *can* God be just?

In this passage, as briefly once before (16:19), Job's belief in the justice of God comes to the surface. He lurches from seeing God as his enemy (19:11–12) to believing that God will be his defender (verse 25; RSV and NIV have 'redeemer'). Later he will lurch back again, but for now his conviction is that, though sickness will destroy his skin, he will live to see God 'on my side'.

But Job's insight goes even deeper than this. He is also convinced that a God who can thus vindicate him must one day 'stand upon the earth'. Job glimpses, without fully understanding, that God will eventually put suffering in a new perspective by coming to stand where people stand, by sharing human frailty and becoming a sufferer himself.

The Message of the Psalms

John Goldingay

If we want to learn to express ourselves in God's presence in praise and prayer, there is no better place to look in the Bible than the Psalms. They teach us how to worship—not by telling us how, but by showing us how, as the writers express themselves in praise or protest, telling what God has done and proclaiming his greatness.

- Praise. Many psalms rejoice in God's activity as creator—of the whole cosmos (see Psalm 97), the world in which we live (see Psalm 104), and our privileged place in God's creation (see Psalm 8). They also rejoice that he is involved in the everyday life and experience of ordinary people (see Psalm 103), for God's activity does not just belong to great events of the past, such as the exodus, or to great events of the future, when his purpose for the world will finally be achieved. God is the God of the present.

In the present God is the creator, still breathing his creative breath into the world, watering it each day with his rain. He is Lord of everyday life. The Psalms describe creation in a variety of ways: one common theme is that at creation God overcame all the powers of chaos that sought to resist his will, so that disorder now has clear limits set to it. This constitutes a promise that the disorder and evil which can threaten to overwhelm our lives (and the life of the whole world)

will not be able to do so.

The Psalms proclaim that the God of Israel is God of the whole world. It belongs to him, he rules it, he cares about it, and the whole world is challenged to worship him. When the Psalms say that God is Lord of the world, they seem to be making claims that are not true in the world as we see it. But these are claims about a lordship of God which we believe will one day be a visible reality, even if it is not so now.

The God whom the people of Israel worshipped was both the creator of the world and the one who had especially committed himself to them. Their response is both deep, enthusiastic joy, and awed humility. The Psalms consistently illustrate these two sides to praise. Some praise is noisy and enthusiastic; it is also clear that praise involves us bowing ourselves down in awed silence (see Psalm 95).

- Protest. The people of God often find that there seems to be a gap between the faithfulness and power which our praise acknowledges and the calamities that actually happen to us. Of course, suffering and defeat are sometimes our fault (see Psalm 130). But this is not always so. One of the most striking features of the Psalms is the way they express the sense of pain and let-down felt in suffering—by the individual (see, for example,

Psalm 22) or the community (see Psalms 89 and 137).

Israel's understanding of life and death is expressed particularly clearly in psalms such as these. To 'live' is not merely a matter of whether you are breathing or not: in its fullest sense 'life' involves good health, freedom, happiness, fellowship, success, and a sense of the presence of God. Death, too, is not merely what happens when you finally breathe your last, but whenever people no longer experience fulness of life. It is as if death has wormed its way into their life ahead of its time. When the Psalmists pray to be delivered from the realm of death (and later praise God for so delivering them), they do not mean that they need to be brought back from the dead, in our sense, but that they need to be healed or released and to know God's presence and activity in their lives once more, to have life in the full sense restored to them.

The Psalms rarely talk about a fuller experience of life after death (but see Psalm 73). They wrestle with the problem of the suffering of the just and the prosperity of the unjust, and it is in this life that they expect to see justice done and oppression punished.

- Telling what God has done. Our experience of God does not stop when things fall apart. The 'protest' psalms plead with God to turn to us and be the God whom we lifted up in our praise. The Psalms show us a God who acts in response to protest and prayer (see Psalms 18; 30; 118), who has both power and a constant love. He is able and willing to keep the commitments he makes.

In telling what God has done in the Psalms, people's experience of God is expressed in vivid pictures taken from everyday life. In a dry land such as Israel, the experience of thirst may become not merely something unpleasant but a matter of life and death. So longing for God is described as thirst, and God's coming to us is described in terms of thirst being quenched, or of the 'thirst' of the land being quenched by rain. But when rain comes, it can bring floods which threaten to sweep people away. In the Psalms we see danger described in terms of flood, and God as the rock on which a person can climb to safety.

Praising God in the Psalms is a corporate affair. Whether it is praise, protest, thanksgiving or proclamation, it happens together. For the people of Israel the natural place for worship was the temple in Jerusalem, for the God of Israel had promised his people that he would always be available there to meet them. It was therefore a place of joy. To be unable to go to the temple was a devastating deprivation. It was not that people believed God was confined to the temple: they knew that he was the God of the whole world and could be active everywhere. But they also knew that he had promised he would always meet them there, where offerings were made and where his Law was deposited.

- Proclaiming God's greatness. Praise, protest and telling what God has done all address God. But the Psalms also speak out in the name of God to humanity. They remind people of what God has done for them and what he expects of them. They promise his blessing and warn of his judgment. They declare that God's purpose will be fulfilled and that his justice will be brought about (see, for example, Psalms 2 and 82).

In that process, the king of Israel has a key place. In the Psalms, as elsewhere in the Old Testament, the 'anointed one' (the 'messiah') is not originally a figure expected in the future. He is the actual king of Israel, chosen by God, promised his support, and called to commit himself to God's concern for justice. The king is very prominent, not just in the psalms of proclamation, but also in the psalms of protest (which often speak of his defeats and needs) and the psalms of testimony (in which he speaks of the way God has answered his prayers). In fact, the kings of Israel were not very good at reflecting God's concerns in their leadership of the people. From 587BC onwards there were no longer kings ruling in Jerusalem. So it is that the 'anointed one', spoken of in the Psalms and in other places in the Old Testament, became an object of hope. In the coming of Jesus Christ we see those hopes beginning to be realized.

Promise and protest, telling what God has done and proclaiming his greatness, all find their place in Israel's hymnbook. The Psalms are designed for churches and individual believers to model their worship and prayer on. The book begins, in Psalm 1, with a promise of blessing for those who make these writings the object of their delight and meditation.

WHO RULES IN THE WORLD?
Psalm 2

Who rules in the world? God and his servants, or the nations and their rulers?

Zion (another name for Jerusalem) was the place where God promised to make himself known in the midst of Israel. It was there that he installed David and his successors as Israel's anointed kings. His relationship with them is portrayed as that of a father with his firstborn son (verses 2, 6–7). God also planned to reveal himself to the world from the same place, and his commitment to David and his successors included bringing about his 'rule' through his 'son' in Jerusalem. As we see from the opening verses of the psalm, more often than not the nations resisted this dual lordship. But God reaffirms that he will triumph by force if not by persuasion (verses 8–11).

Some time after this psalm was written, Jerusalem came under the power of foreign overlords. Nothing further from the picture in Psalm 2 could be imagined. So the psalm then started to express Israel's hopes for the day when God would make it reality when an 'anointed one' would again rule on God's behalf (the Hebrew word messiah is simply the word which means 'anointed'). And the first Christians proclaimed that these hopes were fulfilled in Jesus. His resurrection and ascension are the guarantee that the promise of Psalm 2 will be fulfilled.

It is important for us to listen for God's laughter (verse 4) and not to be too impressed by the pretensions of world powers which think they can shape their own destiny and that of the world independently of God.

IN ALL THE EARTH
Psalm 8

What is our relationship with the physical world? Sometimes we seem to be the pillagers and destroyers of the ecosystem, lording ourselves over it as if we can do what we like with it. But at other times we find ourselves the victims of earthquakes, floods, volcanoes, and famine. Then it seems that we have no control over the physical world at all—it does what it likes with us.

Psalm 8 puts these thoughts into perspective. Here we have God's view of humanity's relationship with him and with his world. We see that:

■ **The purpose of both heaven and earth is to 'magnify' God, not to meet our needs (verses 1–2).**

■ **We human beings are a central concern of the creator God himself (verses 3–4). We are in a real sense God-like, in the position of authority we are given over creation (verse 59). Yet this authority is *given*, and we are responsible to God for the way we use it.**

Sometimes experience may make us wonder how we can see God as attentively caring in the way verse 4 says he is. Often we will be aware that creation is far from being under our control, as verses 5 to 8 say it is. But in the New Testament we are invited to recall that the man Jesus *has* been crowned with glory and honour because of *his* suffering; and that is the guarantee that all things *will* come under his control (see Hebrews 2:5–9).

WHY HAVE YOU ABANDONED ME?
Psalm 22

Pain and grief need to be expressed; we pay a price eventually for repressing them. A 'protest' like Psalm 22 gives us a way of expressing our sense of hurt, abandonment, rejection, and of being attacked.

Yet it is more than merely a means of getting things off our chest; it is a way of expressing our feelings to God, even if we see him as the one who has hurt and abandoned us.

The opening verse sums up the protest. I am sure that God has abandoned me: but I express it to *him* (which presupposes that really he cannot have abandoned me!) There is irony here, and tension as the psalm alternates between protest and praise. (Contrast verses 1–2, 6–8 and 12–21, with verses 3–5, 9–11 and 22–31.)

The Psalmist invites us to hold on to two seemingly opposed sets of facts: the great truths about who God has always been, still is, and will be; and the reality of my present experience of forsakenness. It is easier in such a situation to deny one set of truths or the other.

But both the protest and the praise appear on the lips of Jesus (see Mark 15:34; Hebrews 2:12).

This psalm reflects the depths of human suffering and the heights of human joy. It is at home on his Good Friday and Easter Day, and on ours.

WHY ME?
Psalm 73

'Why?' People lose their jobs or have their houses burgled, and they wonder why such things happen to them, especially when it seems that people who are less honest or less upright get away with anything. When we ask God 'why?', often we do not find we receive the answers we want. The answer may still remain a mystery. But God does offer us ways of living with the question 'why?'

Psalm 73 affirms that we can bring our whys to God, but it notes that our complaints tend to be mixed up with sin (verses 2–3) and that we may need to have our complaints turned back on us (verse 15). It affirms that when we bring our whys to God, we may need to see what we are protesting against as part of a larger picture (verses 16–17). God invites us to see our world in the context of God's world, and this world in the context of the next (see verses 21–24, 26).

While it affirms that we may bring our whys to God, it shows us that we may then find that they cease to be so important. The psalm begins from what other people have and what we wish we had (verses 3–14). It finishes satisfied with having God (verses 25–26, 28). The New Testament equivalent to those statements is Paul's 'for me to live is Christ' (Philippians 1:21). For the Psalmist and for Paul, it is having everything else taken away that tests the genuineness of our satisfaction with God.

HOW LONG?
Psalm 82

All over the world, believers and unbelievers alike witness the oppression of the needy by the powerful and ask, 'How long is it to be like this?' Here God asks the same question, but without the despair that often characterizes our asking. He is the authority to whom all other lesser authorities are responsible.

Like us, the people of Israel understood heaven by finding parallels with their experience of life on earth. So God gathers, in the manner of an earthly court, with his supernatural subordinates who seem to be the counterparts of rulers on earth. He alone possesses life and power in himself: they possess life only by his grace (verses 6–7). The difference between them and him was so great that Israel hardly ever used the term 'god' to describe them. Only Yahweh was really 'God'. But here they receive the courtesy title which underlines the contrast between them and the one real God.

They are challenged to behave as the true ministers of a God like him, whose character is to be concerned for those who have no one else to look after their needs. The psalm presupposes that they will ignore this challenge. God promises that they will therefore be judged.

Only the last verse of this psalm is actually a prayer. It is a very powerful prayer, simply a challenge to God to do what he has said he will do. It speaks of judgment in a more positive sense. The judging of the world to which it looks forward will be good news for the world. It will mean the implementing of God's just and gentle government in a world currently oppressed by evil powers, earthly and supernatural.

GOD'S FAITHFULNESS TO ISRAEL
Psalm 89

We tend to think that the events of history are caused by human decisions (or mere chance). National triumph or decline is explained in terms of politics or economics or sociology. But the Old Testament more often sees God behind national triumph or defeat (no doubt working through political, economic and social factors). It is such an experience that Psalm 89 starts from, though it is a long time before this emerges.

The psalm begins in praise to God for his love and faithfulness throughout Israel's history, both in creation, and in the experience of those who pray this psalm (verses 1–18). When prayer begins in the context of such praise, there is then something to build on. In verses 19 to 37, the praise focusses specifically on God's commitment to David. Prayer also belongs in the context of God's promises; it includes reminding God of what he has promised.

But then the real theme of the psalm is expressed. It is a complaint at the astonishing gap between the theory of verses 1 to 37 and what has actually been happening (verses 38–51). As verses 1 to 37 reach the heights in proclaiming who God is and what he has promised, verses 38 to 51 plumb the depths in attributing just as directly to God this recent calamity. He has all the focus in verses 1 to 37, and he is still the focus as they look at their affliction. It is the fact that *he* has let them down that hurts most of all. As is common with the Psalms, we cannot identify the particular events that Psalm 89 originally referred to, but that is not the point. It was the kind of prayer that could be prayed in the context of any national disaster.

In a psalm of protest, the actual plea (verses 46–51)—the part corresponding to what we would call prayer—is short and to the point. God is simply asked to remember and to turn his face to his people again. Exactly what he does is left to him.

SHADOW OF THE ALMIGHTY
Psalm 91

On the day I write, the newspaper reports the suicide of a much-loved television personality, whose voice 'always conveyed steady reassurance and comfort ... If he died desperate, then we are standing on sand and I wish he hadn't told us.'

Psalm 91 shows us where our true security lies. Here, as elsewhere in the Psalms, the Psalmist expresses his praise of God and his trust in him by addressing people (with God no doubt assumed to be overhearing) rather than God (with other people overhearing). Here a general statement (verse 1), a personal confession (verse 2), a direct promise (verses 3–13) and actual words from God (verses 14–16) combine with one purpose—to declare the security of those who make God their refuge. It is a psalm of trust, not directly telling God that we trust him, but telling others that he is trustworthy.

The variety of terms for God is worth noting: 'the Most High' and 'the Almighty' suggest his power; 'the Lord' (actually 'Yahweh', the name specially revealed to his people) and 'my God' suggest his personal care. 'Shelter', 'shadow', 'refuge', 'fortress' and similar words express in concrete images what these two aspects of God can mean to us.

But is the psalm true? Those who trust God experience illness and calamity as much as anyone. A good example was the murder of five missionaries in Ecuador in the 1950s. Yet the widow of one, Elizabeth Elliot, entitled her husband's biography *Shadow of the Almighty*. It might have seemed that if anyone's life disproved Psalm 91 it was Jim Elliot's, yet his widow affirmed that somehow it was still true. God pulls me away from an individualistic, 'private' faith into one which shares his concerns. God works for righteousness and justice on behalf of the oppressed. And he invites me into an even more searching confession: that he rules not merely in personal life, but in world history and through the heavens, (verses 9–12). So worship invites me into an awe before God's holiness and a surrender to his love; or an awe before his love and a surrender to his holiness.

I end where I began (verse 2). But it is not really the same place, because of the journey I have travelled.

THE LOVE OF GOD
Psalm 103

What draws me into worship? Here it is an awareness of the good things God has given me (verses 1–2). First, forgiveness (verses 3, 8–12): God sees the sins which appal us and which we hope we hide from others, and takes the risk of keeping on forgiving. He overflows with mercy—he cannot keep it in. He removes our sins as far away as infinity rather than let them come between us and him.

He is the source of all healing, sustaining, renewal and love that I experience (verses 35, 13–18). He knows our frailty and weeps with those who weep or grieve or fear. He is the guarantee that, if we do not experience all this in fulness now, we will in time.

But God is not just that for us individually (verses 6–7). When I am forgiven and healed and sustained, I share in the experience of God's people through the ages, and I belong with them. And the God of forgiveness and healing is also the God of liberation and justice: he will not let me be satisfied with my own forgiveness and healing.

GOD THE GREAT CREATOR
Psalm 104

It is difficult to take creation for granted. Gazing at the stars on a clear night, or surveying the horizon from a ridge of hills, or seeing the ocean pound against cliffs, or examining minute life-forms through a microscope, or watching exotic creatures on a wildlife programme, all make us wonder at the marvels of the world in which we live.

There is a dark side to creation which also makes it impossible to take creation for granted: the sea pounding a lifeboat to pieces, the earth quaking and destroying a town, a virus bringing affliction to young and old, and the fact of death which brings an end to the life of every creature.

Psalm 104 sets both aspects of creation into perspective by seeing them in the context of God as creator. If creation is so wonderful, then how wonderful is the God of creation, who not only gave it life at the beginning, but continues to sustain it as gardener, feeder and waterer, keeper and herdsman. He is Lord of light, clouds and wind, and the gentle provider for bubbling stream and growing grass. He not only fulfils all that people need, but also cares for creatures who are remarkable in their own right.

He watches over creation's dark side too: seeing at the beginning that the deep did not overwhelm the world; creating darkness with its dangers as well as daylight; turning Leviathan (seen in the ancient world as a fearful embodiment of the powers of evil and disorder threatening to overwhelm the world) into a toy monster, exercising his power to take back the life that only he can give; sometimes making the earth shake again to remind us that its stability is his gift.

Creation cannot be taken for granted. Still less can the God of creation.

GOD'S LOVE ENDURES FOR EVER
Psalm 118

People do not always experience God's protection from pain and defeat. Here, however, is a testimony from someone who *has* known that protection.

Despite the absence of directions, it is not too difficult to work out how different people are taking part in Psalm 118. The central figure is the king, testifying to the Lord's deliverance in battle (verses 5–7, 10–14, 17–19, 21–22, 28). The priests bless him as he returns to God's house to give thanks (verses 20, 26–27). Perhaps

the challenge in verses 1 to 4 and 29 comes from them, too. The people join in his praise and share in his confession of trust in God (verses 8–9, 15–16, 23–25).

The psalm shows us the way in which the people of Israel or its king, or an ordinary person who has been ill or under pressure, comes back to give God the praise when he has answered their prayer. The experience of defeat or illness raises the question whether God's love really is as constant as we say in our praises. When God answers our prayer (often when we thought he had stopped listening), we are convinced once more of God's faithfulness, and can use this conviction the next time some negative experience threatens to bring us down. A psalm of thanksgiving or testimony such as this gives public expression to what God has done. So it builds up the faith not only of the one who has experienced the answer to prayer, but also of all those who hear what God has done.

THE WORD OF GOD
Psalm 119

Is God someone who delights in giving people orders? Or a liberal parent who just likes doing nice things for people?

In Psalm 119 we are being told how to live God's way. 'Laws', 'statutes', 'commands', 'decrees', are among the favourite words of the psalm, yet the commitment expressed in it is based on love (verses 47–48). We take God's word seriously because we believe it truly reflects who he is and how the world is. Not only that, but by serving God and following his ways we find freedom (verse 45).

Following God involves being willing to look at the areas of life where his expectations of us might be different from the world's. The world may put us under physical or moral or social pressure to change our position, and in this situation God's word as promise also comes to be of key importance (for example, verses 41–42, 49–50, 147–48). We are called to pray under pressure, as the psalms often do, pleading 'renew my life!' (verse 25). The pressure is both external and internal, in the question of whether God's promise is true. (In verses 71 and 75, for instance, who is the Psalmist trying to convince?)

Those who do what God commands can claim God's promises, and those who experience the fulfilment of the promises will be people who go on to fulfil the commands (for example, verse 146). God is both the blessing God and the commanding God. He draws me to an obedience which is awed but joyful (verse 7) and to a trust which is joyful but awed (verse 38).

BY THE WATERS OF BABYLON
Psalm 137

For many people, one of the most troubling features of the Bible is the apparent vindictiveness of many of the Psalms. We can accept other aspects of the way the Psalms speak to God: praise, thanksgiving, prayer, even perplexity. But what of the kind of devastating request that verses 7 to 9 make here?

What made people pray like that? They were not simply insensitive and unspiritual: the moving and poignant lament of verses 1 to 6 makes that clear.

And they were not wrong in believing that God judged oppressors: both Old Testament and New Testament affirm that. They were not unaware that God cared about other nations: many psalms make that clear. Neither (to judge from the New Testament) were they wrong to pray for their oppressors' punishment: we find that in Revelation 6.

Both Revelation 6 and this psalm are prayers of people who have been deeply afflicted by other human beings. We should hardly allow ourselves to feel too superior as we consider their prayer if we have not had to cope with their kind of suffering. Apparently God was accepting enough of their prayer to allow it to find a place in his book. We are allowed to express the most unacceptable feelings to God.

But will God answer the prayer? How does it relate to Jesus' 'Father, forgive them?' Actually, prayer for forgiveness cannot be prayed except in the light of the cross. Even after what happened when Jesus died on the cross, people can still choose to experience either God's forgiveness or his judgment. (Jesus himself echoes Psalm 137:9 in Luke 19:44.) The cross makes forgiveness available; but it is people's response to it that determines whether the exiles' prayer is answered, or whether Jesus' prayer is answered instead.

GOD IS EVERYWHERE
Psalm 139

In this psalm we sense an extraordinary contrast between the deep devotion to God in verses 1 to 18 and 23 to 24 and the deep hatred of verses 19 to 22. This is why verses 1 to 18 often get used on

their own. But it is all one psalm: so how
is it possible to move from such
devotion to such hatred?

The Old Testament prophets rebuked
the people of Israel because their
devotion was *not* accompanied by a
hatred of evil. Real devotion to God will
express itself in a loathing of wickedness.
In fact, the psalm does not seem to have
specific wicked people in mind; it is
talking of wicked people in general. And
it is not talking about our personal
enemies, but about God's. We are not
expecting God to treat our enemies as his,
but accepting that God expects us to treat
his enemies as ours. Believers prove their
sincerity by hatred of evil.

Indeed, in the context of verses 19 to
24, the earlier part of the psalm appears
in a new light. The wicked are those who
think they can get away with anything;
however, saying the psalm involves
being watched closely by God, to
establish that we really do reject the
wicked and all their ways (verses 23–
24). Verses 1 to 18 show us what such
openness to God means.

The fact that God knows all about us
(verses 1–6), can reach us anywhere
(verses 7–12), and has always been
involved even in the innermost aspects
of our lives (verses 13–18), is presented
as straightforward fact. Our Bible
translations have difficulty in keeping it
that way, and present some verses as
reassuring, others as worrying. The
psalm itself implies throughout that it is
both a wonderful and a solemn thing: we
cannot get away from God. But because
he is who he is, what could be a
suffocating stranglehold is actually
something extremely liberating—if we
are committed to what is right and just,
and remain stoutly hostile to evil.

The Message of Proverbs

David Clines

If you open the book of Proverbs at random, you will probably find yourself reading unconnected, isolated sayings, each one sentence long in two lines of poetry (if your Bible shows the parallel poetic lines). Some of these proverbs are famous and pithy: 'Pride leads to destruction and arrogance to downfall' (16:18); some seem rather obvious: 'Smiling faces make you happy, and good news makes you feel better' (15:30); some startle you with an exciting idea or a new image that immediately impresses you with its truth: 'Beauty in a woman without good judgment is like a gold ring in a pig's snout' (11:22).

What is most surprising, however, is that so few of these proverbs seem to have anything to do with God. When God is mentioned, he seems to be rather in the background. He hates evil-minded people and loves those who do right (11:20), he sees what happens everywhere (15:3), but he does not seem to be very active in the world of humans. He blesses the poor (10:22) and gives them long life (14:27), and he protects a widow's property (15:25); but on the whole it is not God but the decisions we make for ourselves that determine our destiny. You don't need to be a believer in God to see the wisdom in Proverbs. And that's how it should be. The Bible has no monopoly on truth. What God says in the Bible is not always original and earthshattering; it sometimes tells us what we have already found to be true.

The wisdom of Proverbs is to show us that there are underlying patterns in life which are not obvious. The first time anyone sees pride leading to destruction, for example, it does not occur to them that this may be an *example* of anything; it is just a one-off event. Without the proverb it may take many such episodes for us to see a common theme. We might have been thrown off the track by noticing early on in life cases where pride did *not* seem to lead to destruction. Now that we have the proverb as one of our resources for living, even though we know it will not always be true, we cannot help asking now, whenever we see pride in someone, Is that person heading for a fall? Asking it of ourselves, too.

There is more to Proverbs than that, though. In chapters 1 to 9, the wisdom of Proverbs—the way to live life with understanding and sensitivity (1:2–6)—is praised as a gift from God. The God of Proverbs may not

Proverbs OUTLINE

necessarily be intervening miraculously in people's lives from hour to hour, but in a hidden way he touches them at every moment. The chief ingredient in wisdom is the sense of God (1:7), a reverence for the God who made us the way we are and the world the way it is. Behind even the apparently secular proverbs stands a truly religious attitude to life.

THE VALUE OF PROVERBS
Proverbs 1:2–5

This introduction is the book of Proverbs' own view of itself. It is mainly about people and their needs, not about grand theories, religious principles, history or feelings.

It recognizes its own limitations, and does not claim to be God's plan of salvation or the truth about the universe. It is a book about everyday life, and 'educational' in the broadest sense.

Proverbs is basically addressed to young people. In chapters 1 to 7 the reader is actually called 'my son', the speaker being a father or teacher. It goes without saying that the way a person starts out in life greatly influences what happens to him or her.

The speaker in Proverbs reminds his 'son' of how, when he was little, his father would urge him to 'Love wisdom and she will keep you safe. Getting wisdom is the most important thing you can do' (4:3–9).

It is not intellectual wisdom that Proverbs is talking about, but practical understanding and know-how in everyday relationships. It majors on the fundamental morals and principles society needs for its stability.

Wisdom is about not having to find everything out for yourself by making all your own mistakes. It is about drawing on the accumulated experience of others to add to your own personal experience. Reading Proverbs offers a forest of signposts to those who are willing to learn.

WISDOM—GOD'S COMPANION
Proverbs 8:1, 22, 30

'Listen! Wisdom is calling out...
'The Lord created me first of all,
the first of his works, long ago...
'I was beside him like an architect,
I was his daily source of joy,
always happy in his presence...'

It takes an imaginative leap to see everyday wisdom as God's companion at creation. Wisdom is pictured here as God's female assistant, not only designing the universe as a skilled architect but enjoying a loving and joyful relationship with the Almighty.

The poet does not, of course, mean us to believe that there literally was such a creature, but persuades us imaginatively that for God, too, wisdom is not an efficient but rather soulless means of controlling the world, but a highroad to enjoyment. To understand is to enjoy. To act skilfully is to have fun. The wisdom that penetrates to the heart of things and leads to appreciation and enjoyment is the first thing God ever created. Without it he could not have made the delightful, rich and meaningful world we live in.

We are not born with this wisdom, but have to acquire it. Not that it need be hard to find. Wisdom herself says: 'I love those who love me; whoever looks for

me can find me' (8:17). What she offers
is maturity and sense (8:5) She appeals
first to the immature—the 'simple'—to
develop their experience of life by
learning from others who have put
down their experience in proverbs. And
then, since no one has lived long enough
to know it all, she addresses herself to
humankind, 'everyone on earth' (8:3),
to take her 'refresher course' in living.

The Message of Ecclesiastes

David Clines

Ecclesiastes could be described as a question mark in the margin of Proverbs. While Proverbs shows wisdom to be the path to life, Ecclesiastes asks: And what is *life* the path to? Answer: Death. What value has anything in life if in the end death cancels out all values?

For Christians, who believe in an afterlife, this may seem a non-question. And there is a sense in which right living has its true reward in the afterlife. But Ecclesiastes' question still holds: Since death is the end of what we have worked for on earth, what is the point of striving? 'You spend your life working, labouring, and what do you have to show for it?' (1:3). In the natural world things are perpetually renewed, the rivers running into the sea and returning to the place where they began (1:7), but human life cannot be renewed. When it is ended it is ended.

This is not pessimism. For Ecclesiastes, death is part of the life-package that God has given each of us. Even though death negates the values of life, that is part of God's design. It does not negate them while we are still alive. Wisdom is still better than foolishness (2:13), even if the wise and the foolish come to the same end. Life is still a gift from God even if in the end God will take it away. This is a sturdy kind of faith, that encourages right living and an appreciation of God's world even in the absence of a Christian kind of hope. Ecclesiastes can be a bridge between the worlds of believers and unbelievers. And it does believers no harm to ask themselves what their aims in this life are, apart from the life they hope for after death.

EAT, DRINK AND BE MERRY!

Ecclesiastes 5:18

'This is what I have found out: the best thing anyone can do is to eat and drink and enjoy all one's activities during the short life that God has given us. This is humankind's package!'

Here is no fatalism, no resignation, no materialism, no selfish living for pleasure. Here, rather, is a truly religious view of life that sees it as God's gift. The

Ecclesiastes OUTLINE

The argument of Ecclesiastes weaves about so delicately that no simple outline can be presented. Here are some of the main elements of the book:

1:1–11 Unlike the natural world, human life comes to a final end

1:12–2:26 What does it all add up to?

3:1–15 A time for everything

3:16–22 Injustice

4:1–7 Observations. What does it all add up to? (again)

4:8—6:9 Life is God's gift

6:10—12:8 The limitations of human knowledge

12:9–14 The bottom line. The best life is guided by God's commandments 'package' we have is full of the most varied activities—weeping and laughing, mourning and dancing, seeking and losing, tearing and sewing (3:18). If God has given it, the most important thing is to use it, and enjoy it. Life does not exist for the sake of something else, but for the sake of the people who are living it.

Against those people who tell us that God wants us to suppress or deny our instincts for life or joy or fun, Ecclesiastes insists that the true way to 'remember' or honour our Creator (12:1) is to savour the life he has given us. Not that Ecclesiastes recommends self-indulgence or immorality, for one of his baselines is: 'Fear God and obey his commandments' (12:13). But on the other hand, it is absurd to take it to extremes: 'Don't be too good or too wise—why kill yourself?' (7:16).

As long as we live within the guidelines of God's way, he prefers us to live relaxed rather than anxious lives: 'Go ahead—eat your food with enjoyment, drink your wine with a merry heart. God has already approved what you do! Let your garments always be white, and don't stint the oil you anoint yourself with!' (9:7–8). That is not a fashion tip, but an encouragement to live joyfully.

The Message of Song of Songs

John J. Bimson

The Song of Songs is a set of love poems. Although it is a short and very beautiful book, it is not easy to decide how many characters are speaking in addition to the two lovers, nor is it clear whether Solomon himself is one of the characters or not. Yet the intensity of the feelings expressed by the rich poetic imagery is plain for all to see.

The exchanges between the two lovers are often so intimate, and so bold in their descriptive detail, as to offend some tastes. This strongly erotic language, coupled with the absence of any obvious religious theme, has made the book difficult for many people to accept as part of the Bible. So what is this book?

- Is it an allegory? Many down the ages have made it acceptable by treating it as such. The rabbis took it to be about God and his love for Israel; the Church Fathers took the male lover to be Christ, and the woman to be his bride, the church, or the individual believer. Since many have reaped deep devotional benefits from this kind of approach, it would be wrong to decry it totally. However, there is nothing in the poems themselves to suggest that this is their primary meaning.

- Or is it simply a collection of love-poems? A growing number of scholars have been content to treat the Song straightforwardly as just that.

Probably they were for use at a marriage-feast. These poems speak to us about the nature of physical love. By celebrating human sexuality without shame, they remind us that it is God-given and wholesome, to be neither denied nor abused. Our sexuality is not an accidental result of sin. God intended it for us from the beginning. It is part of the creation which, at the end of the Bible's first chapter, God declared to be 'good'. Nowhere is its goodness shown more powerfully than in the Song of Songs.

Song of Songs OUTLINE

1:1—2:7 The bride's longing for the bridegroom
2:8—3:5 Love increases
3:6—5:1 Their love is consummated
5:2—6:12 The bride's desire for the bridegroom
6:13—8:4 The bridegroom's desire for the bride
8:5–14 The durability of love

The Message of Isaiah

Dwight Van Winkle

If we want to understand what this great prophetic book means, and apply its meaning to our own world, we need to understand the people to whom these prophecies were first spoken—their needs and their beliefs. But the prophecies had more than one audience, because this book of Isaiah covers a long time-span. So we must look at the people of Israel at three stages of their history, each related to one great disaster, when the Babylonians destroyed Jerusalem and took most of the people into exile:

• The first prophecies, chapters 1 to 39, were addressed to the people of Jerusalem some years before the city fell.

• In chapters 40 to 55 are prophecies addressed to the people in exile in Babylon.

• Last come prophecies addressed to Israelites who returned from Babylon to rebuild the temple and the city (chapters 56 to 66).

• Before Jerusalem fell, its people were confident that God would never allow their city or their land of Judah to be destroyed. They had their reasons for thinking this. God dwelt in Zion (the term means first the temple and then, by extension, the whole city) so how could it be overthrown? But Isaiah challenged this thinking. The city was full of wickedness. Its people exploited the weak (see 1:21–23; 5:7–8; 10:1–2); they imagined sacrifices without sincere repentance could turn away God's anger (1:10–17 is a key passage for this). Isaiah warned them that God would use foreign nations to destroy the city.

Also, the people put false confidence in God's agreement with their line of kings, the covenant first made with King David. God had promised that the line of kings would not fail, and that he would protect the land. But the people conveniently forgot that this promise had a condition: 'If your sons keep my covenant . . .' Isaiah challenged these false hopes as well. The king would be established only if he stood firm in his faith. Yes, God longed to give his grace to the people through their king, but this could only happen if the king trusted God.

The prophet saw only two possibilities. King and people could trust God and be blessed. Or they could fail to trust him, and find judgment rather than salvation. Chapter 1 verses 18 to 20 brings out the choice. God wanted to be reconciled with the people. Did they want this too, and would they obey him? Then he would forgive them and they would prosper. But if they refused him and turned away, only destruction awaited.

The people and the prophet differed in their idea of how Judah should respond to God, for the reason that Isaiah was impressed with the holiness of God where the people as a whole were not. The story of his call (chapter 6) shows that this was so from the beginning. One of his favourite terms for God was 'the Holy One of Israel'. For Isaiah, God was far greater than humanity, perfect in his moral purity. And because God was holy, he demanded holiness from his covenant partner.

This was why the prophet saw Israel's confidence in Zion and its kings as false. And he was convinced that the Holy One of Israel could use the foreign nations either to bless or to destroy his people. In the end destruction came, at the hands of Babylon in 587BC.

This message to Israel before the exile sounds a warning to us today. God is still the Holy One. If we imagine we can believe in him but not respond to him in faithful obedience, then we have got God wrong. He demands holiness and moral purity from his people.

- During the exile in Babylon, the deported Israelites had some deep questions to ask about why this disaster had happened. Was it because Marduk, chief god of Babylon, had defeated Yahweh, usually translated 'the Lord', the God of Israel? Or had God been unfaithful to his promises? Or had he rejected his people for ever? The prophecies in chapters 40 to 55 give answers to these questions.

Had the Lord been defeated? No. He was creator of the heavens and the earth (40:12–31 is a matchless account of this). As the prophet points out several times, the Lord had predicted that Emperor Cyrus of Persia would overcome many nations, including Babylon, so their God directed history. And anyway, no other god existed. The idols are nothing; 'there is no God apart from me'. These chapters contain the clearest statements of 'monotheism', belief in only one God, to be found in the Bible. So if all these things were true, the Lord could never be defeated.

Had God been unfaithful, then? No; Israel had. The exile was God's just response to Israel's sins. As chapter 43 verses 22 to 28 make clear, the people had failed even to offer proper sacrifices, and their leaders had disobeyed God. That is why the nation had been destroyed. God himself was not unfaithful.

Did this mean God had rejected Israel for ever? The prophet had words of comfort for people who thought so. 'Speak tenderly to Jerusalem, and proclaim to her that her hard service has been completed . . .' God had pardoned them; he would no longer remember their sins. He would even make his 'servant' Israel 'a light to the nations', who would save both those Israelites left in their homeland and those foreign nations that submitted to Israel.

These answers, and the whole message of these chapters, should encourage us still today. God is the greatest power in the universe and he keeps his promises. He is always ready to forgive us. Armed with this comfort, we should serve God by telling the good news in word and deed to those outside the community of faith.

- The prophecies to Israel after the exile came to people faced with an enormous task. They were to rebuild, not just the city and the temple but also the community of faith. The prophecies in these chapters aim to encourage those daunted by the task with the hope of a bright future. 'Arise, shine, for your light has come' is the beginning of chapter 60, full of promises of restoration, with the nations serving Israel. Then why was this restoration so long in coming? Chapters 58 and 59 explain: God would not answer their prayers or respond to their fasts because they had still not stopped sinning. They still exploited the weak. The Israelites' future, now as much as before the exile, depended on their response to God. If the Israelites responded in faith by keeping the law and protecting the weak, then God would save them.

These last chapters of Isaiah also speak to us today. God wants to establish his kingdom among us. Then why are our prayers not answered? Why are we so spiritually powerless? Is it because we, too, are disobedient? If we were to obey God and help the oppressed, we would see the rule of God in our midst.

The Holy One still requires holy people. But he remains ready to forgive us and to recommission us as his servants.

SONG OF THE VINEYARD
Isaiah 5:1-7

In these verses the prophet imitates a secular song. In his song he likens the vineyard to Israel and God to its owner. The owner spared no effort and expense in creating the perfect vineyard. But in spite of his best efforts, the vineyard yielded only sour grapes. In verses 3 and 4, the prophet, speaking for God, the owner, asks the citizens of Jerusalem and Judah what he should do with this vineyard which yields only sour grapes. He declares that he will utterly destroy it. Nothing but briars and thorns will grow on it.

In verse 7 Isaiah interprets the song. The vineyard stands for the nations of Israel and Judah. Even as the vineyard was to produce delicious grapes, Israel and Judah were to bring forth justice and righteousness. And even as the vineyard produced only sour grapes, the people brought forth only bloodshed and mourning.

This parable is a condemnation of Israel for its social sins. The people should have been concerned with establishing justice and righteousness. But they did not live up to their calling. Instead of justice and righteousness, they were involved in exploiting the poor and needy. We can see this in chapter 1 verse 23 where the Israelites exploited widows rather than defending them. Or in chapter 5 verse 8, where the landowners were only interested in enlarging their estates and building bigger houses, squeezing out those less wealthy than themselves.

These verses have profound implications for us today. As God's people, we should be concerned with establishing justice and righteousness. We should treat people fairly in our private dealings. But we should also try to ensure that the whole society we live in, both national and international, works for justice and righteousness. The poor and the oppressed must be treated both fairly and mercifully. When God drinks our wine, will it refresh him or will he spit it out?

CALL OF ISAIAH
Isaiah 6:1-8

Isaiah's call to be a prophet came in a mighty vision of God. He was in the temple at Jerusalem after the death of King Uzziah, 742BC, when he saw the seraphim standing guard beside God and was transfixed by their words 'Holy, holy, holy', repeated three times to express the superlative holiness of God. God is completely incomparable. No one and nothing is equal to him.

Experiencing the holiness of God, Isaiah realizes that he does not live up to God's holiness (verse 5). He recognizes that he does not honour God with his speech and that he shares in the guilt of his society which does not honour God with its speech. He does not excuse himself by pleading that he is just a product of his society. Instead, he recognizes his responsibility both for his own sins and those of his culture. His guilt and sin disqualify him from God's service. But the seraphim touch his lips with a burning coal taken from the altar and assure him that his sins are forgiven and his guilt is taken away. In verse 8, Isaiah overhears God's deliberations with his council of angels. Who will be God's servant? Isaiah volunteers with the words, 'Here I am, send me.'

As Christians, we are called to be God's servants. We ought to recognize God's holiness and our sinfulness. Before we can serve him properly, we need to accept his forgiveness which was shown in Christ. Then, like Isaiah, we are able to volunteer to serve God. He is our holy God and Master and we are his forgiven servants. We may not be prophets, but we are part of his church, called to work together to make his message known to the world.

IMMANUEL
Isaiah 7:10–17

Judah was enduring an invasion by Syria and Israel (the ten tribes of the northern kingdom). During this time several conversations took place between Isaiah and King Ahaz. Isaiah wanted to assure the king that he had nothing to fear. If Ahaz trusted in God, God would rescue Judah. Verses 10 to 17 record one of these conversations. Isaiah, speaking in God's name, tells Ahaz to ask for a sign to assure him that God will deliver Judah. Ahaz declines God's offer; he does not want to put God to the test. God's response shows that this was not

the king's real motive. Ahaz did not request a sign from God because he did not want to obey God.

Isaiah proclaims that God himself will give Ahaz a sign. A woman has conceived and will bear a son named Immanuel, which means 'God is with us'. This would have been a sign of assurance since the presence of God gave assurance of victory. Isaiah adds that before the child is old enough to make intelligent choices, the land of Israel and Syria will be deserted. However, since Ahaz refused to trust in God, according to verse 17 Judah would be delivered from Israel, only to be conquered by Assyria. God took Ahaz's response with utmost seriousness.

The New Testament identifies Jesus as Immanuel (see Matthew 1:23). In Jesus, God is with us. The presence of God can assure us of salvation or judgment, depending on our response to him. God holds out these two distinct futures, and our response will determine which future comes to pass. Like Ahaz, we have the choice. If we want salvation, which only God can bring, we must trust him and be willing to obey him. If we choose to rely on ourselves rather than on God, we are choosing to face God's judgment.

THE GREAT KING
Isaiah 9:2–7

This famous prophecy was given at a coronation—either Hezekiah's or Josiah's. On such occasions, prophets would honour the kings in exalted language, using the metaphor of father and son to refer to the relationship between God and the king. Coronations were times of great optimism. The nation recognized the wonderful future that was waiting if the king responded rightly to God.

In verses 2 and 3, Isaiah draws a contrast between the darkness of despair which had been experienced under the previous king and the joyous salvation which could be ushered in by this new king. The joy of the coming salvation will be like the joy of harvest and the joy of the spoils of war. In verse 4, Isaiah expresses the hope that the king will free Israel from foreign oppression, even as Gideon freed it from the Midianites. In verse 5, the instruments of war will be destroyed since peace has made them obsolete.

Then Isaiah follows the common practice of comparing the king to God's son. Just as the Egyptians gave throne names to Pharaoh, Isaiah proclaims the names of the king:

- **Wonderful Counsellor** refers to the king's great wisdom.

- **Mighty God** is better translated 'Divine Warrior' and refers to the king's supernatural skill and strength in battle.

- **Everlasting Father**, or better, 'Father for ever', reflects the hope that the king will look after his people even as a father looks after his children.

- **Prince of Peace** indicates that the king will bring peace, prosperity and well-being to his people.

No Israelite king ever fulfilled this wonderful promise, but Jesus fulfilled it perfectly. And so Christians have identified this great king with Jesus. He is the 'great king', and we should join him in making his kingdom known.

DAVID'S GREAT DESCENDANT
Isaiah 11:1–9

The previous key passage celebrated a coronation. This passage looks forward to the coming of a great future king. Jesse was King David's father, so the 'stump of Jesse' (verse 1) refers to a time when the kings of the house of David will have been cut down. In other words, this is a prophecy about the days after Babylon had overthrown Jerusalem. The prophet anticipates a new 'shoot' from the stump of Jesse, a future king for Judah.

Verse 2 lists seven Spirit-given graces that will empower this king. Then in verses 3 to 5 the prophet describes the king's wisdom, so deep that he will know his subjects' inner desires and motives. He will support the poor and needy, and 'smite the violent' (a better translation than 'smite the earth'). Righteousness and faithfulness will be his royal clothing.

Verses 6 to 9 picture a totally different natural realm in this reign. The great king will bring in a new world order character-ized by peace, a peace mirrored among the animals and between animals and people. There will be no more violence because everyone will know God.

The prophet looks to a great future. Judgment is not God's last word. He will not let human sin and folly triumph.

The New Testament takes in these images of kingship and a new world order under the idea of the new creation which Jesus has brought in. We do not yet see such a world, but we will see it when Jesus' kingdom fully comes. Until then, we work with our king for the poor and needy, and do everything we can to shape the world as he wants it.

THE INCOMPARABLE CREATOR
Isaiah 40:12–17

After the Israelites had been deported to Babylon, many of them doubted the power of God. They believed that Marduk, the god of Babylon, had won a victory over Yahweh, the Lord, the God of Israel. This chapter contains several speeches in which the prophet disputes with the exiles about this. He reminds them of the hymns they sang in the past. In their hymns they sang that God alone had created the heavens and the earth. The prophet points out that you cannot believe at one and the same time both that God created the heavens and the earth and that he lacks power.

These verses provide a good example of such disputation speeches. In verses 12 to 14 the prophet puts a series of questions to remind the exiles of their faith that God created the universe. Who taught God how to create? The Lord alone created the heavens and the earth and he needed no advisor. Based on this belief, the prophet concludes in verses 15 to 17 that compared to Yahweh the nations and, by implication, their gods, are to be reckoned as nothing. Israel should be assured of the power of God.

Often we, like the exiles, sing in our hymns words that we do not fully believe in practice. In particular, we sing that we believe God created the heavens and the earth even though we, like the exiles, doubt his power. If we really believed that God created the universe, we would always look to him to give meaning to our lives and not try to find our purpose elsewhere. And we would never imagine that anything could have a power over our lives greater than God's.

MY SERVANT
Isaiah 42:1–9

This is the first of several passages in this section which introduce God's 'servant'. God delights in his servant and will help him to succeed. Through God's Spirit the servant will bring justice to the nations. The servant will not become discouraged. He will be full of gentleness as he brings forth justice. The nations will wait with hope for the servant's justice and teaching.

In verses 5 to 9 God speaks to his servant. God is the Creator of the universe and of humanity in it. God tells the servant that he has called him to bring people into covenant relationship with himself and to reach out to the other nations with his salvation. Verse 7 speaks of 'bringing out prisoners from the dungeon', which refers to the exiles from Babylon. God is concerned that all humanity should recognize him as God. And he reminds the servant that he has predicted the new things that the future will hold.

Who is the servant? In the remainder of Isaiah chapters 40 to 55 the servant of the Lord is identified with Israel. And also, words used here to describe the servant are used of Israel in other passages. So the 'servant of the Lord' probably refers to Israel. The prophet proclaims that Israel will be liberated from exile and will have the opportunity to bring God's salvation to the nations.

Israel never completely fulfilled this role, but Jesus fulfilled it perfectly. And so the New Testament identifies Christ as the servant of the Lord (see Matthew 12:18–21). It is one of the great pictures for him in the New Testament. Christ mediates the new covenant and brings salvation to the world. Christians must share in this ministry. We, too, should be agents of blessing for humanity while we have the opportunity.

GOD ENCOURAGES HIS SERVANT
Isaiah 49:1–6

God's servant, here definitely identified with Israel (verse 3), speaks out to the nations in this passage. He is very clear that God has called him for a purpose, to be an effective secret weapon (verse 2). Through him God will show his glory.

But verse 4 reveals that God's servant is discouraged. Despite all God's preparation, his mission does not seem to be getting very far. He feels he can only commit his cause to God.

In verses 5 and 6 the servant hears words of deep encouragement from God. His ministry will have results beyond what he could expect. Not only will the exiles return to their homeland and restore the broken spirits of the Israelites left behind in the ruins of Judah, but also Israel, God's servant, will be the means by which other nations will be saved.

As we saw in the previous key passage, the New Testament calls Jesus Christ God's servant, taking on Israel's mission to bring salvation to the Jews and to all nations. And the Christian church is linked to him in this mission. Christians have a ministry of reconciliation, and as we try to fulfil it we can learn from God's servant in this passage. When we feel that our best efforts are futile, we too can commit our cause to God. He can and will work through us to achieve far more than we can foresee.

THE SUFFERING SERVANT
Isaiah 53:1–12

In this, the best known of the 'servant songs', we meet God's suffering servant, who suffers pain and death to redeem guilty people from their sins.

The first six verses are set in the mouths of unidentified people who speak as 'we'. They have changed their minds about the servant. Before they had thought him a worthless person who deserved his suffering. But now they have come to realize that he is suffering innocently, and on their behalf.

In the next verses, the prophet agrees with this confession. The servant suffered quietly for the sins of his people. After he died, he was buried with 'the wicked' (a better translation than 'a rich man'). Verses 10 and 11 say that God made him suffer for other people's guilt, and that he will be raised from death. God will exalt him because he was prepared to suffer and die for many people.

Is the servant still to be identified with Israel, as in the earlier servant passages? It would be surprising if he was not. The probable explanation is that in verses 1 to 6 the prophet speaks for those Israelites not taken into exile, still living in poverty in Jerusalem and Judah. They considered themselves more righteous than those deported to Babylon. But the exiles' liberation from Babylon will lead their fellow Israelites to change their minds about them. In the prophet's mind, the exile was like death and the return like resurrection. He hoped that the return would bring Israel back together, united under the leadership of the exiles.

But whatever the precise meaning in the prophet's mind, Christians have naturally identified the suffering servant with Jesus. He was rejected, he suffered on behalf of others, he was raised from death. We can rejoice even more than the Israelites at the salvation God's suffering servant has won for us.

And also we should make him our model. If we remain faithful to God, even in the face of undeserved suffering, we may help those around us to turn to God.

THE TRUE PEOPLE OF GOD
Isaiah 56:1–8

Who are God's people? The Israelites after the exile were, not unnaturally, very particular about this: they, and only they, belonged to God.

But in this passage, the prophet maintains that the true people of God are those who follow his teaching. They are those who 'maintain justice and do what is right'; they keep the demands of God's covenant. This applies even to the outcast. In Jewish culture foreigners and eunuchs were considered to be outcasts who were disqualified from membership in the community of faith. According to verses 3 to 8, even the foreigners and eunuchs who love God and who obey him are to be included as members of the true people of God. God's people are those who do God's will. The temple should be a house of prayer for everyone who obeys God.

The New Testament takes up this idea by insisting that the church is made up of all who respond to God in loving obedience. As long as a person joins himself or herself to God through Christ, he or she is a part of the true people of God. God works with the poor and the despised to form his own people. Therefore, we should accept into our churches and into our friendship everyone who responds to God, regardless of race or social standing.

We need to realize that we remain the people of God only so long as we respond to his grace by keeping justice, by following his righteousness and by holding to our covenant relationship with him.

WHAT GOD WANTS FROM HIS PEOPLE
Isaiah 58:1–12

This chapter takes up a theme found often in the prophets. What kind of worship does God want from us?

The Israelites at this time were not slow to worship. They kept fasts and times of prayer. But, so they complained, God had not honoured their fast by answering their prayers (verse 3). The prophet responds by pointing out the inadequacy of their fast. True worship demands more than words and ritual. God only accepts worship from people who strive for the well-being of the poor. The Israelites' fast has not had the desired result because they have oppressed their workers, quarrelled and committed acts of violence. They have used the courts to enslave the poor, as verses 6 and 9 are best understood. All of these acts were committed while they were keeping a fast to God.

The kind of self-denial that God desires is a self-denial on behalf of others. God wants the people of Israel to free the oppressed and share their food with the hungry, their shelter with the homeless and their clothing with the poor. If they will do this, God will bless them and bring about their restoration.

Why do our prayers so often seem to go unanswered? Why do our churches so often lack spiritual vitality? This passage provides an answer which may be difficult for Western people to accept. We may not be openly involved in exploiting the poor, but we, like our culture, practise self-indulgence. We do not make significant sacrifices for God, much less for the poor. Too often our gifts and acts of charity stop short of meaningful self-sacrifice. We give gifts so long as they do not jeopardize our lifestyle. We do not become involved in freeing the oppressed and feeding the hungry to the point that it damages our self-interest.

The worship God wants from us involves self-sacrifice. If we will love God and love our neighbour until it hurts, we can expect God to bless us by answering our prayers and by bringing restoration and vitality to our churches.

THE YEAR OF GOD'S FAVOUR
Isaiah 61:1–11

This chapter rings with joy because of a great promise God has given to the prophet. God has commissioned him to proclaim a message of comfort. He is to announce to the nation of Israel that God will save them from their adversity and change their mourning into rejoicing. He refers to this coming salvation as 'the year of God's favour and the day of his vengeance' (verse 2). The phrase 'day of his vengeance' means God taking action against Israel's enemies.

In verses 4 to 9 the prophet heaps image upon image as he encourages the people. He describes the glorious future awaiting them. The ruined cities will be rebuilt. The foreign nations will serve the people of Israel and honour them, since they will recognize that God has chosen this nation to be their priest. Instead of shame, Israel will receive honour. God will bless the people of Israel so much that the nations will recognize their unique status, so fulfilling his promises given to Abraham that through his offspring all nations would be blessed. According to verses 7 and 8, God will save the Israelites because his righteousness is offended by the way the nations have oppressed them. The chapter ends as the prophet rejoices in the national salvation the Lord will bring.

Luke's Gospel, in chapter 4 verses 16 to 21, tells of Jesus reading this passage in a synagogue and applying it to himself. He, like the prophet, had been sent to proclaim the good news to the afflicted and the oppressed. What is more, Jesus believed that the year of God's favour had now arrived; it had come in the 'kingdom of God' which he was bringing into the world.

Christians have a message for the afflicted and the oppressed, to be proclaimed both in our words and in our deeds. The fulfilment of God's promise of salvation has come in the person of Jesus Christ.

The Message of Jeremiah

Andrew Igenoza

The world today is as confusing and uncertain as ever. Many people live in fear of a global holocaust. The developing nations, particularly those of Africa, face political and socioeconomic instability. There are ideological claims and counter-claims. There are the different religions. Which is the right religion, or church? Can different religions be practised at different times? Who is the real God? How may he be known, and what should be our relationship with him? What are the consequences of wrong attitudes towards God and our fellow human beings?

These are pressing questions. But they are not just for today. The prophet Jeremiah lived about 2,600 years ago in the kingdom of Judah. Born into a priestly family, he was called by God to become a prophet in 626BC when he was about twenty years old. This book records his career.

The God of Jeremiah is the God who establishes and faithfully keeps his covenant with his chosen people. This covenant, a special agreement, is made so that people can really know him and give their lives to him in proper obedience. But the Israelites have broken the terms of this agreement many, many times. Even so, God promises to establish 'a new covenant'. He will put his Law within them and 'write' it upon their hearts. They will all know him and he will forgive their sins, wiping them all away.

The promise of the 'new covenant' is at the very centre of the message of Jeremiah. Knowing God in this new way makes all the difference between the true and faithful God, and all other gods and ideologies. The New Testament states that this new covenant was established through what Jesus Christ did when he died on the cross. This God of the covenant is unique, living and everlasting, unlike the idols of the other nations. He is the creator and the sovereign ruler of the whole universe. He is utterly limitless—being both 'at hand' and also 'far off'. People cannot hide themselves from him. He fills both the heavens and the earth. (See 27:5; 10:16; 10:3; 23:23–24.)

This all-knowing, all-seeing God searches the hearts of every individual. His love is everlasting, but at the same time he is just and must judge. This God can be encountered if people seek him whole-heartedly. True guidance, which so many people seek, is offered by the God of the Covenant through his 'Law' and through 'the words of my servants the prophets'. (See 17:10; 31:3; 1:16; 10:24; 29:13; 26:5.) In Jeremiah's time the Law was something near our first five books of the Bible.

Through Jeremiah, God tells his people that if they 'call' upon him and pray to him whole-heartedly, he is ready to answer and disclose to them 'great and hidden things'. In his covenant, God has the power to heal and restore individuals and whole nations. So Jeremiah could pray: 'Heal me, O Lord, and I shall be healed; save me, and I shall be saved, for you are the one I praise' (17:14). The healing and salvation offered by God has a broad effect in physical, psychological, emotional, spiritual, economic and even political terms. Health and healing will be part of the blessings of the new covenant. But at the time of Jeremiah, the condition of God's people appeared to be incurable—beyond healing. (See 8:8,12; 30:12–13.)

What had gone wrong? They had forsaken their God and begun to serve other gods (2:13). They were mixing the worship of God with the worship of other gods. They burned incense to the Canaanite god, Baal, and went after other gods. Then they would go into God's temple and say: 'We are safe!' Their disloyalty towards God and their divided interests led to their abandoning their faith, in utter rebellion against God.

Religious disloyalty because of fear, pressure or serious crises is a deep-seated problem among the African people. Many are baptized, confirmed and bear 'Christian' names but later turn away to serve the ancestors and other nature deities. They break their covenant with God. Jeremiah says this is wrong.

The moral and social evils in Jeremiah's nation were an inevitable result of disloyalty to God. These included oppression, violence, wickedness, sexual immorality, murder, falsehood, theft, and so on. The consequence, which Jeremiah foresaw,

Jeremiah OUTLINE

would be exile, physical removal from their country. They would be dispersed among other peoples by their invaders and conquerors. Before this, there would be famine, pestilence, drought and war.

Jeremiah's era was one of the most turbulent in the history of his people. Within forty years as a prophet, he witnessed the reign of Judah's last five kings and a governor. On the foreign scene, Assyria was eventually destroyed by the rising power of Babylon in 612BC. Meanwhile, Egypt was challenging the military might of Babylon and Judah and the surrounding small nations were seeking their place in these super-power struggles.

At times the kings of Judah pledged loyalty to Babylon; at other times, they were drawn into the Egyptian camp. Jeremiah's unpopular message remained the same—Babylon would gain supremacy, and any nation that would not yield to Babylon would suffer famine, disease, invasion and eventual deportation.

Jeremiah's message naturally drew very sharp reactions—both from the ruling class, including prophets and priests, and from the ordinary people. Many times his life was threatened—and once he was left for dead in an underground well. The scroll on which his words were written was destroyed by King Jehoiakim, and had to be rewritten.

In his sufferings, Jeremiah prayed, wept, was filled with self-pity, accused God of deceiving him and called for vengeance upon his tormentors. But Jeremiah's faith in God never diminished, nor did he compromise his message. Though he was apparently restrained from praying for his people, he continued to do so (14:7–12). Jeremiah's faithfulness and consistency are at the heart of his message.

The prophetic voice, even if unpopular, should not be silenced on sensitive national issues and foreign policy options.

In all his troubles, Jeremiah was delivered from death, and he lived to see his predictions come true. But Jeremiah still had hope for his people. Though the Babylonian captivity would last about seventy years, they would return to their land. Babylon itself and other nations of the earth would be punished. Jeremiah also looked far beyond Judah's return— to the time of the 'messiah', a time of peace and economic prosperity. Jerusalem shall be holy and its inhabitants shall return to God whole-heartedly. Gentile nations shall also share in the blessings. With the coming of Jesus Christ these blessings are already being realized. The message of Jeremiah is of universal and eternal relevance.

A CALL AND A COMMISSION
Jeremiah 1:1–19

Jeremiah was born into difficult times. International tension was high; society was decaying. But Jeremiah was a young man who was spiritually and morally alert, chosen by God, even before he was conceived, to be a prophet—God's messenger to the nations. Like Moses, Jeremiah protested. His problem was his youth: 'I don't know how to speak; I am too young' (verse 6). However, God assured him and gave him power for the task.

The call of Jeremiah shows us that youth, inexperience, or ignorance of public speaking technique are apparently no hindrances to God. In Zaire, Simon Kimbangu, who vehemently protested, like Jeremiah, was called in 1918 when he was twenty-nine. What God expects from his messengers are willingness, spiritual, mental and moral sensitivity, alertness and obedience. God calls his people to be 'prophetic' voices in their various walks of life. Our societies are decaying and Christians must all act, as Jesus said, like salt—to preserve, to heal, to give 'flavour' to the world around them. Like Jeremiah, God assures them of his strength and guidance.

God communicated with Jeremiah not only through visions, dreams and words but also through his common sense, his intuition and observations. The almond tree (1:11–12) was a sign of spring. Here was a message for Jeremiah. Just as Jeremiah's people 'watched' for the blossoming of the almond tree, so God was watching over his word to fulfil it. It was as sure as the seasons. God speaks through simple natural events to people who are alert.

Jeremiah's vision of a boiling pot facing away from the north (verse 13) signified judgment on Judah through an invasion from the north (Syria), as a result of their idolatry. Jeremiah was to proclaim everything he was commanded with all boldness. He would suffer and be stiffly opposed by the kings, the nobles, the priests and the people of Judah; but God assured him of his presence and deliverance. God's ambassadors need to be faithful to his word and be bold in declaring it to people. They are assured of God's help.

AN UNFAITHFUL PEOPLE
Jeremiah 2:1—4:2

In the Old Testament, the relationship between God and his chosen people, Israel, is seen as a 'marriage' (verses 2–3). But instead of worshipping the true God, the people have turned away to worship idols—they have been unfaithful and committed adultery (verse 20). The picture-language of this passage is vivid, underlining the horror that God feels when his special covenant-people turn away from him towards worthless gods. What is more, as long as the people of Israel remained in that state, there was nothing they could do to take away their sin (verse 22).

The people of Israel begin to give different excuses, and to contradict themselves, claiming they have not sinned (verse 23), or, on realizing the falsity of this claim, that the situation is hopeless (verse 25). They even go so far as to call their idols their maker—'You are my father', 'You gave me birth' (verse 27)—but when they are in deep crisis, they remember to call God 'My father, my friend from my youth' and call out 'Come and save us!' (2:27; 3:4).

But this unfaithfulness was not just true in Jeremiah's day. One example can be found in contemporary Africa. The idea of one true God who is 'Father' exists, but scant attention is paid to him. Instead the focus is on ancestral and nature gods. But when in deep crisis, the traditional African remembers to appeal directly to God.

Many educated Africans, brought up in mission schools, now declare their independence of God and of his church. Reason and self-effort become their idols. Either guilt is explained away, or their position is seen to be beyond repair. In their home villages they join in idolatrous and ancestral worship; in the big cities they show up in church sometimes and call upon God to save them. When overwhelmed by problems they seek help from the diviners and medicine men. They also go to the prophets of the numerous African Independent Churches without giving thought to repentance.

'How lightly you gad about, changing your way!' says Jeremiah. Jeremiah's message was to tell God's people to 'return' to God (4:1) by turning away from sin to their God who loves them deeply.

A SERMON IN THE TEMPLE
Jeremiah 7:1—8:22

This sermon was specifically meant for the people who went to the temple to worship, who claimed to be 'believers'. How often it is wrongly assumed that everyone in the church is all right—and the 'sinners' are outside. But no! Jeremiah calls on the temple worshippers to change their ways, and not just have a superstitious trust in the temple and its rituals (7:34).

This makes it clear that anyone who claims to be a worshipper should show it in their moral conduct. Worshippers should be just, and should care for the alien, the orphans and the helpless. They should not kill innocent people or worship false gods. Then—and only then—will God take pleasure in their worship. Right there in the temple there were people who had stolen, murdered, committed adultery, sworn falsely,

worshipped other gods, and even sacrificed their children—and yet they continued to believe that everything was all right with them. The temple rites had become nothing more than magic spells to ward off evil. Jeremiah's verdict was that the temple would be destroyed.

The point Jeremiah wanted to make is that God looks for obedience rather than sacrifice. He is not saying that sacrifice is wrong, but religious rituals without obedience to God's moral laws are meaningless.

The message to the people is clear: for refusing to listen to the numerous prophets sent to them, their doom is sealed (7:25—8:22).

Jeremiah's sermon serves as a warning for people who have a superstitious trust in the 'ceremonies' of religion without a corresponding commitment to serve God and a change in moral attitudes. It is often claimed, at times with a fanfare, that Africans are a very religious people. Research suggests that there are about 20,000 converts to Christianity every day in Africa. The churches may be full and worship may look very lively. But what is the *quality* of their religion? Can it stand Jeremiah's test?

WORTHLESS IDOLS
Jeremiah 9:23—10:25

God's people were meant to be different from their neighbours. The most important thing in life was to have an intimate relationship with the living God, and not to trust in human wisdom, riches or achievements which might easily replace God (9:23–24). The customs of other nations were to be avoided because of their pagan associations. God's people, too, were not to be alarmed 'at the signs of the heavens'—thunder and lightning, falling meteors, comets, heavenly portents—which were worshipped as gods.

The Canaanite god of storm and fertility, Baal, and his consort Ashtoreth, 'the queen of heaven' (7:18), were such nature gods. Child sacrifices were made to Molech. These gods and goddesses who were stumbling-blocks to God's people are pictured by Jeremiah as being false and powerless, the creation of human imagination, the works of craftsmen. They are like scarecrows which neither move nor speak. As they can do neither good nor evil, God's people should not be afraid of them (10:5), and those people who make and worship them are both stupid and foolish (10:8,14).

Africa is a place where there are obvious examples of regional religious worship—shrines, groves with partly buried pots, iron implements, skulls and bones, protective charms and personal deities of destiny, with all sorts of associated customs. These customs and symbols of religion are taken very seriously. How then can an African who is steeped in his local and tribal traditions be convinced that the gods are 'worthless, a work of delusion' (verse 15)? It is only in the power of 'the living God and the everlasting King' (verse 10), shown in his crucified and risen Son, that the powers behind idolatry and the customs associated with it can be exposed.

PRAYERS, MEDITATIONS AND COMPLAINTS

Jeremiah is often called 'the weeping prophet'. He was also a praying and meditative person. His prayers, meditations and complaints are quite unique (see especially 4:19–26; 8:18—9:3, 10:19–25, 11:18—12:13; 14:7–22, 15:10–12; 17:14–18; 18:18–23, 20:7–18). In them we have an insight into the personal religion of the prophet.

Jeremiah talked of his anguish, his grief and tears, because of his people's refusal to repent, and because of the catastrophe which he knew would overtake them as a result (4:19-26, 8:18—9:3). He pleaded with God on behalf of his people, praying for judgment of the nations who were to bring about Judah's downfall. In his prayers, he completely identified with his people, confessing sin on their behalf (10:20; 14:7–9) and making God's covenant with Israel the basis of his plea for mercy (14:21).

Jeremiah also prayed for God's vengeance against his numerous persecutors. These enemies of truth had become hardened by sin and were ripe for judgment. His prayers only confirmed what God had already said he would do. In perplexity, Jeremiah raised the problem of the prosperity of his wicked persecutors, who merely paid lip-service to God. He had no choice but to place himself entirely in the hands of God, who knew him through and through (11:20; 12:3). So Jeremiah prayed for his own life and protection (15:15), and for relief and salvation from his troubles (17:14).

Jeremiah also bemoaned his personal fate as a prophet. He had become a laughing-stock and so complained bitterly against God (20:7; 15:10; 15:18; 20:14). Perhaps Jeremiah's many complaints were not pleasing to God, and he had to be urged to 'return' to God for restoration, but in all his trials, he had God's assurance (15:20, 21).

God's messengers must not be afraid to stand alone—though they may be mocked. They must carry on praying to God for their people, whatever happens. They ought to weep on behalf of their people to avert calamity. Vengeance on the ungodly rests with God (see Romans 12:19; Hebrews 10:30) and in the spirit of Christ we should bless and not curse.

BAD SHEPHERDS AND A RIGHTEOUS KING
Jeremiah 21:1—23:8

The rulers of Judah (or shepherds, as they are called in most translations) were failures. Weak, wicked or shortlived, none of them proved to be good. In the light of this failure, Jeremiah prophesied the coming of God's ruler: the righteous Branch (most translations). The remnant of God's 'flock' would be gathered, and this king would rule them wisely, with justice and righteousness. Under him Judah would be saved and Israel secure (23:3–6; 33:14–16). He alone would be God's ideal ruler. Earthly kings may fail but this king on David's throne would never fail.

Jeremiah's prophecy began to be fulfilled in the birth of Jesus Christ, who will 'reign over the house of Jacob for ever' and of whose kingdom 'there will be no end' (Luke 1:31–33). With the second coming of Jesus, Jeremiah's prophecy will find complete fulfilment

(see Revelation 22:12–16 for the description of Jesus as the root and offspring of David).

Most earthly rulers are a gross disappointment. When, for example, African countries were gaining political independence their peoples were filled with hope. The new rulers would lead them to the Promised Land. But these rulers, whether military or civilian, have in most cases failed woefully. Bad policies, acts of injustice and large-scale corruption have resulted in serious economic, political and social instability. The situation appears to be getting worse.

But God's people in Africa and indeed world-wide, need not put their trust in earthly rulers who so often let them down. Hope in the saving work of Jesus Christ, a king whose reign is both universal and eternal, provides the necessary encouragement to God's people to improve their own conditions and those of their countries, until this righteous king finally comes.

FALSE PROPHETS
Jeremiah 23:9–40; 28:1–17

There are many prophets and churches making conflicting claims today—how do we know the true prophet or the right church? Prophetic movements and churches keep on multiplying, particularly in Africa. The situation was no less bewildering to any critical observer in Jeremiah's time. Many may have thought Jeremiah was a false prophet. Right from the start he had running battles with those who 'prophesied falsely' (5:31) in the name of Baal (2:8; 23:13). These prophets had considerable political influence in the royal court and were greedy for unjust gain (6:13; 8:10). They prophesied lying visions, worthless divinations, the deceit of their own minds in God's name, though God had not sent them (14:14–15; 23:21). They gave their hearers, even those who despised God's word, a false sense of security (23:17). They themselves were adulterous and strengthened the hands of evil-doers, so that no one turned from his wickedness (23:14). Worse still, they carried out their immoral deeds in God's temple (23:11).

True prophecy was not a matter of private opinion or personal wish. The message was given by God and was sometimes unpleasant to the prophet (17:16). Only divine call and inspiration could make a man a prophet; apparent sincerity was not enough. The false prophets did not possess the divine word because God had not called them. They relied on 'lying dreams' rather than faithfully proclaiming God's word (23:25–32).

The false prophets failed all the tests for judging prophecy. By worshipping other gods, they failed the test of right doctrine (see Deuteronomy 13:1–5; Exodus 20:2–6). With their corruption, wickedness and adulteries, they failed morally (see Exodus 20:13–17; Deuteronomy 5:17–21). In addition, their prophecies were never fulfilled. The lives of these false prophets did not match up to the lives of the true prophets who went before them (28:8).

True prophets like Jeremiah faithfully proclaimed God's word against idolatry and immorality. His life was morally upright, and God's word was a delight

and all-important (15:16). Importantly too, Jeremiah's prophecies were fulfilled, some of them before his very eyes (28:16–17; 32:24). These prophecies had a great impact and still do. The words of a prophet should be consistent with God's written word, the Bible; and a prophet's character and lifestyle should be sound. The moral and spiritual impact of a prophetic ministry on the lives of those who hear should be assessed. As Jesus says, 'You will know them by their fruits.'

INTO EXILE
Jeremiah 25:1–14; 39:1–10

The certainty that Judah would go into exile is one of the main themes of Jeremiah. Jeremiah saw the fate suffered by Judah at the hands of the Babylonians as the ultimate punishment for idolatry and immorality. Taking a nation into exile was designed to destroy the whole fabric of the political, economic and cultural life of the nation, wiping out all local traditions. An exiled nation was meant to lose its identity.

As Jeremiah predicted (25:8–12, for example), Jerusalem with the entire kingdom of Judah was sacked by Nebuchadnezzar's army, and the temple and all the buildings were burned with fire (39:8). The most important and useful people were deported, leaving only a few of the ordinary people to till the land. That the distinctive culture of Judah did not disappear, and people did not merge with the Babylonians, was due to Jeremiah and other prophets. In this, Jeremiah won a great spiritual victory.

He announced that after a life-span of seventy years, God would bring back his chosen people to the Promised Land (29:10–14). In the meantime, they were to live normally in the country of their exile, and be prepared for a long stay. But certain individuals and their descendants were to perish in exile (29:31–32; see also 20:6; 27:10, 15).

What the exile means for us today may be a difficult question. For the Hebrews of Jeremiah's time, it meant punishment and a means of discipline which involved their physical movement and dispersal. In history, wars, colonization, trade in slaves and so on have always caused mass movement of people across tribal, national or even continental frontiers. Africa is not left out in this. Even now, the refugee problem persists. Are these punishments for human excesses and wickedness? Has God's church always been alive to her responsibilities? When communists, militant Muslims and other anti-Christian groups overrun people and countries which have formerly been Christian strongholds, can it be seen as a form of exile, a serious punishment for the failure of the church?

In a sense, all of God's children are now experiencing a form of exile. Peter and the writer of the letter to the Hebrews in the New Testament referred to Christians as exiles on earth. Certainly, the worst form of exile is to be forever cut off from the presence of God because of perpetual rebellion.

THE TIME IS COMING . . .
Jeremiah 29:1–14; 30:1—33:25

Jeremiah knew that the exile would be long, but that it would eventually end, and God's people would be restored to their land (29:10–14). This prospect gave him the necessary motivation to write down his prophecies (30:1–3).

God will destroy all the nations among which Israel is scattered; '. . . but I will not destroy you. I will not let you go unpunished; but when I punish you, I will be fair' (30:11). During the restoration, the city of Jerusalem will be rebuilt and the palace will stand where it used to be. God's chosen nation will once again plant, feel merry and enjoy the fruit of their labour (31:4–5). Not only that, but God will make a new covenant, full of blessings, for his people (31:31–34; 32:39–40). And, even better, there will be a righteous king, a descendant of David, who will reign justly and bring peace (33:14–16).

As things got worse, Jeremiah's hope of restoration shone brighter. He demonstrated this in a dramatic way by buying a piece of land, even though he was under guard, at a time when everything—including the economy—was collapsing. This was 'in faith' and trusting God's promise that 'houses, fields, and vineyards will again be bought in this land' (32:15). God promised abundant prosperity and security (33:6). These glorious promises are repeatedly emphasised in Jeremiah. The first official restoration of the land from exile was in 537BC.

But for Jeremiah, restoration meant far more than resuming life in the Promised Land. It looked forward to

the ideal future, the time of the
Messiah, when not only the northern
kingdom (Samaria) would have a part
(31:4–9) but the Gentile nations
would also have a share in God's
blessings (3:17; 16:19). This is a
picture of the kingdom of God in
which people from all continents on
earth, including yours and mine, shall
have a part. (See Revelation 7:9–10.)
The message of Jeremiah was not only
about judgment for sin but also about
hope for all people, both in the present
world and in that which is to come.

The Message of Lamentations

Andrew Igenoza

In modern society people can still be moved by the plight of individuals, but we find it hard to grasp the impact of calamities that come on entire communities or societies. The idea of corporate solidarity which pervaded the Hebrew and the ancient African people is fast disappearing. Yet when disaster strikes our own lives, we can grieve so much as to lose hope totally or become suicidal.

The book of Lamentations is a corrective to both these extremes. It is one of the most tragic books in the Old Testament. But at the same time hope and consolation keep springing up in its verses. Jerusalem has fallen and the remnants of the people are left in its ruins. The writer is totally drawn in to the plight of his people.

The structure of the book is unusual. The first four chapters are acrostics representing the twenty-two letters of the Hebrew alphabet, one verse for each letter, except chapter 3, which has three verses for each letter. Chapter 5 has twenty-two verses but is not an acrostic. Perhaps this structure conveys that the sin and pain of the people are from *aleph* to *tau*, from A to Z. It serves to encourage completeness in the expression of grief, the confessing of sin, and the instilling of hope.

The book is still read aloud annually in Jewish synagogues.

Chapter 3 contains the heart of the message. The poet is full of agony and calls on God for help, but God shuts out his prayers (verses 7 to 20). But then he recalls a truth that rekindles his hope: 'The Lord's compassions never fail. They are new every morning...' (verses 21 to 31). God will not cast off his people for ever. On the strength of this belief, the poet calls for prayers of penitence 'until the Lord looks down from heaven and sees' (verses 40 to 50). He finally receives the assurance that God has heard and drawn near (verses 55 to 66).

Lamentations tries to express in words the enormous grief which the Jews were feeling. God, and faith in him, are taken very seriously. Such an attitude is the only source of hope.

Many African nations in recent times have faced extreme hardship through war, drought, famine, refugee problems or appalling economic mismanagement. Do African Christians despair or become indifferent? Or do we identify with our people while retaining our hope in God?

Lamentations OUTLINE

The Message of Ezekiel

Geoffrey Kimber

When God first called Ezekiel, he was a refugee in Babylonia, married but with no career. He had been born in Jerusalem into a priestly house in the days of Josiah, the last Godfearing king of Judah. When Josiah died, his religious reforms went with him, and the verdict of 2 Kings on each of his

Ezekiel OUTLINE

successors is the same: 'They did evil in the sight of the Lord.' The shocking new foreign paganisms that they brought in must have been a continuing subject for outraged debate in Ezekiel's priestly family home.

When Ezekiel was twenty-five, King Jehoiakim, who had put his faith alternately in Egypt and Babylon, and not at all in God, tried once more to change sides. Nebuchadnezzar of Babylon responded by invading Israel and taking 10,000 of the Jews into exile—including Ezekiel.

Five years later (in the year that Ezekiel had always expected he would follow his father as a priest in the temple) God called him to be a prophet and pastor to his people in exile in Babylonia. For the next twenty-two years he spoke God's words to the exiles and sent messages to the remaining people back home in Jerusalem.

Ezekiel's book is the tidiest of any of the prophets and is in beautiful date order, stating both where and when many of the prophecies were delivered. The first half of his book covers the five years leading up to the final siege of Jerusalem, and is mainly messages of judgment to the Jews, both in the homeland and in exile. The turning-point in his book is when Jerusalem finally fell to Nebuchadnezzar, which vindicated all he had said so far.

After this he turns in the second half to the future and to two main issues: the judgment of God on the nations around, including those nations he had used to punish Israel; and God's future plans for Israel and its final restoration as the people of God.

Five great themes of timeless importance emerge from his book:

- The 'otherness' of God. God is quite different from us. Ezekiel above all the prophets is aware, through his priestly background, of the glory of God. Yet in his highest and most explicit opening vision he does not claim to have seen God, or his glory, or even the likeness of his glory, but only the appearance of the likeness of the glory of God. It is easy these days to try to bring God down to our size, to make him a friend or buddy. But God is still beyond all our imagining.

- The sovereignty of God. Ezekiel lived in an age of disillusionment. It was easy to think that God was dead, or had at least forgotten to do anything. Life seemed a meaningless mess, with world affairs out of control and God's people suffering as a result. And yet Ezekiel's favourite name for God is 'the sovereign Lord'. For Ezekiel, God is sovereign, meaning that he is in overall control. Nothing slips through his fingers, nothing is forgotten. The kaleidoscope of confused events actually fits together to make a consistent picture—if only you have the key.

  The whole basis of Ezekiel's ministry is that the sovereign Lord has spoken to him and given him that key.

  We, too, may be bewildered by national or personal events. We, too, need Ezekiel's message that God is sovereign. Our God reigns in world events as well as in our hearts.

- The wages of sin. The Israelites thought that because God loved them he would ignore their sin. Ezekiel saw that they were a people who ignored God's laws, trusting in secular powers and worshipping idols that claimed to bring material blessings and offered licence for lust. He stated clearly that their complacent idea of God was wrong. God would judge and punish all these sins.

- Personal responsibility. The Israelites made the mistake of blaming others, such as their ancestors, when things went wrong. Ezekiel says clearly that God will judge each person separately. No one will receive God's judgment or his mercy as a group. No one is tied down by his past or his culture. Each may turn in repentance to God and find God's acceptance.

- A people renewed. There are many parts of Ezekiel's pictures of renewal and restoration, especially in his final vision, that are hard to understand. But one clear thread is his concept of Spirit-fllled renewal bringing life to the spiritually dead. His final vision is of the people of God ordering both their worship and their land according to his will; a praising, obedient people of whom it may be said: 'the Lord is there.'

GOD'S COMMUNICATOR
Ezekiel 2:9—3:15

What are the qualities that all preachers of God's truth need? This story of Ezekiel's call to be a prophet illustrates four primary qualities:

- Good preachers know God. The starting-point for Ezekiel's call was a close encounter with God himself and a fresh realization of his greatness and holiness. This realization was to motivate and direct his whole ministry.

- Good preachers have absorbed the message. All good teachers have made God's truth something inward to themselves before they hand it on to others. Ezekiel expressed this particularly dramatically: God had told him to eat it. It was a bitter and difficult message, but because he had the courage to take it into his own life, it produced sweetness inside and nourished him.

- Good preachers know their hearers' situation. Ezekiel said nothing until he had sat seven days with the exiles. He sat silently, listening to them, finding out their situation and their feelings. He was overwhelmed as he sat, either by what he observed or by the task God had given him—or probably both. But at the end he was able to direct God's message clearly and relevantly to the exiles' real life experience.

- Good preachers can stand being rebuffed. Ezekiel's audience were a hardhearted, rebellious lot. They considered themselves God's people and generations of prophets had already struggled in vain to make them hear. Proclaiming God's message, then as now, could be tough. But God promised to make Ezekiel just as tough as his audience, and told him he need not be afraid of them.

And what is the message? The message is from God. The words that filled the scroll on both sides were God's, not Ezekiel's. And he is to begin each message with the words, 'This is what the sovereign Lord says.'

Our preaching must not only be relevant, it must also be God's word to that situation, and it must be delivered with God's authority. Ezekiel took this lesson to heart and in all of his prophecies we find this phrase which is his trademark, 'This is what the sovereign Lord says.'

THE MODEL PROPHET
Ezekiel 4:1–17

Some years ago an American evangelist used to walk from town to town struggling under the weight of a heavy wooden cross. More recently a vicar in Birmingham, England, drew attention to the plight of an imprisoned Russian Christian by spending Lent living in a reconstruction of her cold cell, wearing similar thin clothing and eating the same poor food.

Ezekiel was almost the only writing prophet to do what these men in our own time have done: he became a sign to the people. He acted out over periods of hours or months various significant dramas.

Sometimes he acted out something which his audience would have to do themselves later on, like packing his belongings and escaping to exile (12:1–7). Sometimes God needed to explain the drama—like joining two sticks together (37:15–28) or cutting up his hair (5:1–17).

Some of these actions seem quite reasonable to us. Others have caused commentators today, and quite possibly his contemporaries, to doubt Ezekiel's complete sanity. Of course, we do not know whether Ezekiel kept the drama up twenty-four hours a day like the

Birmingham vicar, or whether he went home at sunset and started again the next morning.

In the present chapter, Ezekiel found a public place outside his own door or in the market-place, and acted out his dramas so that all could see God's message. The message was in four parts and our chapter gives us the first three:

■ **First Ezekiel built a model of Jerusalem under siege (verses 1–3).** This prophesied the siege of Jerusalem which was soon to come.

■ **Then he lay on one side for 390 days and on the other for forty days (verses 4–8).** This symbolized the sin of Israel and Judah and the number of years of that sin, or of its punishment.

■ **Next he was commanded to live on a very poor, ritually unclean diet (verses 9–17).** This foretold the living conditions of the Jews both during the siege and later in exile.

The meaning of these messages is elaborated in later chapters, some of which we shall examine. Perhaps, however, we should take encouragement also from Ezekiel's method. Ezekiel believed in role play and drama. He was the master of the multimedia presentation. He knew that people learn best when a number of their senses are involved, not just the ears. He also knew how to get the whole town talking about his sermon!

GOD'S TOUGH LOVE
Ezekiel 16:1–63

What have divine and sexual love in common? Some may find this a highly distasteful question. Many did in the time of Ezekiel. Yet before Ezekiel's time another prophet, Hosea, had taught that God was Israel's loving husband, and spent his ministry condemning her as an adulterous wife. Here and in chapter 23, Ezekiel uses this same image. The chapter makes five main points, that apply equally to us today:

■ **God's love (verses 1–14)**. Israel was the abandoned newborn child of disreputable parents, but God in compassion rescued her and gave her life. Later when she was grown, he loved her and made her his wife, making her rich, beautiful and famous. God's love for us is far more profound and personal than we can ever realize.

■ **Israel's adultery (verses 15–34)**. But Israel became proud and committed adultery by making love to idols instead of to God (verses 15–19). She even gave her children to these idols as human sacrifices (verses 20–22). When she was in trouble she did not turn to God for her needs but entered into adulterous relationships with foreign powers—Egypt, Assyria and Babylon in turn. Sin is far more appalling to God and also more agonizing than we can understand.

■ **Her punishment (verses 35-43)**. Therefore God is going to give Israel the punishment laid down for an unfaithful wife: he will strip her naked and have her stoned to death. Sin always deserves God's punishment.

■ **Israel's true nature (verses 44–52)**. In fact Israel is part of a worthless family. Samaria, the northern kingdom, was her sister, and—horror of horrors—so is Sodom, that Israelite byword for shameless depravity. Sin is not something superficial; it is inherent in our very nature.

■ **God's continuing love (verses 53–63)**. Yet God still loves Israel and will eventually renew the marriage vow, make atonement for her sin and restore her. God still loves sinners, and paid the price for their sin.

This image is strong stuff which some may not easily stomach. And yet it is used again in the New Testament, both in Ephesians, where Christ, as husband, loved the church and gave his life for her, and in Revelation, where by God's miraculous grace the church is presented to Christ as a perfect bride.

THAT'S NOT FAIR
Ezekiel 18:1–32

The Israelites were suffering and they felt that it was not their fault. The law of Moses had said that God often punishes children for the sins of the fathers, and their prophets had often told them that the whole nation had to suffer because of the sins of a few. As a result, the Israelites were now complaining that God was not fair. Ezekiel says that personal responsibility is just as real as national and family responsibility. At the end of the day, each of us is responsible to God for our own lives. It is true that whole nations suffer because of the follies of their leaders, and often whole families are scarred by the sins of one member, yet God is just and will reward each of us for our own behaviour. The person who sins is the one who will die (verse 4).

A three-generation example is worked out of a good man (verses 5–9), his bad son (verses 10–13), and his good grandson (verses 14–18). We see how each will be judged on his own behaviour and his attitude towards God, sex, money and other people. The lesson of personal responsibility for sin is summed up again (verses 19–20). The person that sins is the one who will die.

We, like the Israelites, can try to hide behind the group sometimes. We blame our sin on our upbringing, our environment, our friends. ('I never had a chance'; 'It's what everybody's doing'; 'I got into bad company'.) As if this excused us. The message of this passage is that we cannot sidestep our own responsibility for our own behaviour.

The second half of the chapter brings hope. What if a person wants to change? Ezekiel makes very clear that if a man turns his back on his old bad way of life, God is waiting to forgive him, because he actually hates punishing the guilty.

On the other hand, if a good man turns to a life of sin he can't get by on his previous good record. God will judge him.

The chapter ends with an urge to action. Repent. Turn away from the past. It also brings us to the nub of the matter: You need a new heart and a new spirit (verse 31).

A HISTORY LESSON
Ezekiel 20:1–29

This chapter sets out clearly what has been wrong with Israel all the way along. In it Ezekiel shows how God works in the nation's history.

The elders of the Jewish exiles often came to visit Ezekiel, perhaps because they took seriously what he had to say. This chapter is one of several that begin with them sitting down in his house. Today they seem to have brought a question which God refuses to answer directly because of their sin. Instead they get a history lecture.

Two great themes emerge in the lecture: God has chosen Israel; Israel has rebelled against God. We are shown how the pattern has repeated itself at least four times:

■ **The story begins in Egypt,** where God chose Israel, but they preferred Egyptian idols (verses 4–9). So God took them away from temptation into the desert and taught them his ways (verses 10–12).

■ **Even in the desert they still rejected him,** so he refused to let them enter the Promised Land and kept them in the wilderness (verses 14–16), still continuing to teach them (verses 17–20).

■ **But still they rebelled, and God finally left them to experience for themselves the horrors of paganism and child sacrifice (verses 21–26).**

■ **Yet when he brought them into the Promised Land of Canaan, they headed straight for the pagan hilltop shrines and continued their idolatry.**

Through deliverance, teaching, the rigours of the desert and the horrors of paganism, God had consistently tried to bring them to know him, and they had equally consistently refused. The judgment outlined later in this chapter had become inevitable. How does this history apply to us today?

We can see first of all that for Ezekiel sin is not primarily about how we treat people and things. Sin is rejecting or ignoring God. The Israelites gave their attention and enthusiasm to idols instead of to him. We today can also ignore him and give our time to other things.

We can learn lessons also about God himself. God wanted to bless the Israelites, to make them rich, to guide them with laws so that they might live and prosper and be in relationship with him. We see him feeling both anger and pity for them in their sin, as today he still feels anger and pity for those who ignore him. We see too, that each time the final decision was taken for the sake of his name—God was concerned that other nations should learn what he was like. God was communicating through history, wanting everyone to know that he is the only God.

THE WATCHMAN
Ezekiel 33:1–20

Jerusalem has fallen. Ezekiel's warnings of coming judgment are complete, for that judgment has now begun. A new work lies ahead of him: explaining exactly why God has punished the people and bringing a promise of final restoration for Israel. God now recommissions Ezekiel for this second part of his task.

At the beginning of his ministry, God had commissioned Ezekiel to be a watchman (3:16–21). Now he does so again. A watchman has two duties: to watch and to report. Not for him the busy life of action and involvement. He must sit apart from the people, passive but alert, straining to see and to hear what lies beyond the horizon for others.

Whatever he discovers, he must proclaim clearly to all. If he does not, he is responsible for the resulting tragedy. If he does, then he cannot be called to account. Whether they accept what he says or ignore it, that is not his responsibility. He has done his work as a watchman (verses 1–6).

As a prophet of God, Ezekiel's job was to listen for God and to hand on his messages to the people. especially to warn the wicked of what lay ahead if they did not change (verses 7–9).

Previously (chapter 18) the Israelites had resented Ezekiel's warnings, feeling they were being punished for things they had not done. Now in their punishment, they realize the extent of their own sin and are overwhelmed by it (verse 10).

Ezekiel's message to them makes three main points:

■ **God does not enjoy punishing people.** He does not rub his hands in glee at the thought of another wicked person ripe for punishment. In fact, he hates it, and is longing that we should repent and live.

■ **It is never too late to change.** The Israelites felt enmeshed in their sin and its consequences, that God had made up his mind about them and closed the file. Ezekiel says God never closes our file. We can always turn. And if we do, God will remember none of our past sins (verse 16).

■ **There is still need for warning.** Some still had a false sense of security. They felt they were so righteous that they could get away with sin. Ezekiel makes it plain that God punishes those who turn to sin, however good their past record.

At the end, Ezekiel pauses to listen to their reactions. Some have taken in what he is saying. Others ignore him. Either way, Ezekiel has spoken what he has heard from God. He has been a faithful watchman.

NEW LIFE IN OLD BONES
Ezekiel 37:1–14

The Israelites were in exile, broken, dispirited, their nation annihilated. There could be no future for Israel. Israel was dead.

And yet when everyone was finally sure that there was no hope, God began to give Ezekiel promises that he was going to bring Israel back to life. In the previous chapter God had promised to cleanse the Israelites from the sins of the past, to bring them back to their land, and to put a new spirit—his Spirit— within them. Now Ezekiel is given this amazing visionary picture of this renewal. God can still make the dry bones of his people live. Two prophecies are involved:

■ **Ezekiel prophesies to the bones.** God's people must hear his voice.

■ **Then he prophesies to the breath.** (The words 'breath', 'wind', 'spirit' in

Hebrew are the same.) Ezekiel is in fact praying to God's Spirit to enter his people, bringing the new life without which no reform can bring lasting change.

The result is that, instead of a group of bedraggled, hopeless refugees, we see a vast army of whole people.

How was this vision fulfilled? In part this happened when after fifty-nine years the impossible happened and Emperor Cyrus allowed Ezra and the exile community to return to Jerusalem and start to rebuild the city and the temple. The returned Jews never again lapsed into paganism. They had indeed a new heart and attitude.

We may also see its fulfilment at Pentecost, when God poured out the Spirit of his new covenant on Jews from every part of the world assembled in Jerusalem.

God delights to take the dry bones of people everywhere, to let them hear his voice and experience his Spirit, to fill them with his wonderful new life.

THE WATER OF LIFE
Ezekiel 47:1–12

In the final eight chapters of his book, Ezekiel records a vivid vision that God gave him some years after his main ministry. In this vision God showed him what he most longed to see—the temple, beautifully restored and with the splendour of God's glory returning to fill it again (43:1–5). Ezekiel must have savoured each moment of the vision as he was conducted around by an angelic being and told some of the regulations and measurements. Finally he is brought back to the main entrance where he began, and he sees what this new temple will produce—a river of water.

Now the river is a picture used widely in the Bible, from Genesis chapter 2 to Revelation chapter 22, where we read, in a clear reference to Ezekiel, of 'the river of the water of life'.

Ezekiel sees three things about this water:

■ **Its source (verses 1–2)**. It comes from the temple, where God himself is worshipped.

■ **Its strength (verses 3–6)**. It does not diminish, but grows deeper and stronger the further it goes.

■ **Its results (verses 7–12)**. It flows into the deadest part of Israel—the valley of the Dead Sea, and, as in the vision of dry bones, it brings surging new life where before there was only decay.

In the water, fish breed again—fish of every kind and in prolific numbers. At the water's edge, trees flourish where there was only barren saltiness before, and these trees provide both food and healing in abundance every month of the year, because they are supplied directly from the temple, from God himself.

This is all a marvellous picture of the life-giving work of God's Spirit. The passage has a world-wide note in it: the fish are of every kind and come from the Great Sea, the Mediterranean, that flows far beyond Israel. Revelation confirms this, saying that 'the leaves of the tree are for the healing of the nations'. God's Spirit, poured out in the water of life from the place where God is worshipped, is for everyone, everywhere.

The Message of Daniel

Daniel Berkovic

At first reading, Daniel may seem a very strange book. It partly tells a story, and partly tells of things to come outside that story. It belongs to the tradition called 'apocalyptic' which means 'uncovering' or 'revealing'. Such writing was very popular in the years between the testaments, but parts of Ezekiel also use this visionary style, and the second part of Zechariah. Above all, the book of Revelation is apocalyptic. The book of Daniel seems to be told in a way that would have been particularly relevant to the years of the Maccabees (see *The Deuterocanonical Books*). So some believe it was written at that time, using a story from the old days of the exile in Babylon.

Daniel, a Jew exiled from his homeland, is taken to be a royal servant in the court of King Nebuchadnezzar. From an early age, he lives in a society where people are interested in collecting all sorts of knowledge. As many imperialistic peoples do, they have convinced themselves of the superiority of their culture, and have succeeded in crossing national and cultural boundaries with their modern, progressive outlook. And so they have gradually got rid of old-fashioned ideas and gods, seeing them as too small for their multiracial and multicultural society.

Daniel OUTLINE

Daniel's purpose is to show their mistake, because his God, the one true God, is greater than all their human achievements. To ignore him is to have a distorted picture of the world. Daniel shows how God stands outside time and yet controls and guides it. He is sovereign, the only true 'superpower', who can be worshipped not just by one little tribe but by the whole world. There are many examples today of governments and leaders trying to make society uniform and monolithic. Exclusive ideologies are imposed in many parts of the world, and dissent is suppressed. In such countries, those who have a personal faith are disadvantaged. There is a need for men of God like Daniel to show in word and action the power of the almighty God and his control over the lives of people and of nations.

In the book of Daniel we learn four great truths about God:

- God is in control of his world. The king believed that his royal commands would shape history and make progress for his people. Under the influence of his decrees, everything would get better and better. But Daniel reveals God to be the sole maker of history. Whether people recognize it or not, he has created the world and is in control. He is guiding history towards its end—not a humanity perfected by its own efforts but one that will finally see and recognize God for who he is.

- God gives signs and wonders to those he has chosen to work for him. The book of Daniel is full of supernatural acts and visions which always confirm that Daniel's God is powerful and active. Through the agency of his personal relationship with Daniel, God breaks through into human life in dramatic ways.

- God is faithful. The early part of the book tells of the pressures put on Daniel and his friends to give up their worship of God, which does not fit in with the king's scheme of things. It is completely unacceptable for them to bow down and worship anyone other than the king, and disobedience means an immediate death sentence. Yet through it all they are faithful and loyal to God, believing that the God they serve will save them and be faithful to them.

- God will reign over all. The visions in the second part of the book show that God's kingdom can only be brought in after the rule of evil has been over-thrown. So history as we know it will have one day to come to an abrupt end. The present age will give way to a new age, which will be everlasting and indestructible (7:14). Daniel's vision is of a battle taking place simultaneously on earth and in the spiritual realm.

REVEALER OF MYSTERIES
Daniel 2:1–49

In Nebuchadnezzar's kingdom great respect was given to arts which we could describe as psychic or occult. In this example, the king has had a dream. He appears unreasonable in his demand (verse 9) that devotees of these arts should first tell him his dream, before interpreting it. Yet those who claim supernatural powers must prove themselves; if they cannot, they are discredited. Nebuchadnezzar is stepping outside the boundaries of ordinary reality. He is entering a world in which only spiritual powers can answer him for 'no one can do it for you except the gods'. And yet the king is only a 'religious' man in the broadest sense, for in his kingdom are the influences of various religious practices and he does not belong to any in particular.

Daniel's spiritual life contrasts sharply with the king's.

■ **He is concerned for others apart from himself,** and shows great presence of mind when the captain of the king's guard begins to round up all the wise men to kill them.

■ **He shares the problem with his friends** and together they seek God's answer.

■ **God has given him the understanding of visions and dreams** and can speak to him in a direct way. Thus, in verse 19, 'the mystery was revealed to Daniel in a vision'.

Daniel's prayer of thanks highlights the difference between human power and God's power. The nature of God is to 'reveal things that are deep and secret; he knows what is hidden and in darkness' (verse 22).

Now Daniel as the mouthpiece of God tells the king what has been revealed to him. He makes it clear that he can do this, not because he is wiser or better than other men, but because God, the revealer of mysteries, has enabled him. And this is not primarily for Daniel's advancement but because 'the great God is telling your Majesty what will happen in the future' (verse 45). The true man of God can see more clearly than any practitioner of occult arts.

THE FOUR BEASTS
Daniel 7:1–28

From here onwards Daniel speaks of his own experience of visions given him by God. Although the earlier stories also revealed things about God and his sovereignty over rulers and history, these chapters are the core of the apocalyptic message. In verse 2 Daniel says, 'I saw in my vision…'; he becomes the 'arch-visionary' of the remaining chapters.

The vision in this chapter is the central one. It describes four beasts coming out of the sea, which many have thought to represent four successive 'superpowers' in the years leading up to this book's date of writing—the Babylonian, Medean, Persian and Greek empires. Each beast is more dreadful than the one before, but the fourth is 'powerful, horrible, terrifying'. Each of these great beasts is an embodiment of destruction. Yet Daniel also sees a vision of almighty God described as the 'ancient of days' (verse 9), one who has been living for ever. The beasts, though allowed to live for a time, are overthrown and slain.

In verse 13 one called the 'son of man' is introduced, who is to have 'authority, honour and royal power' over people of all nations and languages. This title was taken by Jesus, and perhaps he had this passage in mind. The kingdom of God can only come after the worst of evils has been overthrown (verses 24 to 26). But the new age will be everlasting and different from all previous ones.

The Message of Hosea

Julio Zabatiero

The prophet Hosea, born in the northern kingdom, came soon after the prophet Amos. His message takes its tone from the bitter experience of his own marriage. Victim of his wife's unfaithfulness, Hosea dramatized the 'adultery' and unfaithful-ness of the people of God. As a merciful husband receiving back his adulterous wife, Hosea personified God's mercy, willing to receive again his people if they would only repent and turn again to him.

Hosea's preaching takes place against a background full of political instability (no less than four kings rapidly succeeded each other violently by means of successive coups), moral corruption, and religious decadence. The injustice denounced by Amos a few years previously repeats itself in Hosea's day, with military violence, idolatry, and the corruption of priests and prophets.

Hosea's messages are two-pronged:

- he condemns unjust social and economic practices (see, for example, 4:2);

- he speaks out against idolatry, practised by the people, and fed by the false teaching of the corrupt priests and prophets.

All of Hosea's oracles are marked by a passionate love and a profound experience of fellowship with God which, when faced with oppression and idolatry, is outraged. He uncovers the intimate relationship between idolatry and social and economic injustice.

The priests and prophets who instructed the people of Israel were in the service of corrupt kings. They taught anything for money—except the true biblical teaching which proclaims the character of God, the Liberator, as holy, just and pure. We can see from Hosea, and other prophets such as Amos and Micah, that this message of justice and holiness is not tolerated by violent and unjust governments because it is seen as highly subversive. So it is that oppression and idolatry go together because unjust political regimes need false religions to

Hosea OUTLINE

1:1 The context of the book

1:2–3:5 Hosea's marriage, a picture of God's suffering

4:1–8:14 Israel's crimes
4:1–3 Oppression
4:4–10 False priests and prophets
4:11–19 Idolatry
5:1–15 Corrupt leaders
6:1—7:2 Insincerity
7:3–7 Corruption in the palace
7:8–16 Israel and the nations
8:1–14 Rebellion and idolatry

9:1–14:1 Israel's punishment

14:2–9 The promise of restoration

support them. In the light of true worship of God, people would not accept injustice in silence.

In Latin America the theological currents known generally as the 'theology of liberation' have emphasized the relationship between the Christian faith and the concrete historical situations in our long-suffering continent. This is the fruit of a profound experience of God, as Christians have learned to recognize the deep compassion of God for the downtrodden and weak. Whether or not we adopt this theology wholly, the Latin American Christian people are committed to living Christianity in an active form, in love and in reality. For us, the message of Hosea is very relevant. We live in countries whose recent governments have been violent and oppressing. We have seen the increase of non-Christian religions which are winning our people with their idolatrous practices and their promises of salvation for the despairing. We cannot remain silent before such a picture of despair which we see throughout our continent.

Hosea announced that God's will for his people is that they should show forth love and justice (see 2:21, 22; 6:6; 10:12) and be faithful to their God, not betrothing themselves to idols, nor creating regimes which oppress the simple.

In Latin America we are attempting to put into practice the love and justice which come from the true knowledge of God. We are inviting Christians of all continents to do the same to the glory of our Lord. 'Who is wise? He will realize these things. Who is discerning? He will understand them. The ways of the Lord are right; the righteous walk in them, but the rebellious stumble in them' (Hosea 14:9).

RITUALISM AND CONVERSION
Hosea 6:1–6

This passage divides into two parts: in the first three verses the Israelite people are speaking, in the second three verses God makes his reply. In this passage Hosea declares that God does not accept a religion marked by empty rites, and meaningless formalities. While the words of the people seem to show a real trust in God and his salvation, they are actually false because they are not accompanied by a lifestyle which reflects the righteous life that God requires of his people.

God, who knows all about us, saw the Israelite people for what they were: 'Your love is like a morning cloud, like the dew that goes early away.' The live religion of the God of the covenant had been substituted with the empty formality of rituals in the temple, by great celebrations and countless sacrifices. God rejected this: 'For I desire steadfast love and not sacrifice, the knowledge of God, rather than burnt offerings.'

In a way similar to Hosea's time, a great many Christian churches today are more preoccupied with liturgical ritual, doctrinal niceties and institutional progress, than with living a just, holy, and pure life. What God requires of us is different. He wants 'love' to be expressed in action, marked by the practice of good works and a clear manifestation of justice (see, in the New Testament, 1 John 3:11–24). He also desires 'knowledge'—not merely intellectual knowledge, but a personal and intimate knowledge of God, characterized by loving, just and compassionate behaviour, as we imitate Jesus Christ.

God, the Liberator, who 'became human' in Jesus Christ, does not accept empty and ritualistic religion. He does not accept the songs, the emotions and expression of people who, under an appearance of piety, allow injustice and oppression to continue in their own nation, and in many, many countries in the world. True Christianity unites worship and doctrine with love and justice. Little or no good is achieved by proclaiming a gospel which is individualized, spiritualized—diminished.

The church's mission is to announce the true gospel—the gospel of the God who reigns over all the nations with justice and equity, of the King who intervenes in human history in favour of the downtrodden and defenceless, against the evil powers which keep people enslaved.

Love and a personal knowledge of God; not sacrifice and rituals. That is God's will.

IDOLATRY AND POLITICAL POWER
Hosea 8:4–7

In this short passage, Hosea denounces the close link between sinful governments and popular idolatry. In verse 4 the prophet refers to the several coups which happened in the short history of Israel. In about 250 years, eighteen kings, of ten different dynasties, took the throne. And all of these dynasties were disposed of violently.

These power-struggles, along with social injustice, were the fundamental causes of Israel's religious decadence.

The priests and prophets, with the responsibility to teach according to God's 'word', were bought off, and their teachings served the ideology of the royal family in power. Such oppressive and unjust regimes could not tolerate true faith; and they promoted the people's move towards idolatry as they fell prey to the religious manipulations of the corrupt priests and prophets.

God rejected the Israelite kings, the priests and prophets, and finally the Israelite people too, who had given in to idolatry and abandoned the just and liberating character of their true God. The prophets sent by God announced an irrevocable judgment. In 722BC this was fulfilled. The northern kingdom, Israel, came to its end, destroyed by the Assyrians.

If people cannot see God bringing justice, they will try to find it elsewhere. In Brazil the biggest growth rate in the number of 'converts' to the Afro-Brazilian religions (Umbanda, Candomble, Macumba) has coincided with a period much like Hosea's Israel. There has been a political and economic regime of an oppressive character, dominated by an élite, supported by international capital and a powerful ruling class. This regime was responsible for the alarming rise in poverty of the Brazilian people. Despite being the eighth biggest economy in the world, around 70 per cent of Brazil's population lives in utter poverty, under-employed, underfed, ill and without hope. The country which previously could call itself 'the biggest Catholic country in the world' now holds the largest number of converts to non-Christian religions.

The God of justice, the Father of Jesus
Christ, calls his church to fight against
idolatry, and to preach true faith in Jesus,
the only way of salvation. In our time, one
way to fight against idolatry is to resist
oppressive regimes with the weapon of
love, and to struggle alongside the people
for social justice. Announcing the
kingdom of God is done through
liberating words and acts generated by
faith in the Lord Jesus Christ.

The Message of Joel

Geoffrey Kimber

How do you react to news of yet another natural disaster? Pictures of famine in Africa often make us wonder if there really is a loving God in charge.

Most of Joel's book seems to have been written when Judah, with its agricultural economy, had just lost a whole harvest to an enormous plague of locusts. Joel vividly describes the locusts moving across the countryside, systematically engulfing and destroying everything, erasing the rich green landscape and leaving a grey desert behind. There was absolutely nothing left—nothing to eat, nothing to store, nothing for cattle food, nothing to offer God. A catastrophe like this would be remembered for generations.

Such disasters did not confuse Joel. He understood both the love and the demands of a holy God. The people had drifted away from him and now he had sent this to recall them to their senses and to himself. It was not the farmers who had sinned but the whole community. Today equally, it is not the African peasants who have sinned but the whole world community, ourselves included. Joel's call to his times should be a call to ours also—repent.

Joel outlines what true repentance is. It is not ritually tearing your clothes, but having your heart break, being taken over by an overwhelming grief. Repentance is also a group activity, where the whole community comes before God in anguish over sin.

All this is pretty sombre stuff, but Joel is essentially optimistic. He knows that God, who is agonizing over his people's coldness, is going to respond warmly and magnificently if they do return to him. He is planning to give them back everything the locusts have destroyed, and far more besides.

Finally, Joel turns to the future and has a vision of the blessings of our own New Testament age. At the end of chapter 2, he sees that God's Spirit is going to be poured out on people of every race, and that wonderful signs will accompany this. On the day of Pentecost, Peter reminded his audience of how Joel, more than any other prophet, had foreseen the Spirit's coming.

Joel's final verses are reminiscent of Ezekiel's last vision when he sees a fountain of water cascading out of God's house, bringing pardon and blessing to his people.

Joel OUTLINE

1:1–2:11　The plague of locusts
2:12–27　The call to repentance and God's loving answer
2:28–3:21　Future judgment and blessings

The Message of Amos

Julio Zabatiero

Amos, herdsman and peasant, was called by God to announce a hard message to the powerful people in the kingdom of Israel. This powerful ruling class had broken their covenant with God, severely oppressing their people, and exchanging their faith in God for empty and meaningless rituals in great religious ceremonies.

By the time of Amos, Israel had become a superpower. The king, Jeroboam II, had conquered several countries which were paying heavy tributes. He had restored the international trade routes through Israel and created wealth by charging customs and road tolls. As a result, a small and powerful élite which allied itself to the royal house had arisen to dominate the people of Israel. Not only that, but many priests and prophets grew rich and influential as they attributed political success to the hand of God.

In order to preserve their riches and maintain their authority, this economic élite, together with the royal house, created a series of mechanisms by which to oppress the people:

- corruption in the courts of justice (5:7, 12);

- creating big estates, thus enslaving small landowners (2:6; 3:9–15; 5:11);

- degrading the needy (4:1);

- charging high prices for basic commodities (8:4–5);

- demanding costly offerings and sacrifices in the worship of God (5:21–23).

They took from the people their land, their food, their dignity, and their very faith, as they threw great parties and banquets in their mansions (4:1–3; 6:1–7; 8:9–10). The religious leaders, mere observers of all that was happening, lost their 'prophetic voice' and failed to speak out for God, becoming defenders of an official, lifeless, and loveless religion (5:18–20; 7:10–13).

Amos was different. He announced the destruction of Israel because of these sins. A foreign army would destroy the towns and take their inhabitants into captivity. Nothing would avert God's judgment (see, for example 3:11–15). Only the poor amongst the people would later be restored as a nation, under the unified government of David's descendant. There would be a new kind of economic order,

Amos OUTLINE

marked by justice, liberty, and peace amongst the nations (see 9:7, 11–15).

Today, again, God's voice is heard, speaking against oppressive political regimes. Latin America, for example, has been dominated by military regimes and so-called democracies which keep millions of people in poverty, famine, and despair. False religions spring up because the church of Christ has not been faithful in proclaiming the liberating message of the Bible. From Amos we see that the good news of the kingdom of God is directed to the poor, the weak, the hungry, and to those who suffer injustice and oppression because of an unjust economic system.

God has not gone absent. He is always on the watch, and will judge the nations for their mercilessness. Christians must work to transform unjust social structures, eliminate the need for military powers which consume millions of dollars and millions of lives, and create a new social order. From Amos we see that the poor, the weak and the downtrodden are God's chosen agents in bringing about this dream. Moved by faith in Jesus Christ, and not by human ideologies, they will work to make this world a better place to live in. The God who became a human being gave his own life for humanity and desires that all people should be fully human.

THE PRACTICE OF JUSTICE
Amos 5:4–6, 14–16

The message of Amos prophesied the end of Israel, which came less than forty years after his preaching. But God, ever faithful to his covenant, had offered the Israelite élite an opportunity to repent. If they wished to avoid God's judgment they had to seek him; but not with sacrifices, offerings and ritualistic festivals, that served only to cover up their sins (see 5:21–23).

To seek God, according to Amos, meant (and still does mean today) to practise justice and eliminate oppression. As Paul taught in the New Testament, faith must be translated into action both in our personal lives and in the life of nations. To 'seek good' means to do good to your neighbour: the poor and the peasants driven from their land. To 'love good' means to detest violence and, especially in our world of nuclear weapons, to fight effectively for peace—without arms. To 'maintain justice in the courts' means to avoid corruption in the courts of law, where the rights of the poor are defended. Justice also calls for international relations to be corrected—with the rich nations paying just prices for primary resources and agricultural products which they import from underdeveloped countries. It calls for Third World debts to be treated with justice and not with avarice.

The Christian faith demands faithfulness to the will of God, and faithfulness to God and Jesus Christ demands justice in human relationships, at a personal level, at a national level, and at an international level. Faith should expose rather than cover up social injustice, and the injustices of the present world economic order.

Christians today are called to act firmly against unjust social practices. Justice, peace and love are true Christian values; not profit and military might, nor technological advance. When human accomplishments are used for good, and not for evil, this is what it means to 'seek the Lord, the God of Hosts'.

The Message of Obadiah

Dick Hines

At a time when there seems to be little room for justice or moral considerations in the chaotic and cut-throat world of international relations, God's message to Obadiah concerning Edom takes on fresh relevance.

For centuries the Edomites (who were descended from Esau, Jacob's twin brother) hated Jacob's descendants. They took pitiless delight in their destruction (verse 12), seizing upon it as an opportunity for cowardly revenge (verse 14) and economic advantage (verse 13).

But God rules over all nations and will judge all nations, with a compassionate concern for the welfare of all his people. To nations which behave like Edom the warning is: '... your deeds will return upon your own head.'

The Message of Jonah

Dick Hines

Does God have favourites? Does he care about what happens to different nations? And what does he think about countries or people who apparently take no notice of him or his standards? These questions are all examined in the story of Jonah.

Nineveh, the capital of the Assyrian Empire, had become for the Jews something of a byword for cruelty and godlessness. When God called Jonah to go and speak out against Nineveh's sin, it was a sign that although God was offended by their evil ways, he was concerned to warn them of impending judgment. God's concern for Nineveh contrasts strikingly with Jonah's cowardly reluctance to co-operate with God. But the God whom Jonah claimed to worship is seen to control the sea, the weather, the outcome of an impromptu lottery, even the feeding habits of a large fish! So much so that the runaway Jonah, thrown from the ship by terrified sailors, was saved from drowning in response to his desperate pleas, and was given (rather unceremoniously) a second chance to do what God had told him to do.

The Ninevites' response to Jonah's message was overwhelming. 'From the greatest to the least' they had such a change of heart that their threatened destruction was averted. But why wasn't Jonah pleased with his successful mission?

Slowly but surely the reason becomes clear. Jonah's outburst against God for the way he showed mercy to the Ninevites who repented reveals a proud, self-centred and vengeful spirit. Here is a man whose most passionate feelings can be aroused over the death of a common, leafy plant which shaded him, but who responds to the fate of many thousands of human lives with a cold and unconcerned disregard.

The message of the book is unmistakable. God, the creator and controller of this world, looks upon one world, and upon all people with equal compassion and concern. Indeed, it was to 'all nations' that Jesus Christ commanded his disciples to take the message of God's love and forgiveness. In Jesus' parable of the prodigal son, God is pictured as a grieving father, longing and looking for the return of his son. The story of Jonah tells us that God longs for all people to turn to him in the way the Ninevites did so long ago. And Matthew's Gospel records that Jesus commended them for doing so (Matthew 12:41). But what if every single one of God's people were like Jonah?

Jonah OUTLINE

1:1–17 Jonah disobeys God

2:1–10 Jonah's prayer from inside the big fish

3:1–10 Jonah goes to Nineveh; the people repent

4:1–11 God's mercy on Nineveh; Jonah's anger

This unusual and dramatic story is unsettling. In an age when it is so easy to slip into a smug and complacent attitude about the well-being of others, the challenge is unavoidable. In Paul's letter to the Corinthians, God's people are called 'God's fellow-workers'. Rather than remaining unconcerned or trying to hide from their responsibilities, Christians are called to be actively involved in God's loving purposes for all people.

The Message of Micah

Julio Zabatiero

Micah, who lived in a small country village in the southern kingdom of Judah, was called by God to announce the sins of the religious and business leaders who governed Judah (1:1; 3:8). This was at a time when a great religious reform had taken place, restoring ritual purity in the worship of God and the removal of idolatrous altars from the hills of the country.

Yet this religious reformation had not affected the way individuals behaved nor the social and economic structures of the country. The sins denounced and condemned by Micah were:

- the oppression of small landowners whose lands were taken violently by the landed aristocracy (2:1–2; 3:1–3);

- bribery in the courts to defend the interests of the magnates (3:11; 7:3);

- dishonesty in business, violence and lying by the rich (6:9–12; 7:2–4).

The royal house, which had promoted the religious reformation, used violence, oppression and every kind of injustice to keep itself in power and make more money (3:9–10). Families were broken up by covetousness and by violence, and friendships no longer had meaning (7:5, 6). The priests and the prophets were religious mercenaries, preaching for money, and using religion to silence the voice of the oppressed and to justify the violent fury of the rich, the judges, and governors (2:4–6; 3:4–7, 11; 6:16).

Because of all this, Micah, full of the Holy Spirit, announces the destruction of the kingdom of Judah which would ultimately make way for the creation of a new, just society, truly following God, and not observing only rituals (1:16; 3:12; 6:13–16; 7:13).

After the destruction (which actually occurred in 587BC), the prophet's 'utopia' (which Micah compared to the exodus) would come into being (see chapters 4 and 5, 7:11–20). Then a new political and economic order would come about. Through faith in God the nation would be rebuilt. The strong hand of God, his outstretched arm, would accomplish these things.

Micah's Spirit-inspired dream was not limited to Judah but was of a new international order, in which the superpowers would be subject to the small kingdom of Judah, fountain of faith in God and of a new, just, and humanizing society.

Micah OUTLINE

1:1 The context of the book
1:2–16 God condemns idolatry
2:1–3:4 God condemns the oppressors
3:5–12 False religious leaders
4:1–5:15 God's future kingdom
6:1–8 The Lord's court
6:9–7:10 The oppressors are condemned
7:11–20 God's mercy

In chapter 5 verses 2 to 5 Micah announces the coming of a powerful and just leader who is to bring it about. He would come from Bethlehem, an insignificant little town in the country. The New Testament (see Matthew 2:6, for example) identifies this leader with Jesus Christ. In his earthly ministry Jesus inaugurated the universal kingdom—the 'rule' of God on earth, the fulfilment of Micah's dream. The Christian church, the community of the kingdom of God, is called to share in building this new kingdom, fighting against all political and economic organizations which maintain the fortunes of a few and the suffering of a majority of the world population. Will the church fight against human ideologies and utopias to bring about Micah's dream?

WHAT GOD REQUIRES
Micah 6:1–8

The Lord, through his prophet, calls on the people of Judah to take part in a judgment. God asks the people why they have abandoned him; has he, God, fallen short in anything? The people cannot answer, because they have forgotten their God who had delivered them from the land of Egypt.

The reforms that had brought about the restoration of worship in Judah had been only superficial. 'Will the Lord be pleased with thousands of rams, with ten thousands of rivers of oil?' (verse 7). No, God has no need for his worshippers' sacrifices; and rituals cannot purify a person.

What is the will of God? 'He has showed you, O man, what is good. And what does the Lord require of you? To act justly and to love mercy and to walk humbly with your God.'

■ **To act justly.** God demands of us that our courts be honest, that laws be carried out, that the rights of the poor and homeless be defended; that financial crimes be judged with severity and that corruption in government be brought to an end.

■ **To love mercy.** God expects unity and mutual care in society, where doing good is a constant habit, welcomed by its citizens, and where there would be no abandoned children, lonely old people, unemployed slum-dwellers, prostitutes, or criminals.

■ **To walk humbly with your God.** God wants all people to submit to him through faith in Jesus Christ. The message of the church, to be spread to all nations, is a call to a commitment to Jesus Christ, as people respond to what he did for us when he died on the cross, in that great act of selfless love.

How shall we present ourselves before God? With our hands full of sin—both the things we have done, and the things we have left undone? Or with our hands full of the good works which God prepared for us in Christ Jesus?

The Message of Nahum

Dick Hines

Nahum's message from God, made some time in the late seventh century BC, concerned Nineveh, the capital of Assyria, a 'superpower' of the day. The city of Nineveh was denounced as a place of violence, corruption, idolatry and witchcraft (3:1–4). From here godless rulers directed a greedy and cruel military expansion, exploiting the surrounding nations. Indeed, the prophet's own people were being oppressed by the Assyrians.

But the God in whose name Nahum spoke—at whose presence the whole world and all its people are said to tremble (1:5)—declares an end to Assyria's domination. Later, as Nahum foresaw in his vision, Nineveh was completely destroyed (2:1–10; 3:12–18).

There are two contrasting messages here which echo down to today. To nations whose foreign policy resembles the tyranny of Assyria, God fiercely declares 'I am against you' (3:5). Yet a tender whisper of hope may also be heard; for this same God is a good God, and Nahum assures us that '. . . he cares for those who trust in him' (1:7).

The Message of Habakkuk

Geoffrey Kimber

Habakkuk was a man with a problem. He lived in Judah in days when violence and conflict were everywhere, and there was no justice in the courts. But that was not his real problem. The thing that really got him upset was why God was allowing it. We today are often shocked that the government or the police allow people to get away with things. Habakkuk was shocked that *God* seemed to let justice be undermined.

Much of his book is more like a private conversation with God than a normal prophecy. In the opening verses he puts his problem to God: 'Why do you tolerate wrong?' And God answers that justice is on its way—the Babylonians are going to punish Judah.

This answer poses more problems for Habakkuk than it solves. He knows God is too holy even to look on evil, so how can we say that the ghastly behaviour of these murderous Babylonians is actually God's justice in action? Hence Habakkuk's second question: 'Why then do you tolerate treacherous people, and in particular, the Babylonians?'

The answer seems to be that the Babylonians will also in turn get their just deserts. God is certainly not blind to their sins, and the series of five woes (2:6–20) probably refers mainly to them.

In the psalm that concludes his book, Habakkuk meditates on the great things God has done in the past. But in some ways this just makes his problem about the present seem worse. Why is God not active now, when people need him so much? In the end, Habakkuk's faith wins out over his fear in a great final acclamation of faith. Even in the face of economic collapse and ecological disaster, he will still rejoice in God.

Habakkuk's problems may be ours today also. When we see evil in our world, we often ask ourselves why God lets it go on. Bible stories about his great deeds in the past, even news of what he is doing today in other places, may tantalize rather than reassure us.

There is an African saying: 'Seeing something is better than hearing about it.' We may long, like Habakkuk, to see a bit of action from God. Instead we may have to learn three important lessons which the prophet also learned.

- God's sense of timing is different from ours. Yes, he is just, but that does not mean things will always happen when or even how we expect. We have to trust that God will act at the right time.

- Our part, like Habakkuk's, is to wait, to stand in our proper place and to watch with patient faith.

- We must learn to rejoice in God for himself, not because he makes us happy or solves our problems. Then we, too, will find God is our strength, and that we can rise in joy above every situation.

Habakkuk OUTLINE

The Message of Zephaniah

Geoffrey Kimber

Was Zephaniah simply one more in the tradition of prophets of doom? Or did he have something distinctive to say?

There was certainly much in his society to make him cry judgment. The eight-year-old King Josiah had inherited from his grandfather Manasseh a totally corrupt society. Manasseh had been a fanatic for paganism; altars to Baal and Molech were everywhere and temples had been built to sun, moon and stars. The people, especially the rich, had loved paganism's salacious fertility rites and human sacrifices. With it all went a preoccupation with wealth and a blind eye to the oppression of the poor and weak members of society that resulted, without which the wealth might not have been so extreme.

But what did God think about all this? God's day was coming. His anger at this arrogant sinfulness and his deep sorrow over what was happening to his own people were going to find expression. God's day was going to be a bit like a pagan ceremony, with Judah in the leading role—as sacrifice. Or like a blacksmith's shop, with Judah as the pig-iron and God as the fire. All the proud and arrogant, all those indifferent to God, would be destroyed. The remainder would emerge purified.

This was God's plan for the Judah that Josiah inherited. How do you think he feels about our societies? Are we equally indifferent to morality, equally obsessed with wealth?

Only one kind of person was going to survive—the humble: 'I will leave within you the meek and the humble, who trust in the name of the Lord.' Zephaniah urges them to seek God, and to seek him urgently, as those who despair of their times. Have you ever lost something vital—perhaps your key, or your wallet? You search and search, overturning everything until you are not sure whether you are searching or springcleaning. That is the kind of wholehearted search with which we should seek God.

A rich reward awaits those humble enough to search. God hates sin but he loves people. He is waiting to take delight in those who seek him, and to reassure them. Zephaniah pictures God singing in his joy, like a young man singing as he goes to meet his beloved!

Anger and love. This prophet tells us that God feels both emotions towards his people. We need to hold both in our understanding of his character.

Zephaniah OUTLINE

The Message of Haggai

Michael Butterworth

People's morale was low. Nearly twenty years before, they had been liberated by Cyrus of Persia, and returned to their homeland rejoicing, inspired by promises of a great future. God had foreseen the exile and its end after seventy years. He was in charge. He had brought them home and would bless them.

But, after a while, the promises began to seem rather long-term. The people were free, it was true, but it was a struggle to stay alive (see 1:6, 8, 10). As a result of this hardship, the people concentrated on themselves. Rebuilding the temple was an unthinkable luxury. They had started work on it soon after returning from Jerusalem but work had come to a standstill because of local opposition.

Into this situation came the prophets Haggai and Zechariah. 'Put God first,' they said. 'You spend your energy on your own concerns. No wonder God has not blessed you. But his promises still stand. The blessing will come.'

It is easy to give up and become discouraged when God's promises are slow to come about. It is then that we are tempted to put ourselves first and act selfishly. Some time prior to 1947 some British troops stationed in Pakistan had undertaken to build a church. However, when the time came for their families to join them, they stopped work on the church building in order to prepare quarters for their families. Very reasonable! But local people saw the message: 'God comes second.'

Obviously God does not need a house. He does not *need* anything we can offer. But he graciously invites us to express our love for him in concrete, practical ways. Our use of time and money often says more than our most eloquent words.

In 1970 nearly 10 million refugees streamed into India from Bangladesh (East Pakistan). The cathedral at Calcutta had been involved in relief work for some time, but it now became necessary to store supplies in the main body of the cathedral. Surely God was pleased with this use of 'his house'. The book of Haggai challenges us to remember that our actions and our failure to act have implications. Do we put God first in all things? And what do the people around us make of our actions?

Haggai OUTLINE

1:1–12 The first prophetic message: 'Show that you put God first by rebuilding the temple.'

1:13–15 Zerubbabel and Joshua get the people working

2:1–9 The second prophetic message: 'My Spirit is with you. The house will be more glorious than before.'

2:10–19 The third prophetic message:'The people are unclean, but now I will bless.'

2:20–23 The fourth prophetic message: 'Kingdoms overthrown; Zerubbabel is God's seal on the people.'

Haggai repeated God's promises of blessing to the people. The enemies of Judah wanted to stop the work on the temple; they ended up paying for it to continue.

The book ends with a prophecy to Zerubbabel, governor of Judah. He will be like a signet ring, engraved with the king's seal and used on official documents to signify the king's approval. His ancestor, King Jehoiachin, had been like a signet ring thrown off, taken in exile to Babylon, never to return. The line of King David seemed to have been rejected, and God's promise to make his house 'kings for ever' to have failed. Zerubbabel is a sign that this is not so. The signet ring is back on God's finger.

The Message of Zechariah

Michael Butterworth

Jesus made use of several passages in Zechariah. That alone motivates us to get to grips with this difficult little book. It divides into clear sections (see Outline) which need separate consideration.

The prophet Zechariah was involved with Haggai in encouraging the depressed people of Judah and Jerusalem to believe in God's promises, to put him first, and to express that by rebuilding the temple. He also received eight 'dream visions' (chapters 1—6) which speak more specifically of God's purposes. The enemies who devastated Judah will themselves be punished. God is in the midst of his people again and will protect them. Zerubbabel the governor, and Joshua the high priest are symbols of God's continuing promise to send an anointed one, a 'messiah', who will be both king and priest. He is referred to as 'the Branch' (see 3:8 and 6:12).

In chapters 7 and 8, in reply to a question about fasting, the people are challenged about the attitudes of their hearts. Zechariah reminds them of their failures, but also of God's covenant promise: 'They shall be my people and I will be their God.' Only then does he answer the question: the fasts will become feasts, and people from everywhere will come to 'seek the Lord'.

The final chapters of the book are divided into two parts, each headed 'An Oracle'. These chapters deal with the climax of God's purposes. His enemies will be judged—and even turn to him

(see 14:16–19); the house of Israel will be cleansed from sin (13:1); the Lord will be acknowledged as king over all the earth (14:9).

The most amazing feature of these chapters is the appearance of a man who fulfils God's purposes and wins a great victory—through humble obedience and suffering: 'Your king comes to you, righteous and having salvation, gentle and riding [not on a war horse but] on a donkey' (9:9).

Zechariah OUTLINE

A. 1:1—8:23 Prophecies from the time of King Darius 1

1:1–6 'Return to me'

1:7–6:8 Eight visions and other prophecies
1:7–17   The four riders
1:18–21   The four horns
2:1–13   The measuring line
3:1–10   Joshua the high priest
4:1–14   The gold lampstands and the olive trees
5:1–4   The flying scroll
5:5–11   The woman in the basket
6:1–8   The four chariots

6:9–15 The 'Branch'

7:1–8:23 A question about fasting

B. 9:1–11:17 A later prophecy
9:1–10:12   God triumphant
11:1–17   The Shepherd-King

C. 12:1–14:21 The final victory

And yet his rule will extend to the ends of the earth (verse 10). All four Gospel writers make reference to this prophecy, when they describe Jesus riding into Jerusalem on a donkey (see key passage *The Shepherd King*).

Throughout the book of Zechariah there are strong references to the promise of a 'messiah'—the one who would come to save them. Now that we have the New Testament, and the Messiah has come, Christians believe that this figure was Jesus. But the Jews of his time did not recognize him. They neglected to read Zechariah: it was difficult to understand, and did not describe the sort of Messiah that they wanted.

The book is still difficult, and still awaits complete fulfilment. 'The Lord will be king over the whole earth.' Chapter 14 verse 9 is regularly used in many synagogues today. Christians are able to share their understanding and expectation of the fulfilment of this prophecy with others.

UNFIT FOR GOD
Zechariah 3:1–10

In this vision, Zechariah is shown Joshua, the high priest, clothed in filthy garments. He is not fit to stand before God. Satan is quite right there. Joshua is a 'picture' of all of us—we are all 'dressed' in filthy clothes: none of us is 'clean' enough to be acceptable in God's holy presence.

However, Joshua does not try to cover it up, or to justify himself, or promise to do better in future. God himself takes away the filthy clothes and puts rich clothes and a clean turban on him.

The high priest was the representative of the people. The vision shows that they had sinned grievously against God. The book's message throughout makes plain that their exile to Babylon is richly deserved. But God goes beyond judgment to save his people who turn to him.

The people were not punished because they shared in human sinfulness, but because they sinned grossly. Nevertheless, the New Testament emphasizes that all of us, however 'good', stand before God in filthy clothes. This picture of Joshua is picked up by other Bible writers: the wedding guest with the wrong clothes who is cast into outer darkness, the elders in heaven, dressed in white; those in Sardis who have not dirtied their garments.

Joshua also has another meaning. He is described as 'a burning stick snatched from the fire', saved by God from total destruction. In this way he foreshadows Jesus Christ who 'carried' our sins, suffering the judgment we deserved from God, but coming through it victoriously. God promises Joshua, the high priest, that 'I will give you a place among those standing here' (verse 7). This reminds us that Jesus, the great high priest, 'lives for ever to plead with God' for us.

THE SHEPHERD KING
Zechariah 9:9–13; 12:10—13:9

The writers of the New Testament had no doubt that the second half of Zechariah was recording prophecies about the Messiah. Two important 'pictures' are used: king and shepherd.

Both stand for the leader of God's people. Even if the prophet Zechariah had some historical leader or leaders in mind while he was writing, these pictures still help us understand the role of Jesus as God's chosen leader.

Zechariah writes a lot about shepherds and sheep—deploring the lack of a good shepherd, and looking forward to one who is to come. The description of the coming king in chapter 9 also refers to the Messiah.

There is another feature to add to this. When Zechariah talks about the victory of God's people over their enemies in chapter 12, he says that God will pour out on the house of David and Jerusalem a 'spirit of compassion and supplication', so that when they look on me ('him' in some versions) whom they have pierced they will mourn for him, as for an only child. This is remarkable! Could Zechariah have foreseen that Jesus would be pierced by a spear while hanging publicly on a cross?

There is a difficulty in understanding these prophecies and their contexts. For example: Jerusalem at the time of Jesus was surrounded by enemies and ruled by Romans. But it did not become a 'blazing pot in the midst of wood' (12:6). We can interpret this in two possible ways:

■ It refers figuratively to the victory of God's people over their spiritual enemies.

■ It refers to events still to come, probably connected with the return of Christ.

If we keep in mind what we *know* about Jesus' first and second comings and allow this knowledge to guide us as we read Zechariah we shall not be led astray but will be enriched in understanding.

The Message of Malachi

Michael Butterworth

The prophecy of Malachi is addressed to the sort of people who greet every piece of news and every warning with a contemptuous shrug.

Even though they are descendants of Jacob, chosen instead of Esau and his descendants (Edom), all they can say is 'What good has it done us?' Malachi invites the people of Israel to compare their condition with Edom's—God 'loves' Israel; 'hates' Edom. He is referring to Israel's special relationship with God, his 'chosen' people. Edom, by comparison, has been rejected. The covenant with Israel is a major theme in Malachi.

But the people of Israel despise 'the covenant of their fathers'. Even the priests have corrupted 'the covenant of Levi' and no longer bother what sort of animals are sacrificed. The poor ones burn just as well, so why not save the good ones for breeding? The people have behaved as if God wasn't there. But he knows all that they do and he has withheld his blessing.

Malachi selects certain sins for special mention. One example is mixed marriages (chapter 2). It is not mixed race—Ruth was from Moab, and Moses married a Cushite wife—but a foreign religion that matters.

Corrupt religion in the family means corrupt generations to come. Paul in his letter to the Corinthians confirms that this is still a live issue for Christians.

Divorce is mentioned—it also represents the breaking of a solemn covenant. The church has varied in its attitude, sometimes emphasizing the ideal of lifelong one-partner marriage, sometimes emphasizing God's understanding of human weakness. Both are important—though both can be abused.

Malachi contains fearsome warnings of a day to come when evil will be purged from the people and their priests (see key passage *God's Messenger*). But even in this context God extends a generous invitation: 'Put me to the test and see if I will not ... pour down an overflowing blessing.' The wrong way to 'test' God is to complain and to challenge his authority, as the people of Israel did in the desert. The right way is to observe his commandments and look for blessing.

The book ends with a warning of a curse. Many have wanted to soften this last verse of the Old Testament. But it

---

Malachi OUTLINE

puts into sharp relief the amazing fact that our salvation is through Jesus Christ who, in Paul's words, 'became a curse for us' on the cross.

GOD'S MESSENGER
Malachi 3:1–5; 4:1–6

'Malachi' means 'my messenger' or 'my angel' but there seem to be two others mentioned in chapter 3 verse 1. 'My messenger' comes to prepare the way for 'the messenger of the covenant'. The first of these is clearly identified in the New Testament as John the Baptist who prepared the way for Jesus, the Messiah. The other title 'messenger/angel of the covenant' only occurs here but it has meaning as a reference to Jesus, who made the 'new covenant' with his own blood.

Whether Malachi knew he was speaking of the Messiah is another matter. When Moses saw the burning bush, recorded in Exodus 3, it seems that the 'angel of the Lord' who appeared to him was God himself. An expression that can mean 'God' or 'God's messenger' is highly suitable for Jesus. So the prophet says that a day of judgment and purification is coming, heralded by a special messenger. This was fulfilled in the coming of Jesus and John the Baptist.

There is much discussion about what we are to expect before that day comes. There are difficulties of interpretation. The message of Malachi is not obscured by these difficulties: it reminds us to live as people who expect Jesus to return!

THE PROPHETS IN HISTORY

There were prophets in Israel from early days. Moses was the first and greatest; Samuel was a prophet; Elijah and Elisha feature strongly in the books of Kings. From the 8th to the 5th centuries BC, the prophecies of the foremost prophets were collected into books which have survived. These prophets fall into 7 groups, according to their setting in the history of Israel and Judah, and their enemies, first Assyria, then Babylon.

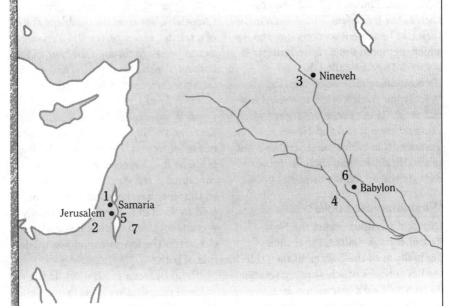

1 **THE NORTHERN KINGDOM**
Amos and **Hosea** condemn the sins of Israel in the years before Samaria falls to the Assyrians (in 722BC).

2 **THE SOUTHERN KINGDOM**
In the years following Amos and Hosea, **Isaiah** in Jerusalem and **Micah** call the Judeans to live justly. (Micah also prophesied to Israel.)

3 **ASSYRIA AND ITS FALL**
Jonah is the story of a prophet sent to Nineveh. **Nahum** exults in Assyria's fall (in 612BC).

4 **BABYLON'S DOMINANCE**
Jeremiah warns that Jerusalem will fall to the Babylonians because of the nation's sins. **Zephaniah** also prophesies during this time. **Habakkuk** asks why the cruel Babylonians are allowed to prosper.

5 **JERUSALEM'S FALL AND AFTER**
Obadiah foretells Edom's doom after its people took advantage of Judah's misery. The book of **Lamentations** records the suffering that followed Jerusalem's destruction (in 586BC).

6 **EXILE IN BABYLON**
Ezekiel prophesies to the Jews exiled in Babylon, both before and after Jerusalem falls. **Daniel** records the story of a Jewish exile. **Isaiah** in Babylon foretells the exiles' return home.

7 **THE EXILES RETURN**
Haggai, speaking in 520BC, urges the returned exiles to rebuild the temple. **Zechariah** does the same, then continues to prophesy through the following years. **Malachi,** prophesying some 50 or 60 years after, once the later groups have returned home, recalls the people to righteousness.

(Nobody knows when **Joel** prophesied.)

The Deuterocanonical Books

Thomas W. Franxman

Bibles from Roman Catholic sources—such as the Jerusalem Bible—contain in their Old Testament sections some books which are not in Bibles from Protestant sources. They are called the 'Deuterocanonical books' (not the 'Apocrypha', which refers to something different). These books are sometimes printed between Old and New Testaments in Bibles for general use, but in specifically Roman Catholic Bibles they are spread among the other books.

What are these books?

During the centuries after the New Testament was written, the church gradually fixed the 'canon' of the Bible: the list of books which were recognized as carrying God's inspiration and authority. It so happens that during the two centuries after Christ's birth, the Jews themselves were not completely at one over the 'canon' of their own religious literature. Thus Christians inherited a double tradition of the number of books placed by the church in the canon of the Old Testament.

A list of twenty-two or twenty-four inspired books seems already to have been current among Palestinian Jews by the end of the first Christian century. This shorter, or Eastern, canon was also the preference of many prominent Christian writers and did not contain certain writings and additions to already recognized books which some Jews and, after them, a good number of Christians

willingly accepted as inspired. For Christians, however, the double tradition of a shorter and a longer Old Testament canon persisted through the time of the Fathers, the medieval period and on into the sixteenth-century Renaissance.

On 8 April 1546, the Ecumenical Council, summoned by the Bishop of Rome and sitting at Trent in Italy, issued one of its decrees. The centuries-long use made by the church of writings not contained in the shorter canon was taken as showing that the reverence originally paid to them in the Jewish community was a recognition of their inspired character. The longer canon was made a rule of faith.

Sixtus of Siena (1520–69), in his 'biblical introduction', was then able to speak of Old Testament books which are 'canonical now and in the past' and those which are 'canonical now but previously not universally accepted'. He thus introduced the still current distinction between 'protocanonical' and 'deuterocanonical' books, or books from the second canon. Jewish religious literature which neither Jews nor Christians consider canonical has, by contrast, come to be known as 'apocryphal', and really this term should be restricted to this sense.

The Deuterocanonical books have real importance. Mainly this is because they are part of the Bible for many Christians. But the collection also contains, among much else, primary sources for the historian (1 and 2 Maccabees) and a wealth of material representing much that is best in Israel's Wisdom tradition (Ecclesiasticus, Baruch, the Book of Wisdom). The summaries that follow are particularly for those less familiar with these books.

Additions to Esther and Daniel

The ancient Greek translation of Esther incorporates six sections which are additional to the Hebrew text. These either expand the familiar story or offer alternative presentations of it. One of these additions gives a more spiritual thrust to a story that rather lacks this dimension, by quoting prayers from Esther herself and from her kinsman Mordecai.

An addition comes into Daniel, also from ancient Greek versions. In chapter 3, the story of Shadrach, Meshach and Abednego in the furnace, there are an extra 68 verses, many of which take the form of a hymn sung by the three heroes.

The books below are placed in the order in which they commonly appear in Roman Catholic Bibles.

Tobit

This book begins with a first-person account of Tobit, an Israelite exiled in Nineveh, who holds an important post under the Assyrian Emperor Shalmaneser. An accident renders him blind.

Then, in the main part of the story, the focus shifts to Tobit's son, Tobias, who is sent on a journey to Media to recover a deposit of money his father made there. His travelling companion, Azarias, turns out to be the angel Raphael. In Media, he sues for the hand

of Sarah, a kinsman's daughter and banishes a demon who has killed seven previous bridegrooms. He marries her, returns to Nineveh and sees Tobit's blindness cured. Tobit eventually dies, and Tobias returns to Media.

This is a delightful little story, associated with Israel's Wisdom tradition.

Judith

This story is set among events which did not in fact occur historically, so we must take it as an instructive legend. It concerns General Holofernes, deputed by his 'Assyrian' king to make wide conquests. His success rightly alarms the Jerusalem authorities, who send out warnings. One such is received by the otherwise unknown town of Bethulia. Holofernes besieges this town.

Judith, a beautiful widow of Bethulia, makes her way to Holofernes' tent and charms out of him an invitation to dine. Later, left alone with the drunkenly sleeping general, she cuts off his head and takes it back to the town. Next day, the shaken Assyrians are easily routed.

The story recalls the death of Sisera in the book of Judges. It celebrates in its own way the providence of God.

1 Maccabees

This book is a history of the Jewish struggles which took place in Palestine between the years 175 and 134BC.

Antiochus IV Epiphanes, ruler of that portion of Alexander of Macedon's former empire which included Palestine, becomes more and more the oppressor of the Jewish population. The priest Mattathias leaves Jerusalem with his five sons and eventually becomes the leader of the resistance movement which he leads until his untimely demise in 166. The leadership then passes to three of his sons in succession. Among his achievements recounted in this history, the rededication of the desecrated temple and the victory over the forces of Nicanor are memorable enough to merit yearly commemoration thereafter. Judas himself perishes on the battlefield in 160BC.

The next portion of the history is concerned with Jonathan Apphus, youngest of Mattathias' sons, who succeeds his brother and, eight years later in the October of 152, assumes the office of high priest which he and his Hasmonean successors will retain. After leading the resistance to the oppressive Seleucid dynasty for seventeen years, he is captured at Ptolemais in 143, and later murdered.

A leaderless people now turns to Simon Thassi who remains head of the movement until his assassination in 134. High priest by succession to Jonathan, he is appointed the officially recognized governor and commander of a nation independent for the first time in four-and-a-half centuries.

2 Maccabees

Here we find a second treatment of the same period covered in 1 Maccabees. It is a condensed version of a five-volume history by Jason of Cyrene. The book opens with the text of two letters from Judean Jews to their fellows in Egypt. The treatment is briefer, and only goes as far as Judas Maccabeus' victory at Nicanor. But it is more detailed on the decline of the high priesthood and the persecution of the Jews which led up to their rebellion.

The Book of Wisdom

Sometimes known as 'the Wisdom of Solomon', this is a book whose anonymous author develops his themes rather in the style of Job or Ecclesiastes.

The author's praise of Wisdom concentrates first (1:1—6:21) on the reward of immortality which Wisdom gives. 'But the upright live for ever, their recompense is with the Lord, and the Most High takes care of them' (5:15). Then (6:22—11:1), in the person of Solomon, the author undertakes to describe the nature of Wisdom and his pursuit of her: 'What Wisdom is and how she was born, I shall now explain; I shall hide no mysteries from you, but shall follow her steps from the outset of her origin, setting out what we know of her in full light, without departing from the truth' (6:22-24).

The Israelites' wandering in the desert was a time when 'what had served to punish their enemies became a benefit for them in their difficulties' (11:5). This is the basic theme of the rest of the book (11:2—19:22) and is worked out in five sets of contrasts: water from the rock instead of water turned to blood, quail instead of frogs, gnats, flies and locusts; manna instead of rain, hail and fire; the pillar of fire instead of darkness; the greatness and glory of Israel over against the crippling affliction of the tenth and final plague.

Ecclesiasticus

This is the longest of the Deuterocanonical books. It is sometimes known by its author's name, Ben Sira (or Sirach). The author uses verse couplets, embodying an obvious truth or some universal experience. This style is familiar to those acquainted with the book of Proverbs. Ben Sira employs these sayings as building blocks as he develops themes of varying length, considerable variety and great number.

The book is not organized in a fashion which makes a summary outline of its contents possible. But two passages of some length, one at the beginning and one at the end of the collection, are both important and typical: 1:1–29, the praise of Wisdom (whose concept dominates the author's work) and 44:1—50:24, the praise of Israel's great men.

Baruch

Baruch was secretary and confidant to the prophet Jeremiah, and this book carries his name. But, in fact, it is made up of quite distinct sections, each of which may well stem from a different writer. An introduction is followed by a two-part prayer (1:15—3:8), set in the time of the Jews' exile in Babylon. There follows a poem celebrating the place of Wisdom in Israel's greatness (3:9—4:4). The poem identifies Wisdom with Israel's Law. The third part of the book is a long psalm (4:5—5:9), aimed at encouraging the Jewish nation.

There are three other Deuterocanonical pieces, which are to be found within other books.

The Letter of Jeremiah is included as chapter 6 of Baruch. It is a letter reminiscent of the one the prophet wrote to the exiles in Babylon (Jeremiah 29). An anonymous author warns against idolatry.

Susanna and **Bel and the Dragon**, which are placed in Roman Catholic Bibles as chapters 13 and 14 of Daniel, are set in Babylon. The first is a short story of a beautiful woman whose life is saved by a young boy called Daniel. The second is in two episodes, in both of which the Daniel whom we know from the book of that name successfully opposes aspects of Babylonian idolatry.

The New Testament

The New Testament Library

JESUS AND THE FIRST CHRISTIANS

THE LETTERS

THE NEW TESTAMENT

A VISION

The Gospels are selective biographies of Jesus, put together to show who he was and what he came to do. This is why there is so much about his death and resurrection. Many miracles are included, showing what it means that God's 'kingdom' (his rule) has come in Jesus. He often taught in parables, everyday stories about what happens when God's kingdom comes. Jesus taught that people can know God personally; he calls us to follow him as disciples on the way of freedom.

Matthew
Mark
Luke
John
Acts

Paul, one of the first Christians, wrote in reaction to the questions which arose from the societies in which Christians lived. We read about some of these in Acts. As well as giving us a glimpse of the early church, he also gives us principles in working out the gospel today. He often begins by outlining the gospel which has brought them freedom, before showing how this affects their lives in particular ways. Each of the other letters brings its own message— Hebrews: why Jesus is better than any other way to God; James: integrity in faith, speech and action; 1 Peter: how to cope with hardship; 1 John: the tests of true faith.

Romans
1 Corinthians
2 Corinthians
Galatians
Ephesians
Philippians
Colossians
1 & 2 Thessalonians
1 & 2 Timothy and Titus
Philemon
Hebrews
James
1 Peter
2 Peter and Jude
1 John
2 & 3 John

Revelation is an 'apocalypse', literally an 'uncovering'. The writer often quotes similar writing in Daniel, Zechariah and Ezekiel. The visions refer to people and events the readers would know about, but a coded language was used which only the faithful would understand, not their persecutors. The colourful symbols of good and evil show how the powers of evil can attack God's people, but God will finally overcome them.

Revelation

PLACES OF
THE GOSPELS

ITUREA

● Caesarea
Philippi

● Ptolemais

TETRARCHY
OF PHILIP

SYRIA

Chorazin
●

Bethsaida
●

Capernaum
Gennesaret ●

Lake Galilee

Cana ●

Tiberias ●

GALILEE

● Nazareth

● Nain

● Caesarea

DECAPOLIS

*Mediterranean
Sea*

River Jordan

Aenon near Salim ●

SAMARIA ● Sychar

● Antipatris

● Joppa

● Gadara

PEREA

● Lydda

Jericho
●

Emmaus ●

Jerusalem
●

Bethphage ●
●

Bethlehem ● Bethany

JUDEA

*Dead
Sea*

IDUMEA

NABATEAN
KINGDOM

The Message of Matthew

Kai Kjaer-Hansen

The first Christians were Jews who came to believe that Jesus, a Jew from Nazareth, was the expected Messiah and the Son of God. When they became believers in Jesus they did not meet a new God, but they came to know God in a new way. They did not abandon their Jewishness, but realized that God's promises had been fulfilled in Jesus.

In all probability Matthew's Gospel was written by such a Christian Jew. He tells us that a new age in history has started with Jesus. With Jesus the 'kingdom of heaven' is at hand (other writers call it the 'kingdom of God'), and a new power is at work through him. The Old Testament era has ended; the time of Jesus has come. But still there is a connexion between these periods, because it is the God of Abraham, Isaac and Jacob who reveals himself and works through Jesus.

- A central theme of this Gospel, then, is that Jesus fulfilled the Old Testament. Matthew often uses what are called 'formula quotations'. He tells us of an event in Jesus' life and then quotes an Old Testament verse, introduced by a phrase like 'so was fulfilled what was said through the prophets...' There is no doubt in Matthew's mind that Jesus' heavenly Father is identical with the God of Israel.

Many attempts have been made in Christian history to reduce the Jewish elements of the Gospels. But in all of them, and most of all in Matthew, the elements of Judaism and Palestine are unmistakable. Jesus is a Jew and born of a Jewish mother. His family tree cannot be separated from the history of Israel. And so it is not strange that, since the time of the Reformation, this is the Gospel which has most frequently been translated into Hebrew in an attempt to give back to the Jews the Jesus whom the Christians have received from the Jewish people. Still today there are many Jews who can

identify with the questions Matthew raises. An example is Jesus' relationship to the Law and the Jewish tradition. Jesus said that he had not come to abolish the Law and the prophets but to fulfil them (5:17–20). He interpreted the Law with divine authority—'You have heard that it was said . . . but I say to you . . .' He also criticized the religious leaders for putting their tradition above God's commandments.

So the drama of salvation is enacted in Jewish history. Jesus addresses himself primarily to the people of Israel. It is an exception if he deals with a Gentile, such as a Roman officer's boy or a Canaanite woman. Yet still Jesus' message has a universal aim that includes all people. After his death the disciples are to continue preaching the gospel to the Jews until his return. Israel must hear and acknowledge Jesus, not deny him. But they are also to 'go and make disciples of all nations' (28:18–20).

In this way there should be believers of both Jewish and Gentile origin in Jesus' church. Matthew also emphasizes that Jesus will build his church and give it a part of his power (16:18–20).

It seems likely that the Gospel was written in an environment where Jewish and Gentile Christians belonged to the same church, but with Jews forming the majority. Many scholars share the conviction that Matthew's Gospel—as we now have it, written in Greek—was composed in Syria, north of Israel, in the years after Jerusalem was destroyed in AD70. From ancient times the Gospel has been attributed to Matthew, who has been identified with Matthew the tax-collector whom we hear about in chapter 9. It is hard to be completely sure in such matters.

- But on Matthew's central theme, who Jesus is, there is no uncertainty. The many different titles and names of honour speak their own clear language, not least 'Messiah', 'Son of God', 'Son of man'. But to Matthew a name such as Son of God is meaningless without the background in Isaiah 53 of God's suffering servant. Like the servant, Jesus gives his life as a ransom for his people; that is the kind of Messiah he is. And so a key word for the work of Jesus is 'service' or 'ministry', and this key word is applied also to the disciples, even though they had great difficulty understanding the greatness of Jesus' service and their own.

In the first chapter the very name Jesus indicates what kind of salvation he is to bring. He is given the name Jesus because he is to save his people from their sins (1:21). It is not the story of a superman or hero Matthew is preparing us for, but the story of God's Son, who becomes a servant to save lost humanity from sin. Through him 'God is with us', the meaning of another important name, Immanuel, which tells us from the very first chapter in what terms we are to identify Jesus.

Who is Jesus? Matthew answers by telling us about Jesus' words and his deeds. Both in what he said and in what he did, he showed his divine authority. His words and acts can lead to faith, even though they can also be met with disbelief and contempt. Many religious leaders chose the latter. They explained away his miracles as done in collusion with Satan (12:24).

It is of utmost importance to realize that Jesus demands a sort of obedience towards himself and his word which is very like the obedience God demanded of his people in the Old Testament. Jesus' words are to be obeyed as the word of God; a disciple of Jesus must be willing to risk his life for his sake; such a disciple must acknowledge Jesus and not deny him. God made these demands of his people in the Old Testament. Now we hear that those who believe Jesus, who hear his words and are obedient to him, have already accepted the God of Israel and are allowed to call him Father as Jesus does.

The Jesus Matthew presents us with demands that people believe in him and serve him. And he does so with divine authority. To a modern reader of this Gospel, the big problem is not so much who Jesus is—Matthew has answered that perfectly clearly—but rather whether we will let Jesus have full authority in our lives.

If we compare the Gospel of Matthew with that of Mark (which Matthew may have known), we often see that Matthew's stories are shorter than Mark's, but his sayings are longer and gathered in larger units.

Many attempts have been made to explain the structure of Matthew's Gospel. One of the most popular ways of division centres around the five great speeches Jesus gives, in chapters 5 to 7 (the Sermon on the Mount), chapters 10, 13, 18 and 24 to 25. The main point behind the division is that these five speeches, combined with what leads up to them, show Jesus giving us a new form of the five books of the Law, just like Moses in his time.

The weakness in this way of dividing Matthew's Gospel is that it makes Jesus appear just a great Law-giver, when he is much more than that. The division used in the accompanying outline has scholarly support:

- 1:1—4:16 The Person of Jesus Christ, the Son of God.

- 4:17—16:20 Jesus Christ is publicly proclaimed.

- 16:21—28:20 Jesus Christ's suffering, death and resurrection.

As already mentioned, in Matthew we meet a Jewish-Christian writer whose Gospel originated in a church with many Jewish Christians. And the questions dealt with are no less relevant to Christian Jews of our own time. But this does not mean that the Gospel is without significance for Christians of Gentile origin, for Jesus is the same today as he was then.

Whether you live fifty or 1,950 years after the events described, in a way it does not make a great difference. The important thing is to get a firm hold of the fact that Jesus has the same power now as then, and that his promises stand unshaken. When, for instance, Matthew tells us that Jesus once came to the rescue of his disciples 'of little faith' out on Lake Galilee (8:23–27), he does so precisely because he believes that Jesus will come to the rescue of his disciples 'of little faith' in the same way today. And today he gives us a share in his serving power—power to serve him, and those around us.

Jesus, God's Son, has made it possible to become a child of God and call God 'Father', and that is the best thing that can happen to a person.

JESUS' FAMILY TREE
Matthew 1:1–25

It is very tempting to skip the long list of names at the beginning of Matthew. It can seem a boring introduction. And yet Jesus' family tree has its significance. It reminds us that the story of Jesus took place on this earth and not in the world of myths. It is the God of Israel who acts, and a miniature version of Israel's history is being presented. Each of the people mentioned has his or her own history, very often far from praiseworthy—just like our history.

In the Old Testament the mistakes and sins of God's people are not concealed, not even if your name was David and you were a king. His offence against Uriah, whom he had killed to get his wife, is also apparent in this genealogy (verse 6). If you take a closer look at the history of these people in the Old Testament, you will see that God is dealing with sinful people. They are a part of the family tree which is meant to show that Jesus is a Jew of royal birth, of David's line.

But he is more than that. He is the Son of God, conceived by the Holy Spirit, and he is Mary's child (verse 20).

The virgin birth cannot be 'proved'. Later some Jews as well as Gentiles spread stories that Jesus' father was a Roman soldier. Matthew's testimony is very different: Jesus' real Father is the God of Israel. Many modern people find the virgin birth hard to accept. But a close study of the claims of Jesus and his extraordinary life has led millions to the conviction that the virgin birth is telling us a vital truth—Jesus is the Son of God.

In obedience to the command of the angel of the Lord, Joseph makes Mary's child his son, and he does so by giving him the name God has decided for him: Yeshua—Jesus. The explanation of that name shows that Jesus is to save us from sin. This name, together with the other name, 'Immanuel' (verse 23), which means 'God with us', teaches us that God's mission in Jesus Christ is to rescue us from sin. Coming as he does as the *final* name in the family tree, Matthew's deliberate point is that Jesus surpasses all the other great people in the story of humankind. He alone is Saviour.

JESUS IS BAPTIZED
Matthew 3:13–17

Baptism is for sinners. John the Baptist knew that. Alongside his preaching of judgment, he baptized people with 'the water of repentance' (verse 11). This is why he hesitated when Jesus appeared, wanting to be baptized.

Since Jesus was conceived by the Holy Spirit, he had no sin to confess. John knew that Jesus, who was coming after him, was stronger than he was. John was the one who ought to be baptized by Jesus, not the other way round. But Jesus insists on following God's plan and is baptized by John.

Baptism is for sinners. And the sin-free Jesus is baptized! *Our* baptism presupposes a confession of sin, otherwise baptism is pointless. Through faith and baptism we become the children of God. (See the article on *Baptism*.) But Jesus does not become the Son of God by his baptism. He already is the Son of God.

By his baptism Jesus laid the foundation for our baptism, in which we are baptized for the forgiveness of our sins. And by his own baptism the sin-free Jesus shows his solidarity with sinners. He is consecrated to his earthly task, which ends in death when he gives his life as a ransom for us. Just as death was the right beginning for his heavenly rule, so was baptism the right beginning for his earthly task as a servant of sinners. And the voice from heaven proclaims that Jesus is God's Son and echoes the description of the Lord's suffering servant in the prophecy of Isaiah.

■ **Jesus is the Son of God,** so says the heavenly voice. In the Old Testament both the king of Israel and the people of Israel can be called the son of God. But between Jesus and his heavenly Father there is an all-inclusive relationship. He has been given everything by his heavenly Father.

■ **And Jesus is the Lord's suffering servant.** The voice quotes a 'servant song' from the prophet Isaiah. No matter which name is used about Jesus in the Gospels, the main idea is always that with his life he serves mankind.

The people of Israel and the king of Israel proved to be disobedient sons of God like the rest of us. Jesus, on the other hand, proved to be God's obedient Son. When Jesus was tempted in the desert the devil tried to tempt him into disobedience. But here and in his death Jesus remained the obedient Son, and for that reason disobedient humanity can become God's children.

FOLLOWING JESUS
Matthew 4:17–22

The kingdom of heaven is at hand in Jesus. That is why we can already 'enter' it, and why Jesus can say to people with God's own authority: 'Follow me.' This passage is about following him (see also 10:1–42, 16:24–26 and 19:16–30).

The four fishermen by Lake Galilee left their nets immediately and followed Jesus. Now they were to be 'fishers of men' for the cause of the kingdom.

When a person is called to be a disciple the initiative lies with Jesus. In those days, if you wanted to be a disciple of a great Jewish rabbi, you had to take the initiative yourself. It was different with Jesus: he called twelve disciples ('The Twelve') (10:1–4) and equipped them to carry out his assignment.

Often we delude ourselves into believing that it is by our own efforts and initiative that we are Christians. But the real reason that faith is created and discipleship established is different. It is God who has worked in us through his word and his Holy Spirit. Both our need of God and God's love are greater than anything we can possibly express.

The four fishermen followed the call at once, but it was not always like that. The rich young man, for instance, went away sorrowful when he heard the same call (19:22). Since then, a lot of other people have done the same thing because they thought that the cost of following Jesus was too great.

When you follow Jesus as a disciple there are costs. It is a question of denying yourself, taking up your cross and following Jesus—whatever it costs (16:24–26).

Everybody who is a disciple of Jesus here on earth is promised fellowship as a member of a new family, and eternal life at the end (19:27–30). But Jesus does not tempt us with dreams of outward success or benefits in this life. His followers have been told to serve as he once served them. If people called him a little devil, they would do the same to his disciples. A disciple must be satisfied with the same lot as his master (10:25).

How does outward success in life help if you miss life itself (16:26)? Service by following Jesus—that is life, even though it may end in a dishonourable death.

THE SERMON ON THE MOUNT
Matthew 5:1—7:29

The Sermon on the Mount is not just an expression of 'simple teaching' which you can be over and done with in a hurry. A Christian can never be over and done with it. In different ways we are repeatedly pulled up sharp by its words. For here speaks somebody with divine authority (7:29). Nobody, not even the prophets in the Old Testament, dared say 'You have heard that it was said . . . *but I say to you.*' Only Jesus can say this, because he is the master of the Law and its right interpreter.

Some people have claimed that here Jesus puts forward a radicalized Judaism, that he gives a new Law which is harder to keep than the laws of the Jews. But we are never told that we become God's children by keeping the teaching Jesus gives us. Others have claimed that the Sermon on the Mount is primarily intended to make us recognize our shortcomings, for, these people say, we cannot keep these demands anyway. Still others claim that Jesus expected the world to come to an end very soon, and the Sermon on the Mount therefore expresses the ways the disciples were to follow in the time before the catastrophe. Interpreted like this, the Sermon becomes almost irrelevant to us because we do not live in such an atmosphere of catastrophe. But in fact the Sermon is not characterized by such an atmosphere. On the contrary, it is governed by the truth that in Jesus the kingdom of heaven is at hand.

You cannot understand the Sermon on the Mount without using the right key. This key is found in the Beatitudes, or 'blessings' (5:3–12), and also in the words that the disciples are 'the light of the world' (5:14–16). They *are* so; they do not become so by living according to the new ways. If we look at the Sermon without this key, the result will be completely wrong.

First we receive God's gift, then we meet God's demands. This is what God's kingdom is like. The blessings give the disciples, 'the poor in spirit', a part in the kingdom of heaven. It is a gift given freely, with nothing expected in return. So the Sermon is primarily addressed to the disciples, to those who have had their sins forgiven (6:12), who have received a part in God's good gift of salvation by praying for it (7:7–11), and who have entered the narrow gate that leads to life (7:13–14). The ways of the new age are to be realized among Jesus' disciples.

So the Sermon on the Mount is primarily instructions for Jesus' followers. For Jesus' disciples, his words become a promise of the new possibilities in life that are at hand for those who have been made new by accepting God's kingdom. But at the same time God's pure will, which Jesus preached, becomes judgment on those who have removed themselves from God and live their own lives with their own norms.

We are all affected by the words of the Sermon, in one way or another. When Jesus says, for instance, that a person who gets angry has committed murder, and a person who looks at another lustfully has already committed adultery, then sin is understood so radically that we are *all* included (5:21–30). Particularly arresting is the warning that Jesus will say, at some point, that he does not know some of those who have performed great miracles in his name (7:21–23).

We cannot be over and done with the Sermon on the Mount in a hurry. It comforts us; it also makes us uneasy. It warns us against treating this world and its norms as if they were good enough. It says: 'You are the light of the world— now go and shine!'

THE MIRACLES
Matthew 8:1—9:38

At the end of chapter 7 we saw the divine authority in Jesus' teaching. Now, in these two chapters, Matthew shows us that God's power also fills Jesus' actions. Ten miracles are recorded here. What place do the miracles have in Jesus' work?

■ **They are a sign that God's kingdom is at hand in Jesus.**

■ **They express God's mercy.**

■ **They point towards a future when God's kingdom will reach perfection, and there will be no more sin or illness.**

Most of Jesus' miracles brought *people* to wholeness (healing the sick, exorcizing demons, raising the dead), but sometimes he also showed his power over the natural world. In chapters 8 and 9 we find examples of both these kinds.

With his divine compassion, Jesus cares for people. And yet it is not people who are at the centre of the stories. Many interesting details about them and what happens to them are not explained by the evangelist; a modern news reporter would have elaborated on these things. It is Jesus who is the focus of the miracles.

He is like a medical teacher at a hospital. While he treats the patient he explains and reveals what is going on, although it is not the illness but the healing that is explained. The words he speaks as he works the miracles illuminate the healer, the healing and the patient. In this way Jesus appears as the great doctor.

But he is different from ordinary doctors. A key to understanding the deeper meaning of Jesus' miracles is given in the healing of the paralytic (9:1–8). Without diminishing the healing itself, attention is directed towards the forgiving of sins. First Jesus tells the paralytic he is forgiven. The religious leaders react by accusing him of blasphemy. Then Jesus heals the man to show that when he forgives sins it is not empty talk. (Elsewhere Jesus warns against assuming that sin and illness are always connected.)

Jesus' miracles and his forgiveness of sin can be received in faith or rejected in unbelief. The religious leaders of the time could not deny that Jesus worked miracles. But they explained them by claiming that he was in collusion with Satan (12:24). When they demanded that he should prove himself by performing an unambiguous miracle, he refused (16:1–4). He would not be mistaken for a mere miracle-worker.

Every side of Jesus' ministry raises questions of belief and unbelief. This is also the case with his miracles and the deeper reality they reveal. Jesus is the great doctor of body and soul who forgives sins on God's behalf.

LAST JOURNEY TO JERUSALEM
Matthew 16:21–23; 17:22–23; 20:17–28

On his last journey up to Jerusalem Jesus taught his disciples about his coming death. Three times he predicted it, and the disciples were shocked to hear it. Peter advised him not to take the path of suffering and even 'rebuked' Jesus (16:22).

Like the other disciples, Peter did not at that time understand the significance of Jesus' suffering and death. They had hoped that Jesus would be a political Messiah, who would throw the hated Roman occupation force into the Mediterranean.

But Jesus said to Peter, 'Get behind me, Satan', repeating what he said when he rejected temptation in the desert.

Even after the third of these predictions the disciples had not understood very much. James and John asked him if they could have the best seats in God's kingdom. So Jesus had to instruct them that whoever wants to be great has to learn to serve (20:20–28).

Jesus' suffering is unique. He gave his life as a ransom, so that we could become God's children. But he is also a model for the way his disciples should serve others.

Only later did the disciples understand the deep significance of Jesus' death and become willing to expose themselves to mockery for their faith in their crucified Saviour. When they preached about it they did not hide the fact that his death on the cross was a dishonourable one in the eyes of his contemporaries.

In the light of the resurrection the disciples later realized that Jesus' death on the cross was the greatest possible expression of God's wonderful love. How God must love us to let his only Son die for us on a cross!

THE GREATEST ONE OF ALL
Matthew 22:41–46

Have you ever heard Jesus measured against other great figures in world history? It often happens that Jesus is made smaller than he is. In the Gospels, however, Jesus is portrayed as greater and more significant than all the great figures of the past.

- **He is greater than his ancestor David.** For David calls the Messiah 'my Lord' (verses 43 to 45). Jesus is not only a descendant of David, he is also David's Lord.

- **He counts for more than Jonah and Solomon** (12:41–42). And John's Gospel rates him *greater than*

Abraham (John 8:53–56). Jesus is of greater significance than all the great examples in the Old Testament who point towards him and with whom he is compared.

- **He is greater than the temple, and Lord of the sabbath** (12:6–8). Within the biblical concept of reality any comparison turns out to be to the advantage of Jesus.

- **He is also greater than his contemporary, John the Baptist.** Jesus rates John 'more than a prophet'; in the history of mankind nobody greater than John has appeared (11:9–11). And yet Jesus is stronger than this great man (3:11).

So we need to be careful how we compare Jesus to other figures. It is best to let him be what he is: greater than all the great.

He and his words demand an obedience similar to the obedience God demanded from the people of his covenant ('You have heard it said . . . but I tell you . . .'). No one else in the Bible demanded such obedience to themselves. So why does Jesus do so? Is it a sign of megalomania? Or of blasphemy? Or is it a sign that it is through him that we meet God? If we receive Jesus in faith we receive God who sent him (10:40).

A FINAL COMMAND
Matthew 28:16–20

The last words of the Gospel are not just intended to round things off in a sensational way. Here we find a binding command, given by the crucified and risen Jesus. The disciples are commanded to make disciples, to teach and to baptize. There is a wonderful coherence in the words Jesus uses, as is obvious from the four times the words 'all' or 'always' appear:

■ **Jesus has all the power.** Here on earth he had already been given all things by his Father (11:27). Now he gives to his powerless disciples a part in his serving power. They are not to use his power to harm anyone or to benefit themselves, but for Jesus' sake and for their fellow human beings.

■ **They are to make disciples of all nations.** This task is still not complete. There are still many people who have never heard the good news about Jesus accurately, even those who live in a 'Christian' country. The task is a corporate one; no individual disciple can reach everybody. But every disciple can reach some, and in that way everybody can be reached. For it is cruel to keep for yourself the best you have been given.

■ **They are to teach people to observe all Jesus has commanded them.** We must pass on a truly biblical Christianity—Jesus as described in the Gospels and explained in the whole New Testament.

■ **And then the wonderful promise, 'I am with you always'.** We are not alone when we are working for Jesus.

At the beginning of the Gospel we read that Jesus is 'Immanuel, God with us'. And now, through Jesus, God is with us.

The keeping of this great command is a continuing story. The first chapter was written by the first Christians. Other chapters have been added since. The final chapter cannot be written until the great day, and in that conclusion we also will play a part.

What will it say in that concluding chapter? Matthew has done his part so that we can get to know Jesus. But some people need to be told the gospel of Jesus in a way only I can tell it, or only you.

The Message of Mark

Graham H. Twelftree

It is generally agreed that Mark was the first Gospel to be written—a short, fascinating and fast-moving story. In his introduction Mark tells us it is the 'good news' about Jesus Christ. One of the main themes is 'discipleship', which makes it relevant to any Christian seeking to follow Jesus today.

We do not know for sure who 'Mark' was, for the name was common in the Roman world. Chapter 13, with its predictions of the destruction of the temple, is our main clue as to when the Gospel was written. Unlike Matthew and Luke, who used Mark as a source and wrote after the destruction of the temple in AD70, Mark is not coloured by the events. Yet in view of the frankness with which Peter is depicted, which would make most sense after his martyrdom in

Mark OUTLINE

1:1–13 The beginning of the good news of Jesus

1:14–8:21 Jesus' work in Galilee
1:14–45   The power and authority of Jesus
2:1–3:12   Jesus' freedom and authority
3:13–19   Jesus commissions the Twelve
3:20–35   Misunderstanding who Jesus is and who may belong to his family
4:1–34   The disciples learn through parables
4:35–5:43   The disciples learn through Jesus' miracles
6:1–6   Jesus misunderstood again and rejected by his own people
6:7–13   Jesus sends the Twelve on mission
6:14–29   Interlude: the death of John the Baptist
6:30–8:21   The disciples misunderstand Jesus' teaching and miracles, even though a non-Jewish woman trusts Jesus to heal her daughter

8:22–10:52 The gradual understanding of Jesus' teaching about himself and discipleship
8:22–26   Blind eyes, at first, only partially opened
8:27–30   Peter states that Jesus is the Messiah

8:31–9:1   Jesus' first prediction of his death misunderstood
9:2–13   Jesus is transfigured; the disciples misunderstand
9:14–29   The disciples fail in their mission
9:30–41   Jesus' second prediction of his death misunderstood
9:42–10:31   Wise sayings and teachings on discipleship
10:32–45   Jesus' third prediction of his death misunderstood
10:46–52   Jesus completely opens the eyes of a blind man who becomes a disciple

11:1–13:37 The last days in Jerusalem before the cross
11:1–11   Jesus' triumphant entry into Jerusalem
11:12–33   Jesus' teaching and action about the temple
12:1–44   Parable and questions
13:1–37   Teaching on times before the end

14:1–16:8 The death and resurrection of Jesus
14:1–72   The last acts of Jesus
15:1–21   The trial of Jesus and the death sentence
15:22–47   Jesus is crucified, dies and is buried
16:1–8   The resurrection

the persecutions of Nero in AD64, it seems that Mark was written after this date—in the late 60s AD.

Mark's purpose in writing his Gospel was to encourage the Christian community as it followed the way of Jesus. From the selection of stories about Jesus and the teaching given on such subjects as what makes a person unclean, divorce and forgiveness, we can see that the teaching here is directed principally to the disciples, not the world. Even the occasions where Jesus is portrayed 'calling' the disciples seem to be included for the encouragement of the community in its mission, rather than to win outsiders as followers, because it is always linked with the invitation to be involved in mission, in reaching out to the rest of the world with the good news.

Without question Jesus is the key figure in Mark's story. He is portrayed in a number of ways:

- The name 'Jesus of Nazareth' shows Jesus to be a true human figure. He has a family who believes him to be out of his mind; he gets angry and assertive, he becomes disappointed and screams out in the pain and loneliness of death.

- Jesus never uses the term 'Christ' (God's chosen or anointed one) of himself and is reluctant to accept it without the implication that he must suffer. Only in the 'shadow' of the cross does Jesus accept the title when he is openly declared 'the Christ, the King of Israel' as he hangs on the cross.

- At key points in the Gospel Jesus is represented as God's Son, because of his special relationship with God that went beyond the confines of human existence and had implications for the welfare of the world. He tells demons and the people he heals not to reveal his true identity as Son of God. Mark shows Jesus keeping his identity hidden, until the time came when it could be clearly seen that his nature and mission from God involved suffering and death.

- The Greek phrase 'Son of Man' in Jesus' native language, Aramaic, meant 'a man' and was probably used as an indirect way of referring to oneself. Mark has used the phrase to emphasize the continuity between the humble earthly ministry and suffering of the man Jesus with the one who has the authority of God to forgive sins and will come again in power and judgment.

The identity of Jesus is portrayed in the first part of the Gospel, in what appear like case studies. Mark shows his readers that Jesus has authority over evil spirits; can forgive sins; is a teacher. Jesus teaches about fasting, the sabbath, divorce, wealth, civil obedience, the greatest commandment, discipleship and the future. He also takes away fear and brings peace and calm; he is the one who heals and tells us of God.

In the central section of the Gospel, Mark concentrates on Jesus' teaching about himself and especially about discipleship. One of the puzzles of Mark's Gospel is why he says so much about the disciples, compared to the other three Gospels. Another puzzle is what Mark actually says about the disciples. For example, they are portrayed as not understanding the teaching of Jesus or Jesus' attitude to children. Most importantly, the disciples do not understand what Jesus says about suffering. So Jesus turns and rebukes Peter: 'Get behind me, Satan, because your thoughts are not of God but of men.' Also they are shown as not understanding Jesus' actions, nor do they remain faithful to him. But Mark's picture of the disciples is not all dark, for he also shows them as successful in their mission. Rather, he portrays the disciples as patterns of discipleship. It is as if Mark is saying, when you read my book about Jesus you will get most out of it if you see yourselves as one of those disciples.

In turn, Mark draws attention to different aspects of discipleship:

- A disciple is someone called by Jesus to leave, or let go of, someone or something in order to follow him.

- A disciple is someone called to be with Jesus. The whole of the Gospel portrays a group of people who follow Jesus closely and are constantly with him.

- Discipleship involves being sent out on mission, both to preach that people can turn from their sins and to cast out demons and heal people.

- The journey of discipleship is the way of the cross. It involves saying 'No' to self and 'taking up one's cross'; living as if in the last hours of life; a life already belonging to God.

- Discipleship involves failure, but also forgiveness. The disciples are portrayed as failing in their mission, in their relationships with each other, and in Peter's denial that he even knows Jesus. But Peter is shown as repentant and the message from the empty tomb is that Jesus will lead the disciples, even Peter.

The largest section of Mark's Gospel is taken up with the story of Jesus' trial, death and resurrection. This also casts its shadow over the rest of the Gospel.

The revelation and understanding of who Jesus is and what he came to do has been gradual but is complete at the cross. The chief priests and the teachers of the law unknowingly declare him to be the Christ, the King of Israel, and the Roman soldier recognizes that 'truly this man was the Son of God'. Jesus has taught, and now it is seen, that his special appointment from God is not a mission of force or an unassailable declaration of God's power but a life of humble service and suffering. Thus Jesus' identity and God's power in him are only visible to the eye of trust in God. The suffering and death of Jesus show God giving himself for us. But what happened to Jesus shows something that is always true of those who try to serve God—there will be suffering, but it will be the gateway to new life.

JESUS' AUTHORITY AND POWER
Mark 1:21–28

We are not told anything about what Jesus taught in the Capernaum synagogue; simply that the people who heard him were amazed, for he taught with an authority unlike that of the scribes. These teachers of the law, who interpreted the traditional laws that helped apply the laws of Moses to daily life, had an authority which arose out of the tradition which they preserved.

Jesus' authority was direct from God. Throughout this Gospel we can see that Mark portrays Jesus' unique relationship with God and how that raised questions in the minds of those around him.

People with an 'unclean spirit' would not have been allowed in the synagogue, so the symptoms of the man's sickness were probably not always obvious. However, on being confronted by Jesus, the demon is dramatically exposed. In our own world, the various aspects of evil, not least the demonic dimension of sickness, are also exposed when Jesus comes into the situation.

The demon tries to protect itself from Jesus with the formula: 'What do you want with us?' In other words, 'Keep away from *us!*' The plural here may mean that the demon is speaking for the whole world of spirits. The demon uses names for Jesus—'Jesus of Nazareth' and 'Holy One of God'—as a way of trying to gain power over him. Jesus is recognized by the powerful unseen evil forces of the universe as their destroyer. This shows us that we have nothing to fear from the unseen destructive evil forces in the world or in our lives, because the coming of Jesus signals their defeat. Jesus retaliates with the command: 'Be quiet (or muzzled) and come out of him.' The demon leaves violently—as sometimes happens in exorcisms today.

Mark notes that the people marvel not just at the miracle but at the new teaching associated with it. In many growing churches in the twentieth century, miracles cause people to ask questions about Jesus, and his reputation spreads.

JESUS FORGIVES SINS
Mark 2:1–12

This is one of Mark's 'case studies' in which he shows us who Jesus is. Here Jesus is the one who has the right to forgive sins.

The four friends of the sick person are said to be so confident in Jesus that they went to unusual lengths to bring the two of them together. Do we go to similar lengths to see that our friends meet Jesus? The roof of this one-storey house, approached by an outside staircase, was probably made of cross-rafters overlaid with branches and covered with hardened mud.

Jesus recognizes that the confidence which the four helpers (and the man?) have in him is sufficient grounds for the man to receive forgiveness. Our lives show many expressions of the need for forgiveness—a sense of guilt, anger, broken relationships and sickness. These things are not always the result of our sin or anyone else's. However, it seems that in this story, sin had had a profound and debilitating effect on the man's body.

The word used here for 'forgiveness' means 'to be released or relieved of sins'. This is the same word Mark has used of the disciples 'leaving' things and people when they were called to follow Jesus. Mark is perhaps underlining that Jesus releases us from the things we cannot leave behind as we would wish—sin and sickness—so that we can follow him.

Like other stories in this section of Mark, Jesus meets opposition from the religious authorities. They knew that the right to forgive sins was the prerogative of God alone, so that Jesus' action was, for them, blasphemy. They failed to understand that Jesus was more than an ordinary person. We also fail to understand who Jesus is if we do not allow him to forgive our sins. After the man had been healed, Mark says that everyone in the crowd (including the scribes?) recognized that in what Jesus had done God was to be praised.

EMPOWERED BY THE HOLY SPIRIT
Mark 3:20–30

In these stories and sayings, we see some examples of charges brought against Jesus. Even Jesus' family thought that he had gone mad! But in verse 22, the most horrific charge is brought against Jesus: that he is possessed by Satan, or the devil, and in his power casts out demons. The word 'Beelzebul' ('Lord of the house') may have been coined on the spur of the moment, but its meaning is obvious: another word for Satan.

Jesus' answer is to point out that it would be impossible for him to exorcize evil spirits in Satan's power, for that would mean that Satan was destroying Satan. It would be like a country or a family fighting itself, and in any case would mean the end of Satan. Jesus uses picture language to explain what takes place in his exorcisms. It is like someone entering a strong man's house, binding him and plundering his house. In exorcism Jesus sees himself as binding Satan in order to plunder his property—that is, to rescue people who are in Satan's grip.

The saying in verse 29 that 'whoever blasphemes against the Holy Spirit will never be forgiven' has caused untold anguish among Christians. A leading

expert on this Gospel says: 'We can say with absolute confidence to anyone who is overwhelmed by the fear that he or she has committed this sin, that the fact that they are so troubled is itself sure proof that they have not committed it.' It is not a saying directed against genuine doubt or questioning, but against those who understand the work of the Holy Spirit in Jesus yet deliberately misrepresent Jesus' work as of the devil. This saying in Mark's Gospel is set against the background of criticism from the scribes and makes for a warning to contemporary church leaders and teachers.

LEARNING THROUGH PARABLES
Mark 4:1–20

Jesus here teaches in parables, and then explains why. Parables are sayings or stories, usually about ordinary life and having more than one meaning.

The story is about a Palestinian farmer. He would have carried a container of seed and cast out seed with his free hand. Then the field would have been ploughed, or the seed buried by driving animals across it.

The parable contrasts three unproductive soils with the good soil. There is the soil on the path where villagers had crossed the field during the year; the rocky ground, where unseen limestone is close to the surface; and soil having thorny weeds which grew faster than the grain. The yield of the good soil is extraordinary when compared with the average of seven and a half.

For Jesus, this story was probably about his apparently futile mission with its setbacks and difficulties. But in spite of them, Jesus is confident that God will bring about a triumphant 'harvest'—the glorious dimension of the Kingdom of God still to come. We can also take this parable as telling of the eventual triumph of God in our mission despite present failure, opposition and uneven success.

In verses 10 to 12 Mark inserts some material about the purpose of parables. People may hear about the secret of the kingdom of God yet not understand. At first sight, this seems strange, but it is in line with the whole of Jesus' ministry. While it was open for all to see and hear, it was at the same time 'veiled' in his humble service. An attitude of trust in God was required to see who Jesus is and what his teaching meant. If God's message in Jesus was not 'veiled', people's freedom to believe or not would have been denied.

Mark interprets the seed falling on various types of ground as various kinds of people's reaction to the message of God. The stumbling blocks are spelt out as Satan taking away the message (verse 15); trouble or persecution (verse 17); and worries about this life, love for riches and the desire for things (verses 18–19).

THE MISSION OF THE TWELVE
Mark 6:7–13

At last the twelve disciples are sent out. In chapter 3 verses 13–15 Jesus is said to have chosen the Twelve to be with him and to be sent out to preach and to have authority to drive out demons. Then comes an important section of teaching and of observing Jesus. After this teaching and experience the disciples are sent out. Being with Jesus is the preparation for mission.

Earlier in the Gospel, Jesus is shown as having authority over evil spirits. Now he shares that authority with the Twelve. Mark believed that exorcism was an essential part of the mission of the church. They are sent out in pairs, probably because the Law of Moses stated that the truthfulness of a testimony was to be established by two witnesses.

The principle of total dependence on God remains true for all time. In shaking the dust from their feet, the disciples would not only dissociate themselves from unreceptive people but also warn them that all obligations to them had been fulfilled.

Oil was used as a medicine. For Mark it was also a symbol of joy, comfort, spiritual nourishment and the presence of God. The disciples' successful mission involved not only preaching that people should repent or turn from their sins, but also exorcism and healing. Is our mission the same today? Or have we surrendered our belief in the supernatural?

THE SUFFERING MESSIAH
Mark 8:27–38

This passage shows that a true understanding of Jesus involves following him in a sacrificial way. Previously the disciples had not understood who Jesus was. Now they begin to understand. But when the disciples know who Jesus is, they cannot face what that means for Jesus and for their own discipleship. For Mark, following Jesus is a journey—to the cross.

As is often true in our time, Jesus' full identity was not recognized by even those who saw and heard him. Even his closest associates, who understood he was 'the Messiah'—God's unique chosen messenger—were not to speak about this. For, as the story shows, they did not understand that suffering was an essential aspect of Jesus being the Christ.

Suffering is also part of being a follower of Jesus. But to carry one's cross does not mean to take on unpleasant tasks. As the readers of Mark were well aware, it means, like those condemned to crucifixion, having one's life in the hands of another, living as if in the last hours of life. In being a disciple of Jesus there is a reversal of the roles accepted by most people. The one who finds life here and after death is the one who is not ashamed of Jesus but abandons his life for him and for the good news.

A MODEL DISCIPLE
Mark 10:46-52

Earlier in the Gospel, in chapter 8, there is an account of a blind man who, at first, saw only partially. Now, following a section containing much teaching on discipleship, comes a story of sight completely restored. Bartimaeus is an example of enlightened discipleship.

In the Old Testament and in Mark's world, blindness was a symbol of mental and spiritual blindness and it was expected that in the age of the Messiah God would open the eyes of the blind. Bartimaeus is a beggar—without known resources—so he can only say to Jesus, 'Take pity on me.' The name 'Son of David' is particularly appropriate for God's special messenger, for in Jesus' time it was associated with the healing work of the Messiah. In the face of people telling him to be quiet, Bartimaeus persists in his trust that Jesus, the revered Teacher, can heal him. It is this trust or faith that enables him to receive his sight from Jesus.

If the question of Jesus, 'What do you want me to do for you?', helped the man make clear and strengthen his trust, it can be a lesson to us of the need to be specific in our trust in and requests of Jesus.

In the final line of the story, Mark is probably saying that the appropriate response of anyone who has received from Jesus is to become his follower. Bartimaeus, once sitting on the edge of the road, now follows Jesus 'on the road'. This road leads to a place of suffering and death.

TIMES BEFORE THE END
Mark 13:1-37

The disciples want to know when the temple will be destroyed and about the events leading to 'the end'.

In chapter 13 verses 5 to 23 signs of the end are mentioned, sometimes in the form of warnings.

■ **There will be Christian leaders trying to mislead Christians.** They will draw attention to themselves with miracles and wonders which are no guide to truth or God's approval of them.

■ **There will be world conflict and natural disaster.** But we are not to be alarmed for they are like the labour pains that herald the joy of new birth.

- **For the followers of Jesus there will be suffering and persecution from the state, official religion and one's own family.**

- **The good news preached to all the nations will be a sign of the end,** even though the world will not necessarily become more Christian.

- **The 'awful horror' or 'the abomination that causes desolation' mentioned in the book of Daniel.** This referred to the pagan altar placed in the temple by Antiochus Epiphanes in 168BC. In Mark it probably means that another foreign power is expected to desecrate the temple. The destruction of Jerusalem and the temple eventually took place when the Romans burnt and dismantled the city in AD70. Severe as the end times may be, God has actually curtailed the suffering out of love for his people so that they will not be destroyed.

Jesus was wrong? In the Western world we tend to think that the end of the present age is at some unknown point along a straight line of history in front of us towards which we travel. It may be better to think that we are travelling parallel to the end, always near to it—like walking along a footpath on the edge of a road—so that at any moment God may come and sweep us up into his future.

- **Only the Father knows when the end will come.**

- **'What I say to you, I say to all: "Watch!".'** Mark emphasizes the point that we are to remain alert or we will be found asleep. The 'signs' that have been given are not to satisfy our curiosity or for us to make calculations of the end. They strengthen trust in God who knows the future and warn us of dangers and the necessity of vigilance.

Chapter 13 verses 24 to 27 is the second part of the answer to the disciples' question. After the signs and warnings, as part of the end itself, the entire universe will collapse. But this is only the framework for the one event which is important—the coming of the Son of Man.

The section chapter 13 verses 28 to 37 has three lessons about the timing of the end.

- **The time of the end is near!** The problem here is that not only this chapter but the New Testament as a whole stresses the nearness of the end. How can we explain this? Was

The Message of Luke

Graeme Rutherford

According to one Gallup poll, 19% of Australians go to church once a week. Yet 80% are said to believe in God (admittedly not all in the God of the Bible). This poll, and polls taken in other Westernized societies, indicate a large disenchantment with the state of corporate Christianity.

Luke, the only non-Jewish writer in the New Testament and a doctor, cannot write of the good news of Jesus without at the same time including the idea of the church.

Luke OUTLINE

Luke is the only Gospel writer who went on to write a second volume, the book of Acts. In it he refers to his Gospel as an account of 'all that Jesus began to do and to teach until the day he was taken up to heaven'. So Luke intends that his Gospel is a record of all that Jesus *began* to do and to teach, and his later book, Acts, is a record of all that Jesus, risen and exalted, *continues* to do and teach through his Spirit in the church.

For Luke, the church is an essential part of God's plan. God had a purpose which did not stop when Jesus returned to his Father. The good news of the gospel includes belonging to the church community. As far as Luke is concerned, conversion to Jesus is, at the same time, conversion to the church. Luke tells us that God's aim from the very beginning was to deliver us from individualism (which is a form of self-centredness) into a community. For the Christian, the church is not an optional extra.

In writing the history of Jesus and his disciples, he is wearing bifocals: their mission is continued into the life of the early church. There are clear parallels in the way Luke describes the ministry of Jesus and his disciples (all that Jesus *began* to do and to teach) and the ministry of the early church (all that Jesus *continues* to do and to teach). In Luke's Gospel:

- Jesus was conceived of the Spirit;

- He refers to the Way of Jesus and his disciples—a journey to Jerusalem;

- The Gospel ends with the ascension of Jesus.

In Acts:

- The church is empowered by the Spirit;

- The church—the Way—is maligned on its journey from Jerusalem to Rome;

- The church continues until Jesus returns.

To look in more detail at the three characteristics in Luke's Gospel:

- The birth of Jesus—conceived by the Holy Spirit. There has recently been a great deal of debate in the church over the interpretation of the opening chapters of Luke. Some have questioned the historical reality of the virgin birth, claiming that the birth stories were symbolic and mythological. But we should not overlook the force of Luke's preface. He specifically tells us that he is not setting out to compose a pious work of fiction. He may be selecting his facts to bring out the truths he wishes to present, but he insists that it is with facts that he is concerned. He claims that he has 'carefully investigated everything from the beginning' and that he has received his information from 'those who from the first were eye-witnesses and servants of the word'.

There are three features of Luke's account of the conception and birth of Jesus which we can focus on. The account is a genuine product of the apostolic age. There is no evidence to suggest that Luke was ever published without the first two chapters. There is a 'Jewishness' in the style and language. As we read we feel we are still in the Old Testament. The hymn we find on Mary's lips echoes Hannah's song at the birth of Samuel, recorded in 1 Samuel. The narratives are certainly not later inventions, they ring true.

Second, Luke's account is sober and simple. There is no hint of the crude elements which existed in the pagan stories of the time about the gods having sexual intercourse with human women. Instead, there is the utmost reverence and restraint.

Last, Luke's account is independent of Matthew's. Both Luke and Matthew agree on the virgin birth. (The term 'virgin birth' is misleading. The birth was normal and natural. It is Jesus' conception which was abnormal and supernatural.) Matthew's account appears to tell the story from Joseph's angle, Luke from Mary's angle. While Matthew describes Joseph's anxiety over Mary's pregnancy, Joseph's dream, the visit of the wise men, and the flight into Egypt, Luke tells the story of the angel's annunciation to Mary, her visit to Elizabeth, the journey south to Bethlehem, the birth in the stable and the visit of the shepherds. Each account would be largely inexplicable without the other. The two accounts are independent but complementary. Both bear clear witness to the virgin birth of Jesus.

● The Way of Jesus and his disciples—a journey to Jerusalem. The theme of travel or journey is an important one for Luke. It has been said that for Mark, discipleship meant 'being with' Jesus, whereas for Luke it is to 'journey with' Jesus, to be always on the move: towards Jerusalem, and then to the ends of the earth. The theme of a journey is present early in the Gospel—'Mary arose and went with haste into the hill country, to a city of Judah.' Then there is the journey to Bethlehem and the presentation of the infant Jesus in the temple in Jerusalem. The clearest expression of the theme comes in a long central section of the Gospel, sometimes called the 'travel narrative' (9:51—19:45). This is nearly half the book! Lastly, the theme reappears at the end of the Gospel in the two disciples journeying to Emmaus (24:13–35).

The theme of travel is one with which Australians like myself can readily identify. Great distances separate many Australians from their cultural origins in Europe or Asia. Within Australia itself, large distances separate the capital cities. The interior of the country is one vast empty desert. As in many other countries, national meetings and conferences are forever facing the so-called 'tyranny of distance'.

But though the theme of journey may appeal to Australian understanding, the destination of Jerusalem and what it meant for Jesus certainly does not! 'As the time approached for him to be taken up to heaven, Jesus resolutely set out for Jerusalem,' Luke tells us. Jesus' steadfastness in going to Jerusalem represented a courageous acceptance of the cross. It is fascinating to notice the way in which Luke, the Gentile writer, emphasizes Jerusalem in his Gospel. He refers to Jerusalem thirty-one times as against thirteen in Matthew, ten in Mark and twelve times in John. Luke's Gospel is absorbed with a journey whose destination is Jerusalem. (If you are interested in following this further, read 9:51, 53; 13:22; 17:11; 18:31; 19:28.)

If, as Luke suggests, the Christian life can be thought of as a journey, there are many in life who are on the wrong road. Jesus' parable of the Pharisee and the tax collector in chapter 18 depicts the right and the wrong way. The Pharisee preens his righteous character and his good deeds. But self-righteousness and self-congratulation cut no ice with a holy God. The trouble was not that he was not as far along the road as he thought he was—he was on the wrong road altogether. It did not matter how far he went along the road of 'self-salvation'. He would never reach his destination that way. Whereas the tax-collector cast himself on the mercy of God, the Pharisee relied on his own merit.

Luke insists that what Jesus accomplished in Jerusalem is the root of salvation. Only through his death can men and women be brought to a right relationship with God. That is why Jerusalem is the crucial destination of Jesus' journey throughout the Gospel. Nothing must deflect him from that path. It has been determined by God.

But Luke also makes clear that salvation only becomes available to individuals as they turn to God and embrace it by faith. This faith and trust in Christ's work on the cross leads in turn to a wholehearted following of Jesus. Small wonder that Jesus urged people to count the cost. Such an adventure is not to be undertaken lightly. It hits hard at our apathy and our self-satisfaction.

There are many hazards along the Christian road. Greed and material possessions are a major hazard. In Australia, as in many countries which were colonized, the greed of early European settlers for sheep, wheat, cattle and mining violated the land rights of the aboriginal people. Only in recent times have white Australians begun to face up to their greed. Jesus' words are a perpetual warning: 'What good is it for a man to gain the whole world, and yet lose or forfeit his very self?'

The journey with Jesus requires no looking back. Hesitant, half-hearted, headturning followers will make little impact. Journeying with Jesus means going 'to Jerusalem', and to the cross before going to heaven.

- The ascension—transition from Luke's Gospel to Acts. Luke alone tells of the ascension—very briefly in chapter 24 of the Gospel and again more fully in Acts 1:9–11. As with the virgin birth, many today believe that the ascension is a myth or legend without any basis in history. They are convinced that in an ordered world governed by uniform laws, a human body cannot defy the law of gravity by rising upwards. Nor—they further argue—can any sort of body, consisting of molecules and atoms, simply disappear into thin air. But scientific objections are inappropriate. Scientists investigate the orderliness of the universe. It operates according to a pattern and therefore they can predict its behaviour, dealing with what happens 'according to precedent'.

Luke, however, is dealing with the unprecedented. Ascensions don't usually happen! Given that he was writing about an extraordinary character—'the Son of God'—who became a man at a definite time, is it not understandable that at a definite time he should also be seen to have passed into a wider existence?

To sum up. Luke writes of God's great plan in history. He traces Jesus' genealogy back to the beginning of creation. Jesus' life is overshadowed by a journey which led steadfastly and purposefully to Jerusalem. Alone among the four Gospel writers, Luke goes on to write a second volume.

For Luke, the church community was an integral part of God's plan. In the accounts of the ascension he unites the past, the present and the future. It is a beautifully unifying truth. It spans the centuries which separate the Jesus of history from the coming King. It assures us that, although his life on earth took place centuries ago, Jesus has not forgotten the world to which he came. He continues to rule. His work in Jerusalem has been accomplished. But the work of proclaiming his salvation must go on until Jesus comes back in the same way as he was seen to go into heaven (Acts 1:11).

WHOLENESS
Luke 1:67–69

Looking good and keeping fit has become a near-obsession for Westerners. For many people physical health and well-being is far more important than spiritual health. Yet the 'wholeness' which is another of Luke's favourite themes includes the wholeness of our physical bodies.

What does it mean to be made whole? Is this what Luke had in mind when he spoke of salvation? Can we equate 'salvation' with 'wholeness' of body, mind and spirit? That would appear to be too much of a short cut. For Luke, salvation is mainly concerned with how we think and act rather than what we have.

In Zechariah's song the salvation which God gives us through the promised Messiah 'that we should be saved from our enemies' is understood in terms of serving God 'in holiness and righteousness'. And John the Baptist will 'go on before the Lord to prepare the way for him, to give his people the knowledge of salvation through the forgiveness of their sins'.

In the healing miracles of Jesus the word 'saved' can often be translated as 'made well' or 'whole'. But the word is also used of rescue from drowning ('Save us Lord, we are perishing') and from death ('He saved others: let him save himself'). Clearly Luke's theme of salvation was not a guarantee of freedom from every kind of nightmarish situation including disease, drowning and death. Jesus could say 'your faith has saved you' to the cleansed Samaritan leper, but his cure was not his salvation—it simply portrayed the meaning of salvation.

But Luke also shows Jesus as concerned for people's physical and mental health. Jesus was moved with compassion for those who were in bondage to disease or demons. 'Wholeness' in terms of all-round health was his concern. This means that Christians are involved in many different areas of health and healing within the wider context of giving people the good news of Jesus in the 'knowledge of salvation'.

MARY—FIRST AMONG BELIEVERS
Luke 2:19; 2:51

Mary, the mother of Jesus is presented as a model for all disciples. Luke shows how she receives God's word with reverence, struggles with its implications, ponders it deeply and lives it out. She, above all, is the one who 'hears the word of God and does it'. Her greatness lies in the fact that she is a woman of faith.

Luke skilfully makes this point in the way he describes Mary 'treasuring in her heart' the things concerning the birth of Jesus. Mary's two appearances show that she has indeed treasured what has been revealed to her. Luke deliberately presents Mary as the model of the faithful one.

Luke's Gospel tells more than the others the gracious, courteous attitude of Jesus towards women, and the place they occupied in his ministry. It stands in marked contrast to contemporary Jewish attitudes.

Among the Gospel writers only Luke writes of the prophetess Anna; the widow of Nain; the woman who was a sinner; the ministering women, Martha and Mary; the woman whom Satan had bound for eighteen years; the daughters of Jerusalem who wept. Clearly Jesus related to women with ease. These can be found in 2:36–38; 7:11–17, 36–40; 8:2–3; 10:38–42; 13:10–17 and 23:27–31.

In Luke's stories women are frequently the first to come to faith. The Easter narrative in chapter 24 highlights the fact that women were the first to come to believe that Jesus was risen from the dead and the first to proclaim their faith in him. While the men remained a safe distance from the burial place, fearing for their lives, some women watched carefully where their King was buried (23:55–56). As witnesses of the burial of Jesus, they played an important part.

Among believers the barriers of caste, class and gender have been broken down. In Acts, Luke demonstrates the equal partnership of men and women in the church. Such a partnership was never intended to be temporary! Even today churches are struggling to work out what this means.

GOOD NEWS FOR A MULTI-CULTURAL SOCIETY
Luke 2:32

Luke's Gospel challenges the concepts of God that were held by the world of his day. God is the God of all the nations. When Luke, a Gentile, traces Jesus' family tree, he goes back, not to Abraham, as does Matthew the Jew, but to 'Adam, the son of God'. Luke sees the good news about Jesus as relevant to the needs of the entire human race. It is no petty thing, done in a corner and of no significance. He is writing of a gospel that must be taken to the very ends of the earth.

When Jesus' parents presented him in the temple as a baby, the aged prophet Simeon welcomed him as the one destined to be 'a light for revelation to the Gentiles and for glory to your people Israel'.

This cosmopolitan approach of Jesus is seen first in his contact with the Samaritans. The Jews despised the Samaritans, and so the story of the Good Samaritan incensed them. Jesus also rebuked James and John when they suggested that an unfriendly Samaritan village should be wiped out with apocalyptic fire bombs. In Jesus' encounter with a group of lepers, all ten were cleansed. Only one was truly saved. And he was a Samaritan.

The love of God embraces Gentiles. In Jesus' last words at the end of the Gospel, he instructs his disciples that 'repentance and forgiveness of sins will be preached in my name to all nations, beginning from Jerusalem'.

None of this means that salvation comes to people automatically. Jesus refers to division, a sifting of people. A person must decide for Christ. Jesus says a day will come when many 'shall seek to enter in, and shall not be able'. Luke's point is that 'all without distinction *may* be saved'. It does not mean that 'all without exception *will* be saved'. The door is open. But if a person is to enter, it is necessary that they should receive their salvation by faith (see 7:9; 8:48; 17:19; 18:42).

Jesus has much to say to our multicultural society.

JESUS AND THE SPIRIT
Luke 4:18

'The Spirit of the Lord is upon me, because he has anointed me to preach good news to the poor.' At the conclusion of the reading Jesus calmly tells the congregation in the synagogue that these words from the prophet Isaiah are fulfilled 'today'. This is perhaps the key reference to the Holy Spirit in Luke's Gospel, the one which stands as a beacon shedding light over the whole of Jesus' ministry. It could scarcely be made clearer that Jesus is the bearer of the Spirit and accomplishes his mission in the power of the Spirit. In this Jesus is unique.

During Jesus' time on earth God's Spirit was not available to others. John the Baptist knew that his work was to prepare people for the Messiah. 'I baptize you with water. But one more powerful than I will come ... He will baptize you with the Holy Spirit and with fire.' Jesus was not only the unique *bearer* of the Spirit: he was also the unique *dispenser* of the Spirit. But he did not baptize with the Holy Spirit until after his death and resurrection.

It becomes clear that the Spirit will be available to his followers as they start to spread the good news about Jesus.

In chapter 11 of Luke's Gospel the Holy Spirit is the great gift poured out on the day of Pentecost, recorded in Acts 2, but not before. There are seventeen references to the Spirit in the Gospel but fifty-eight in Acts. Why is it that Jesus alone is filled with the Holy Spirit in the Gospel? (All the other characters mentioned in the account of Jesus' birth are examples of the working of the Spirit in the Old Testament sense rather than in that of the New Testament.) Why are not all the disciples intoxicated with the Spirit as in the days of Pentecost?

The answer is important. The Spirit was tied up with the person of Jesus, the 'funnel' through whom all later experience of the Spirit would come. Until Jesus had died for the forgiveness of sinners and been raised victoriously to life, the Spirit which rested upon him was not available to be passed on to others in that way.

JESUS—FRIEND OF ALL
Luke 5:30 and 7:30

One of the themes which is constantly repeated in Luke's Gospel is Jesus' friendliness and his ability to get on with all sorts of people.

■ **He was a friend to the down-and-outs.** The scribes and Pharisees were always complaining that 'this man receives sinners and eats with them'. Jesus is found in the company of a notorious woman who revolted the soul of self-righteous Simon. He enjoys a meal in the home of Zacchaeus, the most hated man in Jericho. True to his mission he remains the friend of social misfits to his last breath, promising paradise to one of the criminals crucified with him.

For many Christians today it is easy to be a Pharisee, to have a judgmental attitude towards our culture that cuts us off from it. Church people have been appallingly respectable for far too long. It is a travesty of the attitude of Jesus. He was a friend of the poor and the failures. How many such people are our friends?

■ **He was a friend to the up-and-outs.** Luke does not present us with a picture of inverted snobbery. In no other Gospel does Jesus associate so often with well-off people. He accepts hospitality from them and eats at their dinner parties. Three times we see him as a guest in a Pharisee's house, and among his friends is the wealthy and distinguished Joseph of Arimathea. Jesus' followers included Joanna, the wife of Chuza, Herod's steward, a member of 'high society'.

Jesus was neither aloof nor class-conscious. In Jesus' eyes, the quality of a relationship was more important than social background.

TRUE SPIRITUALITY
Luke 11:5–13

Our modern hustle and bustle places us in the grip of what has been called 'universal fatigue'. People are constantly complaining about how tired they feel. Our bodies, nerves and even our lives pay a frighteningly high price for the haste-ridden, clock-dominated booked-up way of life that we have chosen for ourselves. But there is an alternative.

Many of us recognize a need in our lives for quiet contemplation. Luke's understanding of spirituality is expressed in dramatic form by the way in which he places back-to-back the stories of the Good Samaritan and Mary and Martha in chapter 10. Unhurried communion with Jesus (Mary) leads to a form of service which is no mere do-goodism (the Good Samaritan).

At all the great moments of his life, Luke shows us Jesus at prayer. Jesus prayed at his baptism, before coming into conflict with the Pharisees, before selecting the Twelve, at the transfiguration and during the crucifixion. Luke alone tells us that Jesus prayed for Peter in his ordeal. If you are interested in looking at Jesus' prayers, see 3:21; 5:16; 6:12; 9:29; 22:32; 23:46.

Only Luke recounts the prayer parables of the Friend at Midnight and the Unjust Judge (11:5–13; 18:1–8). The first parable may serve to underline Luke's teaching on prayer. Because we have failed to take into account the cultural context, the parable has often been thought to teach the need for persistence in prayer. But, understanding Middle-Eastern custom, the message of the parable is almost the exact opposite.

In effect, Jesus says to his Jewish audience, 'Can you imagine a friend at midnight, unwilling to lend a loaf of bread?' Most of us have no difficulty in that. 'Yes,' we say without hesitation. But the cultural context requires a 'No.' In Middle-Eastern hospitality, such a response would have been unthinkable. The point of the story is this: if no Middle-Eastern neighbour would behave like this—how much less God!

God is not reluctant or begrudging. Such a picture of him is grotesque. He is more willing to answer our prayers than we are to ask. True spirituality does not require the use of techniques of prayer. The power of prayer is seen to belong to God, not to our words or methods or states of mind. He is not elusive or reluctant to hear. He is Father.

SIGNS AND WONDERS
Luke 11:20

Jesus' miracles aroused controversy—to the point where people once accused him of driving out demons 'by Beelzebub'. Luke makes a close connexion between the miracles and the kingdom. 'But if I drive out demons by the finger of God, then the kingdom of God has come to you,' replied Jesus. (See also 9:2; 9:11; 10:9.) Many Christians today overlook this connexion and fail to find a balanced biblical view of the miracles, producing two extremes.

First, there are those who are sceptical and suggest that the miracles recorded in Luke arose from legend and were added to the Gospel in later times.

Some critics have pointed to the similarities between Luke and *The Life of Apollonius of Tyana*. Because the life of Apollonius has some parallels with the life of Jesus, it is often assumed that the author, Philostratus, is the source of Luke's miracle accounts. But there is a major flaw in this theory. Philostratus, writing 150 years later than Luke, was commissioned by the Empress Julia Domna to write a tract to magnify the importance of Apollonius over Jesus. The borrowing has gone in the opposite direction!

Then, there are those who describe miraculous intervention with unabated enthusiasm. They draw a straight line from the miracles of Luke to the church today. Their position becomes one of fantastic sensationalism.

Luke's association of the miracles with the kingdom means that we are not pushed to either extreme. The kingdom has come in embryo, ambiguously, in the person and ministry of Jesus—'the kingdom of God is among you' (17:21). Yet the kingdom is future and the disciples are to pray, 'Your kingdom come.'

This means that a line can be drawn from the Gospel miracles to our ministry today because the kingdom has come. But the line will not be a straight one. The kingdom is veiled and incognito. At times our prayers will be answered with what can only be termed 'signs and wonders'. At other times, there is frustration, ambiguity, and no healing. The line between Luke and today is not apparent to us at all. God is sovereign and he will not allow us to plot a straight graph.

A WEEK IN JERUSALEM

About a third of each Gospel is set in the final eight days, between Jesus entering Jerusalem on Palm Sunday and rising from the grave on Easter Day. The events of that week are the focal point of what God has done for humanity. Because he gave Jesus to die for us and to rise again, we can find peace with God.

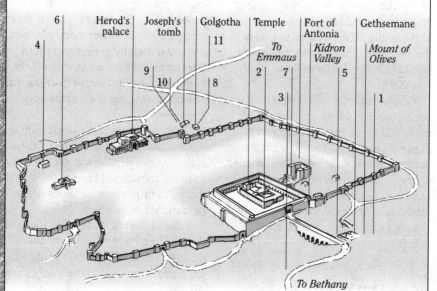

6 | Herod's palace | Joseph's tomb | Golgotha | Temple | Fort of Antonia | Gethsemane

4 — 11 — To Emmaus — Kidron Valley — Mount of Olives

9 — 10 — 8 — 2 — 7 — 5 — 3 — 1

To Bethany

1 Palm Sunday
Jesus arrives for Passover week, entering city via Mt of Olives, welcomed like a king. Drives merchants from temple. To Bethany for night.

2 Monday to Wednesday
Days teaching, mainly in temple. Back to Bethany for nights, probably at house of Martha, Mary and Lazarus.

3 Wednesday evening
At Bethany, Mary, Martha's sister, anoints him with ointment to prepare him for burial.

4 Thursday
Peter and John prepare room for Passover meal. In the evening Jesus and the Twelve eat Last Supper – a day early perhaps because he knew he was to die.

5 Thursday night
In Garden of Gethsemane Jesus is tempted to avoid death. He is arrested, betrayed by Judas.

6 Early Friday morning
At high priest's house, tried by Jewish council. In courtyard Peter denies him. Judas commits suicide.

7 Friday morning
Tried before Roman Governor, Pontius Pilate. Crowd calls 'Crucify him!' Tortured by soldiers.

8 Friday noon to 3 pm
He is crucified at Golgotha, 'the place of the skull'.

9 Friday before dusk
Buried in Joseph of Arimathea's tomb.

10 Early Easter Sunday morning
Mary Magdalene, some other women, then Peter and John find the tomb empty – he has been raised from death.

11 Easter Sunday afternoon
Jesus appears to 2 disciples on road to Emmaus. Explains Messiah must die and rise again.

WHEN WILL JESUS RETURN?
Luke 13:6–9

Many today have abandoned the simple hope that Jesus will return to this earth in power and great glory. Some regard it as an outmoded superstitious belief; others object on historical grounds. Their objection runs like this. The first Christians expected that Jesus would return in their lifetime, but by the time Luke wrote his Gospel three decades had passed and still he had not come.

And so, these people argue, since the early Christians were evidently mistaken about the *time* of Jesus' return, they were probably mistaken in the *fact* as well. They say that Luke sets out to correct the idea that the time of Jesus' return is near. What are we to say in answer to this argument?

First, nowhere does the New Testament claim that Jesus would return in the lifetime of the first Christians. Indeed, Jesus himself told his disciples that he did not know the day and the hour of his return.

Second, passages which speak of the nearness of Jesus' second coming must be carefully interpreted. The life, death, resurrection, ascension and second coming of Jesus all belong together as God's complete plan for the salvation of humanity. For this reason the interval between the time when Jesus became a man on earth and his second coming can be described as 'short', however long it might last. So Luke has not abandoned the idea of the 'end' being near.

Third, the reason why Jesus' return is delayed is explained in the parable of the barren fig tree in chapter 13. This tells of an owner who speaks of cutting a useless tree down, but the vine-dresser is reluctant to do so. He asks for one more year, promising to do everything possible to make it bear fruit. The parable stresses God's reluctance to punish sinners. The end is held back by the patience of God, giving opportunity for repentance.

To sum up. When are we to expect Jesus' return? According to Luke, 'sooner than we expect and later than we expect'. Sooner, and therefore we must be prepared. Later, and therefore we must be patient.

TRUE JOY
Luke 15:1–32

If we were to estimate prosperity according to the number of public holidays conveniently arranged on a Monday, my country, Australia, must be reckoned among the wealthiest. It is 'the Land of the Long Weekend.' Leisure is slowly taking over from work as the dominant organizing principle of Australians' lives. Like the rich fool in Jesus' parable our motto is—'take life easy, eat, drink and be merry.'

But, as that parable teaches, this lifestyle is doomed to disappointment. Such frothy, instant happiness contrasts strikingly with what Luke has to say about joy in his Gospel, sometimes described as 'the Gospel of joy'. Perhaps chapter 15 focusses the theme best for us. It has been called 'the most joyful chapter in the whole of the Gospel of joy'. It tells of the lost sheep, the lost coin and the lost sons—plural, since both sons were lost. Here we have an insight into the joy that God has in forgiving those who recognize their own sinfulness and their need of him.

It is not surprising that in this Gospel the birth of Jesus is surrounded with songs—Mary's song; Zechariah's song; the angels' song and Simeon's song (to be found in 1:46–55; 1:68–79; 2:14 and 2:29–32). Only the book of Revelation contains more songs.

Just as the Gospel opens with joy, so it closes on the same note. After Jesus returned to his Father in heaven the disciples returned to Jerusalem 'with great joy' as they looked forward to the fulfilment of Jesus' promise of the gift of the Holy Spirit. The secret of Jesus' own joy is to be found in the inspiration of the Spirit (10:21). Joy is in some way connected to the work of each person of the Trinity—Father, Son and Holy Spirit.

The joy Luke describes is no ephemeral pleasure. When the seventy-two disciples return from their mission in chapter 10 Jesus says to them, 'Do not rejoice that the spirits submit to you, but rejoice that your names are written in heaven.' Nothing can beat such a joy down. Not even death.

JESUS OUR CONTEMPORARY
Luke 24:13–35

Death is something we prefer not to think about. In my own country, Australia, and many Westernized countries, people are protected from death and suffering to a large extent by welfare schemes and modern science. The government is relied upon to stand between the individual and a threatening environment. The usual plea is, 'Why doesn't the government do something about . . . ?'

But a result of our higher quality of life is that it is harder to face death, pain and limitation when they do intrude, despite frenetic attempts to avoid them. Death is the great unmentionable (though in aboriginal culture traditionally death is an accepted and integrated part of life.) The Gospels alone give the answer.

In the Gospels Jesus is shown to be the contemporary of every generation and culture. Christianity does not live on nostalgia. Jesus relates to today. Nowhere does the Easter story speak to us so clearly as in Luke's account of the walk to Emmaus.

In telling how the eyes of these two disciples were opened to recognize the risen Jesus, Luke also shows us how disciples of any age or time may have their eyes opened to Jesus' presence. When Jesus, unrecognized, joins the disciples as they walk, they are without hope. The bottom has dropped out of their world.

Gradually their eyes are opened. As they listen to Jesus they begin to realize what fools they have been. The cross, far from being a tragedy, was a triumph. It was the climax of God's purpose, not a disaster. The moment of recognition comes when they invite him to eat with them, and 'he took bread, gave thanks, broke it and began to give it to them.'

These two had not been present, as far as we know, at the Last Supper. But it seems Luke is telling us of the most normal ways people meet the risen Jesus today—in his words and in the Jesus meal (holy communion).

Luke's message is vitally relevant in a culture afraid to speak of death. Many will not look to meet Jesus in this way but God's hands are not tied. By the Spirit, through the church, he reaches out in surprising ways, as we see in the book of Acts.

The Message of John

R. Wade Paschal Jr

The Gospel of John is frequently the first Gospel given to new Christians or to people enquiring about Christianity. The simple language and the bold presentation of Jesus as God's Son make this Gospel helpful for the young in faith. The first verse of the Bible that many Christians memorize is John 3:16: 'For God so loved the world that he gave his only Son, that whoever believes in him should not perish but have eternal life.' This eloquent summary of God's plan of salvation is typical of the Gospel as a whole.

John OUTLINE

However, as we go along in our Christian faith and begin to read John again, alongside the other Gospels, this simplicity disappears. We cannot help but ask ourselves, 'Why is John so different from the other Gospels?' It is not simply that John differs from the others in style and chronology. The depth and grandeur of Jesus' authority comes across more starkly in John than in the other Gospels. The number of incidents narrated are fewer, but the drama of the conflict over Jesus is heightened.

I remember talking with a Jewish man who was considering becoming a Christian. 'When I read Matthew, Mark, and Luke,' he told me, 'I could understand Jesus and his teachings and agree. But when I came to John I had to say, "What is this? This is too much to believe!" ' The other Gospels allowed my friend to view Jesus mainly as a prophet and teacher, and this was acceptable to him. But John allowed no such luxury. John confronts us with what is implicit in the other Gospels: Jesus was more than a teacher and prophet. He was the Word of God in human form.

We can divide the Gospel into three main sections:

- Chapters 1 to 12, on the ministry of Jesus, deal with the problem of faith.

- Chapters 13 to 17, the teaching on the last night, are addressed to believers.

- Chapters 18 to 21 are about the trial, crucifixion and resurrection of Jesus.

The burning question in the first twelve chapters is, 'What do you believe about Jesus?' We can view these chapters as a series of dramas about people who either accept or reject Jesus. The Gospel begins with the call of the disciples (chapters 1 and 2). Chapter 3 defines the fruit of faith in Jesus as rebirth in the Spirit. We then see the drama of rebirth in the example of the Samaritan woman in chapter 4. Chapters 5, 6 and 7 portray a series of controversies between Jesus and various groups. The hostility towards Jesus begins to grow in these chapters. In chapter 9 we find examples both of faith (the man born blind) and rejection (the Pharisees). All of this leads up to chapter 12 where the rulers decide to crucify Jesus at the same time as he enters Jerusalem and the crowds proclaim him king. The problem in deciding for or against Jesus is not only what he does (his miracles are generally accepted as good things) but who he says he is. In the words of chapter 5 verse 18, 'This was why the Jews sought all the more to kill him, because he not only broke the sabbath but also called God his own Father, making himself equal to God.'

Jesus' claims for himself in the Gospel stretch the faith of his hearers. He tells Nathanael that heaven will open up and the angels of God will ascend and descend on the 'Son of Man'. When he tells the Jews, 'Destroy this temple, and in three days I will raise it up,' he is really talking about his own body as the temple of God. He tells the Samaritan woman he is the Messiah, and he tells Nicodemus that when he is 'lifted up' (or crucified) he will draw all people to himself. He claims to have the authority to judge and give life, and that his flesh will give life to the world. He claims to have existed before Abraham, and to be greater than Jacob and Moses. When Thomas asks the way to God, Jesus says, 'I am the way, the truth, and the life; no one comes to the Father, but by me,' and ends up by saying that to see him is to see the Father. In short, the Gospel is claiming that the whole of God's revelation and all his plans for salvation are summed up in Jesus. And 'faith' means to accept that Jesus is God revealed as a human being and that his death on the cross was God's plan for salvation.

The teaching on the last night (chapters 13 to 17) changes the focus of the Gospel from the problem of faith to the problem of living as a believer once Jesus has died and risen again. In the main these chapters stress two points:

- First is obedience. Disciples of Jesus can expect hard times and persecution because of their faith. The key to getting through hard times is perseverance and obedience. Only those who continue to obey Jesus will find the peace and joy he offers.

- But the disciples are promised God's help. Jesus will give the Holy Spirit to believers to help them persevere, and to help them remember his teachings and apply them to the problems at hand. Jesus is about to leave his disciples, and he promises them that they are not forgotten by the Father. Indeed, the Father will listen to their prayers and answer as they remain obedient to him. The end result will be that the disciples themselves, through their example and witness, will lead new people to faith in Jesus and continue their Master's work.

Chapters 18 to 21 tell the story of Jesus' arrest, trial, crucifixion and resurrection. Chapter 21 is perhaps an epilogue added after the death of the 'beloved disciple' who was the authority for the Gospel. The death of this disciple (traditionally understood to be the apostle John, but unnamed in the Gospel) evidently caused some problems in the community for which the Gospel was written. Chapter 21 brings out that it is obedience to Jesus which matters most, not the life of their revered leader. The Gospel bears witness to Jesus and it is faith in him alone that saves people and transforms their lives.

The lingering images of the Gospel portray a community that worships Jesus as the living Lord. We are meant to remember the vivid examples of faith: the Samaritan woman running back to her village to proclaim the Messiah; the blind man falling at Jesus' feet to worship him; Peter confessing his faith in Jesus as the crowds drift away; and Thomas calling Jesus 'My Lord and my God' as he is confronted with his Master risen from the dead.

This is the faith that the Gospel seeks in all people. Yet it is not a faith easily found. John, most of all the Gospels, recognizes that Jesus made far-reaching claims and that faith is a struggle. The Samaritan woman must work through prejudices of race and sex and her own sin, before she believes. The blind man moves step by step through objections before he worships Jesus. Peter has to fight to understand what Jesus meant by saying 'eat my flesh and drink my blood'. And Thomas overcomes his doubts that anyone could really be raised from the dead.

John recognizes that doubt and sin are not necessarily the enemies of faith. If we honestly confront our doubt and sin, Jesus offers us real life. Prejudice, unthinking traditionalism, and self-righteousness are the real enemies of faith. The Gospel is a daring call for faith. Jesus is not only human but God in a human life. This is a radical statement, not easily accepted. Yet for those who believe in Jesus he is 'the way, the truth, and the life'.

LIGHT BATTLES WITH DARKNESS
John 1:1–18

The Gospel is going to be about a man, Jesus. But these eighteen verses place his life in a cosmic framework. There could hardly be a more bold and audacious beginning. The subject of the Gospel is to be the nature of the Divine himself— God and nothing less than God is at hand. The Word is Creator of the universe and everything depends on him. Yet the Word faces opposition within the world he has created. There is a darkness that opposes the light, although the light is not overcome (verse 5). It is one of the sad ironies of the Gospel that many who ought to rejoice in God refuse him when they see him face to face (verse 11).

The reason for this conflict lies precisely in the bold claim that 'the Word became flesh and dwelt among us'. The ideas in this passage form a frontal assault on Judaism. It opens with the claim that the Word is divine. Then verse 14 proclaims that this divine Word is a person, Jesus the Christ. This is a big claim for anyone to accept, and would present radical problems for a Jew.

To make matters worse, this person takes the familiar foundations of the Jewish faith and replaces them. In the Old Testament, the glory of God represented God's presence in the temple or the tent of meeting in the wilderness days. Now we read, 'The Word became flesh and dwelt' (the Greek can also be translated 'pitched his tent') 'among us, full of grace and truth, and we beheld his glory . . .' In place of God in the tent or temple, the Word now lives in a human body.

In the same way, John boldly states that Jesus replaces the other pillar of Old Testament faith: the Law. 'The law was given through Moses; grace and truth came through Jesus Christ' (verse 17). Before Christ the Law was the means of relationship between God and his people. Now we become the people of God as we believe in Jesus as God's Redeemer (verse 12).

The gospel of Jesus Christ proclaims nothing less than that the nature of God has come in a man to save his creation. But salvation does not come easily. The story of John's Gospel will be a story of conflict—of faith and hatred. But the end of the story is given at the beginning: darkness does not overcome light. Light and life win through, and are given to all who believe.

YOU MUST BE BORN AGAIN
John 3:1–21

Nicodemus paid Jesus a visit. We are not told why, but we can deduce from Jesus' words that he came to ask a question something like, 'How can a person be a part of God's coming kingdom?' Now Nicodemus has a positive opinion of Jesus: 'No one can do the signs that you do, unless God is with him.' But he is unprepared for Jesus' reply. When Jesus says, 'You must be born again', Nicodemus has no idea what he means.

The Greek word often translated 'again' can also mean 'from above'. It is this latter sense which is really important here. Jesus is saying that sharing in the kingdom of God does not depend on such familiar human qualities as wealth, education or birthright. Being a part of God's kingdom is a matter of the Spirit, it is a heavenly rebirth given by God (verses 5 and 6). The kingdom of God comes when heaven invades the human realm through faith.

But how is a person born from above? The answer is hinted at in verses 14 and 15. These verses look back to an event in the Old Testament book of Numbers. The people had sinned and as punishment were attacked by poisonous snakes. God told Moses to fashion a bronze serpent and lift it up, so that those who looked at it might be saved from the venom. Now Jesus will be lifted up on the cross. Those who believe that he is God's Son will be saved in a new and much deeper way from their sin.

In this sense Jesus becomes the great dividing point of history, as verses 17 to 21 make clear. God's intention is to save the world through his Son. But for those who reject this offer of life and salvation, the condemnation of the old world of death and sin remains. For those who come to him in faith, the gift of new life in the Holy Spirit is given freely and totally. But there is an alternative: to remain in death and darkness and sin. When you come face to face with Jesus you must make a choice, for him or against him.

A WOMAN IS BORN AGAIN
John 4:1–30

The story begins simply enough. Jesus stops, tired and thirsty, by a well in the Samaritan region. A woman appears to draw water. When Jesus asks for a drink of water she responds sceptically, for Jews and Samaritans are historic enemies.

Jesus' words confuse the woman: 'If you knew the gift of God and who it is that asks you for a drink, you would have asked him and he would have given you living water' (verse 10). The woman's response is almost sarcastic: 'Where can you get this living water? Are you greater than our father Jacob, who gave us the well?' The answer is yes—Jesus is the giver of eternal life.

From this point on we see in the woman the steps of the new birth. Jesus asks her 'Where is your husband?' This is a call for repentance; Jesus goes directly to her point of sin. Evidently, the woman is willing to admit and turn away from her wrongdoing. She calls Jesus 'a prophet', recognizing that he speaks the truth.

Her question 'Where ought people to worship?' (verse 20) is natural enough. The temple is where people who repent offer sacrifices in order to restore their relationship with God. Jesus, however, does not send her to a place of worship. True worship is now no longer a question of place, but of worship 'in spirit and truth'. In other words, Jesus is the incarnation of God's truth and the giver of the Spirit, so he is the new 'place' of worship. We no longer go to a place to worship but to a person—to Jesus.

The final step of the new birth comes at the end of the scene, in verses 28 to 30. Before, the woman was an outcast and a loner. Now she rushes back to her village to witness to Jesus and lead others to him. This is the stuff of the new birth—a life redirected from sin to telling others about Christ.

BREAD OF LIFE
John 6:1–71

Chapter 4 saw Jesus gladly accepted; this chapter is a portrait of rejection. It begins with the people's enthusiastic response to the feeding of the 5,000. 'Surely this is indeed the prophet who is to come into the world' (verse 14). Evidently these people believed that the coming Messiah would be a Moses-like figure—repeating many of the miracles Moses performed. They were remembering a promise in the book of Deuteronomy: 'The Lord your God will raise up for you a prophet like me from among you . . . and I will put my words in his mouth.' The feeding of the 5,000 seemed like Moses' miracle of the manna, and these people are willing to make Jesus their Messiah-King (verse 15).

Jesus responds to their enthusiasm with an offer much like he made to the woman at the well in chapter 4. 'The bread of God is he who comes down from heaven and gives life to the world' (verse 33). The people answer positively, again like the woman, 'Give us this bread always.' But there the similarities end. For the bread of life is Jesus himself and to receive this 'bread' they must believe that Jesus has 'come down from heaven' (verse 38).

The people struggle with this. They see him as simply a person like themselves. But Jesus shocks them beyond belief when he says, in verse 53, that they must 'eat the flesh of the Son of Man and drink his blood' to have life. This repels not only Jesus' enemies but most of his disciples. Some remain, not because they understand these words, but because they believe that Jesus is the 'Holy One of God' (verse 69).

What Jesus is saying here anticipates the meaning of the Lord's Supper (or holy communion): eternal life comes to those who believe that Jesus died to save us. Jesus' sacrifice is the means of eternal life. His death gives us life because he is the 'bread of heaven' and God's gift to us.

THE TRUTH SHALL MAKE YOU FREE
John 8:31–59

In this passage Jesus is deliberately presenting his audience with two challenges:

■ **He challenges them about their sin.** These people believe that they are already God's people. They say, 'We are Abraham's descendants and have never been slaves of anyone' (verse 33), and 'The only Father we have is God himself' (verse 41). They may not be 'free' in the political sense, but they are 'free' from pagan superstition. Jesus' insistence, in verses 34 to 36, that they must also be free from sin is offensive to them. When, earlier on they 'believed' in Jesus, they probably meant that they accepted him as a Messiah who would liberate them politically. They do not feel the need for moral or spiritual liberation.

■ **Jesus also challenges them about his own authority.** When he says, 'Abraham rejoiced to see my day' these people scoff in reply, 'Now we know that you are demon-possessed! Abraham died and so did the prophets, yet you say that if a man keeps your word, he will never taste death. Are you greater than our father

Abraham? Who do you think you are?' (verses 52 and 53).

Jesus is indeed claiming to be greater than Abraham. When he said, in verse 58, 'Before Abraham was, I AM', he was claiming to have existed with God before Abraham. More than that, the very use of the phrase 'I AM' claims the authority of God. When God revealed his name to Moses he said, 'I AM WHO I AM.' After that the phrase 'I AM' became so connected with the name of God that it was blasphemy even to say it. The Jews tried to stone Jesus because they understood that by using these words he was really claiming divine authority. If Jesus was simply a man, this was madness and blasphemy and deserved death.

Our dilemma is not so different from that of the Jews of Jesus' day. Until we admit that we sin and are spiritually needy, and until we accept Jesus as God's answer to that need, we will remain trapped by our past. True freedom still comes only when people turn away from their old ways and put their trust in Jesus.

THE LIGHT OF THE WORLD
John 9:1–41

This is both a story of a miracle and a drama of the central conflict going on in the Gospel. The first character is the blind man himself. See how his faith grows in this chapter. When first healed and asked about the miracle he replies, 'The man they call Jesus made some mud and put it on my eyes. He told me to go to Siloam and wash. So I went and washed, and then I could see' (verse 11). Then the Pharisees question him and he

says of Jesus, 'He is a prophet' (verse 17). When pressed again about Jesus he asserts, 'If this man were not from God, he could do nothing' (verse 33). And when finally face to face with Jesus at the end of the chapter he falls down and worships him (verse 38).

Contrast this with the growing hostility of the Pharisees. At first, in verse 16, some Pharisees defend Jesus. But by verse 24 the Pharisees have decided that Jesus' defiance of the sabbath laws is inexcusable and they tell the man healed, 'Give glory to God; we know this man is a sinner.' The inconsistency of this is clear—the miracle clearly belongs to God: how can the agent of the miracle be labelled a sinner?

The irony of the story is that the Pharisees are not conscious of their own 'blindness'; they think they already know the will of God and obey it. But by rejecting Jesus they show that they do not know their own sin and need of salvation (verses 40 and 41).

Both the Pharisees and the man born blind had to make choices. They are the same choices the gospel forces all to make. Everyone is faced with the same set of facts and the same dilemma. Do we believe that Jesus is who he says he is? Do we believe that his miracles are the work of God? Or do we reject him?

I AM THE RESURRECTION
John 11:1–57

Throughout the chapter we sense that Jesus intends all along to raise Lazarus, and for this reason delays going to Bethany before his friend dies. The question asked over and over again in the chapter is found last on the lips of the

Jews in verse 37, 'He gave sight to the blind man, didn't he? Could he not have kept Lazarus from dying?' But healing can only help us so far; it does not solve the problem of death. The answer to death is not healing but resurrection.

This miracle makes it clear that the promise of the resurrection is fulfilled in the coming of Jesus. Faith in him gives life now and the promise of life after death. The resurrection life, as verses 25 and 26 spell out, begins with faith and is not destroyed by the death of the body.

However, the resurrection was not good news for everyone. As the news reached Caiaphas and the chief priests, they saw in it fuel for a rebellion based around Jesus. Caiaphas is unintentionally prophetic: 'You know nothing at all; you do not realize that it is better for you that one man die for the people, than that the whole nation perish' (verse 50). Indeed, Jesus' death on the cross will be 'for the nation'. Because Jesus died for all, the resurrection is promised to all who believe. Caiaphas intends to cut off Jesus' growing popularity through death. What happens instead is that his death brings life to all who believe.

This chapter underlines the power of our hope in the resurrection. We are prone to look on sin, sickness and death as disasters. But the resurrection promises us that none of these things is greater than God's ability to give life. Whatever happens to us, we will not suffer eternal death if we trust in Jesus.

THE FOOTWASHING
John 13:1–17

The roads in Palestine were very dirty. So it was common for a servant to wash people's feet when they arrived at a house. To everyone's astonishment, Jesus takes the servant's place as the disciples arrive to have a meal together.

There are two messages in the footwashing scene. On the one hand the passage emphasizes the example of Jesus: 'You call me Teacher and Lord and it is right that you do so because that is what I am. I, your Lord and Teacher, have just washed your feet. You, then, should wash one another's feet' (verses 13 and 14). As a prelude to the cross, the footwashing scene underlines the sacrificial service that Jesus offered all his life. Those who believe in Jesus must follow his example and serve one another. The love commandment given later in this chapter is built on the meaning of the footwashing: 'A new commandment I give you: Love one another. As I have loved you, so you must love one another' (verse 34). The Christian life is defined in this way as a life of service and sacrifice in response to the love Jesus has shown us in his life and death.

But there is also a second meaning given in Jesus' words to Peter. Peter is at first determined not to have his Lord wash his feet. But Jesus says to him: 'If I do not wash you, you have no part in me' (verse 8). The footwashing in this sense foreshadows the cross in yet another way: Jesus in his death holds out an offer of love which we may humbly accept.

In some ways it is easier to serve than to be served. Peter is repelled by the thought of Jesus serving him. Jesus' death on the cross dramatically underlines that we cannot return to God anything like what he has given to us. Faith demands a humility which accepts the service of one greater than ourselves.

BELIEVE IN ME
John 14:1–31

In some ways verse 1 sums up the whole message of the Gospel: Belief in God means belief in Jesus. For John the two are inseparable. There is no adequate faith in God apart from faith in Jesus. But the time is coming when Jesus will no longer be physically present. How can Jesus be the 'way' to God when he is no longer there?

The answer lies in the two successors to Jesus' ministry named in this chapter:

■ **One successor is the Holy Spirit.** Jesus promises the disciples that they will not be left 'orphaned'; he will send a 'Helper' or 'Counsellor' for them—the Holy Spirit. The resurrection of Jesus will bring not only the promise of eternal life for the believers, but also his living presence through the Holy Spirit (verse 20). The Spirit will help the disciples remember and apply Jesus' teachings to life after the resurrection (verse 26) and to endure with courage the persecutions which will follow.

■ **But there is a second successor, the church.** With the promise comes a commission. Jesus promises that those who believe in him will 'do what I have been doing [and] even greater things than these' (verse 12). So Christians can continue Jesus' work. 'Greater things' does not mean more spectacular—it would be hard to outdo the resurrection! But the world-wide mission of the church does take the ministry of Jesus far beyond the bounds of his earthly ministry. The Holy Spirit is the power for this ministry. Our contribution lies in obeying Jesus and his teaching. Love of Christ and obedience are tied intimately together in this chapter (see verses 15, 21, 23, 24).

For those who follow him, Jesus offers his 'peace' (verse 27). The peace Jesus offers his disciples is not the peace of an easy life. It is the peace of the obedient servant who has the full confidence and support of his master, and carries out his commission effectively and joyfully.

REMAIN IN ME
John 15:1–27

This chapter about Jesus the 'true vine' offers guidance for hard times. The references to 'pruning', 'laying down (your) life', the hatred of the world, and the witness of the believers all suggest a time when Christians will be under pressure because of their faith in Jesus. This is nothing unusual. Jesus stresses that the disciples can expect no more understanding from the world than he himself received (verses 20 and 21). The question is, how do we maintain our faith in the face of opposition?

■ **We must recognize the usefulness of hard times in the hands of our creative Father.** Troubles can be a pruning process by which what is frivolous or inessential in our lives is cut away, leaving the best of our Christian faith to grow and flourish. Like a vine growing new branches which sap its fruit-bearing potential, Christians can develop habits and lifestyles that distract us from our main calling in life. Troubles and persecution have a way of redirecting our lives, inviting us to re-examine our priorities and concentrate on what is really important.

■ **The only way disciples can endure hard times is to remain (or abide) in Christ.** This is the favourite phrase of the chapter. And the key to abiding is obedience. Knowing and doing the will of God is the essential means of remaining in Christ (verses 7 to 10).

■ **As we obey, we also pray (verse 7).** Prayer in combination with obedience produces results. As we obey, God hears our prayers. This assures us that we can find the strength to do God's will even in the midst of hard times.

■ **Finally, loving fellowship is also a means of remaining in Christ.** The only command given in this chapter is to 'love one another as I have loved you' (verse 12). Christians who love each other sacrificially, as Jesus loved, help each other to endure and even to thrive in hard times. The encouragement of other Christians will help us to remain obedient and so prove to the world the power of God's love.

Jesus promises that those who remain in him, who pray and obey, will bear fruit. This 'fruit' takes many forms. It can mean telling other people about Jesus. We also bear fruit when we grow a more Christlike character. But the key is that disciples who grow during the worst of times give glory to God, because their lives are a demonstration of the work of God and the reality of the Christian life (verse 8).

THE FAREWELL PRAYER
John 17:1–26

The Gospels often tell us that Jesus prayed, but this and the Lord's Prayer are the only full-length prayers we have from him. It is a prayer of the Father's obedient Son. Jesus says, 'I have completed the work which you have given me to do, so now glorify me, Father, with the glory which was mine from you before the foundation of the world' (verses 4 and 5). When Jesus asks to be 'glorified', he is looking on to the cross and the resurrection. The resurrection will prove to everyone that Jesus is who he says he is. The cross will not be a shameful death, but a glorious return to the Father where he will take again his position as God's eternal Son.

The prayer characterizes the ministry of Jesus in two ways:

■ **It is a ministry of the 'name'.** Jesus says: 'I have made your name known to the men you took from the world to give me' (verse 6). In revealing God's 'name' Jesus has revealed the will and character of God. The disciples are those who have heard Jesus' words and have believed his message. This separates them from the world, that is, those who have rejected Jesus (verses 14 to 16). Those who remain faithful to the message of Jesus will stand out as different from others. This will cause some to hate them, but God will protect them in their obedience.

■ **It is also a ministry of 'glory'.** 'I gave them the same glory you gave me so that they may be one, just as you and I are one: I in them and you in me, so that they may be completely one' (verses 22 and 23).

The 'glory' of God is God's very life and presence—a presence which gives us joy and love.

The oneness Jesus promises is more than a unity of spirit and feeling; it is a unity which flows out of a common commission. Those who have received the word of God are set aside and empowered by him to share this word with others. Jesus commissions the church in this prayer to carry on his ministry with his power: 'As you sent me into the world, I have sent them ...' (verse 18). As we share our faith with others they, too, will find joy and life through Jesus. We are called to carry on what Jesus began.

JESUS' DEATH AND RESURRECTION
John 19:17——20:29

Like the other Gospels, John refers to the title mockingly put above Jesus' head on the cross: 'Jesus of Nazareth, the King of the Jews.' Only John, however, records that the authorities tried to have this changed to, 'This man said, "I am the King of the Jews." ' This, of course, is the heart of the conflict between Jesus and his opponents. He claimed to be one with God. Was this blasphemy? Or was Jesus who he claimed to be?

Jesus was the 'King of the Jews' in a spiritual sense. He was crucified because he was rejected 'by his own'. But the cross was not the failure of his mission; it was the means to success.

Jesus' final words drive this home: 'It is finished.' The cross completed the work of the Son. Here was obedience to the very end—even the last act of drinking the bitter cup (verses 29–30) was done to fulfil Old Testament prophecy. This was the hour of 'glory', when the Son triumphed over death and over the work of the evil one.

Our response to the good news of the resurrection is summed up in the portrait of the disciple Thomas. At first Thomas doubted the news of Jesus' return: 'Unless I see in his hands the print of the nails, and place my finger in the mark of the nails, and place my hand in his side, I will not believe' (verse 25). Thomas' request is granted, and when he sees the risen Lord he falls in worship: 'My Lord and my God!'

Of course, our dilemma is that we do not see the risen Christ. We can choose to believe that he is our 'Lord and God' on the basis of the witness of others and of the fruit of faith that we can see in others' lives. This is why this Gospel was written: that others may believe by reading what Jesus said and did, even though they were not there to see him. 'These are written that you may believe that Jesus is the Christ, the Son of God, and that believing, you may have life in his name.'

The Message of Acts

Paul Burgess

Acts is a thrilling book. There is no other book quite like it in the whole Bible. It tells how Christianity began. The first scene is of a small group of startled disciples staring after their Master as he rose into the sky. The rest of the book is about how this same band of followers, with the Holy Spirit to guide and empower them, grew in number and influence until, some years later,

Acts OUTLINE

thousands of people throughout the eastern half of the Roman Empire had come to faith in Jesus Christ. Luke, who wrote this book as a follow-up to his Gospel, was a historian. He tells us that his main purpose is to record all that Jesus continued to 'do and teach' through his Spirit-led followers after he himself had returned to his Father in heaven.

Luke was also a doctor, and had a keen interest in the 'group dynamics' of the various characters and groups who appear in his account. His book gives us a fascinating picture of what it was like to be part of the first Christian community—its joys, frustrations, ideals and divisions. The book also gives essential background information to help us understand what Paul was writing about in his letters to the various churches. After reading Acts, no one should doubt the claims Paul made in his letters to being called to be an apostle: an eye-witness to the risen Jesus, with the task of establishing new groups of Christians. (It is clear from the Corinthian letters that this was a question under discussion.) So Acts is a link between the Gospels and the Letters, the two collections of Christian documents that form the bulk of the New Testament.

Though later scribes gave the book the title 'Acts of the Apostles', a better one might be 'Acts of the Spirit'. In Luke's eyes, it is the Spirit of God who directs the disciples in Jesus' work of bringing God's rule into the hearts of men and women. Not only does the Holy Spirit bring the presence of Jesus to his followers, but also, through signs and wonders and preaching, shows unbelievers the power of the gospel to change people's lives.

The book of Acts is an excellent starting-point for a Bible study of the Holy Spirit, showing us how the early Christians' experience of the Spirit developed.

If we study Luke's introductions to both his Gospel and Acts it becomes clear that Luke intended his writing to strengthen the Christian faith of his readers. He aims to assure them that what they had already been taught was well-founded. In doing this Luke provides such a detailed account of the beginnings of Christianity that we can find about three dozen definitions or facets of a Christian. For example, one who has repented, been baptized, forgiven, and received the Holy Spirit (2:38). These and many others are not complete in themselves but all contribute to a full and accurate picture of what it means to become a Christian.

Luke himself was almost certainly a Gentile, though familiar with the Jewish faith. Among the believers, he probably identified with the Hellenists, Greek-speaking converts from the Jewish community. Their worldwide outlook gave them the vision to go out from Jerusalem and share their new-found faith with all people, Jew or Gentile. As Jesus himself said, they would indeed be witnesses 'to the ends of the earth' (1:8). It is interesting to see that the structure of the book reflects the fulfilment of this promise; the gospel was preached first 'in Jerusalem'; then 'in all Judea and Samaria'; finally extending as far as Rome, to which all roads in the 'known' world led.

In many ways Acts is about 'the church in the home'. From the moment that the Spirit comes upon the apostles 'in the house where they were sitting', to the closing verses of Acts where we find

Paul under house-arrest, the home is the place of Christian hospitality. Here communion is celebrated, the gospel is proclaimed and the faith taught. The early Christians met together and prayed together in people's homes. In Romans, Paul speaks warmly of Priscilla and Aquila 'and the church that meets in their home'.

One danger in any religious movement is that it eventually becomes too cosy and inward-looking. But God's people must always be on the move, Stephen told his persecutors as he faced certain death by stoning, recorded in chapters 6 and 7. This means breaking out of institutional and conventional ways of thinking. Stephen challenged the Jews to go beyond the confines of Law and temple and widen their horizons to see the risen Jesus standing 'at God's right hand'. Jesus is the promised Deliverer of all people, so that Gentiles belong as much to God's people as any Jew. This was spelt out in Jerusalem at the first Christian Synod, called to clarify this very point (chapter 15). There is no place for racial discrimination. Salvation is available to all on the same terms, and in Christ Jesus all are one.

The many speeches proclaiming the good news which are so carefully reported by Luke show that different contexts and situations call for different approaches. This not only affects the content, but also style and emphasis. Stephen's speech shows that Christianity, not Judaism, fulfils what is promised in the Old Testament, while Paul's address at Athens points pagans to Jesus, not idols, for a true knowledge of God.

As still happens today, where the gospel flourishes it results in opposition.

Acts outlines the growth of opposition to the good news—by Jews resentful of Christianity, through the threat posed to money-making enterprises and material prosperity, or more directly by Satan and the forces of evil. However, Luke notes that where the powerful word of the Lord is preached, opposition is dissolved and the good news spreads still further.

Luke's account of the early church shows that church history need not be dull! It is an encouragement to God's people as they see how God is always in control, despite trouble and opposition. Acts is a book about mission, God's mission. It shows that his intended purpose will not be thwarted while his Spirit directs his church. Indeed, in chapter 13 we find the first 'missionary society' set up under the guidance of the Spirit, and Barnabas and Saul 'set apart for the work to which I have called them'. This same work continues today—of telling and sharing the good news of Jesus and his kingdom. The same dedication and response are called for from all Christians in today's world.

JESUS TAKEN UP INTO HEAVEN
Acts 1:1–11

Why, after he had risen from the dead, did Jesus leave his disciples? Surely they would have gained from more teaching and training? Instead, after he had appeared several times to assure them that he was alive, Jesus left them to be with God. It was a risk. If he was no longer physically with them, some of them might wander from the way. But by giving guidance and help by his Holy Spirit, he allowed them space to grow up and become independent.

In his last recorded words Jesus tells his followers:

■ **Wait for the promised Holy Spirit.**

■ **Stop speculating about the future.**

■ **Power will come with the Holy Spirit.**

■ **Be my witnesses.** He sets his disciples the task of telling the world that he is alive, is now with God, and will one day come again.

■ **I will come back again.**

John the Baptist had washed people in water to symbolize their need to be cleansed from sin. But in the baptism of the Holy Spirit Jesus promises more than the removal of a guilty conscience. His own Spirit will provide an inner power to enable people to keep God's commands. So, 'You shall *not* kill!' is more than a commandment. It becomes a promise: 'You *shall* not kill.'

At the ascension, the cloud that eventually hid Jesus from their view symbolized the presence of God whose glory is veiled from human eyes. One day Jesus will return to reveal the full glory of God and all who believe in him will be taken up to join him in his glory and enjoy complete fellowship with God.

THE SPIRIT COMES
Acts 2:1–41

Before he returned to his Father in heaven, Jesus told his followers to wait in Jerusalem for 'the power from above'. In the past, the Holy Spirit had only come upon *some* of God's people and then only for a short time. A new era began on the day of Pentecost, when the Spirit came upon *every* follower of Jesus as the permanent guiding influence in their lives.

The Spirit came with what seemed like wind—often a sign of life in the Scriptures—accompanied by fire, symbol of God's presence. Breathing new life into our spirits, the Holy Spirit of God guarantees the presence of Jesus with us.

Pentecost was a major festival and Jews had come from all over the Roman Empire. Originally a harvest festival, Pentecost was later regarded as the day when the Law was given through Moses. The streets were full of the chatter of many nationalities and tongues. Hearing so many different languages being spoken simultaneously must have soon drawn a curious crowd to hear the first-ever Christian sermon! Peter was quick to put the record straight when people tried to explain away what God was doing: no one was drunk!

Since he was speaking to Jews, Peter reminded them of Joel's prophecy: that God spoke of giving his Spirit to *all* his people. Next, he showed how God had proved Jesus:

■ **To be the Messiah** by raising him from the dead

■ **To be Lord** by taking him into heaven to share his own authority over all creation. Yet this was the man whom they had all handed over to be crucified!

Many were convinced by what Peter said and asked what they should do to put things right. Peter told them straight:

■ **Repent.** Turn away from your sins.

■ **Be baptized.** As a sign of sins forgiven, and a new life.

■ **Receive the Holy Spirit.** Receive God's power for right living and the companionship of God.

All this means a new relationship with God which touches *every* part of life, along with a lifelong commitment to follow Jesus.

THE FIRST COMMUNITY OF BELIEVERS
Acts 2:42–47; 4:32–37; 6:1–7

What was it like to belong to the first Christian community? Three thousand new believers obviously needed a crash course about how to live like Jesus, and they drew strength from sharing experience and praying together in their homes. As members of the Jewish community, they continued to attend temple worship, publicly praising God, and everyone who observed their new way of life spoke well of them. It was not just the miracles that demonstrated God's power, but the fact that these Christians so obviously cared for one another. God *must* be influencing their lives. Meanwhile, the regular act of 'breaking bread' in their households reminded them of Christ's body broken on the cross for them.

Did every believer sell his or her possessions for the common good? Probably not, for nobody put pressure on Ananias and his wife to give up their property, while others, later on, still had resources from which to contribute for a famine collection. 'Having everything in common' was not enforced communism but a spontaneous sharing of resources.

There has always been human concern for the poor—from Aristotle to Bob Geldof—but these Christians had the added motivation of expressing the love of Christ for everyone.

The first church administrators were chosen for their spiritual awareness. Their appointment not only allowed the apostles to concentrate on preaching the gospel, but also released gifts of wisdom and discernment. It was not surprising that this more efficient administration led to even more people being converted to Christ.

EXECUTION OF A RADICAL
Acts 6:8——8:3

Stephen, the first to die for his faith in Christ, was one of the seven administrators elected to distribute food. He was no dull church official, but lived out the reality of an explosive message destined to turn the whole world upside down. What was so subversive about this man that what he said threatened the Jewish authorities?

When called to defend himself, Stephen took the opportunity to testify to the true way of worshipping God. He appealed to the history of the Jews to point out that God's presence is not restricted to one country, let alone to one building. God revealed himself to Abraham and Moses on Gentile soil; his dwelling-place was symbolized by a moving tent rather than a stone temple. Even today Christians can easily become attached to buildings and institutions, thus limiting God. Stephen wanted God's people to hold loosely the security of home and a settled identity and follow Jesus, who has the whole world in his hands.

Men of such wide vision, however, are always a threat to those who are imprisoned in their own legalistic attitudes, and are too fond of privilege and security. Failing to recognize God's messengers, the Jews eventually mistook the Saviour of the world for a dangerous enemy of the people. Unable to defeat Stephen by argument, they set up informers to twist his words and blacken his name. Christians under persecution today often face similar misrepresentation.

Stephen's death resulted in the spread of the gospel to Samaria, while his final prayer profoundly influenced one witness to his death. As Augustine wrote later, 'the church owes Paul to the prayer of Stephen'.

SAMARIA: THE OCCULT AND THE SPIRIT
Acts 8:4–25

Samaria appears to have been a place where the occult flourished. Simon Magus practised magic arts while others had come under the direct influence of evil spirits. As these Samaritans listened eagerly to Philip's preaching about the Messiah, many experienced release, healing and great joy. Reports of this reached the church in Jerusalem, always more cautious about unexpected developments than their fellow believers in other places. They at once sent Peter and John to investigate.

Jews did not trust Samaritans. They had different scriptures and a rival temple. The Samaritans had, in the days of the exile, been guilty of associating with the enemy, even marrying pagan settlers. In the eyes of all true Jews the Samaritans were regarded with suspicion, as religious halfcastes. But Philip, following the example of Jesus, ignored this and preached the gospel—with good results.

Yet there was something odd about their new Christian experience. Despite Jesus' promise, proclaimed by Peter at Pentecost, that those who believe shall receive the gift of the Holy Spirit, these people had not done so—until Peter and John laid hands on them.

Perhaps the answer lies in the deceptive atmosphere in which Philip had to work. Samaria, like Ephesus later, was the scene of Satanic deception. Simon Magus may not have been the only one whose eyes were blind to the full implications of the gospel. As happens today, people may appear to be converted and believe in Jesus and yet fail to receive his Spirit into their lives.

The story of Simon Magus has some lessons also for those who desire to serve others in the church. Attaining an influential position through lobbying or even bribery still happens today where leaders are more interested in prestige than in bringing the Spirit to others. Equally it is too easy for pastors to rule over their congregations and cause church life to revolve around themselves. As a famous Scots minister once observed, no one can at the same time show that they are clever and that Christ is wonderful!

LEARNING TO OVERCOME PREJUDICE
Acts 10:1–48

Strict Jews in New Testament times considered all Gentiles to be quite

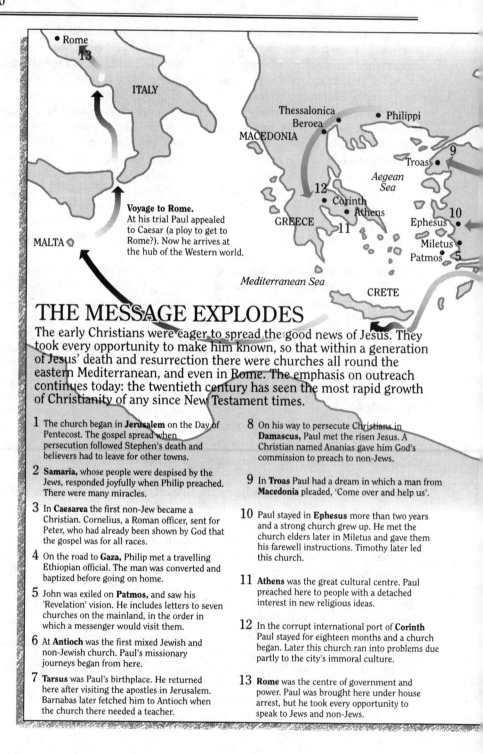

Rome
13

ITALY

Thessalonica
Beroea
MACEDONIA

Philippi

Troas
9

Aegean
Sea

12
Corinth
Athens
Ephesus
10

GREECE
11

Miletus

Patmos
5

Voyage to Rome.
At his trial Paul appealed
to Caesar (a ploy to get to
Rome?). Now he arrives at
the hub of the Western world.

MALTA

Mediterranean Sea

CRETE

THE MESSAGE EXPLODES

The early Christians were eager to spread the good news of Jesus. They took every opportunity to make him known, so that within a generation of Jesus' death and resurrection there were churches all round the eastern Mediterranean, and even in Rome. The emphasis on outreach continues today: the twentieth century has seen the most rapid growth of Christianity of any since New Testament times.

1 The church began in **Jerusalem** on the Day of Pentecost. The gospel spread when persecution followed Stephen's death and believers had to leave for other towns.

2 **Samaria,** whose people were despised by the Jews, responded joyfully when Philip preached. There were many miracles.

3 In **Caesarea** the first non-Jew became a Christian. Cornelius, a Roman officer, sent for Peter, who had already been shown by God that the gospel was for all races.

4 On the road to **Gaza,** Philip met a travelling Ethiopian official. The man was converted and baptized before going on home.

5 John was exiled on **Patmos,** and saw his 'Revelation' vision. He includes letters to seven churches on the mainland, in the order in which a messenger would visit them.

6 At **Antioch** was the first mixed Jewish and non-Jewish church. Paul's missionary journeys began from here.

7 **Tarsus** was Paul's birthplace. He returned here after visiting the apostles in Jerusalem. Barnabas later fetched him to Antioch when the church there needed a teacher.

8 On his way to persecute Christians in **Damascus,** Paul met the risen Jesus. A Christian named Ananias gave him God's commission to preach to non-Jews.

9 In **Troas** Paul had a dream in which a man from **Macedonia** pleaded, 'Come over and help us'.

10 Paul stayed in **Ephesus** more than two years and a strong church grew up. He met the church elders later in Miletus and gave them his farewell instructions. Timothy later led this church.

11 **Athens** was the great cultural centre. Paul preached here to people with a detached interest in new religious ideas.

12 In the corrupt international port of **Corinth** Paul stayed for eighteen months and a church began. Later this church ran into problems due partly to the city's immoral culture.

13 **Rome** was the centre of government and power. Paul was brought here under house arrest, but he took every opportunity to speak to Jews and non-Jews.

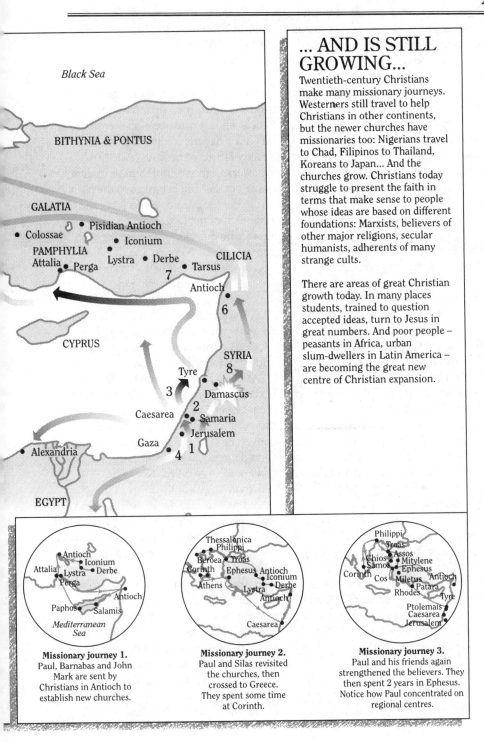

Black Sea

BITHYNIA & PONTUS

GALATIA

Colossae • Pisidian Antioch
• Iconium

PAMPHYLIA
Attalia • Perga • Lystra • Derbe • Tarsus
7   CILICIA

Antioch
6

CYPRUS

SYRIA
Tyre   8
3   Damascus
2
Caesarea   • Samaria
• Jerusalem
Gaza   4 1
• Alexandria

EGYPT

... AND IS STILL GROWING...

Twentieth-century Christians make many missionary journeys. Westerners still travel to help Christians in other continents, but the newer churches have missionaries too: Nigerians travel to Chad, Filipinos to Thailand, Koreans to Japan... And the churches grow. Christians today struggle to present the faith in terms that make sense to people whose ideas are based on different foundations: Marxists, believers of other major religions, secular humanists, adherents of many strange cults.

There are areas of great Christian growth today. In many places students, trained to question accepted ideas, turn to Jesus in great numbers. And poor people – peasants in Africa, urban slum-dwellers in Latin America – are becoming the great new centre of Christian expansion.

Missionary journey 1.
Paul, Barnabas and John Mark are sent by Christians in Antioch to establish new churches.

Missionary journey 2.
Paul and Silas revisited the churches, then crossed to Greece. They spent some time at Corinth.

Missionary journey 3.
Paul and his friends again strengthened the believers. They then spent 2 years in Ephesus. Notice how Paul concentrated on regional centres.

outside the mercy of God, and Peter had much to unlearn from his Jewish past. Even though Peter's experience of Jesus would have freed his attitudes considerably, he still had scruples about eating with a Gentile. He knew also the Old Testament teaching in Leviticus 11, that not all flesh was 'clean' for eating. So his roof-top 'vision' was a turning-point in his thinking. It was also important for the subsequent history of the people of God.

Peter had four days to work out the meaning of what the vision meant. During this time he received Gentile guests into his friend's home, travelled with them, and eventually accepted the hospitality of a Roman centurion, Cornelius, no longer to be thought of as 'unclean', any more than certain kinds of food. As if to sweep away any final doubts, while Peter was speaking, the Holy Spirit came upon these Gentiles in the same way as he himself had received the Spirit at Pentecost.

Luke considered this episode so important that he included it three times in Acts. For us today there are lessons to be learnt in the area of racial and cultural prejudice. 'Respectability' and 'traditional practices' can still be a barrier to newcomers.

Notice also how both Peter and Cornelius saw the wisdom of *involving others* in their historic meeting, as witnesses and for support. Cornelius' positive approach to learning of God is shown when he assembles all his family, even before he himself hears the gospel. Here was a man who expected things to happen.

RESOLVING A CRUCIAL CONTROVERSY
Acts 15:1–35

In the church you will always find some who stand firmly by their traditions and others who seem to question everything. In Luke's day the traditionalists were mainly Hebrew-speaking Jewish believers from the church in Jerusalem. Some of them still belonged to the party of the Pharisees, and saw in Jesus the fulfilment of the Law. The radicals— those who questioned everything— represented by Stephen and the Greek-speaking Christians, had a wider vision for missionary endeavour and welcomed non-Jews into the church. They did not demand that Gentile converts should conform to Jewish religious customs such as circumcision and observance of the Law.

All this upset the more legalistic traditionalists in Jerusalem and some of them began a campaign to standardize things by insisting that every Gentile convert be circumcised. The church was soon divided on the issue, and so a conference was called. Not only Christian unity but the heart of the gospel was at stake. In the final analysis, was a person made pure by obeying God's laws, as the traditionalists claimed, or by accepting God's grace in faith?

It was such an important issue that the entire church, not just the leaders, was involved. They heard from Peter, Paul and Barnabas about the way God was blessing Gentiles, and then James as he quoted from the Scriptures. Eventually, they agreed that things should not be made difficult for Gentiles to join the church—they had as much right to belong as Jews. On the other hand, they should be careful not to offend by their behaviour—a real danger because of the low moral standards and highly idolatrous society that formed their background. It is still important today for new converts to have help in putting their Christian belief into action, without being weighed down with unwarranted rules that do little to help them to think through how their faith will affect the particular circumstances of their lives and relationships.

GETTING THE FULL STORY
Acts 18:24—19:7

Many church-goers are held back in their spiritual progress because they have either a partial or a confused understanding of Christianity. Like Apollos, they can be highly educated and eloquent speakers with a crusading spirit for a Christian approach to the world's problems. Or, like the twelve Ephesian disciples, they can lead a self-contained existence, unaware of their spiritual inheritance, content with leading God-fearing lives.

When Apollos began to explain the Scriptures 'boldly' in the synagogue at Ephesus, a local Christian couple listening to him soon realized that, spiritual man though he was, he had not heard the full story. Rather than put him straight in public, they invited Apollos home and filled him in where his knowledge was lacking. This appears to have been all that he needed, for soon he was on his way to Corinth where he became a great help in building up the church.

The twelve Ephesian disciples were somewhat different. From the moment he met them, it appears that Paul suspected there was something missing in their Christian experience. Not only did they not seem to have any connection with the church meeting in the house of Priscilla and Aquila, but they also lacked any experience or knowledge of the Holy Spirit. A definite commitment to Christ was needed. And so, in the only recorded instance of a 'second baptism' in the New Testament, Paul baptized them in the name of Jesus and laid his hands on them. Their new faith was confirmed by gifts of the Holy Spirit.

As Paul explained, John the Baptist only woke people up to their shortcomings. Many responded to his message by trying even harder to please God—in their own strength. But baptism in the name of Jesus pointed beyond this to the reality of forgiveness and new life in Jesus, plus the promise of strength by Jesus' Spirit to do what in their own strength was impossible.

Ephesus, like Samaria, was a place where superstition and the occult had free rein. It was also, it seems, a place where half-truths hindered would-be Christians from experiencing an effective Christian life.

PAUL'S DEFENCE BEFORE AGRIPPA
Acts 26:1–32

When you have an opportunity to speak publicly about Christ, where should you start? Where possible Paul always began at a point of shared interest between himself and his listeners. Now he stands before King Agrippa and so he emphasizes his orthodox background to these Roman and Jewish civil authorities. He explains his background, former life and conversion, everything leading up to why he is here and what he stands for as a Christian.

The conclusion of his message is simple and direct:

- **'Repent!'** This involves being sorry for what has been done, a change of mind, a new set of values, and a resolve by God's grace to be changed.

- **'Turn to God!'** The whole direction of life is now directed by God, rather than by self as before.

- **'Do deeds to match this new resolve!'** A change of heart results in a change of attitudes and action.

Agrippa's relation to the Jewish faith may have been formal, yet he knew the Scriptures well enough for Paul to appeal to him and ask for confirmation of the truth. In doing this, Paul placed him in an awkward position. If he agreed with Paul he would lose credibility with the Jews; if he disagreed, he would be denying the prophets. Agrippa sidestepped the issue by laughing it off: 'Surely you can't be hoping to make me act the Christian?' In the end it was not Paul who was on trial so much as King Agrippa. The bewildered company left, unable to see why in fact Paul should be standing trial at all!

The Message of Romans

Paul Zahl

The apostle Paul discovered the central core of Christianity. Not that it wasn't already there, implicit in the events of Good Friday and Easter. But Paul was the first to describe the dynamic by which Jesus Christ's presence in people's lives works a miracle. This dynamic is grace.

The letter to the Romans is the crucial reference point in the New Testament for understanding what grace is all about. Only his letter to the Galatians rivals Paul's treatment here of the life-changing good news by which Christ becomes real to ordinary people.

The phrase 'life-changing good news' is a description of grace, for it suggests that human beings need good news, a word from outside our lives, to find a way through our biggest problems. The phrase implies that we are caged into our problems, unable to cut our way through them in any lasting, conclusive way. We need strength beyond our own.

Paul's argument in Romans begins by describing the common ground on which all people stand when it comes to the compulsive problem of 'sin', which means our flawed nature. Although he is

Romans OUTLINE

a Jew and wants to attract the Jewish people to the good news he has been given, Paul demolishes the consciousness the Jews have always had of their unique moral standing with God. In chapter 2 and in a long section of chapter 3, he argues that the problem of humanity's shaky moral standing with God is universal, as deeply underlined for Jews as it is for non-Jews. Paul sees the human race as being locked in a struggle between the ideal our conscience presents to us of being perfect—or, in his language, of obeying God's Law to the full—and the reality of not being able to be perfect. He describes all of us as 'falling short of the glory of God' (3:23).

This portrait of the human condition has struck a chord with everyday people for hundreds of years, and can be compared to the experience of stress.

Modern people are caught between the demand to be perfect (taken in from our culture or from parents, from spouses, from children, from bosses or simply from what is written deep inside us) and the reality that we cannot be perfect. This clash between what we demand of ourselves and what we actually achieve causes a lot of agony. And once we realize that there is a God who asks more of us than we demand of ourselves, the problem becomes worse. In response to this predicament, we develop particular strategies:

- One is the strategy of 'atheism'. This involves getting mad and calling the whole thing rotten to the core. We simply turn our faces to the wall and say we won't play ball.

- Another possibility is the strategy of 'idolatry'. We flee to fantasy—or to another marriage or a new career, or a different place to live—and opt out. We switch our loyalty from God to a person or thing which we think can fulfil our hopes and deliver us.

- Or alternatively we just try harder. Which is what many of us do. If we cannot do it all, then what we need to do is to try harder. In such a strategy the church—or indeed any philosophy of life—can become a kind of coach, exhorting us from the sidelines to keep trying.

Paul does not discard these options because he is partisan about his particular way. Not at all. He just knows from experience that these other options do not work. He has seen their bankruptcy in his own life and in the cultures around him. So he steers his readers towards another way, which he is convinced does work.

That other way is first suggested at the end of the third chapter, then developed to its full impact in chapter 7 and the first part of chapter 8. What he says is this: Jesus Christ took upon himself, on our behalf and in our place, the stress and pain which comes from our failure to be perfect. This is what he did when he died for our sins on the cross. And because he rose again from the dead, he must be God—as no human being has ever done such a thing, before or since. Paul's conclusion is stated in its most essential form in the first four verses of chapter 8: 'There is now no condemnation for those who are in Christ Jesus.' Because God gave his Son to die for us, we live in a relationship of favour with God rather than of judgment.

Paul believes that this relationship of favour rather than judgment conveys confidence to a person (5:1–2) and a kind of hardy personal strength (8:31–39), which is the secret of serenity.

In chapters 9 to 11 Paul goes on to reflect in lofty, almost cosmic terms the role of his people, the Jews, in God's design. He is puzzled, and at the bottom line humbled, by God bringing the life-changing good news to the Gentiles before Israel.

Finally, in chapters 12 to 16, Paul touches on a variety of issues to do with moral life, church life and individual details which are of local concern for the Christians in Rome.

The focus of Romans remains Paul's great exposition of grace, God's unconditional love for the human race, shown in the death and resurrection of Jesus Christ. This is forever in contrast to law, which is all about our own achievement, and by which we seek, unsuccessfully, to establish our own value—or 'personal best'. This focus on grace is the reason the letter to the Romans has spoken at gut-level to people of every culture and era since the day it was written. It is an ancient analysis of humanity's principal problem. It is remarkably close to what Freud and the psychoanalysts are saying, but offers hope where Freud offers only resignation. It is a light into the mind of God, and our own breaking hearts. It is a priceless gift to the world.

THE OPENING SALVO
Romans 1:16–17

Here Paul keynotes the main theme of his letter. This theme, to use old-fashioned language, is 'justification by faith', which is itself shorthand for 'justification by God's grace through faith'. Let's try a modern translation of these words: Our worth comes from being loved unconditionally and put back into relationship with God.

Paul means that the gospel is the life-changing good news by which a person receives salvation. 'Salvation' means being affirmed rather than judged or criticized, by God. God says 'yes' about us rather than 'no'. (See the feature on *Salvation*.) Salvation came to the Jews first (witness the Old Testament); it has now come also to non-Jews. This good news has changed the way people can relate to God, changing it from a way of life based on trying harder and gritting your teeth, to a way of life based on receiving love.

Paul believes this new way of life was foreshadowed in the Old Testament. In chapter 4 he will refer to Abraham, the father of Israel. Here, in verse 17, he quotes from the prophet Habakkuk, where the prophet says that 'righteousness', our right standing with God, comes through faith (rather than through trying harder).

This theme is the core of the letter to the Romans. Our standing or worth is derived entirely from the worth God has given to us, irrespective of anything we do or that belongs to us without God. To bring that closer to experience, no one who is very sick or thinks he is going to die ever tells a friend, 'I wish I'd worked harder in my thirties', or 'If only I'd put more energy into my career'. On the contrary, what people usually say to you at such times is something like, 'If only I'd spent more time with my children when they were little', or 'Why did I make my spouse's life miserable all those years? If only I'd known what a good thing I had.'

It is relationships rather than performance that most of us look back on as the building blocks of a happy life. In the same way, Paul has discovered that his worth is according to how much he is loved (in particular, by God) rather than how much he can love. Receiving, not giving, is the starting-point for a confident relationship with God, let alone with another person. For Paul this is an awesome discovery, a dazzling change in the environment of human experience. In the next seven chapters he develops this discovery.

CONSCIENCE IS NO FUN
Romans 2:12–16

Did you ever see the old Walt Disney cartoon in which Donald Duck is tempted? An angel on his right exhorts him to be good, while a devil to his left spurs him on to do the bad thing. It is a classic picture of evil impulse being cautioned by conscience.

In this passage, Paul begins to expand the notion of Law to include how we perform inwardly as well as outwardly. He says that the people of God, who were given the written Law of Moses, will be judged by that Law. Gentiles, however, who have no written code, will also be judged—but by conscience, which is Law's voice within our souls. 'Whenever Gentiles do by instinct what the Law commands, they are their own law, even though they do not have the Law.' Conscience is something 'written on the (Gentiles') hearts', the stand-in for Law in cultures that have received no Law. The result of this is that the whole world is under judgment. Ignorance of the Law is no excuse, for it is human

nature to know instinctively what is right and wrong.

The Law in this sense is anyone and everyone's standard of performance, whether it is measured against an outward code or an inward instinct. We may translate Law, doing no injustice to Paul's thought, by the word 'stress'—the experience of being an object of many and conflicting expectations. Stress tells me I have got to do it all, to be perfect in everything. It can reduce me to a quivering mass of jelly. It is the feeling of being perpetually under judgment. It causes breakdown and heart attack and ulcers. The experience of stress, then, is the modern world's equivalent of what it means to live under the Law, which accuses everyone who listens to it.

AN EARLY BULLETIN OF GOOD NEWS
Romans 3:19–26

The Law, whether written down or engraved on the heart, is an awesome thing. It judges all of us so that all our excuses dry up and the whole world is accountable to God (see verse 19). Just imagine being caught in the act of cheating in an exam, caught red-handed. You start to turn red, have palpitations and blurt out excuses. Your guilt is painful and obvious, most of all to yourself.

The Law does me no good. It informs me only where and when I have blown it. 'Through the Law we become conscious of sin.' The Law reminds me without pity that I cannot obey it.

So I hate the Law. Have you ever asked someone to stop smoking in a no-smoking area, and been undone by their explosive reaction? 'Sin', breaking the Law, does not like being reminded that it is sin.

Fortunately—and here is an early bulletin of good news from Paul—Law-keeping is not the basis for being loved by God. His standard is perfect, true enough, but all it does in real life is inform me how bad I am. Another way has got to be found if I am ever really to change.

The other way is this: 'God puts people right through their faith in Jesus Christ' (verse 22). Being 'right' means having obeyed the whole Law. It comes to me not through my efforts, but as a gift. Not 'I *am* right' but 'I have been *put* right.' It is the righteousness, or perfect performance, of *another*, God's Son, in my place and now counted to me.

Jesus Christ's perfect performance, his 'expiation' or sacrifice, is a perfect passing grade, completely fulfilling God's standard. When we connect with Christ, his perfection is counted to us. It is like a new set of clothes, given as entry to a coveted social function (like the wedding garment in Jesus' parable).

In short, no one can live up to the Law. We all 'fall short of the glory of God'. Yet the Law must be kept. Jesus Christ, who scored 100 per cent in his perfect life, death and resurrection, is our perfect passing grade, guaranteeing that we are accepted by God.

BEING GOOD FROM THE HEART
Romans 6:15–18

Who wants to be good? It sounds so dull, so Victorian, the opposite of fun. Anyway, good people are usually that way because they think they should be.

'Goodness' often suggests behaviour that runs against what the real me actually wants to do: staying in a marriage, for example, when what people think will really make them happy is finding greener pastures. It is going for what 'I ought' rather than what 'I want'.

For many people, Christianity is a sort of cheering section for people to do 'the right thing'—a sort of spiritual arm of the sheriff's office. The life of Gauguin, the painter, illustrates this. 'Being good' seemed to him to be the straitjacket of the respectable. To stay with his family would have meant staying because of duty and concern for respectability. The 'I want' spelled freedom: Tahiti, a liberated spirit, unrestrained self-expression. Frustrated by his conflict over the good, Gauguin fled to Tahiti for freedom. So he thought.

The apostle Paul sees goodness differently. He realizes that 'goodness' which results from duty is valuable, but that it creates not one iota of happiness. He is convinced that the ideal condition for humanity is when the 'ought' and the 'want' come together, when the thing I should do is the thing I want to do. He will develop this idea in chapter 7.

For now, Paul speaks of his readers being 'obedient from the heart to the standard of teaching to which you were committed' (verse 17). Their obedience is spontaneous and normal, it springs from their real inner longings. Paul sees the life of doing exactly what I want as a form of slavery: I *think* I am free, but I am really acting from compulsion. Freud demonstrated this same fact. We often think we are living, but are really being lived (by patterns buried deep inside us from the past).

'Sin' means being controlled—by impulse and by the guilt that increases the impulse (verse 16). 'Righteousness' is to act from a place of forgiveness, from which I discover that my wants begin to tally with my oughts. Now I know God forgives me, I start to want to serve, and care. Patience, then, can become fun (hard to believe?—it is exactly what Paul is talking about), tenderness a natural, hope second nature, and so forth. In Romans the goal of human life is to enter into an 'obedience that comes from the heart'.

THE NEVER-ENDING STORY
Romans 7:15–24

There are few passages in the Bible that require absolutely no explanation in order to make sense to modern people. But this is one.

Paul portrays the neverending story of conflict within the human soul (or 'heart', as the Bible puts it) between impulse and duty. 'I do not understand my own actions. For I do not do what I want, but I do the very thing I hate' (verse 15). In other words, I end up doing the very thing I know I shouldn't do.

This is puzzling. Did not Greek philosophy teach me that if I know what the good is, I will necessarily do it? And did it not teach me that if I know what the bad is, I will automatically shun it? But it hasn't worked out that way. I am all in knots.

In fact, 'When I want to do good, evil is right there with me' (verse 21). As we saw earlier, Law increases wrongdoing. This is painful. I am trapped between duty and desire. I feel like a character in a film I once saw, caught on a rope bridge

spanning an incredibly deep crevasse, with different adversaries advancing on him from both sides. 'Who will rescue me from this body of death?'

By the way, this passage has been fought over by scholars for many years. Is Paul describing people before they become Christians, or after? Is the conflict between 'ought' and 'want' a universal experience only until a person comes to Christ? Or does it remain the life story of Christians for ever and ever amen?

Christians of almost every school of thought would say from experience that Romans 7 speaks to them after, as well as before, conscious believing begins. There is not one moment when I as a Christian do not still feel caught between the claims of Law and the claims of my will. There are wonderful periods and situations when Law and desire flow together, producing spontaneous action, the 'fruit of the Spirit'. But there are places all along the compass when the two are in conflict. In actual experience I need deliverance 'now' as much as I did 'then'.

THE BURNED-OVER PLACE
Romans 8:1–4

Who can feel ultimately at ease when Jesus calls us in the Sermon on the Mount to 'be perfect even as your heavenly Father is perfect'? Part of growing up, after all, is coming to terms with the gap between my ideals and what I actually achieve. But is living realistically with failure a satisfying pathway to peace of mind?

Paul begins this crucial chapter: 'There is therefore now no condemnation for those who are in Christ Jesus.' The unease of living with failure is here ended. How can this be so? Because (verse 3) 'What the Law was powerless to do in that it was weakened by sinful nature, God did by sending his Son.' The Law could not extract perfect obedience from the human race, because we are temperamentally unable to offer it. How can perfection be achieved without the death of the person I really am? Can I be myself *and* what God wants me to be? No. So God had to create a new way.

God's new way was to send his Son to bear the full weight of his demand. Unlike every other member of the human race, God's Son was perfect. He *could* bear the weight. So in him and in his death, sin (the gap between what God wants of me and what I achieve) was judged. The 'just requirement of the Law' in verse 4—for Paul does not dispute God's right to have perfect children—was fulfilled for us in the Son. So, as we are linked to Jesus, adopted as God's own children, we are counted as fulfilling the Law. At the bottom line, God sees it this way. And his view is all that really matters.

We are a little like the duck hunters who were hunting in a wide-open, barren land in the American South. Far away on the horizon they saw a cloud of smoke. Soon they could hear a crackling sound. The wind came up, and they realized the terrible truth: a bushfire was moving their way. It was moving so fast they could not outrun it. The more experienced hunter began to rifle through his pockets. He soon found what he was looking for—a book of matches. To the other's amazement, he pulled out a match and struck it. He lit a small fire around the two of them. Soon they were standing in a circle of blackened earth, waiting for the fire to come. They did not have to wait long. They covered their mouths with their handkerchiefs and braced themselves. The fire came near—and swept over them. But they were completely unhurt. They weren't even touched. Fire would not pass where fire had passed.

The Law is like the bushfire. We cannot withstand its fierce heat and force. But if we stand in the burned-over place, where Law has already burned its way through, then we will not be hurt. The death of Christ is the burned-over place. The Law has become powerless. 'Thanks be to God through Jesus Christ our Lord!'

A SHOUT OF TRIUMPH
Romans 8:31–39

Paul concludes his long argument about human nature and God's grace, an argument which has now run for eight full chapters, with a great shout of triumph. 'Who can separate us from the love of Christ?' We know that God is on our side, because he 'gave up his Son for us all'.

This intense passage is about God's attitude towards humanity, which is expressed above all in Jesus Christ. Jesus Christ shows that God longs for the good of the human race; he is not a despot. If we did not have Jesus, we would be in the dark about God's mind—his true motives. In fact, we might assume the worst, given his standards of perfection and our congenital inability to meet them. But the Son has come. Therefore, 'Who shall bring any charge against those whom God has chosen?' Or to quote the Gospel of John: 'God came into the world not to condemn the world, but that the world might be saved through him.'

This unshakeable grace of God does not necessarily make the hurts of life any less. These hurts exist whether we know God or not. Experiences such as trouble or hardship or persecution or famine or nakedness or danger or the sword are part of living. Life in the world is very fragile. But the good news of God's love towards us makes it absolutely certain that these things are not judgments. They are not living accusations of how rotten we are. They are, simply, what they are. No more. Despite them God's grace is ours. 'In all these things, we are more than conquerors, through him who loved us.'

We have no need to make our personal tragedies worse by adding to them self-accusation. God is *not* judging the human race through innocent affliction. His judgment was laid to rest when Jesus died. All sin, conscious and unconscious, actual and potential, has been judged by means of that one perfect sacrifice.

The death of Jesus spells the death of judgment on the human race. No bad thing that happens to us can affect the grace in which we stand. This grace is stronger than anything else there is.

SPOKES AND A HUB
Romans 13:8–10

'We love God because he first loved us.' And love between people works the same way. Love begins not in the act of loving but in the act of being loved.

Law had always taught us that if we love, we may expect to be loved, as if we earn love by our own successful loving. In the New Testament, however, our loving comes first from the root of God's loving us, as we are, without condition. It is like this in marriage, or in bringing up a child, or in any kind of lasting friendship. When we are loved as we are, we respond spontaneously. We virtually need to return the love.

Love, then, is no longer a precondition for God's favour but something that flows naturally from our experience of God's grace. And so, as Paul writes in this key passage, 'Love is the fulfilling of the Law.' Love between people and love between God and humanity are the end results of everything God has striven for in the history of our salvation.

It is important that Paul places this insight towards the end of his letter. Had he announced at the beginning that 'love is the fulfilling of the Law', that would have come across to us as a new Law. Love for our neighbour could have become something else we strive to achieve.

But Paul did not start there. What we need, he claimed, is to be loved precisely as we are, locked in our own inability to love. From that seed, God's grace in loving us as we are, through Jesus Christ on the cross, comes the fruit of our love for one another.

Everything depends on God first loving us. This is the horse set rightly before the cart. It can be compared to a wheel with many spokes emanating from the hub. The closer the spokes are to the hub, the closer they are to each other. The further they are from the centre, the further they are from each other. That is how it is with God's love. The closer we are to his grace as the centre, his loving of us as we are, the closer we are able to be to other people. And the further away, the less motivated our loving is and the further away we drift from each other. So it has always been and so it shall always be. God's grace is the centre.

The Message of 1 Corinthians

Graham H. Twelftree

How do Christians deal with divisions in the church family? What attitude should they have to sex and marriage? What place do women have in the church? How does one know if a state of ecstatic enthusiasm is from God? Is speaking in tongues from God or not? What are the gifts of the Spirit? How and when should these gifts be used?

These are some of the questions with which the Corinthian Christians were struggling. They are also very modern questions.

A fundamental issue running through the Corinthian correspondence is Paul's relationship to the Christians at Corinth. They are divided in their loyalty to him as they seek special knowledge, ecstatic experience and the authority of other 'apostles'. Paul's firm reply is that the apparent weakness and foolishness of what happened when Jesus died on the cross, which is also mirrored in the weakness of his own life, is actually the power of God. Our relation to God and our experience of him do not depend on human wisdom and fine words but on our trust in God's power, which he showed on the cross.

Paul deals first with Chloe's report from the church at Corinth. He tells them:

- There is only one Saviour, so there should be no divisions in the church.

- Have nothing to do with immoral Christians.

- Christians should not settle their differences in pagan courts.

Paul ends this section by setting out this principle of Christian behaviour: while everything may be permissible for Christians, because we belong to God, our bodies ought to be used as God intended.

Then Paul answers questions from the Corinthians. In setting out his answers

1 Corinthians OUTLINE

Paul appeals to sayings of Jesus; to Christ as an example; to Christian tradition he has received from earlier Christians; and to Scripture, nature, social conventions and common Christian practice as well as his own authority.

- 'What about marriage? Should married couples refrain from sexual intercourse?' No, says Paul, sexual intercourse is a valuable part of marriage. Only for a short time should couples agree to abstain from intercourse for the purpose of prayer. He also says it is better, because this world is soon to pass away, for Christians to remain as they were when they first became Christians, whether married or unmarried.

- 'Should we eat meat that has been offered to idols?' While an idol is nothing, says Paul, the Christians must be certain that their behaviour does not harm other Christians and that everything Christians do brings glory to God.

- 'What about when we meet together for worship?' Should women wear veils when they take part in worship? Paul answers 'yes' on the grounds of created order, social convention and the practice of other churches.

More importantly, Paul has heard that the meetings of the Corinthian Christians do more harm than good. There are opposing social groups, and richer Christians are not sharing what they have brought for the meal. Paul gives them a warning and directs them to examine themselves. If there is discord when we meet to celebrate the Lord's Supper, we only continue our responsibility for Christ's death rather than receiving benefit from it.

- 'What about the gifts of the Holy Spirit?' At the beginning of chapter 12, Paul says that when someone is motivated by the Holy Spirit Jesus will be praised. He goes on to say that there are many different kinds of love-gifts of the Spirit. They all contribute to the well-being of the one body. A gift of the Spirit has no value apart from the love of the person through whom the gift is given to the body. (See key passages *The Greatest is Love, Gifts from the Holy Spirit.*)

In chapter 14 Paul writes of the importance of tongues—people speaking in strange languages—yet prophecy is to be preferred because it can be understood without an interpreter. Prophecy brings God's message to his people, while the gift of tongues is a sign to unbelievers that they are unbelievers. Paul concludes with some principles for Christian worship: people will come with their gifts, which must contribute in a way which is orderly and builds up the body of Christ, the church family.

- 'Do we need to believe that there is a bodily resurrection?' The centre-piece of Paul's argument is the tradition which he has handed on to them: that Jesus died and that some have seen him, raised to life; the first among many to be raised.

- 'What about the collection for the Christians in Jerusalem?' The reply is that they should set aside a sum each week, in keeping with their income, which Paul can pick up when he returns.

QUARRELLING IN THE CHURCH
1 Corinthians 1:10–31

At Corinth, Christian leaders had become the focal point of quarrelling, as still happens. Some of the Corinthian Christians claimed to follow Apollos, some Peter, some Paul, while others said, 'I belong to Christ.' This last cry probably came from some mystical Corinthians who boasted no human leader but Christ.

Paul's sarcastic response was a reminder that there is only one Saviour who died on the cross! Indeed, Paul had only baptized a few of them and, in any case, they were not baptized as Paul's disciples but as followers of Jesus. They should not claim to 'belong' to anyone—including Christ—in a way that would lead to divisions.

In verses 18 to 25 Paul says that in the rise of quarrelsome parties the Corinthians had overvalued human wisdom, transforming the good news of Jesus into a position to be defended, and so failing to understand the gospel Paul was sent to preach.

There is a modern ring in what Paul says. In verse 22 he says that the Jews look for 'miracles' as people do today when they refuse to trust God until he reveals visible and spectacular credentials. The message of a crucified Messiah is an offence: it is the exact opposite of what people expect from an almighty God acting in strength. Or like the Greeks, who demand proof in the form of skilled human arguments, people in the twentieth century may look to the human mind as the way of understanding how God can be known. Again, the message of a crucified Messiah seems foolish because it cuts across the human attempt to reason towards understanding God.

Despite appearances, to the Christian the message of the crucified Jesus is not one of weakness but of the power of God. It is not foolishness but God's wisdom, his way of saving people.

Paul reminds the Corinthian Christians that even though few of them were wise or powerful or rich or of high social standing, God had chosen them. And so there is no room for quarrelsome boasting.

MARRIAGE
1 Corinthians 7:1–16

Christians at Corinth seem to have taken the mistaken view that God is only interested in the 'soul' or 'spirit', not the human body. This leads to the error that the body does not matter; you can do what you like with it, or else that the body is evil—the cause of trouble.

Paul's answer to their question about marriage is in several parts.

- **There is a gift of celibacy,** and it is a good gift. But people should not try forgoing marriage unless they genuinely have this gift (verse 7). Otherwise there is the possibility of immorality.

- **Marriage includes sexual fulfilment.** Marriages must be complete, not just so-called 'spiritual' marriages. Paul has no disgust with sex. Certainly he does not restrict intercourse to occasions when a child is desired. He is advocating a regular and enthusiastic sex life.

As verse 4 makes plain, we each relinquish the exclusive right to our bodies and give our partners a claim to them. We need to give ourselves to each other to enrich our relationship, and never use our bodies to bargain with. Any one-sided insistence on abstinence amounts to robbing our partners of their rights and ourselves of all God has for us in the beauty of marriage. If a couple agree to abstain from sex for the purposes of prayer, it should be only for a limited time or they will be tempted to immorality.

■ **We should not be dominated by sex,** so that it distorts life. From verse 8 onwards Paul speaks to different groups.

To the unmarried and widows Paul says that it is good to stay single as he does. Few rabbis were single so we would expect that Paul had once been married.

For the married, he has a command from Christ's teaching. Divorce and remarriage are wrong (though read also the article *Marriage and the Family* for the wider Bible teaching).

A married person who becomes a Christian is not made unclean by continuing in marriage with an unbelieving partner. Indeed, the Christian partner is not to initiate divorce because there is a possibility of helping the other to become a Christian. If the unbelieving partner leaves, the Christian is 'not bound' (verse 15), but is free to divorce.

THE LORD'S SUPPER
1 Corinthians 11:17–34

In the early church the 'Lord's Supper' ('communion', the 'eucharist' or the 'mass') took place in the context of a shared meal. The book of Acts shows the early church meeting daily to eat together. At Corinth the Christians met each Sunday, perhaps celebrating the Lord's Supper each time.

The meal possibly began with a Jewish thanksgiving—'Blessed are you, O Lord, King of the universe, who brings forth bread from the earth.' This may have been followed by the leader repeating Jesus' words: 'This is my body which is for you. Do this in remembrance of me.' At the end of the meal the leader would have taken a cup of wine and repeated the words of Jesus: 'This cup is the new agreement in my blood. Whenever you drink it, do so in remembrance of me.' Then everyone would have drunk from the same cup.

However, just because Christians meet together to worship does not, says Paul, necessarily mean that they are doing a good thing (verse 17)! Verse 20 probably means 'When you meet it is not possible to eat the Lord's Supper in the conditions desired by the Lord'. Paul's sharp criticism is due because he has heard that there are divisions among them when they meet. The divisions are probably not like those mentioned in chapter 1, but class divisions between the rich and poor, slaves and free people, with the wealthy getting drunk and not sharing their food, while the poor are hungry and humiliated.

Paul reminds the Corinthians of the tradition he had received from the Lord (probably passed on by earlier Christians) about the Lord's Supper. It is a remembering—a reliving or re-enactment. In remembering the death of Jesus they are proclaiming it. To do so in a way that dishonours him is to remain responsible for the death of Jesus rather than receive the benefits of it.

Paul concludes by urging the Corinthians to wait for each other, to make the Lord's Supper a symbol of Christian unity, not a means of God's judgment.

THE BODY AND THE GIFTS
1 Corinthians 12:1–31

We share a problem with the Corinthian Christians. How can one know whether what one is doing or saying is from the Holy Spirit or not? The problem is compounded because all the potential activities of the Holy Spirit have their counterparts in the pagan world.

Paul's answer comes in verse 3. In any speech from the Holy Spirit Jesus will be glorified as Lord; the people speaking will accept the authority of Jesus and acknowledge themselves as his servants.

The Corinthians seem to have asked about gifts, using a word meaning 'spirituals' or 'spiritual matters' (verse 1). But in his reply Paul uses the word '*love*-gifts'. So what we have come to call 'spiritual gifts' are, in Paul's language, 'love-gifts': tangible expressions of God's love through an individual being motivated by the Spirit to say or do something for the church family.

Paul believed that every Christian has been given some love-gift, some expression of the Spirit, not for their own benefit but for the mutual help of the whole church family. (See more about this in the article *Spiritual Gifts*.)

The list of love-gifts differs from that in Romans chapter 12, showing that there is no fixed number of gifts. Also, the gifts are not restricted to use in worship but are for the whole life of the Christian community. Any words or actions may become love-gifts of the Spirit when they are given, motivated and directed by the Spirit for the good of the whole church family. The way Paul puts his question in verse 30 shows that not every Christian was expected to speak in tongues.

Some important lessons come out of the image of the body:

■ **It is a contradiction in terms to say we are Christians yet not actively belong to a Christian community** (verse 15).

■ **What makes my gift so valuable is not that it is the same or better than the others but that it is unique.**

■ **Different and weaker members cannot be excluded but are needed and are to be cared for.** Paul illustrates this by listing, not offices of the church, but the essential variety of tasks given by God.

THE GREATEST IS LOVE
1 Corinthians 13:1–13

At first glance this lovely passage seems out of place between two chapters on the gifts of the Spirit. But Paul has shown that what the Spirit gives are not simply spiritual gifts. They are *love*-gifts, *charismata*. He also shows that even though some love-gifts of the Spirit may be more obvious than others, they are all essential for the proper functioning of a Christian community. In chapter 13 Paul spells out this point by saying that

even if I possessed many operations of
the Spirit they would be useless without
love.

The love-gift of speaking in tongues
is essential—though overvalued by the
Corinthians (see 14:1–5). However,
without love it is a lifeless, empty vessel
causing unproductive noise.
Prophesying, knowing all mysteries
(perhaps a reference to the gift of
wisdom), knowledge, faith, generosity,
even burning oneself as a religious act,
amount to nothing if they are not
characterized by love. In other words, if
we have a gift of the Spirit it has no value
apart from the love of the person in
whom the gift is evident.

The gifts will not be needed in heaven
any more than a grown person needs
toys. But love never ends and will be an
essential part of the heavenly world. The
gifts of the Spirit bring only partial and
indirect understanding and knowledge
of God, as a metal mirror gives only a
partial and indirect reflection of reality.
But when we see God face to face we will
completely know God as he, now,
completely knows us.

The last verse of the chapter may be
an early Christian saying. In contrast to
the gifts of the Spirit, faith or trust in God
(which enables us to be put right with
God); hope (which is a trust in God in
relation to the future); and love, which
sums up the relationship between a
person and God, remain. Love is the
greatest because it will remain
unchanged and, unlike faith and hope, is
right at the heart of who God is and what
he does.

The Message of 2 Corinthians

Graham H. Twelftree

This letter deals with the pain involved in Christian leadership. How many God-given leaders and, in turn, church families, have been injured by bitter criticism, hurtful misrepresentation and rejection?

In 1 Corinthians chapter 16 Paul says he intended to make a second, perhaps extended, visit to Corinth. This visit turned out to be unpleasant. Relations between Paul and the Corinthians continued to deteriorate so that it seems he wrote a third, severe letter which, if not incorporated into one of the present letters, is lost to us. (We now have only two of the four or five letters Paul wrote to the Christians in Corinth.)

The writing of 2 Corinthians, from Macedonia in about AD55, takes place in the light of Paul's rightful, God-given leadership still being rejected. Thus, by the end of his letter he is planning a third visit in the hope of restoring relations. In that visit he will also collect the money the Corinthians have been setting aside. In 2 Corinthians chapters 8 and 9 he encourages them to persevere in this project.

So the theme of this letter, or collection of fragments, is dominated by a discussion of Christian ministry as one of loving, humble, painful service to which the Corinthians should respond with open hearts (6:3–13).

In his defence, both personal and as a leader, Paul assures them that despite the difficult visit, tearful letter and uncertain plans (1:15—2:4) he has been acting out of love and concern for them.

The test of all ministry is whether or not it reflects the character of Jesus Christ's death and resurrection (4:10–12). In turn, this ministry will be attested to in the lives of those whom the minister has served (3:1–3).

One of the major difficulties for Paul's

2 Corinthians OUTLINE

leadership is that false apostles have intruded on his relationship with the Corinthians. Thus, in chapters 10 to 13 he launches an attack on these people (see key passage *False Apostles, False Gospel*). They had probably made fun of Paul's apparent weakness (10:10). In the light of this, Paul's boasting of his weakness is in order to show the strength of God in his life and ministry (12:9).

How effective this letter was we cannot be sure, but that he eventually failed to re-establish a working relationship with the Corinthians may be indicated by Romans 15:23.

GOD'S CARE WHEN IN TROUBLE
2 Corinthians 1:3–11

There is a common view that the Christian life is free of pain or suffering. But while we still live in this world we will experience these things. Sometimes a Christian will experience God's special deliverance or healing. But, as seen in the life of Paul, this suffering takes on a new significance. It highlights being 'bound' to Christ in his life and death. It can also benefit others and be the means by which we discover and experience God's supporting love.

Relations between Paul and the Corinthians had become strained and the letter is a difficult one. So Paul begins and continues with this generous attitude. He does not wish to hide the fact that he has been suffering, though we cannot tell exactly what happened to him while he was in Asia. Paul's praise is for the comfort that God has given him in his troubles. Just as the sufferings of Christ overflow to him, so his comfort can overflow to the Corinthians.

The word Paul uses to describe his suffering means 'pressure' in the Greek. This 'pressure' obviously had a profound effect on Paul, for it is evident throughout the letter. Christians today are also under 'pressure'—from frustration, disappointment, poverty, broken relationships, other religions, materialism, isolation and persecution. Yet, like Paul, they can also praise God that he has carried and will continue to carry them through. We can also call upon other Christians to pray for us so that they can, in the end, join in the rejoicing of answered prayer (verses 10 and 11).

FRIENDSHIP WITH GOD THROUGH CHRIST
2 Corinthians 5:17—6:2

Paul writes that when people are joined to Jesus Christ they are changed from God's enemies into his friends. Verse 21 explains how this re-making can take place. God's judgment fell on Christ, our representative, who was without sin. And so, when we are joined to Christ, our sins are no longer counted against us. We can now stand in the right relationship with God which Christ enjoyed.

Part of God's initiative in making us his friends was to give Paul, and in turn the whole church, the 'ministry of reconciliation', or making other people friends of God. The church has variously understood this task and has become involved in all kinds of enterprises, from social justice programmes to international peace mediation. While the church must take seriously the social and political problems of our time, Paul understood the ministry of reconciliation to be the preaching of the cross as the love of God for sinners. We must not be side-tracked from this task. A world at peace and free of social problems would still be a world of people at war with God!

Paul sees his task in terms of being an ambassador, speaking not for himself but as God's representative: 'Let God change you from enemies into his friends!' (verse 20). Paul turns to the Corinthians and appeals to them that they should not fail to live out what God has given them. In the light of Paul's strained relationship with the Corinthians, we may wonder if he has in mind the importance of reconciled human relationships as the appropriate response to being reconciled to God.

CHRISTIAN GIVING
2 Corinthians 8:1–5; 9:6–15

In the 'materialistic West' Christians are quick to defend their 'right' to do with their money as they please. Many argue that high taxes remove the need to surrender this part of their lives to God.

In 1 Corinthians chapter 16 Paul had instructed each of them to set aside an amount of money—in keeping with his or her income—so that time and energy would not be wasted with collections when Paul arrived to take the money to Jerusalem. Here Paul urges them to continue this act of love.

In chapters 8 and 9 Paul reveals some helpful principles on Christian giving:

■ **Generous giving arises out of God's love for us.** As the example of the Macedonians shows, generosity does not always arise out of wealth, but sometimes out of distress and poverty. Christian generosity may involve giving beyond our means (8:3).

■ **Giving is a privilege, not a burden** (8:4).

■ **Giving is directed by God** (8:5). The Macedonians were more generous than Paul expected because they had given themselves first to God.

■ **Overflowing with trust, speech, knowledge and love is to be matched by overflowing generosity** (8:7).

■ **Generous giving arises out of following the self-giving example of Jesus** (8:9). Although he was rich, for the sake of others he became poor.

■ If eagerness to please God is the motive for giving, **the gift is acceptable to him in relation to what we have,** not in relation to what we do not have (9:7).

■ **Christian giving is not designed to bring poverty to the giver but to help those in need and to establish equality in the wider Christian family** (9:13–15).

■ **To give sparingly is to receive sparingly; to give generously is to receive generously** (9:6). Paul probably has in mind both spiritual and material blessings (9:10–11).

■ **Christians can trust God.** To hang on tightly to our present possessions is a failure to trust God to supply our needs and to miss out on the liberating experience of his care.

■ **Giving causes thanksgiving.** It not only supplies the needs of others but causes them to give praise and thanks to God (that we have been obedient to him) and to pray for us (9:12–15).

FALSE APOSTLES, FALSE GOSPEL
2 Corinthians 11:1–15

It seems that some Jewish Christians, whom Paul calls 'super-apostles' and servants of Satan, had gone to Corinth with letters of recommendation from Jerusalem.

They had probably been saying that Paul was not to be recognized as an apostle, perhaps even as a Christian. They had criticized his timidity, his unimpressive personality and poor speech and had boasted of their superiority in heritage and in experience of visions. Paul warns the Corinthians that he may not, when he comes, be as timid as he has been (!) and that he is all that the 'super-apostles' say they are— and more—especially in his sufferings! And even if he is not a trained speaker, he does have the knowledge.

■ **Paul is concerned for the life of the Christian community,** for he sees himself as being responsible to present them pure to Christ. However, they have, like Eve, been led astray, not into heresy so much as away from a simple and sincere devotion to Christ. Even though Paul does not say what the different Jesus, Spirit or gospel are which the false apostles are preaching, we can make a guess. They are opposing Paul's preaching of a crucified Messiah who sets people free on the basis of their trust or faith, without any human merit or legal obligations being involved.

■ **Paul is also concerned about his status with the Corinthians as their spiritual mentor.** They have put up with the false apostles, so why can they not put up with Paul who, so far as he can see, only failed to charge them for his services? Nevertheless, even though he believed he was entitled to support, he is glad that he has not been a burden to them, for it will give the intruders something to match in their boasting! Paul's jealous love for the Corinthians leads to his most venomous criticism of his opponent 'apostles'.

The Message of Galatians

Melba P. Maggay

Deep and strong in our nature is the sense that we must somehow do something terrible and hard to find acceptance with God. A religion that does not tell us to walk on fire, eat no meat, pierce ourselves with nails or make a vow to the Virgin to pray a thousand rosaries each year feels somewhat easy and cheap.

Paul's converts in what were probably the southern cities of Galatia in Asia Minor must have felt like this. Some Jewish Christians came to tell them that the gospel they received from Paul was a bit too relaxed in its requirements. These 'trouble-makers', as he called them, had been urging circumcision and the observance of special days and months and years (1:7; 2:3–4; 4:10). Their influence was such that even Peter, recognized leader in the Jerusalem church, feared to stand out against them (2:12–13).

The problem to Paul was partly that Jewish laws and customs were being imposed on non-Jews, a mistake that is repeated in our own day when Western nations impose their cultures and even their own brand of Christianity on other peoples. But more deeply at stake was the integrity of the gospel of grace, the precious idea that 'a person is put right with God only through faith in Jesus Christ, never by doing what the Law requires' (2:16). To go back to feast days and dietary rules is to fall out of line with the truth of the gospel (2:14). It is to slip into a legalism that brings us back to

spiritual infancy (3:23–25; 4:1–2), or to the forced obedience of a slave (4:3, 8). But in fact we are right with God only through Christ's death. To believe this is to be free and not captive (5:1), a child of God and not a slave (4:4–7).

Now that Christ has come, freedom and the power of the Spirit can be had by believing, the same basis on which Abraham was given the promise of blessing (3:6–9). The true children of

---

Galatians OUTLINE

1:1–5 Opening greetings

1:6–9 No other gospel

1:10–2:21 Paul defends himself
1:10–24 His gospel directly from God, not men
2:1–10 His apostleship recognized by Jerusalem leaders
2:11–14 Peter erred in Antioch
2:15–21 Paul, like all Jewish Christians, is justified by faith and has died to the Law

3:1–4:31 Faith and the Law
3:1–5 By faith the Spirit is received
3:6–18; 26–29 The Law and the promise
3:19–25; 4:1–7 The purpose of the Law
4:8–20 A personal appeal
4:21–31 Children of the slave, children of the free

5:1–6:10 Freedom in Christ
5:1–12 Do not go back to the slavery of the Law
5:13–26 Live by the Spirit
6:1–10 Do good and be responsible for all

6:11–18 Final words

Abraham, Paul argues, are those who have received the Spirit by hearing and believing the gospel and have become heirs by belonging to Christ (3:2, 29).

The idea that one does not have to be culturally a Jew to be part of the chosen people of God was so new that Paul was attacked for making up a gospel that is easier and more palatable to people (1:10–11). In reply Paul asserted that his gospel and his authority to preach it were received directly from God and not from any man (1:1, 12, 15–17). His apostleship was to the Gentiles (2:7–8), which qualified him to be authoritative in so far as the gospel related to non-Jewish belief and practice. Far from being popular, his message of righteousness apart from the Law brought persecution (6:12).

One shudders at the thought that Christianity as a religion of grace for all peoples had to stand on very thin ground in the early days. Paul was the only one who consistently preached it, a controversial personality, a late-comer, a notorious persecutor of the faith, a man severely attacked as lacking in apostolic credentials. Yet God used him to hold open for us a way of coming to God without the hardness of minute law-keeping or the narrowness of culture-bound expressions of faith. Without this man's tears and persevering struggle, Christianity could have become just another Jewish sect, a minor tribal religion not very different from all the others whose main teachings have to do mostly with what one may and may not do before God.

The letter to the Galatians shows why Paul insisted so strongly that freedom comes through faith in Christ, not through keeping the Law.

FREEDOM IN CHRIST
Galatians 5:1—6:10

'To be a man,' says one writer, 'is both a crime and a penance.' In our divided selves we wound others because of what we are, and suffer because of what we want to be. In each of us there is this terrible twisted thing that runs haywire and lays waste our lives. At the same time there is a longing for something higher, and a bleak disappointment that our best efforts are not enough to make us better than what we are.

To this tragic sense of our powerlessness comes the good news that we may, by faith, 'eagerly await through the Spirit the righteousness for which we hope' (5:5). God through the Spirit has come to meet us in our need; a power beyond ourselves has come into the world and is breaking window panes and letting in air.

The freedom of Christ brings us a new moral power.

■ **It is power not to sin,** the liberty to abstain from the acts of the sinful nature (5:16–21).

■ **And it is power to be good,** to grow into the fruit of the Spirit's life in us (5:22–26). This is a goodness altogether apart from the Law (5:18, 23); one might as well speak of passing a law to produce grapes out of a mango tree. A person can choose either to dig the barren soil of human effort apart from God, or take root in the fertile ground of life in the Spirit and reap its richness (6:8).

To follow the way of the Spirit is to walk about an earth with the wide and forceful boundaries of love (5:6, 13–14).

One is free, and yet responsible for all (5:13; 6:1–2, 10). The generous commitment to doing good is sustained by the power of God, who sees to it that we reap what we sow (6:7, 9). In the end, says Paul, neither circumcision nor uncircumcision mean anything. Such religious details have nothing to do with the burst of new things God is doing in the life of his people and of the world (6:15).

ALL ONE IN CHRIST
Galatians 3:26–29

Today we are intensely conscious of the rights of women, ethnic minorities and the poor. Inequality and discrimination have by no means disappeared, but many are aware these are wrong and want to see them wiped out.

This was not so in the world in which Christianity came. Greek and Roman civilization was borne on the backs of slaves. And the free Jewish male daily thanked God that he was not a Gentile, a slave or a woman.

In stark contrast, the emerging Christian community crossed all the divisions. Here was a miscellaneous collection of slaves, Roman matrons, soldiers and courtiers, Greeks and Jews of various trades, who were being stretched in their life together to express Paul's belief that in Christ 'there is neither Jew nor Greek, slave nor free, male nor female' (verse 28).

Unity in Christ means here primarily the equal status of being a child of God. One does not cease being a slave, a woman or a Greek on entering this new order of life. But because all share a common inheritance, the relationships are totally new. In Israel, people of the wrong race, sex or class were barred from religious privileges. In Christ these distinctions had gone.

The largely Gentile churches in Galatia were in danger of giving in to traditional Jews who were practising cultural imperialism. They were willing to welcome non-Jews, providing they accepted circumcision and some other Jewish laws and customs. This will not do, says Paul, because the only way of joining Abraham's seed is by belonging to Christ (verse 29).

This principle broke down two of the greatest social barriers:

■ **Slaves were entitled to equal rank in the churches.** And although the pillars of structured slavery were not quickly shaken, established patterns of master/slave relationship were turned upside down. In the letter to Philemon we read of a slave, Onesimus, becoming a fellow church member with his master. At least one bishop of Rome was an ex-slave.

■ **Women were assumed to have an equal religious role with men.** Paul elsewhere wrote of Philippian women 'labouring side by side' with him in the gospel, and he recognized women's right to pray and prophesy in church.

The oneness in Christ of verse 28 refers to equality in more than simply baptism. It speaks of all religious exclusiveness and privilege being abolished. It is not our sex but our basic status in Christ which determines who should play which role in Christian service.

Peter was quite wrong to back away from table fellowship with Gentiles (2:11–13). And the controlling principle of verse 28 shows it is just as wrong to bar a slave (or a non-white) from exercising leadership, or a woman from exercising her whole range of gifts. To do so is to deny the spiritual equality and inclusiveness achieved by the power of grace in the gospel of Jesus.

The Message of Ephesians

Christopher Lamb

The letter to the Ephesians is typical of many of the letters of the New Testament in bringing together two things. It gives an account of what has happened to the world in the coming of Jesus Christ, and it spells out in detail what that is going to mean in practical terms for the lives of people who become his followers.

It means nothing less than a new start for the human race, because the old barrier between God's people and 'the others' has been permanently destroyed. Those previously condemned to live their lives in darkness and ignorance can find immense new resources for living as part of a wholly new group of people—the church. These Christian people are marked by confidence and vitality. At the same time they are willing to give way to one another. All this springs out of the conviction that they have a precious part to play in a huge drama of oppression, danger and rescue. In this story the decisive act has only just taken place, though the Author had planned it, and their part too, from the beginning.

What has been happening is too enormous in scale to appreciate fully, but part of its mysterious meaning is that the followers of Jesus are able to participate in the life which he has secured for them out of his agony and death. They can actually share in his new life, and be called his body, the 'church', those people who have been 'called out' from conventional life to give their daily 'evidence' for him. (The legal language is not accidental. These

people were always in danger from the authorities, despite their innocence. Paul is writing from prison.)

The followers of Jesus are not, like many active people today, so taken up with a single cause that they can think of nothing else. They are more like former addicts or prisoners who have been brought out into a new world of abundant well-being where all the fulness of God's

Ephesians OUTLINE

1:1–3:21   The mystery of Christian faith

1:1–2   Greetings

1:3–14   Christians are chosen to praise God's glory in Christ

1:15–23   Prayer that they may understand their calling

2:1–10   What God's grace has achieved

2:11–22   Jews and non-Jews brought together make a new humanity

3:1–13   Paul's own vocation as a messenger

3:14–21   Prayer for knowledge and growth in God

4:1–6:24   The consequences of Christian faith

4:1–16   The complex way Christ's body (the church) grows

4:17–24   A new person, a new style

4:25–5:5   Appropriate and inappropriate behaviour

5:6–21   Walking in daylight

5:22–33   Putting others first: wives and husbands

6:1–9   Putting others first: children and parents, slaves and masters

6:10–20   Fighting the spiritual battle

6:21–24   Final greetings

creative power is available to them in Christ. Nor are they odd characters with a taste for high-flown religious ideas. They belong to one another and are each being shaped for a particular place and role in a common enterprise—some as leaders, some as ideas-people, some as teachers and helpers of the rest.

A certain style of life is common to all of them, a discipline of mutual respect and care which shows itself in the most everyday affairs and relationships—marriage, family, employment. For something of enormous significance is at stake, and there is a literally superhuman struggle taking place. In chapter 6 we learn there is a war on, and the enemy is not going to be easily defeated. Fighting him will involve the most powerful and sophisticated weapons available, and there is only one source for obtaining them.

Paul sets the Christian calling in the broadest possible context in this letter. This enables Christians to see beyond the frustrations and limitations of our frequently narrow, conventional church life. Through this letter we come into an immense world in which God's purpose is brought through huge cost to triumphant achievement. To this we make our own fluttering human response, tiny in scale but great in meaning.

GOD'S GREAT PLAN
Ephesians 1:3–14

There are not the same local greetings in this letter as in most of the others. Perhaps it was a circular.

Paul writes to small, struggling groups of Christians and puts their lives in the spotlight of the activity of God. For God has—just the other day, it seems—brought off the long-planned coup which has changed the whole meaning of human existence for those who see what has happened in Christ.

As Paul piles words and sentences upon one another in his excitement, we begin to hear what he is saying: that because of Jesus ('in Christ', as he keeps saying) we have been adopted as the children of God. Now at last we can come into our inheritance, free from the barrier that human wrongdoing had placed across that possibility. In Christ that overwhelming objection has been dealt with, and the whole 'estate' is now ours—in principle.

The Holy Spirit is the key to the house we do not yet live in, but can visit. All the richness of what is now, and was always intended to be, ours can be summed up in one word—Christ! It is not a swear-word but a word of beauty and power. It was Jews like Paul who first realized this, but now non-Jews, too, are entering into the same experience and joining in the same chorus of admiration for what God has done.

NO MORE SECOND-RATE PEOPLE
Ephesians 2:11–22

In Paul's world people accepted that some people were privileged and others not. You could not even count on equality before the law. It depended who you were. In our world that is still true in many places, but instead of accepting it, we try to fight against injustice. One of the reasons why we do not just accept such things is this very passage, with its vision of 'a single new humanity'.

Many Jews in Paul's day thought that non-Jews were people ignored by God, having no place in the story of his people and no part in the plans he had for them. This was not just theory. As devout people saw it, the way that non-Jews lived showed that they simply did not know the first thing about life as God designed it. For this reason, such people were prevented, wherever possible, from blundering into Jewish affairs.

One vivid example of this may have been in Paul's mind as he wrote verse 14. The outer court of the temple, where non-Jews were allowed to go, was separated from the inner court, which was restricted to Jews, by a notice in several languages warning 'foreigners' not to go further on pain of death. This barrier between those who belong and those who do not, between the devout and the simple seeker, between the privileged and the unprivileged, is now abolished, Paul claims, by Christ's death on the cross. Christ, as it were, put himself between the two groups and took the effect of their hatred of one another on himself.

This way of understanding a very rich piece of writing from Paul is immensely important for our modern multi-racial societies. The result of Christ's coming is peace. He himself is the peace treaty, and the outcome is something new altogether, a living multi-ethnic house of God.

BUILDING UP THE BODY OF CHRIST
Ephesians 4:1–16

Paul reminds his readers that he is in prison, and that they too should be 'bound' to one another. For they are not just individuals, living life as it suits them. There is a unity in the body of Christ. All belong to one another and are called to work together, each making their own contribution. That unity is part of the oneness in the nature of things which comes from the one God 'who is over all and through all and in all'.

In a world which is falling apart, Christians are called to express and maintain that unity, and to use the gift given to each of them for the sake of the whole. What God wants is mature adult people, and Christ provides the measure which tells us just what that means. We are not to be children, distracted by every latest thing and easily led astray by those with twisted minds. Through Christ, God has provided us with gifts for one another. Some are leaders in action, some in thought. Some can explain things with great clarity, and others are quick to help and care for people in need. There are those whom God uses to plant new faith in people, and those who can help Christians be the people of God. No one is meant to be just a spectator, admiring the others, because the body does not have extra, unused bits.

The body of Christ is a sign of the new creation—a way in which people can come to understand what God intends to bring into being throughout his world. In our day we can see the importance of such a vision for social and political life everywhere. At the same time, we realize how little that vision is actually operating within the church as we know it. The trouble is that we lose sight of the head—Christ—and try to go our own way. We are meant to take all our directions and all our resources from him so that we can help each other and grow bigger and more beautiful together.

BASIC EQUIPMENT
Ephesians 6:10–20

After all the instructions Paul has given his readers, he wants them to recall their resources. To the unbeliever his equipment list might seem like a useless jumble of religious ideas. Stalin asked, 'How many divisions [of soldiers] has the Pope?' But the modern world has proved over and over again that the power of faith in God combined with unflinching moral courage and integrity can overturn the most immovable dictatorships and profoundly unjust governments.

In such a struggle, it does seem that some more-than-human dimension is involved. In the face of mass murder and persistent contempt for human life, it has been shown that you cannot trust those in power to have basic human decency or a sense of reason. Some other force has taken them over, and these qualities are no longer in operation.

Paul knew the destructive energies let loose in that kind of situation, and he did not underestimate them. The only answer is the confidence which the power of God can give. Through this people of faith know that because they desire only God's peace and justice, their cause cannot in the end be defeated. Truth holds them together, their peace with God keeps them stable, faith protects them from despair, and knowing God's plan of rescue keeps alive their hope. Their only weapons are the words of truth and love, fresh and sharp and healing.

Paul needs those words himself. He is a prisoner. At any moment he may be called to trial. The words come only out of long and continuous prayer, the Christian equivalent of military intelligence. Just as superior intelligence wins wars, so the power of prayer can turn around even the most hopeless situation and make it a victory for God.

The Message of Philippians

George Carey

What kind of letter would you and I write to a band of supporters if we were in prison with the death penalty as the most likely outcome? It is very likely that we would wallow in self-pity and plead for help!

Paul was in this situation when he wrote to the tiny church of Philippi in about AD62. He was in prison in Rome on the charge of preaching an 'illegal' faith and Paul knew that execution could be the result if he faced an unsympathetic judge. The Christian believers at Philippi, hearing of Paul's imprisonment, sent him a generous gift to express their love and support for a wonderful pastor and friend. Paul, greatly encouraged, writes this affectionate and grateful letter. And as a good pastor, he does not miss the opportunity to encourage them in the Christian life!

Far from being panic-stricken and fearful, Paul's reply reveals his confidence in his Lord and his vibrant, joyful faith. This is one of the most personal of all Paul's letters and indicates that a very special relationship existed between him and this church which he had founded.

The message of Philippians contains four very special features:

- It is a message of love. Far from wallowing in his misfortune, Paul radiates joy from his prison cell. Sixteen times in this brief letter the words 'rejoice' and 'joy' occur. He opens the letter by saying that he prays for them 'with joy', and his conclusion echoes this outrageous attitude to life: 'Rejoice in the Lord always. I will say it again: Rejoice!'

But what is the ground for this optimism? Is it any more than a brave man whistling in the dark? The answer is clear: Paul's joy stems from his conviction that Jesus Christ is risen from the dead and is Lord of all. What is more, he has proved the reality of his faith on the anvil of experience and he *knows* that whatever others might do to him, he is on

---

Philippians OUTLINE

1:1–11   Greetings, thanksgiving and prayer

1:12–26   Paul's living faith in the face of death

1:27–2:30   Encouragement for the Christians at Philippi
1:27–30   Unity is essential for the gospel
2:1–11   Let Christ's humility mark your life
2:12–18   Let your light shine
2:19–30   Please take care of your Christian leaders

3:1–4:1   Watch out for false teachers

4:2–23   Final words of encouragement
4:2–3   Settle your differences for Christ's sake!
4:4–13   Keep praising
4:14–23   Thank you for your gift; God will supply your needs too

the victory side. That's something to rejoice about!

- It is a message about Christ. Just as a lover cannot stop talking about his or her beloved, Paul cannot stop talking about his Lord. Try reading the letter by replacing words like 'Jesus', 'Christ' and 'Lord' with 'X', and you will be amazed by the centrality of Jesus Christ. It reaches its most magnificent peak in chapter 2 verses 5–11, where Christ's humility is taken as the way we should live.

- It is a message full of hope. Even though he faced the bleak possibility of a savage death, Paul's faith does not waver. He knew that Christ had triumphed over sin and death—so he could exult, 'For me, to live is Christ and to die is gain'. Indeed, his longing was to 'be with Christ'.

- It is a message about Christian growth. It is clear from the letter that false teachers were going around. Paul warns the Philippians to stay well away from those who preach a different faith. But Paul's teaching is positive as well. He shares his own testimony: even though, in following Christ, he has left behind everything that the world values, his ambition is still 'to know him and the power of his resurrection'. His experience of Christian living had taught him how to be content, whatever the circumstances. His declaration—'I can do everything through him [Christ] who gives me strength'—is a challenge to us all.

BE LIKE JESUS!
Philippians 2:5–11

This passage is one of the greatest statements about Jesus in the whole of the New Testament. Many scholars believe that Paul is quoting a familiar Christian hymn of the time, but whether it was written by Paul or not, this breathtaking picture is an expression of Paul's great longing that his friends at Philippi should be the kind of people that their Lord wants them to be. 'Be like Jesus!' is what Paul is saying.

It helps us understand the passage if we see that the story of Adam, the first created human being, lies behind it. Adam was only concerned about himself. He grasped after equality with God, but, instead, sin and death became his reward. Jesus, on the other hand, though he was by right equal with God, did not cling to this selfishly, but deliberately laid it aside in order to save us all.

We may trace four steps down and four steps up in Paul's magnificent expression of Jesus' humility. The story starts off in heaven with Jesus being in the 'form' of God. Then:

- He did not hold on to his rights.

- He gave up all he had.

- He humbled himself, and became a servant.

- He was obedient all the way to death.

And from this 'rock bottom' point, Jesus is:

- Raised to the highest place.

- Given the greatest name.

- Worshipped by the whole of creation.

■ **Proclaimed 'Lord' by all.**

Because many modern Christians think that the passage is about the doctrine of Jesus, we miss the point of Paul's argument. His attention is not on the nature of Jesus as God—that was obvious to him and his readers—but on the way the followers of Jesus should live: Put other people first, live unselfishly and humbly, don't grasp after your rights. This radical discipleship may take us to death, but it will also take us to glory.

PAUL'S TESTIMONY
Philippians 3:4–14

Every Christian has a story to tell about God's love. In this moving passage, Paul shares his story so that others might not be led astray by the false teachers (verse 2) who wanted Christians to adopt a Jewish form of the faith. 'I could put my trust in such things if I wanted to,' says Paul. 'I'm a circumcised Israelite; of the Benjamin tribe; a Pharisee even. What is more, I kept the Law faultlessly' (verses 4–6).

And then Paul drops his bombshell. 'I count all this as dung because I have gained the most precious thing of all—Jesus!' What is more, his ambition is to go on *knowing* more and more and entering deeper and deeper into Jesus' death and resurrection.

This 'knowing' that Paul talks about is the knowledge gained through experience. Just as we get to know a person by sharing and living with them, so Paul's knowledge of Jesus grows through his daily contact with him. Even when he faces suffering and discouragement, he experiences the 'power of his resurrection'. Indeed, for the mature Christian, sharing the sufferings of Christ and knowing the power of the resurrection often come together.

Paul disclaims any idea that he is a perfect and complete Christian (verse 12). His goal, he says, is the 'prize of the upward call of God' (verse 14). Paul's aim is to be like a spiritual athlete, going flat out towards the finishing tape to win the first prize and receive the crown of glory.

But, unlike an athlete, Paul is not concerned about himself. In the Christian 'race' there is not one single 'winner'. Paul's ambition for his friends at Philippi is that each person should be the very best for Jesus.

The Message of Colossians

George Carey

Many today are looking to new religions and cults, to the mysteries of 'inside' knowledge, to all sorts of beliefs, to try to satisfy their spiritual longings.

What would Paul write to an 'ordinary' community faced with these pressures? Colossae was an insignificant town in the valley of the Lycus river in Asia Minor, near the present-day village of Honaz in western Turkey.

Without any question this was the least important church ever to receive a letter from Paul. Why did he write to them? Because he believed the foundation of faith was under attack there.

News had reached him of a dangerous heresy which threatened not only the Colossian Christians but even the Christian message itself. From Paul's reaction, it seems that the people teaching this did not believe that Jesus Christ was the centre of faith, nor that he was God's only Son who had achieved salvation. For them, Jesus was one of many divine beings who brought salvation to mankind.

Paul would have none of that. Jesus Christ is not one of many gods: he is the only one, all in all. This is the theme of his letter to the Colossians.

In the opening chapter Paul uses the most amazing terms to describe Jesus Christ, showing Christ's relationship to God, to the created universe and to the church:

● Christ is 'the image of the invisible God' (1:15). He perfectly reflects the glory of God in a way that humankind can see and understand. This is why the first basic confession

Colossians OUTLINE

1:1–14　Greetings and opening prayer
1:1–2　　Greetings
1:3–12　 Thanksgiving and prayer
1:13–14　Our deliverance through God's Son

1:15–2:10　The supremacy of Jesus Christ
1:15–19　Christ supreme in creation and head of the church
1:20–22　God has reconciled the universe to himself through Christ
1:23–2:3　Paul's ministry in the gospel
2:4–10　Christians should therefore keep their lives founded on Christ

2:11–23　Errors in the church
2:11–12　Circumcision and baptism
2:13–15　God has brought the Colossians to life through Christ's death
2:16–23　Avoid religious practices which move Christ off centre

3:1–4:6　New life in Jesus Christ
3:1–4　　Fix your minds on your new life with the risen Christ
3:5–14　Put off what belongs to your old lives; put on what belongs to your new lives
3:15–17　Christians' lives together, in character and in worship
3:18–4:1　Relationships at home and at work
4:2–6　　Christian prayer and evangelism

4:7–18　Final greetings

of the first Christians was that 'Jesus is Lord'.

• Christ is 'the firstborn over all creation' (1:15). To put it another way, 'In him all things hold together' (1:17).

No more important statement could be made to people in our culture today. We lack a centre for our thinking and our living. Our knowledge is fragmented— the bits do not add up to a coherent whole. But, Paul says, Jesus Christ gives us the uniting principle. He is the key to understanding the universe and the purpose of our lives in it. He is the one who makes sense of everything, who holds it all together.

• Christ is 'the head of his body, the church; he is the source of the body's life' (1:18). The church, as God sees it, is not so much a body of Christians as the body of Christ. This group of people have a mission to represent Jesus in the world. Christ is the church's 'head' in the sense of directing his people, and so continuing his work through them. The church exists to make Jesus known to others, to serve them in his name and to draw them into his family.

The rest of this small letter is really an expansion of Paul's teaching about the centrality of Christ. The main theological section ends by linking faith in Jesus to our everyday lives: 'Just as you received Christ Jesus as Lord, continue to live in him, rooted and built up in him, strengthened in the faith as you were taught, and overflowing with thankfulness' (2:6–7).

The remaining chapters spell this out in practical advice. Jesus was raised to new life, and Christians should live the risen life (3:1). In chapter 3, Paul tells us to let that new life show in our words (8), character (9—10), lifestyle (12), attitudes to others (13), inner life (15), and worship (16—17). It affects our social relationships as well—wives and husbands (18—19), children and parents (20—21), masters and slaves (3:22—4:1).

Paul's letter offers us a glimpse into the life of a small Christian community struggling to work out its faith in a hostile world with many competing forces. It prompts us to ask: Is our Jesus as large as Paul's Lord? For him Christ was the majestic centre of all things, the only Lord and Saviour. Is this the way we see Jesus?

PAUL AND THE SECRET CULTS
Colossians 1:15–19; 2:4–23

What teaching was Paul attacking in this letter? Very probably it was a kind of 'secret knowledge'—a Jewish form of Gnosticism, that many-versioned religious philosophy of the day which tried to make sense of the problem of good and evil.

Many people, then as now, found it difficult to see how a good and powerful God could be responsible for a world such as this. Some forms of Gnosticism believed that this world was under the control of wicked forces which were rebelling against God. Other forms developed an approach which put the 'god of this world' on the lowest rung of a ladder of divine beings which ascended to the transcendent and basically unknowable God at the top.

From what Paul writes it seems that he saw in this four challenges to the Christian faith:

■ **It led to theological compromise.** Christ was not unique according to Paul's opponents. If that is so, then Christianity is no worse but certainly no better than any other faith.

■ **It led to moral abuse.** The famous cry of the early gnostics was *Soma sema*, 'the body is a tomb'. If the body is a tomb for the soul, then logically you either degrade it or despise it. You either beat it into submission (2:23) or you indulge in all kinds of licentious practices because the body does not matter.

■ **It led to false religious practices.** Paul warns his readers about treating religious rules as if these could lead a person to God (2:16–22).

■ **It led to social exclusivism.** Early Gnosticism claimed that those who followed the teaching possessed a wisdom—*gnosis*—superior to the common herd.

We can understand, then, why Gnosticism was such a great menace to Christianity. It demoted Jesus Christ from his central place with the Father and made him just a member of a 'fulness' of beings (compare 1:19). We can begin to appreciate Paul's determination that this false teaching should be dealt a death-blow. The Christian message says plainly that Jesus Christ is available to everyone. It is not a hidden knowledge but a faith open to all. No one is declared an outsider by reason of creed, race, colour or sex.

And we need to practise an open Christianity. We should avoid any club, organization or lodge which has exclusive membership, bound together by secret 'religious' affiliation or secret initiation ceremonies.

THE OLD NATURE AND THE NEW
Colossians 3:1–14

For Paul, being a Christian must result in a changed life. If Christ is Head of all things, and if he has risen from death for us, this has a direct consequence for the way we live. The 'putting off, putting on' analogy in this passage is probably a reminder of baptism, when new Christians shed their old clothes and put on white garments. Life, he is saying, must be a daily baptism, with a daily dying and rising again.

Paul groups the vices and virtues in fives. In verse 5 he commands his hearers to put off the sins of the flesh—immorality, impurity, and so on. Paul, unlike many modern evangelists, will not allow us to believe that becoming a Christian introduces us to an easy and comfortable life. In his opinion, the Christian life is lifelong warfare against the powers of evil.

Another five vices meet us in verse 7, which we may describe as sins of the tongue—anger, wrath, malice, slander and foul talk. Paul clearly expected his readers to work out the extent to which the Christian life had affected social communication.

Why is Paul so insistent about 'putting off'? After all, he was no mere moralist. The answer is given in verse 10. The image of God in humankind,

once spoiled through our fall into sin,
has now been restored through Jesus
Christ. We are therefore a new creation
in Christ, and it is inconceivable that
Christ's people could live as they did
before!

This new creation, with Christ as the
centre, is one of harmony and co-
operation (verse 11). Jesus is the
gravitational pull whch holds us all from
flying apart. This unity of all humanity in
Christ is a revolutionary concept. All
divisions are shattered through Christ's
work—religious, political and social
divisions are gone for good.

Verse 12 tells us which virtues we
should 'put on'. Five are listed:
compassion, kindness, lowliness,
meekness and patience. To this beautiful
series are added two others, forgiveness
and love. Forgiveness is required
because this is what God has given us in
Christ. And at the heart of all these good
things, there should be love.

The passage is a strong reminder that
the Christian life is down-to-earth, to do
with our character and our everyday
relationships. The strong 'putting off'
verses remind us that we belong to God
and we should aim to do what pleases
Christ our Lord, rather than what suits
us. The 'putting on' verse tells us that
our new life is based on the kind of life
which Jesus himself lived.

The Message of
1 & 2 Thessalonians

George Carey

The church at Thessalonica was very young when Paul wrote these letters. We learn from Acts 17 verses 1 to 10 that Paul had to leave the town very quickly after preaching the gospel because of persecution. So Paul had had no chance to build up the new Christians in the faith. However, he was able to leave Timothy behind to encourage and teach them.

Some months later when Timothy rejoined him at Corinth, Paul was thrilled to hear that the young Christians were going on very well. But there was one problem. Apparently they had misunderstood Paul's teaching about the return of Jesus. They thought that any of their fellowship who had already died would not have a share in the future glories promised to them. As a result, they were grief-stricken. Paul therefore wrote at once to clear away misunderstanding and to reassure them that all followers of Jesus will share in his victory. Indeed, the 'dead in Christ' will rise first and will be waiting for those who are alive when Christ comes.

These letters remind us very strongly that Christianity cannot be separated from its great hope—the coming of Christ and the renewal of all things. Although Paul did not know when it would happen—'it will come like a thief in the night,' he says—he knows that Christ *will come* and at a time when he is least expected.

There can be little doubt that Paul longed for Christ to return soon. He knew that it would be a time of the greatest joy and unimaginable happiness—not only because Christians would be united with their loved ones, but more especially because the followers of Jesus would be united with their Lord and Saviour. This great hope spurred Paul on in preaching the gospel and gave him a sense of urgency. Because he did not know when it was going to happen, he went all out to win people for his master.

But Paul also reminds these young Christians that just because Christ might come soon, it gave them no excuse to pack up work, to be lazy or allow their

1 and 2 Thessalonians OUTLINE

1 THESSALONIANS
1:1   Greetings
1:2–3:13   Paul encourages the Christians
4:1–12   Practical Christian living
4:13–5:11   Be ready for Christ to return
5:12–28   Final instructions and greetings

2 THESSALONIANS
1:1–2   Greetings
1:3–12   Praise and encouragement
2:1–12   The events leading up to Christ's return
2:13–3:5   Paul reassures the Christians
3:6–15   Keep on working!
3:16–18   Personal postscript

standards to drop. Paul says that the opposite should result. The coming of Jesus ought to make us holy, godly people, who show the reality of our faith by the quality of our behaviour and work.

From these short letters we can see that the coming of Christ is far more than 'pie in the sky when I die'. Paul's teaching is relevant to today. Because Christ is going to return in triumph we should not neglect justice, holiness and human values; his imminent arrival should encourage us all the more to do everything well for him.

WITH GOD FOR EVER
1 Thessalonians 4:13–18

We all know from experience that to lose hope is to lose everything. The Thessalonian Christians had somehow got the idea that their loved ones who had died would not enter the kingdom of God and that only those alive when Jesus came would share in his joy.

'No!' exclaims Paul. 'God will bring with Jesus those who have fallen asleep in him' (verse 14).

Paul then outlines his teaching on Jesus' return:

■ **Jesus will come at the appointed time.** (This is the meaning of the sounding of God's trumpet.) Paul sees this as the consummation of all things, when God's kingdom will triumph over sin and evil.

■ **Those who have died 'in the Lord' will rise first.** They will take priority over the living.

■ **Those who are alive will be caught up to meet the Lord 'in the air'** along with the risen dead. Whatever that may mean, the heart of the message is that both dead and surviving Christians share the same destiny.

■ **Those who believe in Jesus will be with him for ever.** This expresses the most intimate fellowship possible. Just as Jesus the Word was 'with God' in eternity, so believers will share the noblest fellowship of all.

In the beginning of chapter 5 Paul quotes Jesus' own teaching—that no one knows when he will return. That wonderful event will be as sudden and as unexpected as a 'thief in the night'. It could occur today, tomorrow or in a hundred years. For Paul, the important thing was not *when* Christ was coming but *that he is coming*. This fact should motivate the way Christians live—as a people of hope, joy and holiness.

THE MAN OF LAWLESSNESS
2 Thessalonians 2:1–12

A few years after writing the first letter to the Thessalonians, Paul heard that some of the Christians there believed that the day of the Lord had come. Some had even stopped working and were waiting with great eagerness for the blessing to begin!

To help these believers, Paul adds several new features to the teaching he had already given in his first letter. In this intriguing but mysterious passage, we find his expectation that the sign of Christ's coming would be the rise of unprecedented terror, violence and persecution, led by a 'man of lawlessness' But, says Paul, he will be 'restrained' (verses 6, 7). Who or what is the man of lawlessness, and what restrains him? No one really knows. Some scholars believe that Paul had in mind the implacable Jewish opposition to Christianity, which was restrained by the law and moderation of the Roman Empire. If so, Paul's prediction was not fulfilled in the way he expected, because Christ did not come when this persecution waned. Others say this event is a long time in the future, and believe that it refers to the 'beast' in Revelation 13, who will reign temporarily over the earth before the final victory of the Lamb. We cannot be sure of the exact meaning of the passage, but we can be certain that nothing can withstand Christ's coming victory.

The spiritual value of this great doctrine is to alert us to the fact that before Christ's coming things are going to get very black indeed. Many will be led astray and 'unbelievers' deceived. Be on your guard, says Paul, but take heart that God will have the last word; the kingdom of Christ will 'slay' the forces of darkness.

The Message of 1 & 2 Timothy and Titus

R. Wade Paschal Jr

These three short letters—first and second Timothy and Titus—coming at the end of the letters of Paul, are often called the 'Pastoral Letters'. They are called this because of what they are about. The letters are written to individual Christian leaders and contain advice on how to organize or direct the local churches which Paul has assigned to them as his assistants. The three letters are traditionally considered together because of their similarity of style and outlook.

With all their similarities, each of the letters has its own personality:

- 1 Timothy is the longest of the three and the most loosely organized. The letter reads as if Paul were ticking off a list of problems in Timothy's church at Ephesus, addressing each as it came to mind.

- 2 Timothy is written as a farewell letter: Paul is anticipating his approaching death (2 Timothy 4:6). He uses the letter to defend his (and Timothy's) ministry and to warn that people will begin to turn from their faith.

Timothy/Titus OUTLINE

1 TIMOTHY

1:1–11   The problem of false teachers
1:12–20   God's grace to Paul and Timothy
2:1–15   Instructions on holy living
3:1–16   Instructions for bishops and deacons
4:1–10   Critique of false teachers
4:11–5:2   Personal instructions to Timothy
5:3–16   Instructions about widows
5:17–25   The treatment of elders
6:1–2   Instructions to slaves
6:3–10   Warnings about money and greed
6:11–21   Final exhortations

2 TIMOTHY

1:1–7   Paul remembers Timothy's spiritual heritage and calling
1:8–18   Paul gives evidence from his own life about hardship and faith
2:1–13   Paul charges Timothy to work hard and endure sufferings
2:14–26   Paul warns Timothy to avoid disputes and gently correct the erring
3:1–9   Warnings against evil men who teach for personal gain
3:10–17   Exhortation to follow Paul's example and preach God's word diligently
4:1–8   Paul predicts further resistance to the gospel
4:9–22   Final words

TITUS

1:1–9   Guidelines for elders
1:10–16   The tendency of all people toward corruption
2:1–15   Teachings for men, women and slaves
3:1–8   The grace of the gospel
3:9–15   Closing instructions and requests

- Titus seems like a shortened version of 1 Timothy. But it is clearly tailored to events in Crete (Titus 1:5-16) and includes superb short summaries of the gospel Paul preached (Titus 2:11-14; 3:47).

The letters are practical and straightforward. Timothy and Titus are instructed on how to deal with controversies within the church, how to set up or direct church leadership, how to deal with widows in the church, and other down-to-earth problems. These letters are much like the practical sections of Paul's other letters. The lack of a corresponding theological section may reflect the fact that Paul is writing to two associates who already know what he believes. What they need is help in dealing with problems on the ground.

The central theme of these letters, then, is how to be a Christian leader. This is important for Timothy and Titus, and for the elders whom they are to appoint in the churches. There are three main aspects of this theme:

- The character of a Christian leader. The main thrust in the letters, even more central than the practical details, is the character and way of life needed for responsible leaders. Their task is exacting, as they must enter into right relationship with the different age- and interest-groups in the churches, as well as opposing false teachers. Leaders must show an unassailable probity of life, so that no discredit will come to the gospel. They also need to find strength and fearlessness, which the Spirit will give them (2 Timothy 1:7). Paul himself is the apostolic model for the character God requires.

- How to deal with disputes. The false teaching facing the churches is notoriously hard to define. There seem to have been elements of all the doctrinal controversies evident elsewhere in Paul's letters. The best known antidote to such disputes is regular teaching of orthodox Christian truth. That is why teaching is at the centre of what Christian leaders are called on to undertake.

- Enduring hardship. This crops up throughout these letters, but it is the main subject of 2 Timothy. Again Paul puts forward his own experience as an example. He has had to endure much in a long ministry, and his end is now near. But, far from bemoaning his fate, he remains full of gratitude to God for the privilege of serving the gospel.

Small wonder that Christian leaders everywhere have found these three small letters an inspiration.

The date and authorship of these letters is in dispute. They do not correspond with what is known about Paul's life in Acts, and the language and style of the letters is different from the other letters Paul wrote. However, much of this difference is due to the lack of extended theological sections—sections perhaps not needed given Paul's readers. The theology of the letters is thoroughly Pauline where it is found. Since our knowledge of the end of Paul's life is extremely sketchy, it is quite possible to develop an argument that the Pastorals carry Paul's authority. The letters fit well with the situation in Ephesus in the late AD60s and could well have been written by Paul or under his authority by a trusted friend who knew him extremely well (such as Luke).

CHURCH LEADERS
1 Timothy 3:1–13

In the churches of today there are very varied types of church organization and ministry; this is one of the main factors that separate the denominations. And most denominations try to justify their own church structure from what can be seen in the New Testament churches.

This passage, and its partner in Titus 1:5–9, is a favourite source used to justify almost every form of church government. Yet Paul gives us only a sketchy idea of what he means, because that is all Timothy and Titus needed. So it is difficult to extract a single universal system from what we find here.

One plain fact is that 'elders' (or 'presbyters') were to be appointed. The words 'bishop' and 'deacon' may refer to subclasses of elder. The elders were to act as stewards of the churches, probably directing charity work. (Hence the need for honesty and integrity.) They also served as the main teachers and preachers.

Paul dwells on the character needed for elders. His key concern is the moral integrity of the church leaders.

Paul is well aware that non-Christians will judge the whole church and the validity of the gospel of Christ on the basis of how Christians act. The leaders of the church will be held up for severe examination—and they must dedicate themselves to absolutely blameless behaviour. If even the children of the leaders are not well-behaved, blame will fall on the pastor and the church (as ministers know only too well). Harmony within the church depends on fair, objective and even-handed leadership. When leaders are driven by a desire for recognition or personal gain, the church is sure to experience dissension from those who feel they are unfairly treated by the elders (Titus 1:8–9).

The world is waiting for Christians to fail, so that the accusation can be brought 'See, the gospel really doesn't work. They are no better than we are!' Leaders in the church must take on the burden of bearing the world's scrutiny. It is not a light task and is not to be laid on immature Christians or on those motivated by selfish thoughts of gain or pride. The church needs upright, mature leaders in order to maintain its witness and its own internal harmony.

LIVING THE GOSPEL
Titus 2:1—3:7

Titus chapter 2 is typical of the general practical instructions in the Pastoral Letters. Titus is told to exhort the men to be 'sensible' and 'steadfast'. The women are to be reverent and good housekeepers, not giving way to petty habits of gossip or carrying tales. Young men are to exercise self-control. Titus himself is urged to be a model of Christian behaviour, combining sound teaching with good deeds.

To some, the sex roles described may seem to belong to a different age. And the whole thing may smack of a legalistic and narrow-minded traditionalism. But Paul didn't mean it that way. He saw good deeds and a godly lifestyle as the outflow of our salvation. We are redeemed 'from all wickedness', and so as a natural consequence we become people who belong to God and 'are eager to do good' (2:14).

To continue to sin makes nonsense of our salvation. All the wrong things that belong to our life before Christ are destructive—selfishness, envy, false pride. These things lead us to hate and destroy one another (3:3). If we are saved through Christ, these things must be replaced by love, kindness and goodness. These qualities build people up and make life a good thing.

In chapter 3 verse 5 Paul shows clearly that this is not a new legalism. We are not saved because we do good deeds. We do not even do good deeds under our own power. We are saved because God showed us mercy in Jesus Christ. And we find the power to live a new life because the Holy Spirit washes and renews us and transforms our minds and wills.

The power of the gospel should be visible in the church. This does not mean there will be no conflict or controversy. Disagreements do happen, even between people of good will, because of personality differences and differing priorities.

However, the church should act out of concern for others rather than from self-centred pride. We should be able to disagree and yet still care for one another. If we still have controversies and arguments laced with malice and strife, then that shows how far we are from fully experiencing the mercy of God in Jesus Christ. And that is one good reason why we still need teachers like Titus to remind us how the gospel affects our own lives.

The Message of Philemon

George Carey

This tiny letter gives us a splendid illustration of the transforming power of love. Philemon was a Christian businessman living in Colossae and, like most wealthy people of his time, he had slaves. No doubt as a Christian he treated his slaves very well and he must have felt badly let down when one of them, Onesimus, ran away to Rome. But you cannot run away from God's love. In Rome, the lonely Onesimus met up with Paul and became a Christian.

It is almost certain that Paul wrote this personal letter at the same time as he wrote Colossians, about AD63. The purpose was, of course, to tell Philemon the exciting news of Onesimus' conversion and ask him to forgive the man for running away, and take him back as a Christian brother. He knew that Philemon felt mistreated by his runaway slave and so pleads with him to recognize a change of heart.

Neither here nor elsewhere does Paul ever attack the social evil of slavery. Christianity was too weak at that time to do so anyway. But he does undermine slavery by making all slaves and all free people equal in the Christian family. 'I am sending him back,' says Paul, 'no longer as a slave but as a beloved brother . . . both in the flesh and in the Lord.' There is no mistaking here the radical effects of the Christian message which has power to liberate those bound by all forms of oppression in society. Paul sets us a marvellous example that within the Christian family the transforming nature of love should mark all our relationships. Indeed, this love is strong enough to break down the barriers that human sin builds.

The Message of Hebrews

Joy Tetley

From beginning to end, the letter to the Hebrews proclaims with vivid and penetrating intensity 'the living God'— who he is and what he does. The original background and context of the letter are swathed in mystery, but its essential message speaks loud and clear across the centuries. There could be no more relevant message for us today: the God who is greater than the whole immensity of the universe, and the source of its existence, the God whose divine majesty should excite worship 'with reverence and awe' is the God who in Jesus his Son has laid bare his heart.

When we look to Jesus, we see what God is like. For Jesus 'is the radiance of God's glory and the exact representation of his being' (1:3). And the nature of God as we see him in Jesus is to reach out and communicate (1:1). He longs to draw humanity into that intimate relationship with himself which he had planned from the beginning (see chapter 2), and he is willing to go to staggering lengths to make that relationship a reality for those who will accept it. For in Jesus his Son, God identified himself totally with the human condition and so became utterly vulnerable, subjecting himself to temptation, suffering and death (see, for example, 2:17; 4:15). He opened himself to 'the ravages of sin', feeling the full destructive force of all that had warped his world, and yet was not overcome by it. We can therefore approach God with complete confidence that he himself,

Hebrews OUTLINE

1:1–4 Introductory sentence: God has spoken through his Son

1:5–10:18 Jesus Christ is greater than any alternative

1:5–14   The Son of God is greater than the angels

2:1–4   The need to pay attention to the gospel

2:5–18   Jesus our pioneer

3:1–6   The Son of God is greater than Moses

3:7–19   The need for confident faith and the dangers of unbelief

4:1–11   The promise of God's rest

4:12–16   Open before God

5:1–10   Jesus our great high priest

5:11–6:12   The need to grow in faith and a warning against abandoning Christ

6:13–20   God's promise is sure

7:1–28   Jesus the high priest after the order of Melchizedek

8:1–9:28   Jesus the mediator of a new covenant

10:1–18   The unique sacrifice of the Son of God

10:19–12:29 Faith and perseverance

10:19–39   A call to perseverance

11:1–40   The value of faith and its old–covenant heroes

12:1–2   Looking to Jesus

12:3–11   The training of God's children

12:12–29   Living in the light of the sure and certain hope of heaven

13:1–25 Concluding exhortation, prayer and greetings

13:1–17   A guide to Christian living

13:18–25   Concluding prayers and greetings

through his experience in Jesus, knows what it is like to be a human being, with all its pressures and hardships.

Two things about God, then, leap out at us from this letter:

- God knows. That in itself is a liberating message. But for the writer of Hebrews there is more—much more. God, he asserts, can offer us more than sympathy, encouraging though this is.

- God not only knows; he acts. He offers us a 'new and living way' into his presence, a blessing which carries with it forgiveness, freedom from bondage to the fear of death, the privilege of being God's children and citizens of the world to come, the prospect of fulness of life through all eternity and the experience here and now of moving towards that perfect wholeness of being. In other words he offers the salvation for which he made us. It is an astonishing and comprehensive offer—and all the more so because its cost was willingly and painfully borne by the Son in whom God expressed his own being. At tremendous cost to himself God has acted to break the power of sin and death and to open the way for all who persevere in following Jesus to find their destiny.

Precisely *how* this can be so, only God can adequately explain. Our author, like the other New Testament writers, can only use imagery which would be familiar to his community as he tries to put into words a truth which is more surely taken in through worship and experience than by rational analysis. The imagery on which the writer of Hebrews focusses most attention is taken from the Old Testament tradition of priesthood and sacrifice. It is likely that he was himself a Jew and that those whom he was addressing shared a Jewish heritage. For the modern reader not quite so soaked in the Old Testament, such imagery can at first sight throw up something of a barrier, so it is important to identify the fundamental points being made.

The task of the priest is to help in establishing a positive relationship between humanity and God. Such a relationship is God's dearest wish, and we see from the Old Testament what detailed provision he made to enable his people to communicate with him. A major part of that provision was the system of sacrifices and the priestly activities associated with it, particularly as a way of cleansing from sin (the book of Leviticus is particularly concerned with this). The writer of Hebrews argues that God in his Son has offered a sacrifice which is fully and finally effective. Unlike the sacrifices of the old covenant, which had to be constantly repeated, it is 'once for all'. And it can cleanse a person totally, for the one who offers it is the 'exact representation' of God's being and the sacrifice he offers is himself. God in Jesus is thus both great high priest and spotless victim. This insight is unique in the New Testament. Perhaps we can best express it today by saying that God willingly 'sacrifices' what is closest to his heart, and 'goes through hell', so that we may feel confident enough to enter into loving relationship with him.

Such ultimate sacrifice cries out for response, and the writer of Hebrews spells out in no uncertain terms the need to take advantage of God's astounding offer. Doing so will involve embarking on a pilgrimage; hardship and persecution will by no means be excluded from the journey. But with steadfast endurance and constant looking to Jesus it will surely lead to eternal glory.

GOD HAS SPOKEN
Hebrews 1:1–4

It is as easy today as it ever was to be attracted to false gods or trapped in false or distorted ideas about the true God. This passage speaks of God revealing to us with full clarity what he is really like.

As originally written, these verses are made up of just one sentence—and there can be few more telling opening sentences in the whole of the New Testament. Right at the beginning of his letter, the writer gives us a concentrated summary of his message and his words evoke a response of wondering adoration. This is 'theological poetry' of the highest order.

The sentence is thoroughly God-centred (as should be our faith). God is the subject and all that is said about the Son must be understood in this light. God has communicated in the past 'many times and in many ways', but in his Son he has spoken his final and definitive word. So if we want to know for sure what God is like and how he acts, we must look to Jesus his Son, in whom he expresses himself most completely.

According to these verses, God's Son shares with his Father in making, ruling and sustaining the universe. He is greater even than the angels. He is prophet (God's mouthpiece), priest (cleansing from sin) and king (seated at God's right hand). And in all this he gives us a vision of God—a God of infinite majesty and power who is so full of concern for his human children that he comes down to our level and cleanses us from the dirt of sin.

The rest of the letter will make it clear just how much this cost him. As we ponder these verses, we can only worship and adore this most surprising God.

JESUS OUR TRAIL-BLAZER
Hebrews 2:5–18

In this passage, we see the utter humility of the Son of God and his liberating power. This Son, already described as 'the radiance of God's glory and the exact representation of his being', became totally human, vulnerable to all the pressures of human existence. He was tempted, he suffered, he died and yet through it all he gave us the perfect picture of what God intends human beings to be like.

The writer of Hebrews uses an Old Testament psalm (Psalm 8) to help convey this astonishing truth. God made humanity only a little lower than the angels, to be crowned with glory and honour and to have dominion over all things. As we are well aware, our destiny has not yet been fully realized (verse 8), but in Jesus we see it as a glorious possibility. In going through human experience, and most particularly in tasting death without being destroyed by it, Jesus has opened the way for us to follow. He is the 'pioneer' (verse 10), blazing the trail ahead of us. He is our brother (verse 12), who has shared our common humanity and broken the stranglehold of our mortality (verses 14–15). He is our merciful and faithful high priest who can set aside our sins, unite us with God and bring us understanding help when we are tempted.

Such a message speaks deeply to our suffering world, enslaved on the one hand by potentially all-destructive delusions of grandeur and on the other by a crippling awareness of weakness and failure to love. Jesus can set us free from our slavery. We have only to turn to him.

OPEN BEFORE GOD
Hebrews 4:12–16

When read with any sensitivity, the first two verses of this passage send shivers down the spine, for they proclaim the penetrating and all-seeing sovereignty of God. Absolutely nothing can be hidden from him, and when we experience the activity of the living God through his word, it pierces into the very core of our being. Like Adam and Eve in the Garden of Eden we may try to hide from God our nakedness, our failures, but he will surely find us out. Whatever strategies we may employ to cover ourselves (even using the cloak of 'religious respectability'), God will see through our disguises. Our imperfections lie open to him. And it is to him that we must finally give account. It is a chilling picture of how humanity stands before God.

Yet the remaining verses of our passage (verses 14 to 16) lead us from potential despair to confident hope. The God to whom we must give account is the God who has revealed in Jesus what he is like. And Jesus can identify with us in our weaknesses, he is our high priest at the heart of God, expressing God's longing that we should be one with him.

We have no need to hide. We can approach God's throne 'bravely', or 'with confidence'. The word in verse 16 suggests the boldness of complete honesty. We can come before God just as we are and know for sure that he will not only understand, but also show mercy and give us the grace we so much need.

We simply need to come close to God. Then we will know ourselves accepted, supported and transformed by the God who sees into the secret recesses of our hearts and understands from the inside what he sees.

JESUS OUR GREAT HIGH PRIEST
Hebrews 5:1–10

We see from this passage that the writer of Hebrews is a compelling preacher with a passionately pastoral heart. These verses are rather like a mini-sermon with three main points, exploring the Old Testament theme of high priesthood in the light of Jesus Christ:

■ **Every high priest is appointed 'to offer gifts and sacrifices for sins'** (verse 1). As the writer stresses elsewhere, Christ's sacrifice is final and totally effective. Christ our great high priest is 'the source of eternal salvation for all who obey him' (verse 9). That gives us the deepest reassurance.

■ **A high priest can deal gently with those who are ignorant and make mistakes since he himself is weak** (verses 2 and 3). That is an extraordinary statement, for nowhere in the Old Testament are pastoral sympathy and gentle care presented as a feature of priesthood. The writer's view here seems to be greatly coloured by his experience of Christ the high priest, who 'in his life on earth made his prayers and requests with loud cries and tears' (verse 7). The Son of God knew weakness, fear and anguish from the inside and he was not afraid to express in prayer just how he felt. And so he ministers to us with the sympathy born of personal experience. That should encourage us to trust him enough to follow his example, by coming to God in all the rawness of our feeling and the reality of our human frailty. Like him we shall surely be accepted and heard.

■ **Just as no high priest takes the honour on himself but is called by God (verse 4), so Christ's high priesthood is by God's vocation and appointment (verses 5 and 6).** It is a royal and essentially mysterious priesthood, like that of the enigmatic Melchizedek, mentioned in Psalm 110 and in Genesis chapter 14. It is also the priesthood of one who expresses God's very being (verse 5), so we can trust him with our lives even when our minds cannot fully comprehend.

THE SACRIFICE OF THE SON OF GOD
Hebrews 10:1–18

These verses are sometimes regarded as a summary of the author's teaching. They set before us the shadow and the substance of God's dealings with us.

■ **The shadow is seen in the Old Testament sacrifices.** The first four verses hammer home the message that animal sacrifices cannot take away sins. Outward sacrifices cannot lead to inner cleanliness! Indeed, repeated 'year after year', sacrifices confront their offerers with a vivid, annual reminder of the grim reality of their sin and that they are incapable of escaping from its power. At best, such sacrifices can only be regarded as 'a shadow' of that supreme self-offering of the Son of God (verse 1). A shadow has a direct connexion with the object that is casting it, but it gives only an indirect picture and can often distort the object's basic shape. How foolish, then, to focus on inadequate and potentially distorting shadows when we can find 'the realities themselves' by looking straight into the face of Jesus and finding there God's lasting forgiveness, and inward transformation.

■ **The substance came with Jesus.** In verses 5 to 14, we focus on him—and what a humbling sight we see. We see the eternal Son of God, the 'radiance of God's glory', willingly consenting to enter the world of human experience. We see him taking on a body prepared by God which will be given over to the suffering of death (verse 10), so that we can be 'made perfect for ever' (verse 14). In so doing, he defines true sacrifice as the offering to God of a totally dedicated life, ready for anything that might be required to show God's love to a needy world.

Verses 15 to 18 declare that Christ's sacrifice has brought into being the new covenant, that new order of things looked forward to by the prophet Jeremiah. God will now be experienced within ourselves, ministering that love which both forgives and forgets. It is to the same kind of service that he calls all who respond to his suffering and costly love.

A WARNING
Hebrews 10:26–31

From his letter as a whole, it is clear that the author had an urgent and passionate concern for the community to whom he was writing. Apparently they were in some danger of rejecting the Christian message and thus throwing away all the blessings and benefits it offered. To keep them on the right track (the way of Jesus), the writer stresses all the good results that follow from being loyal to Christ. But also, here and in other passages, he paints a vivid picture of what will follow if people deliberately and cruelly turn against the living God, having once known and received his love. Again the picture of judgment is portrayed in essentially Old Testament imagery (verses 27–29). Today we might perhaps express it in different terms, but the reality remains. What happens to those who accept God and then turn violently against him? (We assume here that it is the true God whom they reject and not some wrongly preached parody.) By their very action they close themselves off from God's loving mercy. To be effective, love and forgiveness have to be accepted.

The strong language of verse 29 leaves us in no doubt that those who shut themselves off from God's love are extreme and wilful in rejecting his Son. They treat him with utter contempt, even though once they were content to receive his gifts. These are not 'everyday sinners': still less are they those whose pain and distress make them feel angry with God. Such are always welcome at the throne of grace and will find there understanding and grace to help. No, these are people who decisively choose to reject God.

It is indeed a fearful thing to fall into the hands of the living God. But if we are aware of our need and of the depths of God's mercy, the only 'raging fire' we shall encounter is the burning and purifying heat of his holy love.

LOOKING TO JESUS
Hebrews 12:1–3

'Let us keep our eyes fixed on Jesus' (verse 2). This phrase puts the writer's whole message in a nutshell. It is Jesus who must be the focal point of our lives, Jesus who is the perfect expression of God. When we look to Jesus we are so drawn by his understanding and encouraging love that we can begin to let go of those things that weigh us down and trip us up (verse 1). Like athletes stripped for a race we can make singlemindedly for the finishing line, where we fall into the arms of one who has run the race himself and can share with us the joy of God.

The race caused Jesus much pain. It brought him hostility, shame and a criminal's death (verses 2 and 3). His followers cannot expect to escape suffering, but they have at their disposal all the resources of God who in Jesus knows the problems from the inside. When they fix their eyes on Jesus, they receive his strength to keep going.

But if the Christian 'race' is not a fun-run, neither is it a competitive first-past-the-post affair. Followers of Jesus are engaged in a corporate marathon in which all go at their own pace and all at the end receive the same heavenly reward. There could be nothing further from the modern world's widespread and enervating 'rat-race'.

The writer speaks of Christians being surrounded by a 'great cloud of witnesses'. Here are the spectators in the stadium cheering on the runners down on the track: a vast sea of faces made up of those who have remained faithful to God through life and death. This great company of heaven, though invisible to earthly eyes, is a living reality, an unseen and powerful supporters' club for those still running the race that is set before them.

A PICTURE OF HEAVEN
Hebrews 12:18–24

Here is nothing less than a vivid impression of heaven. And the amazing message is that followers of Jesus on earth can experience even now something of heaven's lively joy.

The writer points up the wonder of it all by first stressing what heaven is not (verses 18 to 21). He is very likely addressing Jewish Christians, so he uses terminology they would readily understand. Jewish tradition taught strongly that the holy God was unapproachable. Mere creatures, polluted by sin, could not survive a direct experience of God's presence. The precise reference in this passage is to God giving the Law on Mount Sinai (see Exodus chapters 19 and 20), when even Moses, God's chosen servant, trembled with fear.

Alongside this terrifying picture is portrayed the Christian vision (verses 22 to 24). The God who is indeed 'the judge of all' can be approached without fear by those who 'fix their eyes on Jesus' (12:2). Jesus is 'the mediator of a new covenant', the one who opens the way to a new and confident relationship with God whose nature it is to forgive (see the chapter on *Covenant*). Mount Zion, the new and heavenly Jerusalem, holds no terrors for those who trust in Jesus. It is peopled by a joyful community of angels and faithful ones, now enjoying perfect fulness of life. And when Christians on earth take advantage of their free access to the living God they are entering now this city which is their true and eternal home.

What practical difference does it make if we believe the Bible's teaching on heaven? Surely that it gives us a much-needed and healing sense of perspective in an anxious and troubled world.

The Message of James

Enio Mueller

The letter of James seems to have been written to some poor churches, struggling to preserve their purity and faithfulness to Jesus. Their poor members lived among rich people who exploited them in many ways (see 2:15–16), and some of these rich people also belonged to the church (1:10). So there were problems.

In our own day a growing number of Christians in the southern hemisphere belong to 'churches of the poor', and they see many of their concerns mirrored in this letter.

The letter consists of a sequence of what seem to be loosely-connected exhortations, dealing with everyday life. Verses 2 to 8 of chapter 1 set the scene. Trials and temptations must be faced with joy, because that way they lead on to maturity. But this calls for wisdom, which God gives to all who ask in faith. The rest of the letter shows how to live according to this wisdom, especially if you are poor, but also if you are rich:

● Poverty brings its own temptations, and this despite many promises offered to 'the poor'. God has chosen the poor to inherit the kingdom (2:5; compare with the Beatitudes, Matthew 5:3). He blesses them by lifting them up, whereas he blesses the rich by bringing them down (1:9–10; compare with the Magnificat, Luke 1:52–53). The core of worldliness is to let social status influence how we treat

people (1:27; 2:4). Some of the temptations mentioned in chapter 3—jealousy, bitterness, selfishness—are more acute for poor people. And the 'wanting what you cannot have' of chapter 4 verse 2, which leads to so much trouble, comes into the same category.

● Wealth brings temptations, too. The language used of the sins of the rich is

James OUTLINE

decidedly strong. Wealthy people are tempted to live self-sufficiently (4:13–16), to be proud of themselves rather than humble before God (4:6–9), to be friends with the world and so God's enemies (4:4). The richer people get, the more they want, and other people's rights are forgotten (5:1–6). In the well-known discussion of faith and works, the example given of dead and useless faith is when people who have enough neglect those who are poor (2:14–17).

Naturally, material concerns are not the only ones in this letter. But they are central, and should not be spiritualized away. Other parts of the letter, however, are equally relevant to everyone, rich or poor. We should all love our neighbours, live pure and consistent lives in speech and action, resist the devil without and evil desires within. We should wait patiently for Christ to return, expecting the 'crown of life'. A major theme is prayer, especially for wisdom (1:5) and for healing (5:14–18). Prayer should come from right motives (4:1–3) and must be without the doublemindedness of doubt (1:6–8).

FAITH AND WORKS
James 2:14–26

What saves us? Faith or deeds? This passage is often contrasted with Paul's teaching about faith, but that was not the original question. Some people claim to have faith but give no concrete evidence of it. What should we make of their claim? So this is not about faith versus works, but about the kind of faith that belongs to the gospel and salvation.

■ **All Christians have faith.** This whole letter presupposes that faith is an essential part of a Christian's life.

■ **But there is faith and there is faith.** Some people show only an intellectual or 'religious' faith. Demons have this faith, and it makes them shudder. But to some people it seems to give a warm self-satisfaction (verse 16), particularly among the well-to-do.

■ **Can such faith save us?** No. It is good for nothing (verse 16), useless (verse 20), dead (verses 17 and 26).

■ **What, then, is living faith?** Here and throughout the letter this question is repeatedly answered. Real faith will be expressed in action (verses 14 to 17). Faith and deeds are not two independent entities which have to be brought together; real faith requires deeds or it is not real faith. The two are one organic whole. The stories of Abraham and of Rahab illustrate this perfectly, so that the conclusion in verse 24 is inescapable.

■ **What deeds is James talking about?** To answer this properly, we need to read the whole letter, which is about this very question. But verses 15 and 16 give a concrete example—meeting meeting people's physical needs. Abraham and Rahab are examples of people who risked their lives or sacrificed their best for their faith. James illustrates again and again the kind of life which shows the reality of an authentic faith.

THE RICH AND THE POOR
James 2:1–7; 5:1–6

Few themes are more controversial in our times than this one. And this is understandable, because here we touch things essential for our very existence. On one side, the Bible tells us with fair clarity how God intends his creation to be. (It is a repeated theme in the prophets.) On the other, we have the world as it actually is—full of remarkable differences and distinctions between people. We live in a world marked by gross inequality in the distribution of and access to material goods. And this involves Christians as well.

In the message of James, we saw that this problem was at the heart of the church's dilemma. These two passages are among the most explicit.

- **There were apparently very rich people and very poor people in the same church** (5:1; 2:2). The rich were very unjust in the way they came by their wealth and how they treated those who worked for them. We are not told whether these rich people were Christians, but God's word is addressed to them. This is an example of the church's prophetic voice, which always needs to be heard. Read again the strong words in chapter 5 verses 1 and 5.

- **There must be no favouritism among Christians.** Centuries of discrimination between rich and poor have led to deeply ingrained inequalities. And these are often repeated in the church. But this is to be condemned, because in Christ all are equal (see Galatians 3:28).

- **If there is favouritism on God's part, it is towards the poor** (2:5). In the world all the cards are in the hands of the rich, so, to compensate, God is particularly the protector of the weak and oppressed. It is a matter of simple justice.

- **The church has often acted as shown in chapter 2 verses 1 to 4,** insulting the poor (2:6) and 'showing contempt for their Maker' (Proverbs 14:31). It is even worse when Christians act in the way described in chapter 5 verses 1 to 6. It is time to reverse any such tendencies, and to show more love and respect for God by showing more love and respect for the poor of the world.

The Message of 1 Peter

Enio Mueller

Peter—there is good reason to think this letter comes from him—appeals to his Christian readers as 'aliens and strangers' (2:11). The two words he uses were legal terms describing categories of 'second-class citizen' in the Roman Empire. 'Resident aliens' were foreigners with permanent residence but inferior social status, or poor people who never achieved full citizenship. 'Visiting strangers' were people without permanent residence, who were living in a country for some time.

There were, then, legal barriers against immigrants at that time, as there are in many countries today, including Western states. Discrimination, too, against poor countries and against immigrants is felt intensely by those who suffer it.

There are many signs in this letter that the Christians of Asia Minor (modern Turkey) for whom Peter wrote were drawn largely from these groups (see 1:2, 17; 2:18). And so they could feel from their own experience what is true of Christians everywhere, that we are in some ways separated from mainstream society.

Something real and tangible has happened to change the whole course of

1 Peter OUTLINE

our lives—Peter calls it 'new birth' (1:3). We now have a new and high calling in Christ (2:9–10). And our beliefs and lifestyles are no longer the same as those of our fellow-citizens. We have become 'aliens and strangers'.

1 Peter is a letter of encouragement for Christians, helping them find their bearings in a society that seems not to understand them any more, and which presents them with many problems. Through the letter there runs an apparent paradox, which is really the great dilemma of Christians in the world:

- Christians must maintain their distinctiveness, even at the cost of being misinterpreted by their fellows. Indeed, it seems that many were beginning to be persecuted by the state (see, for example, 1:6–7; 4:12–19).

- But, separate though they are, they must not opt out of society. On the contrary, this is where they must live, and live so that everything about them becomes a practical demonstration of the gospel (2:9, 12, 15; 3:1, 15). '... They will have to recognize your good deeds and so praise God.'

LIVING IN SOCIETY
1 Peter 2:11–20; 3:1–12

'Your light must shine before people, so that they will see the good things you do and praise your Father in heaven.' So says Jesus in the Sermon on the Mount, and Peter echoes him in verse 12 of this passage. Then he goes on to show some ways in which this general principle can be put into practice:

■ **Christians should discipline themselves** (2:11). Only then will those who live alongside them in society see in their lives an expression of God. Perhaps, for many now as then, this will be the only way to grasp God's reality.

■ **They should live consistently in society at large** (verses 13 to 17). In public life, the order is: 'For the sake of the Lord submit to every human authority.'

Is this just a repeat of Paul's instruction in Romans 13? There are reasons from the letter to understand it rather differently. One is the reference in chapter 5 verse 13 to Rome as 'Babylon', a code-name used in the book of Revelation for that empire as evil and oppressive, so much so that in Revelation 13 it is pictured as 'the beast from the sea', totally hostile to God. Christians are to be obedient citizens, in other words, but not to carry any illusions about the corruptibility of political power, nor to be naively co-opted by those in authority. They are to act as 'free people' (verse 16), freely choosing to submit to authority, but reserving the duty to obey only God when the two authorities conflict.

■ **They should act considerately in their households,** as servants in 2:18–20; as husbands and wives in 3:1–7. (The idea of a 'household' includes both family and household servants, and can readily cover today's farms, small factories and commercial units. It was the focus for the spread of Christianity in the first century.) Servants (workers) are to act with integrity whatever the circumstances. Wives are to live respectfully and attractively. Husbands should be thoughtful and helpful.

We are all called to 'strive for peace with all our hearts' (3:11), and to live so as to give reality to the 'reverence for Christ' within us.

JESUS, THE SUPREME MODEL
1 Peter 2:21–25

Peter is writing about servants suffering unjustly. This immediately brings into his mind a picture of Jesus, the 'servant of God' prophesied in Isaiah 53, suffering unjustly for us all. He meditates on that passage, and echoes it repeatedly in these verses.

Jesus the servant was blameless, but, partly for that very reason, he was made to suffer. Yet his suffering heals us all. He is the supreme model for all who are persecuted and oppressed.

What mental image do we have of Jesus Christ? It is a vital question, because on the answer will depend how we see ourselves as Christians.

Traditional Western Christianity has, because of its history, seen Jesus mainly as heavenly Ruler and exalted Lord. So Christianity has sometimes become an instrument of domination, or has acquiesced in the West's colonial or economic dominance over other nations.

Latin Americans, under Spanish and Portuguese influence, have often seen Jesus as the sweet infant sleeping in his mother's arms. This image has had a complex pattern of effects on Christian behaviour.

In poor and oppressed countries in today's world, Christians seem to be rediscovering Peter's picture of Jesus the suffering servant. By its nature, this is the hardest one to cope with. It requires that we give up all that the world teaches us is essential to human personality and a successful life.

We are called in this picture of Christ to be not rulers but servants, on the side not of the oppressors but of the oppressed. And having before our eyes the servant Jesus, we must be a servant church, becoming in the world a ferment of love, peace and justice.

The Message of 2 Peter and Jude

George Carey

The letters of 2 Peter and Jude were written late in the first century when false teaching was beginning to be a problem to the Christian church. Two features of their teaching were particularly dangerous. First, they were saying that, as the second coming of Jesus had not happened, clearly the Christian hope was without foundation. 'Where is the promise of his coming?' they scoffed. He was not going to appear. Second, they taught that the really 'spiritually enlightened' person knew that as this world is worthless it does not matter what you do with your body. Morality was therefore a matter of indifference and purity was old-fashioned.

Both 2 Peter and Jude meet this by emphasizing that the promises of God are totally reliable, based on the life and resurrection of Jesus. Even though it might seem that the second coming was delayed, Christians should remember that a day in the sight of the Lord is as a thousand years. God is not slow or slack in keeping his promises. If he delays his coming, it is because he is a merciful Lord who wants as many people as possible to have the chance of salvation.

Such is the writers' concern for the truth that both these letters release the most savage attacks on these false teachers. Their readers are urged not to follow the scepticism and immorality of such teachers but to live upright lives in which the purity, goodness and power of Jesus shine through. 'Therefore,' urges 2 Peter, 'be all the more eager to make your calling and election sure' (1:10). And Jude echoes this exhortation: 'Build yourselves up in your most holy faith and pray in the Holy Spirit. Keep yourselves in God's love' (verses 20–21).

2 Peter OUTLINE

1:1–2   Greetings
1:3–15   Knowing God and his calling
1:16–21   Knowing God's message
2:1–22   False teachers and how to resist them
(this chapter has many parallels with the letter of Jude)
3:1–18   The final coming of Christ

The Message of 1 John

Christopher Lamb

The author writes with great authority to Christians whom he frequently calls his children. He seems to speak from the long experience of an older generation which actually lived with Jesus. He uses that authority both to reassure and to warn his readers.

The truth is that God sent life itself, his own life, into the world in the person of Jesus. So those who share that life will be marked with the same gift of self-giving love. Of course people go astray, for no one is yet perfect, but any hatred is totally out of place. There are those who mislead people, and others who have already left the Christian fellowship, yet all have passed through the same experience of being accepted into the church. So how does one judge who is right?

True Christians can be recognized by their care for others, and their grasp of the reality of Jesus Christ's coming into the world. It seems that some have been causing confusion in the church by saying that Jesus was not fully human, or did not really suffer on the cross. They thought perhaps that he was some angelic messenger, and not truly the Son of God.

John does not develop his letter point by point. Rather he states and re-states his themes like a composer arranging a series of simple notes. You can open the letter at almost any stage and read some variation of his basic message. He wants his readers to be confident that God is love and that he sent his Son to show us just what that means. But he is also concerned that they should not be taken in, but learn to test those who claim to be spiritually guided.

John might have been writing for our own time. For today many people are again searching for a way of life inspired by God, and all sorts of religious groups have become popular. Again we need to apply the tests recommended by John. Are people being taught to love or to hate? Do they simply pass by those in need? What place do they have for Jesus in their lives? If God is a God of love for them, how do they see that love most clearly shown?

1 John OUTLINE

LIVING IN THE LIGHT
1 John 1:5–10

The message that we human beings are sinners looks like bad news. Yet coming to terms with our spiritual state is as important as an honest diagnosis of our medical condition. We have nothing to gain by covering up the truth about ourselves. Once we are naked on the couch of the divine physician and under the light of his examining, we cannot argue with his assessment of our state.

Our personal lives may be much like other people's, neither dramatically sinful nor full of shining virtue. But we still need to repent for the society we live in, for the worldwide injustice which benefits us economically, for the torture, rape and murder which our societies fail to prevent.

If the diagnosis were all there was to help us, we should certainly be reluctant to know the full truth about ourselves. Thankfully, there is also prescription, treatment and cure.

God's light is not the merciless light which only exposes and does not heal. We are called to submit to that light, to relax and be at home in it, and to share our lives with others who have come along the same path. When that happens there is a common energy and purpose running through us all. We become part of one another. And the effect of the death of Jesus continually works through all our lives, purifying and changing and renewing us, like a body being healed. Only one thing is required of us—a fundamental honesty, and a deep intention to search for the healing truth of God and share it with our whole world.

THE CHILDREN OF GOD
1 John 2:28—3:3

Genesis, the first book of the Bible, tells us that God made men and women in his own image. They were not like him in looks, but they were intended to be like him. In spite of the desperate evil in the world, it is still possible to look at human beings and catch a glimpse of what God must be like.

In some followers of Jesus we can already see the family likeness. Our hope is that this will grow in us so that when he comes, he will recognize us as his own. John hints that there are others, 'not of this fold' who are his children too, for 'every man who does right is his child.'

John wrote to tiny Christian communities, probably scattered in the small towns of what is now western Turkey. Most of the people at that time must have been quite unaware of them. The churches survived and grew because of the quality of the lives of ordinary Christian believers and the depth of their convictions. We have inherited the advantages which they and countless succeeding generations have created for us, as well as the mistakes and failures of the past.

Despite the numerical size, and the wealth and influence of the international church, the fundamental situation is no different from that of those first generations. God, for his own reasons, has honoured us in making us his children, to show his likeness to his world and to understand that world as his inheritance to us. We live in the hope of becoming recognizably like him, and we continually exert ourselves to live up to the immense measure of our calling.

TESTING THE SPIRITUAL LEADERS
1 John 4:1–6

There are many gurus and 'people of God' in today's world, both in the Christian and other religious communities. Some are genuinely humble people; some are mistaken; a few are fraudulent or mad. Many are led astray by the flattery of their followers, for it is a heady experience to have your every word treated as a message straight from God. Many people today seem to need a living idol or an infallible guide as an escape from cynicism or despair.

. John warns his readers not to be taken in by every claim to spiritual authority, but to 'test the spirits' to see whether they genuinely come from God. The test is their reaction to the name and claims of Jesus. In John's day, there were those who denied that Jesus had been a genuine human being. This meant that his death was not real, and therefore it did not mean anything and neither did the resurrection. If this is so, then the life of Jesus can only set us an example, alongside other examples. Even if it is the best example, it cannot save us.

Exactly the same view of Jesus is held by many in our own time, especially among those influenced by Eastern religious traditions. It is impossible always to avoid controversy, but Christians have to find ways of asserting the true significance of Jesus without giving needless offence, or denying the genuine elements of truth within other religious traditions. It may sometimes seem impossible, but 'he who inspires you is greater than he who inspires the godless world', and who locks people into a prison of this-worldly thinking. The Spirit of Jesus is the true liberating and converting power in the world.

The Message of 2 & 3 John

Christopher Lamb

It is difficult to reconstruct the situation which these two letters address, but the same false teaching mentioned in 1 John is clearly a problem (2 John 7). The author responds by urging the same command of mutual love (2 John 5–6) and the same assurance that the one who does right is a child of God (3 John 11).

The author expresses much affection for his readers, but there is clearly trouble in the church, and destructive elements among its leadership. The different churches keep in touch with one another by the constant travels of some members, who therefore deserve all support (3 John 5–6). Nevertheless the Elder (who may not be the same as the author of 1 John) is prepared to violate the sacred law of hospitality where 'deceivers' are concerned (2 John 10). For truth matters as well as love. Controversy in the church is nothing new.

2 and 3 John OUTLINE

2:1–3   Greetings to a congregation well-known to the writer

2:4–6   The law of love which you had from the beginning

2:7–13   How deceivers are to be dealt with in the church

3:1–4   Greetings and encouragement to a church leader

3:5–15   Trouble in the church

The message of Revelation

Stephen H. Travis

We none of us need persuading that Revelation is a difficult book. Yet wherever Christians face persecution it speaks with fresh power.

The very first verses explain what the book is, and show us how to approach it.

- It is 'the revelation (or apocalypse)

Revelation OUTLINE

1:1–20 Prologue John announces that he has received from Jesus Christ a revelation of God's purposes in history

2:1–3:22 Letters to the seven churches Christ's messages of warning and encouragement to particular churches

4:1–5:14 A vision of heaven. A glimpse into heaven, where a true perspective is given on the purpose of God and the events of history
4:1–11 All that exists, exists by God's creative will
5:1–14 The saving work of Christ, the sacrificed lamb, is the key to understanding God's purposes. (Out of this follows the rest of the book. The lamb has authority to open the seven seals, and so sets in motion the acts of judgment which come in chapters 6 to 19.)

6:1–17 & 8:1 The seven seals A description of events leading up to the final coming of Christ. (The **seven seals, seven trumpets and seven bowls**—see below—are different accounts of the same period of history, not accounts of three periods following one after another. Each group of seven includes reference to human evil expressed in war and oppression, to natural disasters, to persecution of God's people, and to the triumph of Christ. They echo Jesus' predictions in Mark 13, Matthew 24 and Luke 21.)

7:1–17 First interlude: the church secure in God's care
7:1–8 The 144,000, sealed for protection, represent all God's people
7:9–17 Multitudes from every nation will worship Christ in his triumph

8:2–9:21 & 11:15–19 The seven trumpets

10:1–11:14 Second interlude: the church's task, to witness in the face of suffering
10:1–11 The angel with the little scroll promises no more delay, instructs John to witness to people who refuse to repent
11:1–14 Two witnesses, reminiscent of Moses and Elijah, symbolize the church's prophetic task in face of persecution by the beast, who is antichrist

12:1–14:20 Third interlude: conflict between the church and evil powers This central section of the book sets the conflict between church and state against the background of the age–long battle between God and the powers of darkness. The lamb (Christ) does battle with the dragon (Satan). This is the story of history. But Christ's triumph is certain

15:1–16:21 The seven bowls

17:1–19:10 The fall of 'Babylon' Rome's anti–Christian empire falls prey to its own forces of destruction

19:11–21 Christ's final coming

20:1–10 The reign of Christ and the destruction of Satan

20:11–15 The final judgment

21:1–22:5 The new heaven and the new earth God has prepared a new creation for his people. This new city stands in stark contrast to Babylon, the earthly city which embodies hostility to God

22:6–21 Epilogue Concluding promises and exhortations

of Jesus Christ', showing 'what must soon take place' (1:1). This title indicates that the book belongs to the Jewish tradition of apocalyptic books, which used weird picture-language to describe God's purpose in history and to give hope to the persecuted. There are some apocalyptic chapters in the Old Testament, particularly the second half of Daniel.

- It is prophecy (1:3), addressed to seven churches known to the author. John writes for their situation and expects them to understand his relevance to their needs. But the seven churches also represent the whole church—seven in apocalyptic symbolism expresses completion or perfection. So Revelation is a letter with something to say to us all.

Some readers understand Revelation as a series of detailed predictions—of events throughout history, or of events just before the end of history. But to justify such interpretations people have arbitrarily to identify particular historical events with John's picture-symbols. And how could the original readers of Revelation have understood or benefited from such predictions?

John—probably not the apostle John, but someone otherwise unknown to us—writes to warn that the church will soon suffer oppression by the Roman state. The news from Rome is that the Emperor Domitian (AD81–96) is getting tough with people who question his demand to be called 'lord and god'. John himself has caught the first blast of this new danger. He has been banished to the island of Patmos because his gospel-preaching has offended the authorities (1:9).

Against such a background a question becomes urgent. Where is God in all this? How can we believe in the goodness of God's purpose in face of the apparent meaninglessness of events and the triumph of evil? Who controls the world—God or Domitian? Does ultimate power lie in Beijing, or Moscow, or somewhere else? The book of Revelations responds to these questions, and pulls out some great themes which underlie the whole of history.

- It exposes the nature of evil. Evil is more than simply the misdeeds of individual people. It is embodied with terrifying power in the operations of the totalitarian state. Two symbols express the twin aspects of this sinister control over people's lives. The beast (chapter 13) represents political tyranny. The prostitute (chapter 17) represents economic control. The Rome of John's day embodied both aspects, but they have a long history, both before then and since. And they succeed because they make evil attractive. By imposing order on chaos, political tyranny seems to promise security. Economic progress has all the seductive attractiveness of a prostitute. But the attractiveness is an illusion. Such power over people keeps them away from the truth, defies God and oppresses his people.

- It sets forth the crucified Jesus as the clue to God's purpose in history. Human experience does not depend on cold fate or on meaningless chance. At the centre of history is Jesus, the sacrificed Lamb who by his death opened the way to salvation and showed that God is involved in the sufferings of the world. The Lamb alone is worthy to open the scroll of human destiny and put its contents into effect (chapter 5).

- It shows what is involved in God's purposes: judgment on those who follow the beast rather than the Lamb (chapters 6 to 20); vindication for those who remain faithful to God through suffering and martyrdom (6:9-11); and a new creation in which everything will be set right, and God and the Lamb will be the focus of true worship (chapters 21 and 22).

Meanwhile, what is the role of the church? It is to suffer and to witness. In chapter 11 the church's role as witness to God's truth is represented by two prophetic figures. But the very act of witness provokes persecution (11:7), so that the witnesses are called to a suffering which mirrors the suffering of their Lord. Thus Christians under an oppressive regime have a responsibility to speak the truth about Jesus and about the evil around them. And they must be ready to accept the suffering which may follow. John casts doubt on the rightness of taking up arms (13:10).

John's is a realistic vision. He knows the weakness of the churches (chapters 2 and 3), yet believes that God can sustain them. He knows the power and glory of Rome, yet discerns in it the evil of totalitarian force and the deceptiveness of economic prosperity. He knows how great are the forces of evil which ravage the earth, but he has a clear picture of the ultimate triumph of the cross of Jesus.

JOHN'S VISION OF CHRIST
Revelation 1:9-20

John's great book about the purpose of God in history has its roots in these verses. He describes how, one Sunday, Christ appeared to him in a vision and spoke words of warning and encouragement.

Who is the Christ who confronts him in this way? Already in greeting his readers John has referred to Christ in words which would strengthen the nerve of those facing the prospect of persecution. Jesus Christ is 'the faithful witness' who calls them to witness faithfully despite their suffering. He is 'the firstborn from the dead', whose resurrection guarantees the resurrection of his followers, even if they should be martyred for their faith. He is 'the ruler of the kings of the earth', even though at present earthly kings seem to hold complete power (all these phrases are in verse 5).

Now in his vision John sees the reigning Christ and describes him in Old Testament imagery. In verse 13 he is the one 'like a son of man' who in Daniel chapter 7 verses 13 to 14 received from God a kingdom that would never be destroyed. But he also has the snow-white hair which in Daniel chapter 7 verse 9 belonged to God himself. By such imagery John declares that Jesus is God, one with the Father. Christ is 'the First and the Last' (verse 17—God's own title in Isaiah chapter 44 verse 6). And through his resurrection he holds power over death (verse 18).

This Christ is the one who speaks to the seven churches with all the thundering authority of God (verses 15 and 16). It will be a word of judgment for their complacency (compare with chapter 2 verse 16 for what 'the sword of his mouth' will do). But it will also be a message of reassurance, for Christ holds securely in his hand the seven stars who represent the seven churches of Asia (verse 20). Every Christian congregation, however small and feeble, stands under the searching gaze of Christ, and is held by his hand.

LETTERS TO THE SEVEN CHURCHES
Revelation 2:1—3:20

Before addressing the seven churches about God's purpose in history, the risen Christ has a special message for each of them. We see strengths and weaknesses of churches today mirrored in these short letters. We read of loyalty in face of opposition, and of refusal to compromise over ethical standards. We read also of the failure to behave lovingly, of spiritual complacency, easy acceptance of material comfort and secular morality. Of the seven churches, only those at Smyrna and Philadelphia escape rebuke.

Each of the seven short letters follows a standard pattern:

■ **Address to the angel (the heavenly representative) of the church.**

■ **Description of Christ, the author.**

■ **Description of the church's deeds, followed by praise or criticism.**

■ **Warning of the consequences of unfaithfulness.**

■ **Exhortation to stand firm, and a promise to those who 'overcome' through their faithfulness.**

The first letter can stand for them all. It is addressed to Ephesus, a large church in a great seaport with a population of 300,000. Christ sustains them and keeps his searching eye on them (2:1). He commends them for patiently resisting false teachers who 'claim to be apostles but are not' (2:2). These false teachers were probably of the sect known as Gnostics—referred to as Nicolaitans in verse 6. Because they believed that matter is evil and only spirit is good, they argued that Christians could behave as they liked with their bodies and it would not affect their spiritual salvation. Hence they were 'wicked men' (2:2), advocating immorality in the name of Christian freedom.

Yet the Ephesian Christians themselves have lost the love they used to have. Unless they repent, Christ will 'remove their lampstand' (2:4–5), which means they will cease to exist as a Christian congregation, for where love is absent Christ is unrecognizable. But if they listen to his warning and continue to share in his victory, they are assured of eternal life (2:7).

THE SEVEN SEALS
Revelation 6:1–16; 8:1

Christ opens the seven seals referred to in chapter 5 verse 1. He shows John what the future holds. What happens, happens only by his permission. The seven seals represent, not a detailed survey of specific events in history, but the shape of history as a whole. The pattern of events matches very closely the pattern which Jesus himself described in Mark 13. Catastrophes are portrayed which are part of what we must expect to happen before God's perfect kingdom finally comes.

The first four seals bring four horses and horsemen into view (6:1–8). The white horse represents war; the red one brings the destruction of international strife. The black horse represents famine, and the pale horse, death.

The opening of the fifth seal brings a glimpse of Christian martyrs crying out for God to vindicate them. Whether in ancient Rome or Asia Minor, in the China of the Cultural Revolution or Uganda under Amin or Obote, the martyrs are people caught in the crossfire in the great battle between God and the forces of evil (6:9–11).

The sixth seal leads to natural disasters and chaos among sun, moon and stars. In the Old Testament and in other Jewish literature, as well as in Mark 13, such portents herald the day of God's judgment. When such disasters happen people sometimes turn to God with a new seriousness. More often, perhaps, they want to hide 'from the face of him who sits on the throne and from the wrath of the Lamb' (6:16).

The seventh seal follows in chapter 8 verse 1, after the interlude of chapter 7. After the sixth seal, we imagine that the only thing still to happen is 'the great day of wrath' (6:17) and the final coming of Christ. But instead, we are told of 'silence in heaven for about half an hour'. Why? The silence means that the angels are quiet while God hears the prayers of his people. We may feel helpless in view of the power of the nations, but we can pray. Prayer is part of the process by which God brings his kingdom.

THE TWO BEASTS
Revelation 13:1–18

John sees two beasts. The first appears from the sea and derives his power from the 'Dragon', Satan (verses 1 and 2). He represents evil embodied in the Roman Empire and especially in the emperor himself. He holds sway over people because—like Hitler and other dictators—he seems to guarantee security (verse 4). He even imitates the death and resurrection of Christ (verse 3). The reference to the fatal wound which had been healed probably alludes to the widespread belief that the emperor Nero, who committed suicide in AD68, would return alive to lead armies against Rome. The beast is permitted to dominate the world and to oppress Christians for a limited period (13:58; forty-two months is not meant literally). That permission comes ultimately from God. No tyrant can step beyond the limits set by God, or upset his final purpose.

The beast from the land has two horns like a lamb (verse 11). He is a parody of the Lamb of God, and represents the priesthood of the 'emperor cult'. These priests encouraged worship of the emperor, and so turned people away from Christ. By marking with a number the foreheads of those who give allegiance to the emperor, they imposed economic sanctions on all who refused to submit to the emperor's tyrannical claims (13:12–18).

The number 666, whose meaning would not be in doubt to John's first readers, probably signifies Nero Caesar. In Latin, Greek and Hebrew, letters of the alphabet served as numbers, and so the letters of someone's name could be added up to make a number which was a kind of code for his name. Nero was one emperor whose tyrannical power had caused suffering to Christians. John sees that Domitian is another. Throughout history there have been rulers who have organized the machinery of state to claim from their subjects an obedience which is tantamount to worship. Christians must recognize such totalitarian claims as demonic, and stand firm against them whatever the cost.

THE REIGN OF CHRIST
Revelation 20:1–10

After his description of the final, triumphant coming of Christ (19:11–21), John describes how Christ rules for a thousand years. This sequence has led many to think that this reign, or millennium, will be a literal thousand-year period after Christ's final coming to earth.

But the passage does not say that Christ rules for a thousand years *on earth*. Surely his throne (20:4) is in heaven, like all the other thrones in Revelation, apart from those of Satan and the beast. And the fact that John *saw* this vision after the vision of Christ's coming need not mean that it will *happen* after Christ's coming. It is better to understand the millennium not as a period of earthly rule in the future but as a description of Christ reigning *now*, between his first and final comings.

Christ through his ministry, death and resurrection bound Satan's power (20:2–3; and see Mark 3:27; Colossians 2:15). If the devil has power in the world today, it is only because people are blind

enough to allow him power and influence to which he has no right. We should lay hold of the fact that the risen Christ is ruling now and is working out in history the implications of the victory won at Calvary and on the third day.

While Christ reigns, his triumph is shared by the martyrs (20:4–6), and presumably by all Christ's faithful people. But at the end of this period of Christ's rule, just before his final coming, the forces of evil will make a last desperate effort to thwart God's purposes. And then Satan will be finally and utterly destroyed (20:7–10). The plan of God, which was focussed in Christ crucified and risen, will thus reach its glorious goal.

THE NEW HEAVEN AND THE NEW EARTH
Revelation 21:1—22:15

When Christ comes again the present created order will be transformed to become an environment suited to the perfect and eternal rule of God among his people. The picture-language of these final chapters points to what God has in store for them. This new world will be dominated by the presence of the living God. He will remove sorrow, death, pain and evil. He will be the source of his people's life (21:3–6).

John speaks of the world to come as a city—the Holy City, new Jerusalem. But by a drastic change of image, the city is identified with 'the bride, the wife of the Lamb' (21:9). So the city is the church, God's people gathered in a community of love. On the city's gates are inscribed the names of Israel's twelve tribes, and on its foundations are written the names of the twelve apostles. This affirms the unity of God's people through the ages, both Jews and Gentiles (21:9–14). Like the holy of holies in the Jerusalem temple, the city is a cube, and it is vast (21:15–16). There is no temple in it because it is all temple, filled with the presence of God (21:22). Although no evil will enter this city, all that is good in human life and culture will be taken up into God's kingdom (21:26–27).

In that kingdom the redeemed are sustained by God and the Lamb. They will not spend eternity in idle contemplation: they will serve God and share in his triumph, surrounded by his light. At last the curse or judgment on human sin imposed in the Garden of Eden (Genesis 3) will be reversed in the Paradise of God (22:1–5).

Key Beliefs

The Ascension

When Jesus, his resurrection appearances complete, 'ascended' out of his disciples' sight, he 'returned home' to his Father. One of the greatest spectacles of the ancient world was when a general who had won a major victory returned home with the spoils of war, his defeated enemies trailing behind. Ringing in his ears would be the praises of his people. Paul wrote of Jesus' ascension: 'When he ascended on high he led captivity captive and gave gifts to men.' Jesus returned home in triumph, sin and death conquered through his death and resurrection.

The ascension, then, was a most important event, full of meaning for us today. **It reminds us that Jesus is our risen Lord, our reigning King, and our eternal High Priest.**

■ **Risen Lord.** Peter on the Day of Pentecost preaches, 'This Jesus . . . God has made Lord and Christ.' That is, the resurrection has vindicated the claims Jesus made to be Son of God. He is head of his people, and he pours out the gifts of his Spirit on them. In the verse already quoted— adapting a sentence from the Psalms—Paul makes the moment of Jesus' ascension the point when the church was ready to receive the Spirit, when he 'gave gifts to men'. Risen and ascended, Jesus now makes available to us his power and victory.

■ **Reigning King.** The day of his ascension was Jesus' coronation day. As victor over the powers of evil, he returned to his Father, and now he shares the throne of God. All authority is given to him in heaven and earth. He reigns as King over all those who now call him Lord, and one day he will reign over the whole of creation when he comes in power and glory. But he does not reign alone. To quote the apostle Paul again, 'We have been raised with Christ,' and we share in the destiny to come.

■ **Eternal High Priest.** It is in the letter to the Hebrews that the theme of Jesus as high priest is most clearly expressed. In the Old Testament the high priest came before God bearing the blood of a sacrifice, thus claiming God's forgiveness for the people. Jesus came before his Father claiming the sacrifice of his own life, a sacrifice which need never be repeated. Because of what he achieved, we can 'enter with boldness into the holy place'. Jesus Christ is now our High Priest, our Mediator with God. Through him we offer our sacrifices of praise and thanksgiving to God, and through him we receive God's salvation and blessing.

We can see, then, that the doctrine of

the ascension carries deep significance for Christians which affects our daily living. It tells us that Jesus is Lord of our lives; he holds the present and the future in his hands. But it also brings it home to us that he is our eternal High Priest whose gift of life is full, free and final.

No wonder the New Testament Christians lived such triumphant lives. They were aware that Christ's victory was their victory, and they lived as though it was!

References

Genesis 28:12	John 3:13
Judges 13:20	John 6:62
Psalms 24:3	Acts 1:9–11
Psalms 68:18	Romans 10:6
Isaiah 14:13	Ephesians 4:8–12
Matthew 28:16–20	Hebrews 9:24
Luke 24:50–52	Revelation 7:2
John 1:51	

Baptism

When a new Christian in New Testament times went down into the water of baptism, what was at stake was total commitment. This commitment was being displayed in three different ways, and it presents a challenge to us today.

- **In baptism God commits himself totally to us.** Baptism declares God's love and grace which is expressed supremely in Jesus' life and death. His death was in fact his baptism, which opened the way of life and peace to us. Baptism declares to us that we are forgiven, that we are now God's children and that his Spirit is given to all who follow him. Baptism, therefore, says as much about God as about us; it speaks of his sacrificial love, that he will never forsake us and never let us go.

- **In baptism we commit ourselves totally to him.** In the service of baptism the new Christian is actually stating two things. First, that he or she repents of a sinful past life and is willing to renounce it. Second, that the new owner of his or her life is now Jesus Christ. Paul links together Jesus' death and resurrection and our baptism. The new Christian, by going under the waters of baptism, enters into the death of Jesus and rises from it to share in the resurrection. Jesus' death was his baptism for us; our baptism is a death to the old life. For the New Testament Christian this was no game or play with words. To say 'Jesus is Lord', as each did at baptism, amounted to saying that from now on Jesus Christ came before everything else. They were prepared to face insults, ignominy and perhaps even death because of the love of their Lord.

- **In baptism the church gives itself totally to us.** Baptism is not a private and personal agreement between God and us. It takes place within the family of the church, and without that family we cannot survive as Christians. We need its fellowship, its life and its help. Through his church God's grace comes to us in innumerable ways, leading us into deeper faith and commitment and on into greater maturity. When we talk about the 'sacrament' of baptism we are speaking of two things which are going on at the same time. The outward part includes such things as water, Bible readings, the minister and the congregation. The inner part is what God is doing in the sacrament through his Spirit. That part, like seed sown in the ground, only becomes visible much later on. The classic picture of baptism is as 'new birth', and this is a reality to new Christians because they are aware that through the Holy Spirit they now looks at life quite differently, and belong now to a new group of people.

How far is this New Testament pattern recognizable in our practice of baptism today? This is a question to be asked both of churches that baptize infants and of those that baptize only adults. God wants not half-hearted believers, but men and women who are wholehearted and reckless in their love for him. Do our baptismal disciplines express this element of commitment? Many churches are guilty sometimes of dropping standards in their desire to make 'more' disciples. But those who have not counted the cost will quickly fall away.

We should question as well whether our church is taking its responsibility seriously to love and care for new Christians. Just as we would question the love of a mother and father who did not bother about their children, so with a church which allows people to drift away from its fellowship and is not a welcoming and accepting family. Such a church is not worthy of the trust which God has placed in it.

References

Matthew 3:11	Acts 8:12–16
Matthew 3:13–17	Acts 16:33
Matthew 28:19	Acts 19:3–5
Mark 1:5	Romans 6:1–6
Mark 10:38–39	1 Corinthians 1:13–15
John 3:5	1 Corinthians 12:13
Acts 1:5	Colossians 2:11–15
Acts 2:38	Titus 3:4–7
Acts 2:41	1 Peter 3:21

Breaking Bread

The central act of Christian worship is known by several titles—*Communion*; *Breaking of Bread*; *Eucharist* (which means 'thanksgiving'); *Mass* (which refers to being sent out into the world after the service). Whatever the name, it began as a meal—and that is easy to forget when all you receive is a piece of bread and a sip of wine. The modern communion probably started as believers ate together in each others' homes. Later it may have become formalized and linked with a 'love feast' and later still separated off as a distinct ritual. Whatever its origins, however, it will have carried more or less the same meanings for those who took part.

■ **It was a meal of open invitation.** The original eucharist was the last supper. Quite literally, it was the last supper of all the suppers and feasts which Jesus had held during his ministry. No one had been excluded from those meals. 'This man welcomes sinners and eats with them.' The eucharist was the meal of a community where there was 'neither Jew nor Greek, male nor female, slave nor free'.

■ **It was a meal of fellowship with Jesus himself.** The first Christians would certainly have been conscious of the presence of Jesus with them, however they expressed it: 'He was known to them in the breaking of the bread.' John tells the story of the feeding of the five thousand in a way which calls the eucharist to mind. Those who took part were 'feeding on Jesus, the living bread'.

■ **The eucharist pointed people back to the death of Jesus.** It was not so much bread and wine which were important, as bread broken like Christ's body on the cross and wine poured out like his blood. 'Do this,' was Jesus' command, 'to remember me.' The last supper was a Passover meal, and in the early days at least Christians would be reminded that both Passover and the Eucharist speak of being freed from slavery. Here was a new agreement with God, sealed and delivered in Jesus' blood.

■ **The eucharist was a meal of reconciliation and unity.** 'All of us, though many, are one body, for we all share the same loaf.' Those whom Christ invited to his feast should love one another and care for one another. The behaviour of the rich at Corinth was a scandalous denial of this. They ate their own food and got drunk while poorer Christians went hungry. But in doing this they despised the body of Christ. Again, Peter's refusal to eat with Gentiles at Antioch was seen, correctly, as a total contradiction of the fact that Jesus had broken down all social and racial barriers.

■ **Those who took part in the Lord's supper declared themselves Christ's men and women**. This is why Paul roundly asserts, 'You cannot drink the cup of the Lord *and* the cup of demons.' In some ways the eucharist was much more than a symbol. Some Corinthian Christians ate food which had been blessed in the pagan temple, but this was an act of idolatry if you took seriously the idea of sitting down to eat with Jesus.

■ **The eucharist looked forward to the coming of Jesus in triumph.** Jews would have been used to the idea of the messianic banquet—the great feast at the end of the age where the Messiah would be host. Many of Jesus' parables pick up this theme of a celebration meal. So, according to Paul, every eucharist 'preaches the Lord's death *until he comes*'. It is 'the marriage supper of the Lamb'. Whenever Christians take communion they anticipate that glorious day.

References
Exodus 12:15–27
Exodus 12:43–49
Matthew 26:17–30
Mark 14:12–26
Luke 22:7–20
Luke 24:28–31
John 6:53–58
Acts 2:42
Acts 20:11
1 Corinthians 10:16–22
1 Corinthians 11:17–34
Revelation 19:5–9

The Christian Hope

'I hope so' often signifies wishful thinking, uncertainty or vague optimism. Biblical hope is quite different. It is founded on the character of God and has the ring of confident expectation. It is the exact opposite of hopelessness. Jeremiah bought a field though the Babylonian army which was invading his country was encamped there. His action is typical. 'Destruction cannot be God's last word,' he is saying. 'He will be true to his nature and his promises—in the end. One day life will begin again.' God is very much a God of promises. Abraham is called to go out into the unknown with only the promise of a land, a nation and a blessing to lead him on. But this promise is something to cling onto in the dark times.

Hope turns life into a journey. It is not a recurring cycle but a movement forwards into the future which God has in store. Mere optimism produces false, cheap hopes: 'Zion will never fall'; 'The temple can never be destroyed'; 'The exile will soon be over.' The prophets lashed out at this kind of easy prediction. They set their hopes on the covenant love of God and looked beyond disaster to the fulfilment of his promises. Though their works contain scarcely a hint of a personal life beyond death, yet their confidence issued in beautiful and haunting visions of an ideal king, a new earth, a reign of justice and peace, the unity of all peoples and the city of God at the centre of the world.

For the Christian these visions and promises came true in Jesus. 'Christ is our hope,' Paul writes, and John looks forward to a day when the people of God will see Jesus as he is and be like him. They will live the life of the age to come, in the presence of God. They will know perfect peace and security under the rule of the King of kings. They will be reunited with those who have died. A new heaven and earth will signal the end of sin, suffering and death. God will be all in all.

This hope is grounded on more than feelings.

■ **It was the logic of Jesus' life.** He lived as if there were more to come. His actions were pointers to a kingdom that would not pass away.

■ **As people experienced the love of God through him, they began to realize that God would not throw onto the scrap heap what he held so dear.**

■ **Jesus taught that he would come again.** Many of his parables bear this meaning. It would be a coming as Lord and Judge of the whole world.

■ **His resurrection was the pattern and guarantee of the resurrection of all who were in him.** He was like the firstfruits of a great harvest to come. (See also *Resurrection*.)

■ **The Spirit of God living in their hearts assured the Christians that the promises were genuine.** They had the down payment.

How ought Christians to respond to this? There have always been those who have tried to conjure timetables out of the Bible texts. This is straining for a certainty which is unobtainable. Being too taken up with the intricacies of prophecy becomes codecracking and, at its worst, leads to giving up on this world in view of the catastrophe which is always about to happen. But hope for the future can affect the way we live in the present even when the details are unknown.

Those who live by the Christian hope need not be shaken by every latest fad; their lives have direction and purpose built in. They work to change what is, because they measure it by what will be. They need not be anxious or fear death, since hope is an anchor. They know that nothing done for Christ is wasted, so they do not easily fall prey to despair when they seem to be getting nowhere. They sit loose to this world and its values because it is not their ultimate home. And, perhaps most importantly, they strive to live lives of which they will not need to be ashamed when Jesus comes.

References

Isaiah 4:2–6	Ephesians 1:13–14
Jeremiah 32:1–15	1 Thessalonians 4:13–18
Matthew 24:13–14	2 Timothy 1:12
Romans 5:2	Titus 2:11–13
Romans 15:4–6	Hebrews 6:17–20
Romans 15:13	Hebrews 11:8–16
1 Corinthians 15:51–58	1 Peter 1:3–5
2 Corinthians 1:15–22	1 John 3:2–3
2 Corinthians 4:16–18	Revelation 21:1–22:21

The Church

'For we are an Easter people and Hallelujah is our song,' said Pope John Paul II, and it is not a bad definition of what Jesus intended the church to be. Its bedrock is the resurrection and its message is one of joy. Unfortunately, the church has not always expressed these things in its life. Historically, churches have often stood in the way of people reaching Jesus Christ. Yet at its best the church is something great. Four New Testament images give a clear picture of what God wants his people to be:

■ **The church is the people of God.** Israel was originally chosen to be God's people and his witness to the nations. Because it constantly turned its back on God, a new way was opened up through the life, death and resurrection of Jesus, and all who follow him are now the 'people of God'. They are true sons and daughters of Abraham, because they live by faith, trusting the promises of God.

But was it Jesus' intention to found a church? There can be little doubt that it was. He called twelve apostles around him, and sent them out to make disciples and to proclaim the message of the kingdom. His last act was to tell his followers to go and tell others. According to Matthew, Jesus said to Peter: 'You are Peter and on this rock I will build my church.' A new people was to grow from Jesus' ministry. Either Peter's confession or Peter himself was to be the starting-point of the people of God.

■ **The church is the body of Christ.** Paul was the first to use this phrase for the church and no one knows for certain where he got the idea from. It could have simply been taken from the notion of the human body with each limb and organ having its own function. If so, it is a beautiful picture of each person serving Christ joyfully, gladly and wholeheartedly. Whoever we are we matter to the body, which is the poorer for us not being there.

On the other hand, Paul may have taken the expression from Jesus' words at the Last Supper, 'This is my body.' If so, he is stressing the church's mission to continue the teaching and ministry of Jesus. It exists to be his body in the world; healing, helping, sharing and uniting. The two sacraments Jesus gave us express the meaning of the body, too. Through baptism we join it; through holy communion we are nourished in it.

■ **The church is the temple of the Holy Spirit.** This rich description speaks of the presence of God's Spirit among and in his people. Each individual Christian is filled with God's Spirit and so is the whole body. He is given to us to make us 'holy' and powerful.

Although it is possible to 'quench' the Spirit and 'grieve' him, the Spirit of God is active within the church and working through it. The growth of the church is a tribute to his work.

■ **The church is the bride of Christ.** This metaphor, found in the writings of Paul and in Revelation, looks ahead to the future when at Christ's coming the church will be presented to the bridegroom as a glorious and pure bride. In that day all its imperfections will be removed and it will be a fitting partner for God himself. Wherever it is placed, God's church lives within the dynamic tension between what it is and what it ought to be. The people of God should live more like him, the body must continue to grow, the temple is still being built and the bride awaits the call of the bridegroom.

Three dangers continue to dog the church's story. One such danger is exclusivism—that my church is the only true church. But the church belongs not to us but to Jesus Christ and those who confess him belong to it regardless of denominational tag. Another is tradition. Church tradition is often a great blessing but it may also silt up the channel of God's grace if it is valued above the message of the cross. And a third danger is organization. The church began as an 'organism', like a plant adapting to its environment and new situation. Inevitably, organization began to shape and direct the spontaneous ministries which sprang up. But when a church is overorganized the creative work of the Holy Spirit may be squeezed out and the gifts of God's people may not find expression. Only a church alive to the Holy Spirit will express the joy of the resurrection.

References

Genesis 12:2	Romans 16:3–5
Genesis 17:7	1 Corinthians 1:2
Exodus 19:4–6	1 Corinthians 11:18
Matthew 16:18	1 Corinthians 12:27
Matthew 18:17	Ephesians 1:22–23
Luke 12:32–34	Ephesians 5:23–32
Acts 2:47	Colossians 1:18
Acts 4:32–35	Colossians 1:24
Acts 5:11	1 Timothy 3:15
Acts 7:38	Hebrews 12:22–24
Acts 20:28	1 Peter 2:4–10

Covenant

Covenant is the Bible's word for an 'agreement'. When we make agreements today—legal, social or personal ones—we seal them in a variety of ways, with a legal document, a certificate, a wedding-ring, or even a kiss.

In the Bible four covenants with mankind are mentioned:

■ **The covenant with Noah.** Following the great flood, God promised humanity that he would never send another one. The rainbow was the sign of this covenant.

■ **The covenant with Abraham.** Abraham's trusting faith, which made him risk everything on God's promise, was rewarded by God's covenant. God declared that he would make of Abraham's descendants a great nation. The sealing of this covenant was in the act of circumcision.

■ **The covenant with Moses.** This covenant sprang from God delivering his people from Egypt. He led them out of captivity through his servant Moses and revealed his name 'Yahweh' to them. In this covenant God declared: 'You are now my people and belong to me. You must be holy as I am holy.' At Mount Sinai the covenant was sealed on two sides. On God's side there came the gift of his Law, given so that it might be the framework for life. 'Abide by these

rules,' said Yahweh, 'keep them faithfully and you will honour me and be my delight.' On their part, the Israelites promised to keep these laws and to have no other gods but Yahweh.

■ **The new covenant.** The tragedy of Israel is that they failed to keep God's covenant. In spite of God's many appeals through prophets and leaders, his agreement with Moses was repeatedly broken. The later prophets began to see that the sinfulness and weakness of humanity made it impossible for people to keep their end of the bargain. Through them God began to show that he would introduce a new and everlasting covenant: not an external but an internal one, that is, not written on stone tablets like the Ten Commandments, but on the very hearts of us all. More wonderfully still, it would no longer be limited to the Jews—it was to be for all people.

What the prophets awaited, Jesus fulfilled. His death was the sealing of this new agreement between God and humanity. At the very moment the lambs were being slaughtered in the temple for the Passover meal, Jesus the Lamb of God sealed the new covenant with his own blood.

The covenants mentioned in the Bible show that they come from the gracious, free and generous act of God. He is utterly sure and dependable and he longs for a people to enter fully into his love. Three aspects of his character emerge from the Bible's teaching about God's covenant. He is **Saviour**: he came to Israel's rescue through Moses, he came to our rescue through Jesus Christ. He is **Teacher**: he gave the Israelites guidelines for their relationship with him and he teaches us through his revelation in the Bible. He is **Lover**: he wants his people to love him as deeply as he loves us.

Still today God's new covenant gives meaning, hope and peace. It declares that God's everlasting agreement with us has been made and will not be broken. Whatever difficulty we face we can respond, 'God has expressed his faithfulness in the covenant and he will never let me go.' That faithfulness was sealed through the death of Jesus—such is the nature of God's love. But the covenant is also a covenant of grace— God's love is unconditional. God's eternal covenant is quite unmerited on our part. All we can do is to accept it gratefully through Christ and live it daily.

References

Genesis 6:18	*Isaiah 24:5*
Genesis 9:8–17	*Isaiah 49:8*
Genesis 15:18	*Isaiah 55:3*
Genesis 17:1–21	*Jeremiah 11:10*
Exodus 2:24	*Jeremiah 31:31–34*
Exodus 6:4–5	*Ezekiel 37:26–27*
Exodus 19:1–6	*Zechariah 9:11*
Exodus 24:7–8	*Luke 1:72*
Leviticus 24:8	*Luke 22:20*
Deuteronomy 5:2–3	*Acts 3:25*
Joshua 24:25	*Romans 9:4*
Ezra 10:3	*Galatians 3:15–17*
Nehemiah 1:5	*Ephesians 2:12*
Nehemiah 9:8	*Hebrews 8:6–13*
Psalms 25:10	*Hebrews 12:24*
Psalms 89:3	
Psalms 105:8–11	

Creativity

Strictly speaking, only God can create, since creation is to bring something out of nothing. But the story of God's act of creation does shed some light on the nature of human creativity.

- **Creation involves a product—something 'new' comes into existence.**

- **It results in order and structure in place of what was chaotic and formless.**

- **It ought to issue in something 'good', which in the widest sense is made in praise of God.**

- **There can be no creativity, as the Bible sees it, which is not inspired by the Spirit of God**, whether he is directly acknowledged or not.

On this reckoning Jesus Christ is the truly creative person. In his mighty works people could see the creative power of God. His teaching was heard as a new doctrine because of its originality and freshness. People were 'born again' when they encountered him. The turning of water into wine was a sign of the remaking of the world. In his life, death and resurrection, as Paul saw clearly, a new creation came into existence.

Every true act of creation is a sign of that promise and possibility. In the story of Adam naming the animals we can see humanity ordering the environment, creatively giving it shape and meaning and making a 'cosmos' out of chaos. Adam had this power under God, as his vice-regent on earth. Creativity is also apparent in Proverbs, in the careful and systematic classification of human behaviour. Here is the early social scientist at work, bringing pattern and order into confusion, helping people to 'see' and understand the world in a new way. Psalm 150 points to the creative gifts of musicians who praise God on a variety of instruments. Exodus chapter 31 gives high prominence to a creative designer named Bezalel, a man 'filled with the Spirit of God' along with other craftsmen who used their powers to create and make beautiful the tent of meeting. The accounts of the building of the temple also show the value given to the skilled workman in Israel. And though the Bible says little directly about the artist in words, yet Jesus' own teaching methods show that he valued the world of verbal images and pictures.

Creativity is about more than simply the arts. The worship of the church can be a creative act. Where the Spirit is at work and where there is love and freedom within order and structure, the whole body of worshipping believers can offer a new sacrifice of praise to their Redeemer. Phrases like 'a living temple', 'the multi-coloured grace of God', 'varieties of gifts but the one Spirit', all point in this direction.

Similarly, love is a creative gift—husband and wife are creators. Paul's treatment of Onesimus, the runaway slave, smashed old stereotypes and created new ways of looking at slaves. In love a one-time prostitute broke open a box of precious ointment for Jesus and did something 'beautiful' for him.

Sadly, the creative gift can be buried out of sight and never used to bring glory to the giver, or it can be employed destructively. Wisdom can degenerate into the cleverness that 'puffs up'; the gift of speech can be used for effect rather than for communication. People can build a tower of Babel as easily as a temple. But God calls us to use our creative gifts to the full, with something of the richness that he brought to creation.

References
Genesis 1:31
Exodus 31:1–11
1 Chronicles 16:37–42
Job 28:1–11
Psalms 150:1–6
See also God the Creator

The Cross

The question 'Why the cross?' has haunted the Christian faith from the beginning. The crucifixion was a penalty reserved for criminals, and many non-Christian writers in the first few centuries thought it was a rather sick joke that the Christians preached a crucified saviour. But in spite of the offence of the cross the New Testament and the first Christians did not shrink from declaring proudly and firmly that Jesus' death was God's chosen way of salvation.

But was the cross an accident? At what point in his life was Jesus aware of the cross? We do not know for sure, but it was after Peter had given voice to his famous confession—'You are the Christ'—that Jesus began to talk less about the kingdom and more about his death. What we can say firmly is that according to the New Testament the cross was planned in the purposes of God. God prepared it as the 'highway' home to him.

'Why did the cross have to happen? Why couldn't God just forgive us and let "bygones be bygones"?' some people ask. But humanity's situation was far too tragic for such a trivial response from God. So terrible was humanity's burden of guilt and sin that only God could mend the broken relationship and heal the hearts of us all. The incarnation means that God identified with human need and suffering, and the cross declares that God took all the sin and

shame and dealt with it once and for all in Jesus' death. Paul put it this way: 'God made him who had no sin to be sin for us, so that in him we might become the righteousness of God.'

We shall never fully understand the cross in this life; at the heart of it there is mystery. But God does not require us so much to understand it as to experience it, that is, to discover its benefits. We do know this, that it is God's way of salvation and it has changed the lives of millions.

Here are some of the many different ways people have understood the cross:

■ **Jesus our Example.** For many people the death of Jesus has been an inspiring example of patient and quiet suffering in the face of overwhelming odds. We can take it as a pattern when we are suffering unjustly. In the New Testament writings Jesus' obedience, ending in his death, is marked out as an example of how Christians should react when persecuted or opposed.

■ **Jesus our Liberator.** Although we know Jesus to be someone who removed the sin of the world by his death, it clearly did not have this meaning for those occupying Roman soldiers who put him to death. They saw him as a political agitator. To the Jews he was a 'messianic upstart'. His claims about the coming of his kingdom appeared to challenge the law of Moses. His final entry into Jerusalem as the crowds waved palm branches and cried 'Blessed is he who comes in the name of the Lord' was laden with symbolic meaning. Today many who are fighting oppression, injustice and poverty have taken hold of the cross of Jesus as a model of someone who fought against the forces of evil and conquered.

■ **Jesus our Representative.** A representative is someone we put into a position of power and influence to express our point of view. So this theory sees Jesus as the perfect human being who stands before the Father on our behalf and represents us there. This idea is well caught in Newman's great hymn: 'A second Adam to the fight and to the rescue came.'

■ **Jesus our Sin-bearer.** A dominant view in the New Testament is that Jesus died for our sin. Many have extended this to mean that Jesus died as 'my substitute'. That is, his death was a death I deserved to die; he took my guilt and sin and nailed it to the cross so that I might be forgiven and rise to new life through him.

In these ways and more the death of Jesus has been interpreted for our time. If the resurrection is the heartbeat of the Christian faith, it must be the case that the death of Jesus is its heart. An effective gospel today must present the death of Jesus confidently and clearly. It is still the way of hope, peace and eternal life.

References

Genesis 3:15
Isaiah 52:13—53:12
Jeremiah 31:31–34
Matthew 1:21
Matthew 16:21
Matthew 26:26–29
Matthew 27:27–54
Mark 10:45
Mark 15:21–47
Luke 12:49–50
Luke 22:14–23
John 1:29
John 12:24
John 19:1–37
Acts 2:22–23
Acts 3:15
Acts 4:10
Acts 8:32–35
Acts 10:38–43
Romans 3:23–25
Romans 5:6–10
Romans 8:1–3
1 Corinthians 1:22–25
1 Corinthians 5:7
1 Corinthians 15:3
2 Corinthians 5:14–21
Galatians 2:20
Galatians 3:13

Ephesians 1:7
Ephesians 2:13
Ephesians 2:16
Philippians 2:5–10
Philippians 3:10
Colossians 1:20
Colossians 2:13–15
Colossians 3:3
1 Thessalonians 2:15
1 Timothy 1:15
1 Timothy 2:5
2 Timothy 1:10
Titus 3:4–7
Hebrews 2:14–18
Hebrews 5:7–9
Hebrews 7:26–27
Hebrews 9:12–14
Hebrews 10:11–14
Hebrews 10:19–22
Hebrews 12:2
1 Peter 1:11
1 Peter 1:18–19
1 Peter 2:21–24
1 Peter 3:18
1 John 1:7
Revelation 1:5–7
Revelation 5:9–10

Discipleship

'Disciple' is a 'Gospels' word. Apart from a few references in Acts, the rest of the New Testament prefers to describe the Christian in other terms. But 'disciple' is a good word; it has a simplicity and a concreteness about it. What does it mean?

■ **To be a disciple is to follow Jesus.** Discipleship begins with a call— 'Come to me', 'Follow me'—and to be a Christian is to walk behind Jesus, as Bartimaeus, a blind man whom he healed, followed Jesus 'in the way'. In fact, 'The Way' briefly became a way of describing the Christian community. Jesus leads, whether to the other side of the lake, to Jerusalem or to Galilee, and the call to disciples is 'to follow in his steps', even if this means taking up our own cross behind him.

■ **Following Jesus involves breaking with the past.** The Galilean fishermen left nets and family; Levi had to walk away from the tax office. The rich young ruler was unwilling to make this break. Jesus referred to this as 'hating your life' and 'forsaking all' for his sake. Many in the crowds found the cost too high and 'walked no more with him'.

■ **The word 'disciple' literally means a learner,** and this highlights a third aspect of the Christian life. Disciples have not left school. Jesus invited men and women to take on his 'yoke' and learn from him. In this he was just like the rabbis who taught their students a whole-life package. The twelve are chosen 'to be *with* him'. He offers 'to *make* them fishers of men'. By watching, listening and living with Jesus the disciples learned the secret of the kingdom at a level much deeper than words. They saw Jesus praying, arguing, healing, teaching. Some saw him transfigured or in agony. To be a disciple is to learn from Jesus by sharing every part of his life.

One difficult lesson to learn was that life was to be shared with other disciples as well. The circle round Jesus became a new community, replacing the ties of kinship or status. Jesus' family are those who hear the word of God and obey it. When Peter complained bitterly that he had given up everything to follow Jesus, he was promised a new home and family. The distinguishing mark of this new community was to be its mutual love.

This was no closed community, however. Anyone could join. Though Jesus often taught his followers in secret, yet this was only a prelude to sending them out to preach, teach, heal and exorcize. There was a rhythm of learning and doing. In this way they continued his work. Jesus had promised to make his disciples 'fishers of men'. Once he sent out twelve of them, once seventy, and these missions clearly prefigured the great commission, which he gave right at the end, to them and to every Christian to bear witness and 'make disciples of all nations'.

One final theme emerges from the Gospels—that of weakness and failure. The disciples are typically shown as faithless, dull and uncomprehending. They cannot grasp the truth about Christ's passion, they reject the women who bring children to Jesus, they dispute about who is the greatest, fail to stay awake with Jesus in his agony and at his arrest run for their lives. Some, like Nicodemus, try to be secret followers 'for fear of the Jews'. Judas betrays; Peter, despite his boasts, denies. The churches for whom the Gospels were first written would have read these passages as a call to be faithful and as an illustration of Jesus' warning: 'without me you can do nothing.'

References

Matthew 28:18–20
Mark 1:16–20
Mark 3:13–15
Luke 9:1–6
Luke 9:57–62
Luke 14:25–33
John 1:35–51

Galatians 2:20–21
Ephesians 6:10–20
Philippians 3:12–16
1 Timothy 6:11–16

Faith

Biblical faith is never a matter of believing impossible things. It is responding to a God–given vision, as Abraham did, when he left his home city, not knowing where God would take him.

Faith means 'seeing' the world in a particular way, from an angle God has shown us. To those who refused to see, Jesus' miracles might appear just as wonders or even works of Satan. To the eye of faith they were 'signs'. The man born blind had faith in that he 'saw' who Jesus really was. Some Jews who had sight in a physical sense were unable to perceive that they were in the presence of the Messiah. The centurion in Mark's passion story witnessed the bare facts of the crucifixion and yet saw through them to the deeper truth and so confessed his faith: 'This man was the Son of God.' At the empty tomb John 'saw' the graveclothes and 'believed'.

It is in the thought of Paul that faith is most fully worked out. For him, faith is the encounter of the whole person (not just intellect or just feelings) with Jesus himself (not with a set of beliefs or doctrines). Faith in Christ does not mean ticking off a list of things you believe. It is coming to the end of your resources and crying out to God to save you. It is staking your eternal destiny on his death on the cross. It is trusting him with your life, the 'yes' of your whole personality to Christ.

For Paul, such an act of commitment opens a person's life to all the blessings God has in store. Through faith we are acquitted of our sins and made right with God; we are given God's Spirit to live within us. We are a new creation, with a new purpose, power and hope.

Paul's teaching about faith came under two different kinds of attack. The first emphasized the painstaking keeping of legal requirements in the hope of working one's way into God's good books. Such labour produced only a dismal catalogue of failure. God had already sent his Son to set mankind free from such slavery. The opposite position was as bad. This argued that, provided you believed, you could live how you liked because God's grace would cover all your misdeeds. This was a perversion of the gospel. Neither view had begun to grasp the truth that faith is not primarily our offering to God, but his gift to us.

It is left to James to hammer the point home in a passage which superficially seems to be contradicting Paul. Real faith shows its genuineness by the obedience which flows from it. It always leads to love in action. 'Faith' in the sense of mere intellectual assent or cold orthodoxy is a dead thing. A 'faith' which ignores the hungry, the poor, the widow or the orphan is just a word.

This is not to deny that faith will sometimes mean witnessing to the truth. The Christian believes that certain things are true: God sent his Son, Jesus is the Christ, God raised him from the dead ... As these truths became organized, so 'the faith once delivered to the saints' emerged. Christians are called to contend for this body of truth. Yet, in the end, Christianity is not a set of beliefs or a creed. It is a living relationship with Christ.

References

Genesis 12:1–5	John 6:68–69
Genesis 15:6	John 9:35–38
Exodus 14:13	Acts 2:38–39
1 Samuel 1:15–18	Acts 16:31
1 Kings 17:21–24	Romans 1:17
1 Kings 18:41–46	Romans 4:18–22
Job 1:9–12	Romans 5:1
Job 1:21	Romans 10:6–13
Job 42:2	Galatians 2:20
Psalms 56:3–4	Galatians 3:11–14
Psalms 106:30–31	Galatians 3:23–29
Isaiah 7:9	Ephesians 2:8–9
Isaiah 26:3–4	1 Timothy 4:1
Isaiah 43:1–5	1 Timothy 6:12
Jeremiah 17:7–8	2 Timothy 1:12
Habakkuk 2:4	Hebrews 11:1
Mark 2:5	Hebrews 11:6
Mark 6:5–6	Hebrews 11:8–10
Mark 10:52	Hebrews 12:1–2
Luke 7:2–10	1 John 5:1
John 1:12	1 John 5:4
John 3:15–16	Revelation 3:19–20
John 5:24	

God the Creator

The Bible makes no attempt to prove that God exists. It takes this for granted, assuming that it is self-evident that the whole of creation displays his work. Indeed, the first thing we learn about God in the Bible is that he is the Creator who brought everything into being.

The two creation accounts in Genesis tell us two important things about God and creation. The first is that everything in creation is totally dependent on God. All life belongs to him and we can do no creative act without him. The second understanding is this: God is the sovereign Lord who is independent of everything else. He did not have to create. Then why did he?

The Bible's clear answer is that God created the universe because he loves. Creation flows from his desire to enter into a relationship of love with us all. From our own experience we can understand the link between loving and creating. Just as in a family children are born from love and into love, so God's act of creation springs from his love which brings everything into existence.

In the first creation account (Genesis 1:1—2:4) the accent falls on the creation of all things: 'In the beginning God created the heavens and the earth.' ('Heaven and earth' is a Hebrew way of saying 'everything'.) In the next verses there follows an ascending order of creation from the most primitive creatures to God's most perfect creation—humanity. God's satisfaction at his workmanship is expressed in the statement at the conclusion of it all: 'God looked at everything he had made, and he was very pleased.'

At the heart of this story comes the creation of humanity made in 'the image and likeness of God'. This phrase tells us that there is a difference between us and other living creatures: we bear the stamp of the Creator to show that we belong to him in a very special way. (See further under *The Image of God*.)

In the second account (Genesis 2:5–25) the emphasis falls on this world and on relationships between men and women. This passage develops further the high place humanity holds in creation—to 'rule' the earth as God's stewards and to have responsibility over all life.

The rest of the Bible confirms the teaching found in Genesis and develops it in four ways:

■ **God is at work in his creation.** God did not wind up the universe like a clock and leave it to tick away unattended. He is still at work in the universe caring for it and giving it direction and purpose. Jesus referred to this unceasing care when he said to those who complained that he healed on the sabbath: 'My Father is always working, and I too must work.' Paul echoes this by bringing Jesus Christ directly into God's creative work: through Christ all things have come into being and they are sustained by him.

■ **God providentially cares for everything**. A greatly neglected teaching these days is the doctrine of providence. This belief means that God is intimately interested in every aspect of his creation and our welfare is his delight. Jesus taught in the Sermon on the Mount that 'every hair of your head is numbered', emphasizing that God's love is careful and concerned.

■ **We live in a sin-shot world**. This world has been spoiled through sin. God created all things well but his creation has been marred and spoiled through humanity's rebellion against God. Humanity's fall into sin has affected practically every part of the created order. So Paul says: 'All of creation groans with pain . . . it waits with eager longing for God to reveal his sons.' Because we are part of this sin-shot creation we, too, carry within us the signs of its disintegration—weakness, sickness and death. (See further under *Sin*.)

■ **God is in control**. Although the plight facing humanity is serious, God is in control. The name most constantly used of God in the Old Testament is 'Yahweh', which probably means 'I am that I am' and may be translated roughly as the 'ever-present God'.

The Bible's teaching about creation challenges much of current thinking. It reminds us that this world has meaning; if the universe came into being by chance then there can be no basic purpose behind it, but if God created it then it has a meaning which affects all our lives. It reminds us too that God's creation is to be enjoyed. God has given it to us to take pleasure in it, to admire it and use it enthusiastically without abusing it. It also shows us that God loves and cares for us. Our joy is his delight. Disappointment, disaster and even death cannot affect this one little bit because 'nothing will be able to separate us from the love of God'. His love is such that he longs for us to move from an appreciation of creation to a deeper acknowledgment of a Maker whose beauty and love are expressed most fully in Jesus Christ his Son.

References

Genesis 1:1–2:4	*Psalms 36:5–9*
Genesis 2:5–25	*Psalms 90:1–6*
Genesis 8:22	*Psalms 102:25–28*
Genesis 22:8	*Psalms 104:1–30*
Genesis 45:5–8	*Psalms 115:16*
Genesis 14:18–22	*Psalms 136:1–9*
Genesis 17:1	*Psalms 139:13–15*
Genesis 22:13–14	*Psalms 145:15–20*
Exodus 3:14	*Psalms 148:1–10*
Exodus 15:1–18	*Proverbs 8:22–31*
Exodus 15:26	*Ecclesiastes 12:13*
Deuteronomy 8:7–18	*Isaiah 40:12–31*
Deuteronomy 26:1–11	*Isaiah 42:5*
Judges 6:24	*Isaiah 44:6*
Nehemiah 9:6–25	*Isaiah 44:24*
Nehemiah 9:32–37	*Isaiah 45:18–19*
Job 26:5–14	*Jeremiah 10:12–16*
Job 33:4	*Jeremiah 18:5–10*
Job 33:23–30	*Daniel 4:31*
Job 38:2–41	*Joel 2:18–23*
Psalms 8:1–9	*Amos 4:13*
Psalms 19:1–6	*Amos 5:8–9*
Psalms 24:1–2	*Matthew 6:28–34*

Luke 13:1–5
John 1:1–4
John 5:17
Acts 4:24–25
Acts 14:17
Acts 17:23–31
Romans 1:20–23
Romans 8:18–23
Romans 8:38–39
1 Corinthians 8:6
1 Corinthians 10:26
Colossians 1:15–20
Hebrews 1:1–3
Hebrews 4:11
Hebrews 10:6
Hebrews 11:3

God the Father

Words like 'mother', 'father', 'son' and 'daughter' stand for the richest relationships in human life. We are bound to our parents in a very special relationship of love. We owe them life, because without them we would not exist. But we can go much further than that: if they have been wise and good parents we can be grateful to them for bringing us up in a loving family which has helped us to develop into mature and whole people. It is against this background that we should try to understand what the Bible has to say about God being our 'Father'.

It is strange at first sight to discover that the Old Testament rarely talks about God as Father. It is the New Testament which develops this teaching—God is only known as Father through Jesus the Son. It is a striking fact that Jesus came preaching the kingdom in which the king is a Father. Jesus spoke of his Father as 'Abba'. This is an intimate word, similar to but not the same as our word 'Daddy' Even today in Israel you can hear small children calling out 'Imma' (Mummy) and 'Abba' (Daddy). By using this word Jesus was showing his own personal relationship with the Lord of all and showing that this God is not aloof and distant but close at hand. This must have seemed almost blasphemous to fellow-Jews who placed such an emphasis on God's distance from us. God's name was too sacred even to be uttered, so whenever they came upon the word 'Yahweh' in the Bible they used 'Lord'. But Jesus called him 'Father'—even 'my Abba'!

The first Christians continued this emphasis. Paul, for example, talked frequently about 'the God and Father of our Lord Jesus Christ'. It was also very natural for them to speak of God as 'Abba', because hadn't this been their Lord's practice? This awareness of God as Abba, they realized, came through lives opened by the Holy Spirit. So Paul writes: 'God has sent the Spirit of his Son into our hearts crying "Abba! Father!"'

Clearly, then, two events had to happen before God could be known as Father:

- **He had to come and show himself, not as a distant God, but as Father** of a man who was his very dear Son. Through the ministry of Jesus of Nazareth, God is revealed as Father.

- **Then it has to become personal to us.** We cannot enter God's family without his Holy Spirit entering our lives and starting the new creation within us. This is what Jesus meant when he said to the Jewish rabbi Nicodemus: 'Unless a man is born of water and the Spirit he cannot enter the kingdom of God.' 'Water' here stands for baptism, the outward symbol of belonging to the family, and 'Spirit' means the working of God in our lives bringing us to faith.

It is important to note that when we call God 'Father' we are not suggesting that he is masculine in our understanding of sexuality. God's nature embraces qualities which belong to both male and female natures and the Bible does not shrink from speaking of God's maternal care and love. What the term 'Father' means is that God looks after us as a real parent should. He provides for us, he defends us, he loves us. We should not hesitate to use such a term for God when it was so important to Jesus and handed on to us from him.

In our anonymous world where people are often fearful and insecure, the doctrine of God as Father is exciting and inexhaustible. Jesus lived life aware and confident that he could not drift from his Father's care and love. There is no need for us to pray 'Our Father' and live as though we are orphans.

References

2 Samuel 7:14–15	John 1:14
Psalms 103:13	John 5:36–37
Isaiah 9:6	John 10:15
Isaiah 63:16	John 10:30
Isaiah 64:8	John 11:41
Jeremiah 3:19	John 14:2–7
Jeremiah 31:9	John 17:1
Matthew 5:16	Romans 8:15
Matthew 5:45	1 Corinthians 8:6
Matthew 5:48	2 Corinthians 1:3
Matthew 6:4	Galatians 4:6
Matthew 6:9	Ephesians 3:14–15
Matthew 11:25–27	Hebrews 12:7–9
Mark 14:36	1 Peter 1:2–3
Luke 11:11–13	1 John 1:2–3
Luke 15:11–32	

God the Trinity

The word 'Trinity', used of God, means that the one God has revealed himself as three persons—Father, Son and Holy Spirit. It is not a biblical word and it is surprising, if not actually staggering, that the early Christians developed this doctrine. The reasons which led them to do so are to be found in the New Testament particularly in the way the apostles met with the living God.

■ **A meeting with Jesus Christ.** The first Christians were Jews. Unlike the pagans of their day, they were monotheists, believing firmly in one God who made heaven and earth. Yet we can see in the Gospels the impact the man from Nazareth made on those Jews. His life, his actions and his teaching all conspired to make people ask: 'What kind of man is this? Where does his authority come from?' Then came the time when Peter made his famous declaration: 'You are the Christ (Messiah), the Son of the living God.' Jesus was often evasive about his true nature, preferring the mysterious 'Son of man' description to 'Messiah' and other divine titles. But it dawned on those who surrounded him that the only way to explain this man was by acknowledging that he was in some sense God.

Yet it was the resurrection which brought to a head their thinking about who Jesus was. The sceptical Thomas, after the resurrection, kneels to worship as God the 'man' he had earlier followed: 'My Lord and my God!' Peter preaches on the day of Pentecost, 'This Jesus, whom you crucified, God has made both Lord and Christ.' From the resurrection on, a new way of understanding Christ developed. Those first Christians were in no doubt whatever that Jesus, their Saviour Jesus, expressed fully and visibly the presence of God himself. Paul, one of the earliest writers, calls him 'Lord', 'image of the invisible God', and 'firstborn of all creation'.

■ **A meeting with the Holy Spirit.** Jesus told his disciples that after he had gone he would not leave them comfortless; he would send the Holy Spirit to them. They would have learned of the Holy Spirit from the Old Testament: that power of God which came on people for special purposes and then only temporarily. 'He will abide with you for ever,' Jesus told them.

Pentecost was the start of this disturbing encounter with God's Spirit. He came on a bedraggled company of disciples, formed them into a formidable group of God's storm-troopers and made them a loving, caring family. His role was twofold: to direct the attention of people to Jesus as Lord and Saviour, and to come into the lives of those who turned to Jesus through repentance and faith. So to have the Spirit was to be a Christian. The Spirit is given to Christians so that we may know in our own experience the reality of God, and know the salvation offered in Jesus Christ. (See further the article *Holy Spirit*.)

■ **A meeting with Father, Son and Holy Spirit.** The testimony of the New Testament is that those first Christians experienced God in three ways—as Creator, as Saviour and as the one who came into their lives. So there are a large number of references to the three persons in the Godhead. This verse from Paul's letter to the Romans is just an example: 'I urge you, brothers, by our Lord Jesus Christ and by the love of the Spirit, to join me in my struggles by praying to God for me.' The frequency of this threefold pattern indicates how strongly the thinking of the New Testament writers was influenced by their experience of God. They were not writing carefully contrived and thought-out theological books. Rather, from their lived-out experience flowed the excitement of meeting the living God, the one who had revealed himself as Father, Son and Spirit.

It was therefore quite logical and natural that the doctrine of the Trinity— Father, Son and Holy Spirit as separate and equal partners in God's nature— developed in the centuries after the New Testament was written. This is the reason why we recite creeds about the Trinity. And we, like the New Testament Christians, can experience a

revolutionary meeting with God the Three-in-One.

References

Isaiah 6:1–8	1 Corinthians 12:4–6
Matthew 3:13–17	2 Corinthians 13:13
Matthew 28:19	Galatians 4:4–6
John 14:15–23	Ephesians 2:18
John 15:26	Ephesians 4:4–6
John 16:13–1	Philippians 3:3
John 5:1	Hebrews 10:10–17
Acts 2:33–34	1 John 5:1–12

God's Revelation

Any important discovery about another person may be called 'revelation'. Think of human love or friendship and you will know that from intimacy springs revelation. It is the nature of love to reveal itself.

This is true of God's revelation except that, because he is the 'unknown' God, we cannot discover him at all without his help. Unless he reveals himself we cannot find him. This he does in four ways: through **creation**, through the **prophets**, through the whole **Bible** and, above all, through **Jesus Christ**. Putting it another way: through the seen Word, through the spoken Word, through the written Word and through the incarnate Word.

■ **Revelation which comes to us through creation** is often spoken of as 'general revelation'. This means that God has revealed himself in human history, through the beauty and order of creation, and in our own moral sense. This note is certainly there in the Bible. But we have to realize that such revelation is seriously affected by human sin; instead of creation revealing God clearly, we have a distorted and incomplete vision of him.

■ **Revelation through prophets, through the Bible and through Jesus Christ** is called 'special revelation'. Because of our rebellion against him, God in his love and mercy has sent to us special messengers and prophets to call us back to him. The prophets through the Holy Spirit claimed to bring God's word to his people. Time and again they came crying, 'Thus says the Lord!' In time, the somewhat elusive words of the prophets gave way to the full and final revelation given in Jesus Christ—the incarnate Word, the Word made flesh. The letter to the Hebrews puts it this way: 'In the past God spoke to our forefathers through the prophets . . . but in these last days he has spoken to us by his Son.'

It is the testimony of the Bible and the Christian church that God has revealed himself perfectly and clearly through Jesus Christ. What is the essence of that revelation? That he is our Father and Deliverer and that his Son is the only way to him. The very heart of God's revelation, therefore, is the good news brought to us through Jesus Christ.

A very difficult problem relating to revelation is the place of the Bible. Some scholars argue that the Bible is not itself revelation but rather a record of God's revelation. It points to him. The moment we make the Bible to be itself revelation, they say, we end up worshipping a book instead of a living Lord. While we must acknowledge that this is a danger to be guarded against, it is extremely difficult to separate a record from the revelation it is witnessing to—how can we know the revelation except through its teaching and witness? The Bible is a faithful record and for that reason the Christian church from the very beginning has readily spoken of it as God's word, through which God's revelation in Christ has been conveyed to us. In experience God's revelation can come to us through the very words of the Bible as it witnesses to Jesus Christ.

Christians have no need to be ashamed to confess that in Jesus Christ God has revealed himself finally, fully and perfectly. He is God's last and best Word, and we must carry this controversial message humbly to others, to share with them what we have learnt.

References

Genesis 1:3	Daniel 10:1
Genesis 1:6	Luke 10:21–22
Genesis 1:9	John 1:1–5, 14
Genesis 12:1–4	John 12:38
Exodus 3:1–15	John 16:12–15
Deuteronomy 29:29	John 16:25
1 Samuel 3:1	Romans 1:17–18
1 Samuel 3:21	1 Corinthians 2:10
Isaiah 22:14	1 Corinthians 14:6
Isaiah 40:5	Galatians 1:12
Isaiah 53:1	Galatians 1:15–16
Isaiah 56:1	Hebrews 1:1–3
Jeremiah 1:6–8	1 Peter 1:10–12
Daniel 2:19–30	Revelation 1:1

The Holy Spirit

'I will not leave you comfortless. I will send to you another Comforter, who will be with you for ever.' These words of Jesus, spoken just before he died, are a fitting introduction to that divine being we call the Spirit. He comes to us through Jesus Christ, and he indwells us for ever.

Before the coming of Jesus there was no clear expression of the Spirit. The favourite Old Testament word for the Spirit is 'breath', which probably stands for the powerful energy of God in the world. As 'breath' of God he creates, inspires, gives leadership, empowers, reveals God's word and gives creative ability. The prophets herald the coming of the Messiah who will be anointed with God's Spirit, in an age when all of God's people will be visited with the Spirit of God. But throughout the Old Testament the Spirit came on people for specific tasks and for temporary periods. He did not indwell them permanently.

During the ministry of Jesus the Spirit acted in great power. The Spirit indwelt Jesus fully, and gifts and graces at their very best were to be seen in his life. But the 'age of the Spirit' properly began when Jesus' work had been completed with his death, resurrection and ascension. Jesus, Spirit-filled, then became the giver of the Spirit. He told his disciples that he would not be leaving them alone: 'I will send to you another Comforter, who will be with you for ever.' The Spirit came in power on the day of Pentecost, inspiring the church to proclaim the good news of the kingdom.

There are four very important truths about the Holy Spirit:

■ **He is the Spirit of Jesus.** Although the Spirit has a distinctive personality, his role is never to proclaim himself but to glorify Christ and 'floodlight' the work of Jesus. The Spirit is only satisfied when the beauty and glory of Jesus are lit up by his light. It is not surprising, then, that in the New Testament there is some overlap between the work of the Spirit and the Son—Jesus is said to indwell the Christian but so does the Spirit. This overlap, however, merely emphasizes our central point—the Spirit wants to make us more like Christ.

■ **He is the Spirit of mission.** In the Acts of the Apostles we constantly see the Holy Spirit in action guiding the church, coming in power on the apostles and indwelling all believers. He is interested in enlarging the boundaries of the Christian family and making disciples. He continues to apply the work of Jesus Christ to every new situation and every age.

■ **He is the Spirit of the church.** Without the Spirit there is no church. He who was the distinctive mark of the ministry of Jesus now fills the community of Jesus. No one can be born into God's family without him. He indwells all Christian people and he is the centre of the church's unity and the mainspring of its life.

■ **He is the Spirit of power.** The word often used of the Spirit in the New Testament gives us our word 'dynamite'. That explosive power of God is seen in the Acts of the Apostles as the apostles witness boldly to the resurrection of Christ. That self-same power is expressed through the gifts of the Spirit given to his people.

So where has that power gone today? There is, in fact, plenty of evidence throughout the world today of astonishing growth as the Spirit works among his people. Yet there are also many weak churches and powerless Christians. Two key things should be borne in mind. First, the Spirit can be grieved by hardness of heart, by unbelief and opposition and his work may be quenched or restrained. When the church tries to operate in its own power, that is when it is most weak. Second, remember that the incarnation and the cross of Christ appeared to be very weak. The Spirit does not always take us along the pathways of blessing and power. Sometimes he takes us through the valleys of suffering, opposition and struggle. We should remember that Calvary was as much a sign of power as was Pentecost.

Although no clear teaching about the person of the Spirit can be found in the Old Testament, in the New Testament the Spirit is clearly portrayed as a separate person within the Godhead. In the Acts of the Apostles the Spirit leads the church. He may be lied to, he speaks, he takes direct action. But it in John's Gospel that the personality of the Spirit reaches its peak when he is spoken of as the one who proceeds from the Father, sent in the name of the Son. The special name John gives to the Spirit is 'Paraclete', which comes from the root 'one who gives encouragement and comfort'. This sums up his nature very well.

We should never ignore the Spirit. A Spirit-less church is worse than powerless—it is dead. On the other hand, we should never exaggerate his importance so that he overshadows the Father and the Son. The Spirit exists to give glory to the Son and it follows that a balanced Christian faith will want to rest on the whole Trinity. But we certainly need to allow the Spirit room in our lives to make us more Christlike, and allow the Spirit room in our churches to bring new life, change and development. Clinging to church tradition is sometimes the enemy of the Holy Spirit. He is always on the move and we should not be afraid to travel light.

References

Genesis 1:2	*John 3:6–8*
Genesis 6:3	*John 4:24*
Exodus 31:3	*John 14:17*
Numbers 11:29	*John 15:26*
Judges 6:34	*John 16:7–15*
Judges 15:14	*Acts 2:1–18*
1 Samuel 10:6	*Acts 8:29*
2 Kings 2:9	*Romans 8:2–16*
Psalms 51:10–11	*1 Corinthians 2:11–14*
Psalms 139:7	*1 Corinthians 3:16*
Isaiah 11:2–3	*1 Corinthians 6:19*
Isaiah 40:13	*1 Corinthians 12:4–13*
Isaiah 42:1–4	*2 Corinthians 3:6*
Isaiah 63:11	*2 Corinthians 3:17*
Ezekiel 18:31	*Galatians 4:6*
Ezekiel 36:26	*Galatians 5:22–25*
Joel 2:28–29	*Ephesians 1:13*
Zechariah 4:6	*Ephesians 4:4*
Matthew 3:16	*Ephesians 5:18*
Matthew 4:1	*Ephesians 6:17*
Luke 1:41	*1 Thessalonians 4:8*
Luke 4:18	*1 Thessalonians 5:19*
Luke 11:13	*2 Timothy 1:7*

The Image of God

'Isn't she like her mother!' 'Doesn't the look like his father!' And the new parent glows with pleasure that other people notice the family likeness. Similarly, it was God's intention from the beginning that we should bear the likeness of our heavenly Father. At the beginning of Genesis God declares: 'Let us make man in our image, after our likeness.' The narrative continues: 'So God created man in his own image, in the image of God he created him, male and female he created them.'

Two things require immediate comment. First, 'image and likeness' is simply a piece of Old Testament parallelism pointing to one single reality. Second, we see that the image idea embraces humanity as male and female. Both sexes are equally loved, chosen and called by God himself.

But what does it mean to be made in the image of God? Over this phrase oceans of ink have been spilt. Does it refer to our rational faculties, our moral responsibilities, our spiritual nature? Sensible as each suggestion is, none is really adequate on its own if our relationship to God is left out. This is probably the central idea, that God intended our relationship to him to remain unbroken and that we would grow up within the 'family', to bear the imprint of his nature in all its diversity and breadth.

Two illustrations may help us understand the biblical notion of the image of God:

■ **An image is a stamp of ownership.** Just as a coin might bear the likeness of the Sovereign or President so it was God's desire that the family character of beauty, love and holiness might mark our lives. Although humanity's fall has defaced the image of God in us, it is not obscured totally. Even in the most evil and perverse of people God's image is present and marks that person as really belonging to him.

■ **An image is seen in a mirror.** A mirror remains a mirror even though no one has used it for years but, of course, its nature and destiny are not fulfilled until it is used. Paul appears to draw on this idea: 'We who ... all reflect the Word's glory, are being transformed into his likeness.' That is, those who are in Christ are like mirrors before him, reflecting in our lives the spiritual and moral unity between Creator and creature. Jesus Christ is the only true 'image of the invisible God'. In his likeness we are being shaped, and one day we will be fully like him.

The implications of this teaching are very great and have personal, social and political significance. To us as persons God declares his love and his estimate of our worth. We might sometimes despair of ourselves and might even wallow in terrifying seas of self-loathing. But how can we deny God's regard for us? We are made in his image and that means that he likes and loves us as we essentially are. The idea is very important for social and political thought as well. Here is the basis for Christian concern and action. If we are made in the image of God, then we are equal in God's sight and ought to have equal opportunities for a full, dignified human existence. This is the Christian charter for humanity, and because of it we should fight against all forces of oppression, poverty and ignorance which dehumanize people today.

References

Genesis 1:26

Genesis 9:6

Romans 8:29

1 Corinthians 11:7

1 Corinthians 15:49

2 Corinthians 3:18

2 Corinthians 4:4

Philippians 2:5–10

Colossians 1:15

Colossians 3:10

Hebrews 1:3

James 3:9

Incarnation

'Incarnation' is a technical word meaning that God in Jesus 'took flesh' and became a human person. This great claim of Christians finds abundant support in the Bible.

The Old Testament begins with God creating humanity in his own 'image'. That is, we were meant from the start to walk with God, grow like him and share his nature. But humanity's fall into sin wrecked this relationship and introduced guilt and death. It is the unspoken assumption of the Old Testament that God had to do something about this tragic parting of ways to bring us back to himself. It looks forward to the coming of God's 'Messiah' who would deliver his people from their sins. (See *Jesus the Messiah*.) The New Testament sees Jesus fulfilling that expectation.

The New Testament takes Jesus' humanity for granted. Although his birth was exceptional, he grew as all children do in knowledge as well as physical growth; he experienced hunger and thirst; he knew what it was to feel tired; he learned from experience; there were times when he was ignorant; and he suffered a real death. The incarnation stresses the reality of the human Jesus. William Temple used to say, 'Christianity is the most materialistic of religions'— because of its central message that God has revealed himself in the human life of Jesus Christ.

But equally firmly the New Testament is clear that Jesus was more than human. The total impression of this man's life, his teaching and mighty works, the death he consented to and his resurrection led the first Christians to preach with great excitement that this Jesus was the 'Christ', the 'Lord', the 'promised Saviour', and even 'the image of the invisible God'. The New Testament is compelled, by the impact of Jesus to make the most staggering claims for him, knowing that this would infuriate the Jews and send the learned Greek philosophers into peals of laughter. But the reality of the incarnation was unquestioned by the apostles and as they preached the good news of God's salvation through Jesus Christ they saw its effectiveness in a confident, growing church. In the words of John's Gospel, they believed firmly that the 'Word took flesh and dwelt among us'.

Why did Jesus Christ become a human being?

■ **Because humanity's need requires a saviour.** Christ did not come to us because we needed a social worker. Such was our predicament that he came 'to seek and to save the lost'. God's response to human sin was personally to intervene in our history.

■ **Because God wanted to identify with human sorrows, joys and**

needs. We should never present the Christian faith as though the last week of Jesus' life was the only period that really mattered. The death and resurrection of Jesus were the climax of a life given over for us. He *lived* the cross before he died it. Incarnation therefore means that Christ has now taken our human nature into God's presence as a foretaste of the glory we shall share one day.

■ **Because we need a model for Christian living.** Jesus reveals the beauty of human nature when it is lived for the glory of God. Just as good teachers will hold up to their pupils a model of what they are trying to teach, so God declares to us through the incarnation: 'This is what is meant by the image of God. See my Son's holiness, his joy and goodness, his power and victory over sin. This was my intention for you from the beginning.' Although as far as this life is concerned we shall fall far short of the quality of Jesus' life, nevertheless we should not be afraid of following the practice of the early Christians, who kept before them the inspiration of Christ's life as the way they ought to live.

References
Matthew 1:20–23
Matthew 4:1–11
Mark 13:32
Mark 14:32–36
Luke 2:39–52
Luke 10:21
John 1:10–14
John 4:7
John 6:38
John 12:27–28
Acts 2:22
Acts 10:38–40
Acts 13:23–25
Romans 8:3
Galatians 4:4
Philippians 2:5–11
1 Timothy 2:5
1 Timothy 3:16
Hebrews 2:17–18
Hebrews 4:15
Hebrews 5:7–10
1 Peter 4:1
1 John 4:1–3

Jesus the Messiah

The Hebrew word *Messiah* (with its Greek equivalent *Christ*) originally means someone anointed by God. In the Bible it usually means more: a God-sent rescuer who bursts into a crisis to sort things out.

A longing for a Messiah arises particularly when a people groan under a foreign oppressor, look back wistfully to past glories and cling to a creed which tells them they are God's special people. In the Old Testament, there were hints of the one who would come. But in the bitter days of Israel's occupation, first by the Greeks and then by the Romans, the cry for a deliverer became more desperate and insistent. Occasionally the 'coming one' was seen in spiritual terms but far more often he was a 'son of David' who would win military victories and expel the Romans. Literature produced in earlier persecutions liked to picture him in lurid colours, wielding supernatural weapons. It was this nerve which John the Baptist touched, with his message of one who was coming to thresh the people and baptize them in fire.

Certainly, Galilee was a breeding ground for messianic hotheads. In AD6, for example, Judas of Galilee raised the standard of rebellion in protest at the Roman-imposed census. We can imagine the effect on the boy Jesus as he watched the survivors of this ill-starred campaign limp home, wounded, demoralized, searching for bolt-holes to hide them from Rome's vengeance.

Jesus began his ministry in an atmosphere of intense messianic expectation, but in what sense can he be called the Messiah? Certainly, he displayed messianic qualities. He healed the sick, the lame, the deaf, the dumb and the blind. His sermon at Nazareth—given us in Luke chapter 4 verses 16–21—sounded like a manifesto for a new age. And his triumphal entry into Jerusalem and cleansing of the temple both suggested the actions of someone behaving 'as if he owned the place'.

People also drew messianic conclusions. In John's Gospel a number of individuals recognized Jesus as the Messiah and the crowd once tried to make him king. When the disciples were pressed by Jesus, 'Who do you say that I am?', Peter jumped to the shattering conclusion, 'You are the Christ.'

Yet Jesus disliked people calling him 'Messiah' publicly. He is reluctant to apply it to himself, too. His answer to the High Priest's question at his trial, 'Are you the Christ . . .?' is best taken as meaning, 'Yes, though that would not be my way of putting it.'

Why was he so reluctant to accept the title? Perhaps because a word is known by the company it keeps. 'Messiah' was too tied up with ideas of violence, military might and nationalism to do a useful job. So Jesus linked the term with suffering in an attempt to correct misconceptions. 'Yes,' he seems to be saying, 'I am the rescuer, but my way of delivering you involves dying on the cross.' To the average person, like Peter, this was impossible to understand.

After the resurrection the whole world was changed. The glory, power and victory of the Messiah were now locked into Jesus' death on the cross. Christians could now understand what Jesus had hinted at before. They preached a suffering Messiah, a 'Christ crucified'.

Once the gospel moved out of its Jewish setting, of course, 'Christ' became a foreign word. It gradually lost its original meaning and was used, as it tends to be today, just as another name for Jesus. Which is a pity, because Jesus as the Messiah shows us that God always fulfils what he promises, even if the fulfilment is long delayed.

References

Psalms 72:1–17	Luke 1:32–33
Psalms 89:3–4	Luke 2:11
Isaiah 9:6–7	Luke 4:16–21
Isaiah 11:1–5	Luke 7:18–23
Isaiah 53:1–12	John 4:25–26
Isaiah 61:1–11	John 14:1–15:27
Ezekiel 37:24–25	Acts 2:36
Micah 4:1–2	Acts 3:18–26
Micah 5:2	1 Corinthians 1:23–24
Zechariah 9:9–10	1 Peter 2:21–25
Matthew 21:1–9	
Mark 8:27–30	
Mark 14:60–64	

Jesus the Redeemer

'Redeemer' was a very expressive term in the ancient world. But modern readers 'hear' it as a religious word, although trading stamps and the pawn shop give us a small clue. We may have better luck with the word 'ransom' which, in an age of terrorist activity, is depressingly up to date. 'Ransom' brings the idea of a victim who has fallen into the hands of powerful enemies and a release which involves the payment of a large sum of money.

Similar ideas lay behind the use of 'redeem' in the ancient world. For example, aristocratic Greek or Roman prisoners of war were sometimes 'ransomed' at enormous cost. Again, a slave might buy his freedom by a kind of religious fiction known as 'sacred release', in which he took money along to a temple, where he became part of a sacred story in which the god 'bought him out' or 'redeemed' him.

The Bible is packed with redemption ideas:

■ **Israel had its next-of-kin redeemers,** near relatives who had the responsibility of looking after members of the family when they fell on bad times. So your redeemer might be called on to buy a field from you if you were getting into debt, buy your freedom if you had got yourself enslaved or marry your wife if you had inconveniently died. There were, in addition, dozens of situations where someone might need to ward off a plague or death sentence by payment of money and so 'redeem himself'. The same themes recur through these examples—a victim, a desperate plight and liberation. But always at a price.

■ **In the New Testament Jesus is the Redeemer.** The title draws in all the associations already mentioned. Sin is slavery; it is a plight from which people cannot free themselves. The Law which should be a check-marker for holy living becomes a ghastly reminder of failure. Paul expresses the sense of being a slave and victim in an agonized cry, 'I have the desire to do what is good, but I cannot carry it out...' As so often, the Psalmist states the heart of the problem: 'No man can redeem the life of another or give to God a ransom for him. The ransom for a life is costly, no payment is ever enough.'

The good news is that Jesus, as God incarnate, could find the ransom price. He himself described his death on the cross as giving 'his life as a ransom for many'. It is important not to push the picture beyond its limits. The New Testament never actually says to whom or what the price was paid. But it does make clear that Jesus frees people who are unable to free themselves. And this act of liberation costs God dearly. He never just says of human sin, 'Never mind. Let's pretend it never happened.'

Redemption affects the present and the future. Here and now a sinner can experience forgiveness of sins, freedom from slavery, and a life with purpose to it. At the end of the age, Christians look for total freedom—from the penalty, power and even the presence of sin. And they expect the 'redemption' of the created universe. Meanwhile they are called to live life as marked men and women ('sealed' the Bible calls it), who have been 'bought with a price'.

References

Exodus 6:6	*1 Corinthians 6:19–20*
Exodus 13:12–16	*2 Corinthians 5:14–21*
Leviticus 25:47–55	*Galatians 3:13*
Job 33:24	*Galatians 5:1*
Psalms 49:7–8	*Colossians 1:14*
Mark 10:45	*Ephesians 1:7*
Luke 1:68	*1 Timothy 2:5–6*
John 8:34–36	*1 Peter 1:18–19*
Acts 8:32–36	*Revelation 5:9–10*
Romans 3:24–26	

Jesus the Teacher

If the Christian gospel can change people's lives for eternity, then we have a vital duty to get it across to others. But how is this to be done? Surely the example of Jesus the Teacher is the one to follow.

The rabbi in Jesus' day was held in high regard. He went through a taxing course of training, gathered his disciples (a little like a modern guru), and delivered weighty commentaries on the Old Testament and its application to everyday life. No wonder 'teacher' was an esteemed title.

Jesus was also called 'rabbi' and 'teacher'. He was recognized as one who explained the scriptures, debated them with other experts and gathered disciples. Yet there was a difference. He obviously had had no formal training; he was as happy to teach in the fields or from a boat as in the synagogues; he was not averse to setting aside the Law of Moses if the demands of the occasion required it or making it a hundred times *more* demanding by drawing out its deepest implications.

The typical teacher taught by making scrupulous and painstaking reference to the line of teachers who had gone before him. None would feel free to ignore the line of tradition. But Jesus astonished everyone by the freedom with which he handled the Law and by his personal authority. As a teacher he inspired awe, fear and confidence. On the road to Jerusalem no one dared to ask him any question who had caught a glimpse of his face set like a flint towards the cross. Yet he encouraged an openness to outcasts, taxmen, prostitutes, lepers and children which contrasted with the typically tight rabbinical circle of teacher with disciples. And perhaps most significantly, he called people to follow him as his personal disciples, rather than just to learn the Law. His authority as a teacher did not seem to hang on his learning, his training or his social status.

The ordinary people heard him with delight, which is not surprising when we look at his methods. Jesus revelled in the vivid image and the outrageous picture. He writes in the sand while the respectable demand punishment for an adulteress; he washes his followers' feet to make a point they will never forget. He sets the crowd buzzing with a startling paradox ('not peace but a sword'), a blistering turn of phrase ('whitewashed tombs') or a scandalous demand ('go the second mile'). They may have complained 'this is a hard saying', but they never found him boring.

Jesus was different in two other respects:

- **He put himself at the centre of his teaching** ('follow me'). This would have been distasteful on the lips of anyone else, but was not so on his.

- **He was not interested in information for its own sake.** To

Nicodemus who begins promisingly—'Rabbi, we know you are a teacher come from God'—he replies with a statement which goes to the heart: 'Unless a man be born again he cannot see the kingdom of God.' Jesus' questions are never to be taken at their face value. His parables are never simple stories, despite all appearances. He hinted that since a parable's real meaning could only be 'lived', not mugged up, whether you understood it or not depended on the openness of your heart rather than your intellect or education. There were those who understood a parable well enough, but because of their hardness they were probably worse off after hearing it than before. None of his teaching, least of all the 'beautiful' Sermon on the Mount, was designed merely to entertain the intellect. As many have found since, his words are a revolutionary manifesto and a rock on which to build a life.

References

Matthew 5:1—7:29	Luke 4:16–22
Matthew 13:1–52	Luke 6:39–40
Matthew 16:21–23	Luke 9:1–6
Matthew 18:1–15	Luke 10:25–37
Matthew 21:23–27	Luke 11:1–13
Matthew 22:15–46	Luke 15:1–32
Matthew 25:1–46	Luke 19:47–48
Matthew 28:16–20	Luke 24:25–27
Mark 1:14–15	John 3:1–13
Mark 3:13–15	John 7:14–18
Mark 4:1–20	John 13:1–17
Mark 11:18	John 14:1–10
Mark 13:1–37	John 16:12–14
Luke 2:46–47	

Jesus the Word

The 'Word' is a title for Jesus found almost exclusively in John's Gospel. It was a term with a rich set of associations for both Jew and Greek. In fact John's decision to call Jesus the Word was a brilliant attempt to communicate the truth about Christ in language that would ring bells in both worlds at once.

■ **For the Jew, the 'Word' could only mean the 'Word of the Lord' in the Old Testament.** It was the 'Word of the Lord' which came to the prophets and made them the bearers of a personal message from God to the people. It was by his Word that God made the world. When he said, 'Let there be . . .' something new came into existence. The Word, then, was the communication of what God had in mind. God acted powerfully through it. He had even made the world by it. To receive God's Word and live by it was the way to find life.

■ **In the world of Greek thought, the Word (*Logos* in Greek) was one of the taken-for-granted ideas.** The Stoics, for example, said that the universe was not the result of random forces. It was not a chaos, a mess or a disorder. It had a logic to it. This hidden blueprint ensured that nature followed a regular pattern, that the grass grew, the beasts had their seasons and the stars did not fall from the sky. The reason why things were as they were, the Stoics called Logos. Logos was both the invisible programming and the specific examples of it in the print-out.

About the time of Jesus a Jew called Philo, himself immersed in Greek ideas, took the bold step of connecting the Greek Logos with the Old Testament Word.

■ **This process is not difficult for us to appreciate, since we use words in much the same way.** 'What do you have in mind?' we ask people. And they reply by putting their thoughts into words. We use words to plan our projects, to get things done, to communicate and explain ourselves to others. In one way we can look on our words as separate entities. And yet, of course, they could hardly be more closely related to us. Unless I'm putting on an act, who I am, what I think and what I say are all the same thing.

We can see how brilliantly John built a bridge between two worlds by calling Jesus the Logos/Word. But he was not just using a familiar term. There was one enormous leap forward. John made the incredible claim that the Word of God had become a particular human being: 'the Word became flesh.' 'Flesh' is what humans are made of, it is the stuff that bleeds. So the living, breathing, walking Jesus of Nazareth is the mind of God,

God's thought-processes embodied. Jesus is the means by which God made the universe; he is the working-out of the blueprint.

If someone were to say, on a bleak Monday morning, 'What is life all about?' John would reply, 'Look at Jesus and you'll see what the universe means.' The way God is and the way God works are fleshed out in him. To receive Jesus is to tune in to the universe, to live the way you were designed to live. It is like running with the escalator and not against it.

References

Genesis 1:1–31
Psalms 33:6–9
Isaiah 55:10–11
John 1:1–18
Hebrews 1:1–3
Revelation 19:13

Judgment

Judgment is not a popular idea. It smacks too much of hell-fire preaching and vindictiveness. Yet it is impossible to detach the note of judgment from the Bible. In fact, it is difficult to know why any Christian would want to, because the Day of Judgment is when God will begin his reign, when good will finally overcome evil and we will see the triumph of both justice and grace.

In the Old Testament, belief in a 'Day of the Lord' was well established by the time of Amos. It was seen as a 'good time for all Israel' when God would see that his people were all right. But Amos turned this right round: the nation's sin would make it a day of darkness, not light. From then on it became commonplace for the prophets to preach God's judgment on a rebellious people. This judgment would come in national defeat and deportation, but the experience of exile would refine the people and create a purged remnant through whom God could work.

Alongside this theme lay the idea of a judgment on the nations which oppressed Israel. The literature which came from times of persecution developed this into a technicolour scenario, with God coming in the clouds, judging the living and the dead and bestowing a kingdom on the saints of the Most High. In this way those who were suffering comforted themselves with the thought that 'one day soon' their resistance would be recognized and their enemies vanquished.

And then Jesus came, throwing the whole question of a future judgment into the melting-pot. Because Jesus was God's last word. The end-time had arrived already. Up to a point all the 'future' things—eternal life, last judgment, second coming, resurrection of the dead—are now. As Jesus encountered people he created a crisis, a separation. They were for him or against him. Herod judged himself when he tried to murder Jesus; Pilate condemned himself when he dared to sit in judgment on him; and the cross was the ultimate judgment on the world's values. Paul presents judgment as a process where God allows people to live out the consequences of their own decisions.

And yet there is still a judgment to come. The Bible speaks of a time when the choices people have made will be confirmed. The eternal consequences of accepting or rejecting Jesus Christ will be made clear. God will judge the living and the dead. Judgment is guaranteed by the resurrection of Jesus. It follows his coming in glory. It will result in the overthrow of all that is evil and the triumphant reign of God.

Much of this is described in pictures, but it is important to take seriously the realities to which the pictures point. Jesus spoke of 'outer darkness', 'fire', 'weeping', 'a shut door', of people being 'lost'. Paul also wrote of the Christians' lifework (though built on a foundation which can never be touched) being 'tested by fire', so that they should be careful how they build. And the parable of the sheep and goats pictures the nations being judged by the way they treated Jesus when they met him unrecognized.

If judgment is a reality, then it is hard to go along with those who say everyone will be saved in the end, or there is a second chance after death. But many questions remain unanswered. Are we judged as soon as we die or do we await the Day of Judgment? Is punishment eternal or do only those in Christ survive? What about those who have never heard the gospel? The New Testament does give some clues but a good deal depends on what you make of the picture language.

In any case the Bible is not very concerned with the furniture of heaven and the temperature of hell. It concentrates on a positive truth. Christ has died, and so no one need be condemned. It speaks about being 'justified' by faith in Jesus, which is a picture of walking away from a law-court, free.

References

Genesis 18:25	*Romans 1:18–32*
Psalms 9:17	*Romans 2:6–11*
Isaiah 3:13–15	*Romans 14:10–12*
Ezekiel 18:1–32	*1 Corinthians 3:10–15*
Daniel 12:1–3	*1 Corinthians 4:3–5*
Amos 5:14–20	*2 Corinthians 5:10*
Malachi 2:17–3:5	*2 Thessalonians 1:5–10*
Malachi 4:1–3	*2 Timothy 4:1*
Matthew 3:7–12	*Hebrews 2:2–3*
Matthew 11:20–24	*Hebrews 9:27*
Matthew 13:37–43	*Hebrews 10:26–31*
Matthew 25:31–46	*1 Peter 4:5*
Luke 16:19–31	*2 Peter 3:7–13*
John 3:18–21	*1 John 4:17*
John 5:24–29	*Revelation 20:11–15*
Acts 10:42	*Revelation 22:10–13*
Acts 17:30–31	

Justice

When we look around it seems all too obvious that we live in a very unjust world. **It seems unfair** that the resources of this globe are controlled by one third of the population while the remaining two thirds live on or below the poverty line. **It seems unfair** that in most societies, East and West, there will be found the rich, who own a great deal of the resources and control their distribution. **It seems unfair** that the unjust often go unpunished while the honest and deserving are harshly treated. We have to agree with the writer of Ecclesiastes: 'In this world you find wickedness where justice and right ought to be.'

But this dismal picture is inevitable only when God is left out of our reckoning. In the Bible he is the source of justice. One of the best of the many good things he has given us is a clear moral framework, by which we can live out the kind of life he wants us to enjoy. If we want to use this framework to find the way of justice, we have to focus on two qualities—holiness and love.

■ **True holiness is based on God's holy Law.** 'Justice' is really a translation of the word 'righteousness'. This is a quality of life God wants from us all as we keep his commandments. But this is easier said than done. Only by claiming in faith the forgiveness and new life which God offers us in Jesus Christ can we ever find God's righteousness.

God's Law, then, cannot itself make us righteous. But still, as forgiven people, we make it our aim to live as God requires and to honour his way of living. So God's people will keep his laws and those of their society. We will honour the just claims made on us by others and try to live as honest, reliable and just people.

■ **True justice is based on God's holy love.** Christian love is not a mawkish thing but a fierce commitment to God and his world. It is a love which does more than feel sorry for the needy; it tries to do something for them. When William Wilberforce started his campaign for the abolition of slavery he was not guided by sentimentalism but by clear Christian principles of justice, gleaned from the character of God's love. He knew that the gospel values every person—black and white, male and female—as of equal worth before God. He believed with all his heart that it was morally wrong for one human being to be owned by another, and he felt the scandal of one person being free to live with dignity while another was denied a full human existence. Love broke from Wilberforce as a cry for justice—a cry that spanned his whole life.

True Christianity refuses to be confined within the narrow area of life we call 'religious'. It is a way of life which spills over into our everyday experience, our social life and our political aspirations. If it is a living faith, Christianity will stand at the crossroads of human life and call people to a just God who wants everyone without exception to enjoy his bounty. His people must be committed to justice, standing up for those who are unfairly treated and courageously opposing all evil and all breaking of God's Law.

References

Genesis 18:19	Isaiah 9:7
Leviticus 18:4–5	Isaiah 26:7
Deuteronomy 16:18–20	Isaiah 45:21
Deuteronomy 25:15	Isaiah 59:9
Deuteronomy 32:4	Isaiah 59:14
Deuteronomy 33:21	Isaiah 61:8
2 Samuel 8:15	Jeremiah 4:2
2 Samuel 23:3	Jeremiah 31:23
1 Kings 6:12	Jeremiah 50:7
2 Chronicles 19:6	Amos 5:24
Nehemiah 9:33	Micah 6:8
Job 8:3	Zephaniah 3:5
Job 36:17	Zechariah 7:9
Psalms 7:9	Malachi 2:17
Psalms 11:7	Malachi 3:5
Psalms 19:8	Matthew 23:1–5
Psalms 89:14	Matthew 23:23–28
Psalms 94:15	Mark 6:20
Psalms 99:4	Luke 1:46–55
Psalms 103:6	Luke 10:29–37
Proverbs 2:9	Romans 1:32
Proverbs 8:15	Romans 13:1–7
Proverbs 12:5	2 Timothy 4:8
Proverbs 29:27	1 Peter 3:12
Isaiah 1:17	Revelation 15:3
Isaiah 5:16	Revelation 16:5–7

The Kingdom of God

Every political organization or social group that wants to change society has its manifesto or programme. Jesus' manifesto was the 'kingdom of God'. He burst on the scene about AD30 exclaiming: 'The time is fulfilled and the kingdom of God is at hand.'

What did he mean by this? In the time of Jesus the Jews looked for God to intervene in many different ways. Some longed for a revolutionary, political leader who would overthrow the power of Rome; some looked for a period of peace and prosperity in which they could live in safety and bring up their children without fear; some longed for God to send his Chosen One to establish a kingdom for the Jews at Jerusalem.

But Jesus' idea of the kingdom was very new and very different:

■ **The kingdom was already here**. 'The kingdom of God is among you,' he said; now he had come, the kingdom was here. The mighty works he was doing were signs of the breaking in of his kingdom. To follow Jesus, therefore, meant entering his kingdom.

■ **For Jesus the 'kingdom' was the rule of God in human hearts**, rather than a territory with definable borders, as the word means to us. It means people, not property: people who follow and acknowledge him as Lord. The kingdom, then, for Jesus was a spiritual rather than material reality.

■ **The kingdom became a living reality through Jesus' death and resurrection**. After Peter made his great confession that Jesus was 'the Christ, the Son of the living God', Jesus spoke less about the kingdom and more about his cross. But these are not two separate ideas. The kingdom only becomes a kingdom for us through what Jesus did on the cross. His death is the key to the kingdom, the door by which we enter.

■ **The kingdom in its fulness is yet to come**. It has come in part, but it will only fully come when Jesus Christ returns to reign. In the meantime the church—that part of God's creation which accepts his authority—must continue to preach the message of the kingdom.

It is clear from Jesus' teaching about the kingdom of God (or 'kingdom of heaven' as Matthew calls it) that he was concerned with the quality of human life. We who belong to the kingdom should show it in holy living, by expressing compassion and concern for others, by being 'salt' and 'light' in society. This will involve social and political action, although we must never fall into the trap of assuming that Jesus' kingdom is a blueprint for social change. It is important to remember that Jesus never tried to give a clear definition of the kingdom. By teaching in parables he was disclosing a revolutionary message 'in code', so that the poor as well as the rich, the slave as well as the free, the Gentile as well as the Jew, might enter.

References

Exodus 19:5	Mark 14:25
Psalms 45:6	Luke 9:1–2
Daniel 4:37	Luke 17:20–21
Matthew 3:1–3	Luke 19:11
Matthew 4:23–25	John 18:36
Matthew 6:10	Acts 1:6
Matthew 13:1–52	Romans 14:17
Matthew 16:13–20	1 Corinthians 4:20
Matthew 16:28	1 Corinthians 6:9–10
Matthew 25:1–46	1 Corinthians 15:50
Mark 4:11	Revelation 1:9
Mark 10:23	

The Land

Most people want a place of their own; it is a natural human longing. To say, 'That's my house' or 'That's my land' gives great pleasure, and many more would love to be able to say it. It was this desire that drove settlers in North America out into the wilderness to claim the land, to build their farms and houses and to start a new life in a new world. In a very similar way, the Hebrews set out from Egypt to settle down in a 'land of promise'. But there was one significant difference: the Hebrews believed that their land was given to them by God.

Three great themes are at the heart of the Bible idea of 'land':

■ **God promised Israel a land** where they could find peace and prosperity. 'Go from your country,' said God to Abraham, 'to the land which I will show you.' God's call to Abraham to leave his security in one land and to seek for another was the dream which shaped Israel as a people. This explains why they considered it right to drive out other occupants of the land; all others were exercising 'squatters' rights', while they alone were the rightful inheritors.

■ **The land represented God's presence.** In the Old Testament we find that as God's people settled down in the land so the land itself, and important elements within it, became symbols of God's presence. So to this day three major religions

call the land of Israel 'the Holy Land'. Jerusalem (Zion), its most sacred city and (for the Jew) the temple, as the place where the Ark of the Covenant once resided, symbolize God's personal presence.

Taken on their own, these two themes could lead people to conclude that the land was theirs for ever and they could do whatever they liked with it. And we find this attitude coming out from time to time in the Old Testament when people forgot the third very crucial element:

■ **The land really belongs to God**; the people's task was to be wise and careful stewards. So we find in the book of Deuteronomy many instructions to take care of the land, not to waste or exhaust it. Every seventh year the land should lie fallow to regain its strength. The lesson is drummed in. Because God has given it to you to enjoy, out of gratitude to him you should be generous to others. Let some of your produce go to the foreigner, the fatherless and the widow. Share your wealth with the poor and the foreigner because 'you were once poor and a stranger'. Every third year, one tenth of all produce had to be set aside as a contribution to the needy. God even declares: 'There will be no poor among you.' And every seventh year, slaves should be given the option of freedom and a generous token of the wealth of the land they had helped to produce. God's ownership of the land was symbolically recognized each year through the offering of the 'first fruits', presented in the temple to the Lord.

We can see at once one very important difference between the Christian and the Jew. For the Jews, the land is an essential feature of their faith, but for the Christian what counts is possessing God and being a citizen of heaven. Still there is a belief common to both: whatever patch of land we enjoy, together with the material blessings that go with it, is not to be used selfishly but for God and his people.

This is why Christians should be among those who want the poor to share the riches of this world, why we should be generous and sacrificial in our giving to the needy, and why we should care for the land and use it for God's glory and his people.

References

Genesis 12:1–3	Joshua 11:23
Genesis 13:15	Psalms 85:1–13
Exodus 3:17	Isaiah 1:7
Leviticus 25:8–17	Isaiah 24:1–20
Leviticus 25:23–34	Isaiah 26:1–4
Numbers 14:5–8	Ezekiel 48:1–22
Deuteronomy 6:10–15	Joel 2:22–26
Deuteronomy 8:1–10	Amos 2:6–8
Joshua 1:1–9	

Law

In all societies lawlessness appears to be on the increase these days, yet many still think that if we had complete freedom we would be better off.

But God is a great believer in law! In the Old Testament we see that, following the covenant he made with Moses, his Law (the Torah) was given to the people of Israel so that their lives might express that they were in fact the children of God. (See under *Covenant*.)

It is important to remember that at the beginning the Torah was not intended to be simply a list of dos and don'ts. The Hebrew word *torah* means 'instruction' and it was intended to be a framework for life, a gift of God's grace so that Israel might become in conduct what they already were—the people of God. Unfortunately, human nature is apt to turn a benefit into a barrier and this happened with the Law. By the time of Jesus the Pharisees had hedged the covenant around with 613 laws which the Jews were expected to keep. Jesus condemned the legalists who had made a prison camp of God's Torah: 'The scribes and Pharisees sit on Moses' seat... [but] they bind heavy burdens, hard to bear, and lay them on men's shoulders.'

Jesus' own attitude to the Law is interesting. On the one hand he was prepared to ignore it and even criticize it. Yet, on the other hand, he commended it and obeyed it as having divine authority. This apparent contradiction is resolved when we understand that Jesus believed that he had come, not to condemn or abolish the Law, but to fulfil it.

Jesus fulfilled the Law firstly by showing that love is the fulfilling of the Law. Indeed, he declared the double command to 'love the Lord your God with all your heart... soul... mind... and your neighbour as you love yourself,' to be the perfect summary of the entire Law.

And secondly Jesus showed, by his whole life of obedience to the Father from start to finish, that this was how the genuinely human life should be lived. His death on the cross ushered in the new covenant so the way of salvation now is not by keeping laws but by receiving God's forgiveness through Christ. He and not the Law opens the way between the Father and us.

Is the Law relevant for us today?

■ **The Law is fulfilled in Jesus Christ but this does not mean we can pass it by.** Its inadequacies are clear enough. It cannot lead a person to God, and because of its appeal to standards which are beyond us, only increases our sinfulness. Nevertheless it still remains 'holy, just and good'. Although we are not bound by the 613 laws of the old Jewish tradition, and although the Old Testament ceremonial law is fulfilled in the new covenant, the essence of the moral law as expressed in the Ten Commandments must be kept by us all. We are not made Christian, of course, by keeping them. But we heed them because we *are* Christians and we want to live well for God.

■ **The gospel cannot be properly understood as good news without the preaching of the Law.** Its standard of what God requires is the backcloth against which the gospel makes sense. The church fails when it neglects God's standards of holiness, justice and love.

■ **Paul writes of the 'natural' law written in our hearts.** He means by this that those who have had no chance of responding to the gospel in this life are not condemned automatically by God. Because he is the God of mercy and love, he judges such people by what they have made of the law of conscience within.

References

Exodus 20:1–17	Matthew 5:17–20
Exodus 21:24	Matthew 22:37–40
Leviticus 19:1–37	Mark 2:24–28
Leviticus 25:23–34	Romans 2:12–16
Numbers 15:37–41	Romans 3:20
Deuteronomy 5:6–21	Romans 4:13–15
Deuteronomy 11:1	Romans 5:12–15
Deuteronomy 11:13	Romans 7:4–12
Deuteronomy 11:26–28	Romans 7:21–25
Joshua 24:14–15	Romans 13:10
2 Kings 8:13	Romans 15:1–7
Nehemiah 8:1–18	Galatians 2:16–20
Psalms 19:7–14	Galatians 3:13
Psalms 119:97–112	Galatians 3:21
Jeremiah 7:21–26	Galatians 4:4–5
Malachi 1:6–14	James 2:8
Malachi 3:6–10	

Love

It is not exaggerating to say that love is a description of the whole Christian life.

■ **First comes God's love for us.** In the Old Testament, God loves Israel and rescues her from slavery. Though this love may involve discipline and judgment, yet he has sworn never to give her up: 'Israel' is engraved on the palms of his hands. The people of Israel, for their part, are commanded to love God with all their powers, along with their fellow Israelites and the foreigners among them.

In the New Testament the fundamental fact is that God is Love, and that there is a richness of love within God. Jesus is the Father's 'beloved Son' and the Son loves the Father; the love between them shows the Spirit's presence. Out of that love flows the divine love for mankind, which shows itself in the coming of Jesus and particularly in his death. 'God commends his love in that while we were still sinners Christ died for us.' 'God loved the world so much that he gave his only son.' The cross is an expression of God's love; in no way is it the action of a vindictive deity.

The life, death and resurrection of Jesus are part of one loving rescue operation for humanity. In fact, the apostle Paul speaks of Jesus loving us in a once-for-all, unrepeatable way. He is 'the Son of God who loved me (once, on a definite occasion) and gave himself for me.' In one of the great passages of triumph in the Bible, in Romans chapter 8 verses 37–39, Paul exults in the fact that nothing in all creation can separate him from the love of God in Christ.

■ **Next comes our love for God.** The New Testament says rather less about this, perhaps simply because God's love comes first. But Jesus endorses the great commandment, 'You shall love the Lord your God . . .' And in John's Gospel he emphasizes that we show our love for God by obeying him. The Christian is called to a singleminded love that will cling to God in the face of the attractions of the world or even family ties. And Jesus restores Peter precisely by pressing the question whether he loves him 'more than these' (the other disciples).

■ **Then there follows our love for other people.** Perhaps the most striking aspect of the Bible's teaching on love is that it is presented as a command. It is not primarily a matter of feeling or liking or talking. It has to do with the will. If love is commanded, then to love our family or our neighbour or even our enemy is not something which is up for negotiation. If it is commanded then it is possible.

This is likely to make most people

feel inadequate. But the Bible stresses that our love for our fellows is in the way of a *response*. It is a response to the love of Jesus; we love because he first loved us. It is a response to the Spirit within us, who sheds the love of God abroad in our hearts. It is a response to our being united to Christ as branches are connected to the stem of a vine. Love is his fruit.

Love is the mark of the church. The world is to know the disciples of Jesus not by their zeal or doctrinal purity but by the love they have for one another. Love has to be incarnated—lived out. Christian living is not a matter of working out an ethical system. There is always a specific person, here in front of you, in a concrete situation. Love is the greatest of gifts.

Paul sets love against cleverness, or even knowledge, if by that is meant something secret which only the select few can grasp. Love builds up where knowledge can puff up. Love is a matter of action. It shows itself in a thousand different forms—in hospitality, in greeting, in not being snobbish, in not keeping a score of wrongs, in weeping with those who weep, in encouraging, in giving up your rights, in speaking out, in working together, in seeking reconciliation. It is the 'more excellent way'.

References

Numbers 14:19	John 21:15–17
Deuteronomy 7:7–9	Romans 5:5
Deuteronomy 10:18–19	Romans 5:8
Psalms 86:5	Romans 8:37–39
Psalms 103:1–18	1 Corinthians 13:1–13
Psalms 107:1–43	Galatians 2:20
Psalms 116:1–2	Ephesians 3:17–19
Isaiah 49:16	Ephesians 5:2
Hosea 11:1–4	Colossians 3:14
Luke 6:35	1 Thessalonians 5:13
Luke 10:25–37	James 2:8–13
John 3:16	1 Peter 1:22
John 13:1	1 John 3:14–18
John 14:21–24	1 John 4:7–12

Male and Female

Probably the greatest social revolution of our time has been the emancipation of women. Until this century women were limited to their three traditional strongholds: children, kitchen and church. Outside these areas women could not move without being frowned on. But now women have greater freedom and opportunity in practically every society and this has been of benefit to us all.

But there have been harmful side-effects. Some feminists consider men their bitter foe. And women seem now to be at even greater risk on the streets of our cities, from violent, embittered men.

Against this background, what is the Bible's teaching about male/female relationships?

■ **We were created equal.** In God's sight, men and women have equal honour and standing. Both sexes were made in the 'image of God' and destined for an eternal relationship with our Father. This is the divine charter for human freedom and dignity.

■ **We were created to be together.** The creation story tells us that men and women were not created to be separate and isolated but to be together, absolutely essential and necessary to one another. Apart from one another male and female cannot *be*. **We need each other not only to survive but to be truly ourselves.**

■ **We were created to be different.** The desire for equality may so easily blur the significantly different things we contribute to the human family. Human beings are not the same— and the differences are far more than sexual. They include the way we perceive life, our attitudes to others, the nature of our gifts and our consciousness of sinfulness. Such differences, falsely perceived, can become points of division and bitterness. But when accepted rightly, as part of the way we complement one another, they lead to enrichment and strength.

Christians make a very important contribution to society by working out the Bible's teaching. Take, for example, the way men and women unintentionally threaten one another. Women feel hedged about by age-old traditions and attitudes, which can still make them feel oppressed in church and society. Men can find women's emancipation deeply threatening. 'Brains rather than brawn' is the currency of a modern society and so some men feel undervalued, their strength no longer needed. How can Christians help to confront these feelings, remove the threat and make accepting relationships possible? Even in highly developed societies women sometimes complain that they are not valued as persons by men but as sex objects, particularly at work. Directly contrary to this, the Christian message is of human dignity, treating the person of the opposite sex as a sacred person made by God for God. And the task of the Christian church is to build God's community of love in which hostility, hatred and opposition are replaced by acceptance, trust and respect.

References

Genesis 1:27	Luke 8:1–3
Genesis 2:7	John 4:5–42
Genesis 2:18–25	John 20:1–18
Genesis 3:14–20	1 Corinthians 11:3–16
Joel 2:28–29	Galatians 3:28
Matthew 19:4	1 Peter 3:4
Luke 7:36–50	

Marriage and the Family

'Marriage,' goes the saying, 'is the nursery of heaven.' At least it is meant to be, although no one imagines that all marriages are perfect. Like every other human relationship marriage can be undermined by weakness, sin and selfishness. And if anyone is going to have an enduring relationship of love with another human being, it needs to be worked at and begun afresh every single day.

Despite the ever-increasing numbers of broken marriages, marriage is still the basic social unit in practically every society, and this was certainly God's intention from the beginning. He created humankind in his image as male and female, and it was his will that they should find fulfilment in one another. Paul even uses the loving and holy relationship between Christ and his church as a model for marriage as it should be. And Jesus treated marriage as a lifelong obligation which no one should sever. Divorce is always a terrible break in God's purposes, brought about through human weakness and sin.

But marriage is far more than the relationship of two people. It is the foundation of the family and the centre of a web of relationships which affect each person for good or ill. What does the Bible teach about a good marriage and wholesome family life?

■ **Faithfulness and trust.** In marriage there is only one person we can give ourselves to intimately, and that is our partner. A 'holy' marriage is one in which the other person is sacred and all other men and women are 'out of bounds'. The problem today is that this clear boundary is so often transgressed, sometimes even by Christians. The main cause is the power of sexual desire, to which none of us is too holy to be impervious. A couple who want to be faithful will keep the lines of communication open, building trust and helping each other to steer clear of situations which could become too difficult to handle. Also, the Bible tells us not to defraud one another in the matter of sexual intercourse. We must be willing to consider the needs of our partners and give ourselves willingly and in love, even though we may not always feel up to it. It is rare to find couples prepared to discuss this issue openly.

■ **A disciplined framework.** Love between the sexes is the seed-bed in which true love is propagated for the entire family. That love will express itself in a loving framework of life in which children will grow up to be mature adults themselves. The Bible has some down-to-earth things to say to us. Disciplining children is not always wrong: indeed, punishment appropriate to the misdeed will be necessary at times, so that children are brought up to heed what is right. Punishment which flows from love will never be harsh or cruel. But just because we are parents does not mean that we own our children: they belong to the Lord first. So Paul calls us to work at our family relationships—children to obey, and parents not to provoke or discourage.

■ **Companionship.** The good marriage and happy home is where our best friends are. In that context it should be natural to play, pray, laugh and have fun together—simply enjoying being with members of our own family. So marriage and the family, when they function at their best, can give us a foretaste of what heaven is like, and of the divine family of which God the Father is the head.

References

Genesis 1:26–28	*Luke 20:34*
Genesis 2:18–25	*John 2:1–2*
Genesis 24:62–67	*John 19:26–27*
Genesis 29:15–20	*1 Corinthians 7:10–11*
Proverbs 19:13–14	*1 Corinthians 7:33–34*
Proverbs 22:6	*1 Corinthians 7:38*
Proverbs 23:13–18	*Ephesians 5:21–6:4*
Proverbs 31:10–31	*Colossians 3:18–21*
Matthew 1:18–25	*Hebrews 13:4*
Matthew 19:3–9	

Ministry

Ministry begins when people start to follow Jesus Christ; it is the hallmark of discipleship. Ministry means 'service', and to be a follower is to serve. When the first disciples started to follow Jesus he soon got them to work learning and doing. They entered into his ministry of proclaiming the kingdom just as we also, when we serve others, enter into it. At the heart of the New Testament is this conviction that since Pentecost, when the Spirit came on the waiting disciples, all Christians have gifts and talents to offer their Lord and one another. So important is this point that we can put it this way: the church is ministry.

The whole church is to be a 'royal priesthood'. Although there is only one true priest—Jesus Christ, who died a sacrificial death for us all—the church took over Israel's priestly role of representing God to the world. Yet still there are distinctive ministries which God gives to his people within the wider ministry of the church. The first one we see in the New Testament is that of the 'Twelve', probably to be identified with the apostles. Their identity came from having been with Jesus in his earthly life and witnessed his resurrection. After Pentecost, ministry arose very naturally according to what was needed and as the Spirit poured out his varied gifts. Many of the terms used arise from the nature of the task—the teacher, the prophet, the deacon, the healer, the interpreter and

even the word 'bishop', which means 'overseer'.

No single authorized order of ministry arose in the New Testament. There seem to have been many different patterns of ministry. It was only after the New Testament period that a threefold order emerged—bishop, presbyter (or 'elder') and deacon.

We need to pick out three essential jobs which Christian ministry at its best will perform:

- **Authority.** It is very important for the sake of the body that we obey those who are set over us in the Lord. Although Paul teaches that every Christian is a 'minister', yet he urges obedience to those ministers who have been given authority and that we should recognize clearly their role to lead and guide the church. This is a very important principle for the church today when there are some who think they have the right to depart from the teaching of their churches and found new ones.

- **Service.** Ministry, of course, means service. We have no gifts which are just for us. Ministry is never for ourselves but always for others. Jesus showed us the example by taking a towel and washing the feet of others. Whether it is our lot to preach to thousands or to work as a porter in a hospital, all ministry for Jesus is sacrificial. It is often unrewarding and humdrum, and sometimes its consequences can be painful and costly. But for the Christian it is always worthwhile.

■ **Building up.** Because the church belongs to Jesus Christ, those who have special ministries within the body have a duty to build it up to please him. This happens when there is effective leadership—a growing church will have leaders with vision and clear goals. Gifted teaching also plays an important part, since it is through steady proclamation of the faith that people grow from immaturity to a mature and adult understanding.

But the sacraments also help this process of building up. The first, baptism, is a once-for-all sign of new birth. It is an essential mark of belonging to Jesus. (See further under *Baptism*.) Although it has always been normal practice for this sacrament to be administered by a lawfully-appointed minister, in fact any Christian can baptize if given that responsibility. And the second sacrament, holy communion, was intended to be taken repeatedly as a sign of nourishment (see article *Breaking Bread*). From earliest times the leader of this 'meal' was some one authorized by the body to celebrate the feast on their behalf. It has been common since about the third century to call this celebrant a 'priest'. This word is not acceptable to all Christians, as to some it implies that Christ's work on the cross was somehow not complete. Others are happy with it as long as it merely indicates that the 'priest' is representing the priesthood of the whole body.

The Bible's teaching reminds us that we are engaged in ministry whatever we do—whether we work in the church or in the world. Ministry does not belong only to a special group but to us all. Nevertheless, God does call people to special functions within the body and we should all be alert to the challenge to take up new tasks for him and to use our talents in his service.

References

Exodus 24:13–14	*Romans 13:4–6*
Exodus 28:1–4	*2 Corinthians 3:1–6*
Exodus 28:35	*2 Corinthians 4:1–7*
1 Samuel 2:11	*2 Corinthians 5:18–20*
1 Samuel 3:1–8	*Ephesians 4:11–13*
Psalms 103:21	*Colossians 1:7*
Isaiah 6:1–9	*Colossians 1:23*
Jeremiah 1:6–10	*1 Timothy 1:12*
Ezekiel 44:10–14	*1 Timothy 3:1–13*
Mark 3:13–19	*1 Timothy 5:17*
Mark 10:42–45	*2 Timothy 1:3–7*
John 13:3–7	*1 Peter 4:10–11*
Acts 6:1–7	*1 Peter 5:1–5*
Romans 12:4–8	

Mission

David Livingstone, the famous Scottish missionary-explorer of the last century, was once asked why he chose to be a missionary. 'God had only one Son,' he said, 'and he was a missionary.' It was that fact that made him choose his career.

Mission in fact starts and ends with God. The Bible makes it clear that he is a 'sending' God. He loves his world so much that in spite of our sin and weakness he sent his messengers, he sent his prophets, and finally he sent his Son to establish his kingdom. The entire activity of God in creation and salvation has a mission aspect to it because God's concern flows from his love. He loves us too much to leave us where we are.

Three important truths about mission need to be understood:

■ **Mission is God's work.** It is a mistake to begin with the church. Mission springs from the love of the Father, is given practical expression in the work of the Son and is made effective through the ministry of the Holy Spirit. It is God's outgoing love for the whole of creation, God's work in God's world.

■ **Mission is God's care for the whole of life.** The good news which Christ came to share embraces the whole of reality and takes in not only preaching good news to those who are in spiritual need (evangelism) but also caring for the poor, the needy and oppressed. Mission which stops at the doors of the church is defective, because God's mission is world-centred and not merely church-centred. Indeed the Bible's order of things has God moving out to the world before he moves out to the church.

■ **Mission is God's people caring for God's world.** Because God cares, we care. Because his love has been poured into our hearts, it overflows into his world. Pentecost is the great symbol of this. The gift of the Holy Spirit not only created the church, it made all Christians missionaries and we are all involved in the task of mission.

One way we do this is by simply *being who we are*. The key word is 'presence'. Just as Jesus brought in the kingdom by living among people and showing the compassion of God, so the Christian, by being with others, can bring the presence of Jesus and show his love and goodness.

Another way is by *sharing what we have*. Someone once defined evangelism as 'one beggar telling another beggar where to find bread'. In the task of evangelism we simply share what Jesus Christ means to us and has done for us. It may not be our gift to preach or explain the intellectual dimensions of the Christian faith, but every Christian can tell a unique story of what God has done and is continuing to do.

And yet another way is by *serving*

others. Just as Jesus came to serve, so the Christian gospel becomes good news for people when it is expressed not only in words but also in loving action and service.

'Go into the world and preach the gospel,' said Jesus, and this is still the church's charter. This makes missionary congregations of Christian churches—being, sharing and serving. A church begins to grow when it turns its attention outwards to the world. But that movement away from its own life and concerns may be the pathway into pain, challenge and crisis because it is the movement of the cross. But remember mission ends with God as well as beginning with him. And so we have every confidence that God's purposes are being worked out.

References

Genesis 1:28
Genesis 12:1–3
Genesis 17:1–8
Exodus 6:1–8
Exodus 19:5–6
Isaiah 11:1–4
Isaiah 40:1–5
Isaiah 43:10–13
Isaiah 43:21
Isaiah 58:6–10
Isaiah 59:16–19
Isaiah 61:1–4
Isaiah 66:18
Jeremiah 31:10–12
Jeremiah 31:31–34
Joel 2:1–2
Jonah 1:1
Micah 4:1–5
Zechariah 9:11–17
Matthew 3:1
Matthew 4:23–24
Matthew 9:35
Matthew 28:18–20
Mark 1:32–34
Mark 3:14–19
Mark 6:34
Mark 10:43–45
Luke 7:22
Luke 10:1–11
Luke 15:3–32
Luke 19:1–10
John 1:9–18
John 5:25–27
John 6:35–40

John 10:7–16
John 17:6–26
Acts 1:6–9
Acts 2:37–42
Acts 9:26–30
Acts 10:34–43
Acts 11:18
Acts 13:1–3
Acts 20:18–28
Romans 1:16
Romans 3:21–26
Romans 5:6–11
Romans 10:9–15
Romans 15:15–21
Romans 16:1–16
1 Corinthians 1:23
1 Corinthians 2:1–4
1 Corinthians 9:19–23
2 Corinthians 5:11–21
2 Corinthians 8:8–9
Galatians 1:6–9
Ephesians 1:3–10
Ephesians 2:13–17
Ephesians 3:7–13
Philippians 2:5–11
Colossians 1:15–20
Colossians 1:29
1 Thessalonians 1:8–10
1 Timothy 1:12–17
2 Timothy 2:1–7
2 Timothy 4:2–5

Money

We all need money and most people want a good income to enjoy a decent standard of living. But money in itself is not real wealth. Money is important to us because of the things it can be exchanged for—such as food, clothing and other possessions. There is very little in the way of material things that money cannot buy. And it can also give us power—power to control our own lives and, when there is a lot of it, power over other people.

Because of the power of money there are some who regard it as evil. There is an old saying: 'Money is the root of all evil.' But this is simply not true. The Bible never condemns money. Some of its great characters—Abraham, Joseph, Job, Joseph of Arimathea—were wealthy people. What the Bible does say is that 'the *love* of money is the root of all evils'. Money itself is neutral, but selfishness and greed can make money a source of evil, with inordinate wealth for some at the expense of crippling poverty for others.

This is not all there is to be said, however. From a Christian perspective, money can be a potent force for good as well as for evil. What is a mature Christian attitude towards it?

■ **God expects us to share our wealth and possessions.** On the whole Christianity has an excellent track record on this issue. Of course there are many Christians who have abused their wealth, but many more have given away their wealth to the poor or have diverted much of it to charitable ends. In our own day it is more crucial than ever that we share our resources with those in need. True treasure, said Jesus, is stored up in heaven and not laid up in banks or building societies. It is the wealth of love, generosity and compassion which endures for ever. Christians should be known for their radical self-giving as Jesus is remembered for his.

The Bible lays down one very clear starting-point for our giving and this is known as the 'tithe' (or tenth part). It ought to be our aim to set aside a tenth of our gross pay for God's work. This is where sacrificial giving starts.

■ **The wealth of society should be distributed evenly.** We cannot support any particular philosophy because some of the socialist systems can be as cruel, heartless and impersonal as the capitalism they are keen to replace. A society which embraces a Christian attitude to life will want to uphold the right of every citizen to a dignified, full existence with adequate medical care, education and housing for all. Such a society will divert resources so that those in need can break out of the poverty trap.

The love of money may be a source of evil. But money can also be a tool with great potential for doing God's work. Let us use it well.

References

Exodus 22:25	Matthew 6:25–33
1 Kings 21:1–15	Luke 6:24
2 Kings 12:4–16	Luke 9:3
1 Chronicles 29:1–18	Luke 12:16–21
2 Chronicles 24:5	Luke 16:19–31
2 Chronicles 24:11	Luke 18:18–30
2 Chronicles 24:14	Luke 19:1–10
2 Chronicles 34:9, 14, 17	Acts 5:1–11
Psalms 15:5	Acts 8:18–20
Proverbs 23:4	2 Corinthians 8:9
Proverbs 28:20	1 Timothy 6:6–10
Ecclesiastes 5:10–12	1 Timothy 6:17–19
Ecclesiastes 5:19	James 1:9–11
Ecclesiastes 7:12	James 2:5–7
Isaiah 55:2	Revelation 3:17–18
Matthew 6:19–21	

The Neighbour

The Old Testament laws include many about 'the neighbour'. The neighbour is the person next door or along the street, the fellow-Israelite, the fellow-citizen or, at a pinch, the visitor who has settled down with you for a while.

Such people must be respected as you would respect yourself. They must be loved in the day-to-day details of life. You are not to steal their spouse, life, property or children. You are not to defraud them in trade, withhold their wages, oppress them with exorbitant rates of interest, curse them if they are deaf or trip them up if blind. You are not secretly to shift their boundary stones to gain extra land, nor give false evidence against them in court, nor even covet anything that rightfully belongs to them.

The neighbour laws were just one of the ways in which Israel was to be 'holy' like her God. The community flourished when people loved their neighbours as themselves. When people were set against their neighbours, it signalled the breakdown of society.

The laws on neighbours were well known. The issue in Jesus' day was about who was to count as a neighbour. Where to draw the line was a matter of intense debate. Most agreed the term included the fellow-Israelite and the convert. Some argued that personal enemies did not count, and others taught that you had a duty to push 'heretics, informers and renegades' *into* the ditch, not pull them out. Pharisees, not surprisingly, excluded non-Pharisees. No one dreamed that Gentiles could ever be neighbours. And there was a saying that 'a piece of bread given by a Samaritan is more unclean than swine's flesh.' Everyone continued to define the exclusion zone.

'Who is my neighbour?' a scribe once asked Jesus. This assumes that you have got to draw the line somewhere. In fact, Jesus refused to answer the question in those terms. Instead he told a story, the Good Samaritan, which was deeply offensive to the hearers, since relations with the Samaritans at that time were particularly bad. The word 'Samaritan' was an obscene insult. The scribe, not wishing to soil his lips, could only manage 'the one who showed mercy' as a description of the neighbour. But this half-breed heretic was a true neighbour according to and even beyond the Law. He had compassion on a man who would have shrunk from his touch had he not been half-dead. The neighbours by race, blood, culture and religion proved false. The 'open cheque' the Samaritan gave to the innkeeper showed that he had never learned to draw a limit to compassion or neighbourliness.

The church picked up her Master's teaching. All the Law is summed up in the command to love our neighbour. Even the riff-raff can love their neighbours and hate their enemies. But what James called 'the royal law' helps me see that my enemy *is* my neighbour.

References

Leviticus 19:18
Deuteronomy 15:7–11
Zechariah 8:10
Matthew 5:43–48
Luke 10:25–37
Romans 13:9
1 Corinthians 10:23–33
Galatians 5:14
Galatians 6:2
Galatians 6:10
Philippians 2:1–4
2 Thessalonians 3:11–15
Hebrews 13:1–2
James 1:27
James 2:1–8
James 2:15–17
1 Peter 3:8–12

The New Creation

Anyone who has felt like saying 'Can we start again, please?' knows how appealing is the thought of a new creation. It speaks to just those longings which are most acute: despair at being locked into old patterns of behaviour, weariness of a life that has become meaningless, memories of past sin and failure which drag us down in the present, a profound sense of loss. 'Behold, I am making everything new,' says God in the Revelation vision, and it is like opening the door into another world. It is almost too good to be true.

Nevertheless, this is the Bible's staggering claim. With the coming of Jesus something radically new exploded on the human scene. He said it was like new wine that would burst the old wineskins; like new cloth ripping away from a threadbare garment; like changing water into wine. Crowds accustomed to careful, cautious teaching were transfixed by his freedom and authority. He turned conventional wisdom on its head. After his death and resurrection it became clear that the powers of the world to come had entered this world. Matthew's version of Jesus' suffering and death stresses that something earth-shattering and life-giving has happened. Jesus has opened up 'a new and living way' into the very presence of God.

The rest of the New Testament looks for other pictures—death to life; darkness to light; bondage to freedom.

Paul was deeply impressed by the transformation that took place when Christ took hold of someone. 'If anyone is in Christ . . .' you can almost hear him thinking, 'it can only properly be compared to a totally new creation.' What God did with chaos at the beginning, when he created something 'good' by word and spirit, he does now in the individual.

'New' is the key word of this experience. In baptism new converts broke decisively with the old life. They 'died' in the water and 'rose' in Christ to live in a completely new way. They had a new song to sing and spoke in new tongues. They were free from the old way of trying and failing to keep the Law or just following the 'cravings of the sinful nature'. They were part of a new community, which crossed the boundaries of class, race, sex and which lived by a new commandment of love. All this was such a change that it seemed right to refer to what had happened as putting off 'the old nature' and putting on the new. Christians were people who had been born all over again!

It is easy to give the impression that that was the end of the matter. But although Paul does not dilute his 'new creation' image, he recognizes that the old personality is still alive and active. Part of the point of telling people about the new beginning they had made was that they should then be able to become (in practice) what they were (in Christ).

A new act of creation had taken place. Now the new nature was to be renewed daily in the image of its creator. This was the work of the Spirit of God, but the individual still had a part to play. When Paul writes about God's work in the new person, he nearly always follows it by practical and specific advice about how life is to be lived.

'All things new.' The sweep of the Bible story extends from first creation to last. One day God will create a new heaven and earth out of the remnants of the old. The created universe will be liberated from its present state of decay and frustration. Death, crying, mourning and pain will be destroyed. The old order will have passed away. What such a new creation means is beyond imagination, but the writer of Revelation is sure that the most important thing about it is that God will be at its heart. 'Can we start again, please?' 'Even so. Come, Lord Jesus.'

References

Isaiah 61:1–3

Isaiah 65:17–25

Jeremiah 31:33

Ezekiel 37:1–10

Matthew 18:1–4

Luke 4:16–21

John 3:3–5

Acts 3:19–21

Romans 6:4

Romans 8:18–23

2 Corinthians 5:17

Colossians 3:1–10

Titus 3:4–7

Revelation 21:1–7

Powers of Evil

We live in a world where evil abounds on all sides and at times it seems to have the upper hand. In the Bible evil is regarded as a malevolent force which is personal in character. The Old Testament occasionally appears to regard evil as under God's control, but when we get into the clearer light of the New Testament it is seen as something quite distinct from Almighty God. Jesus speaks of this world as being under the tyranny of the Evil One whom he calls 'the Prince of this world'. Indeed, Jesus' ministry cannot be fully understood unless we take into account the very significant battle he had with the forces of evil from start to finish. He cast out demons, he spoke about the influence of Satan, and he looked on towards his death as the climax of his struggle with the powers of darkness.

This note is echoed in later New Testament writings. Paul, for example, adopts the language of his day and states that the Christian fights against 'the rulers, the authorities . . . evil in the heavenly realms'. The language suggests that behind the political powers of his day stood spiritual 'powers', controlling them just like a puppeteer with his strings. Nevertheless, Paul has no doubt that the cross of Jesus had shattered their power and influence. He uses a graphic image of the hosts of evil, broken and defeated, trailing behind a victorious Christ like beaten armies behind a triumphant Roman general. But this gives little ground for complacency. The struggle with evil continues until God ushers in his kingdom—only then will come the end when Satan will be cast out for ever. In the meantime, the Christian fights against the desperate powers of evil and must put on the whole armour of God if he or she is going to prevail.

But is this language to be believed these days? There are some Christians who regard this kind of language as 'mythological' or pictorial expression, tied to the New Testament's world-view and not meaningful for us today. (Though many in Third World countries are not so distant from the background of 'demons'.) But it is hard to see how we can eradicate this element from the New Testament as it is so prominent there. A better alternative, perhaps, is to live with the tension that there is in the universe a force of evil which exists to frustrate the plans of a holy God and to plant the seeds of evil everywhere. The forces of good and evil are not equal, otherwise where is our Almighty God? But the battle is still on.

Some cautions are in order when we talk about the devil and the demonic.

■ **Not everything that is bad is necessarily demonic.** Great harm is done to Christian witness by over-credulous Christians who have jumped to the conclusion that all pain, suffering, trouble and strife have demonic origins. We should not attribute responsibility to the devil unless there are real grounds for doing so.

■ **No demon can ever inhabit a Christian.** The testimony of the Bible is against this unlikely idea. If the Holy Spirit of God indwells us the powers of evil cannot live alongside him.

References

Genesis 2:9	*Luke 9:1*
Genesis 2:17	*John 8:44–48*
Genesis 3:5	*John 13:2*
Deuteronomy 1:39	*1 Corinthians 5:5*
1 Samuel 18:10	*Ephesians 4:27*
Job 1:6–12	*Ephesians 6:11–12*
Matthew 4:1–11	*Colossians 2:8–15*
Matthew 7:22	*Hebrews 2:14–15*
Matthew 12:22–29	*1 Peter 5:8*
Matthew 17:18	*1 John 3:8–10*
Mark 1:23–27	*Revelation 2:10*
Luke 4:33–35	*Revelation 12:9–10*
Luke 8:2	*Revelation 20:10*
Luke 8:27–33	

Prayer

Most people pray. Some, it is true, only pray when they are in trouble, but statistics show that many people consider prayer important.

For the Christian, prayer is more than a religious duty—it is his or her native air, a lifeline to God with whom he or she has a permanent relationship of love. This relationship is the start of real believing prayer. Paul tells us that it is the Spirit's job to spark off this prayer life in us: 'Because you are sons, God sent the Spirit of his Son into our hearts, the Spirit who calls out, "Abba Father!" '. Because of this new relationship we have as children to God our 'Father', we can always come into his presence, and we know that he cares intimately for us.

Prayer takes many different forms, of course. One helpful outline of the various forms of prayer is in the letters of the word ACTS—Adoration, Confession, Thanksgiving, Supplication (that is, asking). But fundamental to prayer is conversation. Just as chatter, laughter, talking and asking is the life-blood of normal conversation in any family, so God is anxious for us to speak to him and for this conversation to be as natural as breathing. And God is not the slightest bit interested in the type of language we use when we talk to him. He does not demand liturgical or religious expressions, and he does not pick us up when we make grammatical errors! Because prayer is heart-to-heart sharing with someone we love, we should use language which comes naturally to us.

'Lord, teach us to pray,' asked the disciples. Jesus replied by reciting the Lord's Prayer, more or less implying, 'This should be your pattern.' This great prayer breaks down into seven petitions:

- The first three are concerned with **God's glory—'hallowed be thy name . . .', 'thy kingdom come . . .', 'thy will be done . . .'**

- The next three are to do with **our needs—'give us . . .', 'forgive us . . .', 'protect us . . .'**

- Finally we come back to **God's glory—'thine is the kingdom . . .'**

Here, then, is the Jesus dimension in prayer: to begin with God and his honour. He who taught us to say 'Our Father' is the one who knows that we may rely on God with utter confidence.

But why do we pray? If God is a loving Father, why do we need to go to him with a begging bowl? Yet look at the example of Jesus. He told his disciples, 'Ask, seek, knock,' but just before he had said about human needs: 'Your Father in heaven knows that you need them.' He saw no contradiction between the two things, possibly because prayer is much more than asking God for help. In prayer we enter into his concerns for the world, for others as well as for ourselves. It is a dynamic engagement with the resources of God: not twisting the arm of a reluctant God, but joining in God's spiritual battle against all forces which oppose his kingdom. God will expect us, therefore, to go to him with all our burdens and needs because that is what it means to belong to a family.

And will he give us what we want? God will always hear our prayers—of that we can be sure. But his response will not always be in accord with what we want or when we want it. Because he is the sovereign Lord of all, we must leave him to respond 'according to his will'.

We have said that most people pray. But, to God's great sorrow, and our impoverishment, most of us are mere novices when it comes to prayer. We paddle in the shallows of a relationship with God, when he longs for us to enter into the depths of a vibrant and rich prayer fellowship with him. For that to happen we need to spend time in his presence, just resting, contemplating, questioning, seeking—and finding.

In this, as in any great enterprise, we shall need the help and advice of counsellors and spiritual giants who know more about depths of prayer than we do. These days there are many sources we can go to.

Because prayer is power, God wants to raise up 'prayer warriors' so that they may join him in the spiritual battle against all that opposes his will.

References

Genesis 18:22–33	John 17:1–26
Genesis 32:9–12	Acts 4:31
Exodus 17:11–13	Acts 9:11
Exodus 32:11–13	Acts 10:9
Exodus 33:12–16	Acts 12:5
Judges 16:28	Romans 8:16–17
1 Samuel 1:10–11	Romans 8:26–27
1 Chronicles 29:10–19	Ephesians 1:15–17
Nehemiah 1:5–11	Ephesians 3:14–21
Psalms 57:1–11	Ephesians 6:18
Daniel 9:15–19	Philippians 1:9–11
Jonah 2:1–9	Colossians 1:9–10
Matthew 6:7–15	Colossians 4:3
Matthew 7:7–11	1 Thessalonians 3:10
Matthew 26:39	1 Thessalonians 5:17
Matthew 26:41	1 Timothy 2:1–8
Mark 1:35	James 5:16
Luke 9:28–29	1 John 5:14–15
Luke 11:9–13	Jude 1:20
John 14:13	

Prophecy

Is your church a prophetic church? Or
does that seem a strange question? If so,
how far we are from the times of the
Bible when prophets and prophecy had
great importance.

The word 'prophet' comes from a
root which means 'one who speaks for
another', and during Old Testament
times God raised up many people to
speak for him. 'Thus says the Lord' was
their favourite cry. What were the
characteristics of a prophet?

■ **He challenged the people of God,**
calling them to live according to the
covenant. A strong core of morality
runs through prophetic preaching.
God wanted his people to honour,
love and serve him. The prophet
often came with the call to repent.

■ **He interpreted national and
international events.** In times of
calamity and confusion the prophet
played a major role in interpreting
what God was doing in that situation
and how he wanted his people to
behave.

■ **He foretold the future.** This was not
the prophet's central task, and yet
many prophets did predict the future
with remarkable accuracy.
Sometimes they foretold the near
future so that the fulfilment is
recorded in the same book of the
Bible. Sometimes their predictions
did not come true for centuries, as for

example prophecies of the coming
Messiah.

In Jesus Christ all Old Testament
prophecy was fulfilled. He spoke of John
the Baptist as the last and greatest of the
prophets, the 'forerunner' who brought
the whole tradition to its climax in
heralding the coming of the Son of God.

Yet despite this fulfilment of
prophecy in Christ, we still find
prophets working in the early church.
They did not come with fresh revelation,
because all had been fulfilled in Christ. It
would appear that these prophets were
so open to God and so sensitive to the
Spirit that they acted as spiritual guides
to the early Christians.

Prophecy, too, was one of Paul's 'gifts
of the Spirit'. And many churches today
are discovering the importance of the
prophetic element. This is excellent as
long as certain criteria are kept in mind.
All Christian prophecy must be
anchored in the Bible. It will reach
beyond the merely pietistic and should
speak to real needs in the community.
There is a strong social and political
element in biblical prophecy. The
prophet was someone who stood
between God and the whole nation and
called them back to the Lord.

A church may be prophetic even if it
has no 'prophets'. A prophetic church
will try to listen to what God is calling it
to be, to do and to say in its own context.
When faced with social, political and

human problems the prophetic church
will speak God's word clearly and
boldly, standing up for the under-
privileged and downtrodden.

References

Genesis 20:7	Matthew 21:11
Exodus 7:1	Mark 7:6
Numbers 11:26–27	Luke 1:67
Deuteronomy 13:1–5	Luke 4:17
1 Samuel 3:1	John 4:19
1 Samuel 10:11	John 7:52
1 Kings 18:19–39	John 11:51
1 Kings 22:16	Acts 2:17–18
1 Chronicles 25:1–3	Acts 8:30
Isaiah 9:15	Acts 19:6
Jeremiah 23:16–22	Acts 21:9
Ezekiel 3:4–15	1 Corinthians 12:28
Amos 2:12	1 Corinthians 13:9
Zechariah 13:3–4	1 Corinthians 14:1–3
Matthew 1:22	Ephesians 2:20
Matthew 2:2–6	Ephesians 4:11
Matthew 2:15–17	1 Peter 1:10–12
Matthew 11:9	
Matthew 11:13	

Repentance

You do not always reap exactly what you sow. People are not locked into the mistakes and sins which they committed in the past. They are not trapped and programmed for disaster, because it is possible to repent. And when people repent they prove that the past need not determine the future. The Bible even speaks of God himself 'repenting', changing his course of action, in response to a change of heart. Of course this is picture language, but it is a picture which brings hope and possibility into situations of despair.

To repent is, in essence, to turn around: to turn from our own ways and re-turn to God. It was one of the great cries of the prophets in Israel. As the people of God strayed from the right path, murmured against God and his representatives, went after strange gods, broke the covenant by oppressing their fellow Israelites, played power politics in defiance of their vocation and rebelled against the light, so prophet after prophet called them to turn back and return to the Lord.

Sometimes the repentance was slick and easy and the prophet agonized in God's name over the nation's superficiality. Sometimes it seemed as if they were unwilling to repent at all and the prophet thundered judgment. Sometimes the refusal to turn just seemed inexplicable, flying in the face of nature. But despite the elaborate system of sacrifices, it was true repentance that

wiped the slate clean. There was no sacrifice for 'defiant' sin, but when the sinner acknowledged he had done wrong, God himself would have mercy without sacrifice. In the period between the Old Testament and the New, this truth became a fundamental principle of Judaism.

Against this background John the Baptist called the nation back to God, baptizing penitents to prepare for the crisis of the Messiah's coming with fire. Repentance was also at the heart of Jesus' first preaching, with the same note of urgency and crisis: 'The kingdom of heaven is at hand; repent and believe the gospel.' The prodigal son reaches rock bottom, 'comes to himself' and 'repents' when he turns for home and his father's house. The first Christian sermons called on their hearers to repent and put their faith in Christ.

Repentance must always be genuine. Paul distinguished between grief and godly grief, or remorse and repentance. True repentance shows itself when people change the way they live. Tax-collectors are told not to exact more than is right, soldiers not to be extortionate; Zacchaeus publicly offers to restore four times the amount by which he had cheated people.

It is here that the mystery of repentance is found. It may seem as if this is all a matter of human decision. But the Bible writers always recognized that no one has the power to turn unless God turns them. God must create the clean heart. It is God who takes the initiative, whether it is in the wholehearted and scandalous acceptance of the despised tax-collector Zacchaeus or through the kind but searching questions put to the disloyal disciple Peter. Paul writes, 'The goodness of God leads us to repentance.'

It is wrong to call people to repentance in a context of judgment, condemnation and fear. It is often the prodigal son remembering his father's house, the shepherd searching for the sheep, the look on the face of Christ when Peter had denied him, which break the heart and work the miracle.

References

2 Kings 17:13	Luke 24:47
Nehemiah 1:9	Acts 3:19
Hosea 14:1–2	Acts 17:30
Matthew 3:2	2 Corinthians 7:8–10
Mark 1:14–15	1 Thessalonians 1:9
Luke 3:8	Hebrews 6:1–6
Luke 15:7	

Resurrection

The ancient Easter greeting puts it in a nutshell: 'The Lord is risen'; 'He is risen indeed.' Without the fact of the resurrection, the cross would have been an unmitigated disaster. If Christ did not rise from death then the Christian faith is vain and Jesus becomes one more might-have-been.

The resurrection stories stress the importance of witnesses. The disciples saw an empty tomb, a stone rolled aside, graveclothes. They also met Jesus—in an upper room, by the lakeside, on the road, in a garden. The narratives do not seem to make any distinction between the two sets of experiences. The resurrection is presented as a fact, as something which happened, independently of anyone's inner feelings. Does this mean the tomb was empty? No one supposed that an empty tomb proved the resurrection, of course. And 'resurrection' involves more than a dead body come back to life. But matter still matters. 'Resurrection' in a New Testament sense will not allow the bones of Jesus to be in the tomb at the same time as the disciples were experiencing the 'resurrection appearances'.

In fact you can see the Gospel writers struggling with this problem. They are sure that they have met the same Jesus whom they knew before his death. He is not a ghost, his body bears the marks of crucifixion, he even eats broiled fish and cooks breakfast. But they are equally sure that he is not just the same Jesus, a kind of super-Lazarus, come back to life but doomed to die again in time. Sometimes they seem not to be able to recognize him until the penny drops; he stands in their midst although the doors have been locked. We are meant to conclude that Jesus has passed beyond death into another kind of existence in which his body has been transformed.

This gives us a clue to the meaning of the resurrection. For the first-century Jew, resurrection could only mean the end of the age and the dawning of a new world. Resurrections do not happen inside history; they put an end to history. And the new Christians realized that something literally epochmaking had occurred. From now on, time could be split in two, with Jesus at the midpoint.

The resurrection has something to say, therefore, about the past, the present and the future.

■ **Looking back, the resurrection set the seal on the ministry of Jesus.** His life was given an authoritative interpretation. People might ask, 'Did he teach the truth? Was he who he said he was?' The resurrection answered these questions with a resounding 'yes'. Above everything else it forced the inquirer to make sense of a death which otherwise was no more than another Roman execution.

■ **The resurrection affects the present also, because the Christ who rose is still alive today.** Christians are risen with Christ. Many of the resurrection stories have a meaning for now as well as for then. Of course, they are about the first disciples. But they are also about Christians today, who can still walk with Christ on the road to Emmaus, know him in the breaking of bread, be addressed in their grief (as Mary was), in their doubt (like Thomas) or their remorse (like Peter by the lakeside). The resurrection is the guarantee that nothing can separate us from his love.

■ **And the resurrection looks on into the future, as Paul shows in his idea of the 'firstfruits'.** Jesus is the first of a great harvest. Because Jesus conquered death everyone in Christ will be made alive. This truth underpinned Paul's lifework. No one could say to him, 'Life is pointless. We are all doomed to die. Whatever you do will be lost and utterly forgotten.' Paul would have retorted that because Jesus Christ had risen, and because Christians would one day rise, nothing done 'in the Lord' could ever be in vain.

References

Psalms 16:9–11	*Acts 2:29–32*
Isaiah 26:19	*Romans 1:4*
Matthew 22:23–33	*Romans 6:4*
Matthew 28:1–15	*Romans 8:11*
Mark 16:1–8	*Romans 14:9*
Luke 24:1–43	*1 Corinthians 15:3–23*
John 5:28–29	*1 Corinthians 15:35–58*
John 6:39–40	*2 Corinthians 4:14*
John 11:25–26	*Philippians 3:20–21*
John 20:1–28	*1 Thessalonians 4:13–14*
John 21:1–14	*Revelation 1:17–18*

Salvation

Today 'salvation' has become a mainly religious word. To get a full idea of its meaning in the Bible let us use three other words instead—**deliverance, revolution,** and **wholeness**.

■ **Deliverance.** In the Old Testament the Passover Festival stood for God's deliverance of his people from bondage in Egypt. To this day the Passover for the Jews means 'freedom' because God saved them from a desperate plight when nothing else could have helped. Many times later Israel wandered away from its God and drifted into bondage. Then too, the people cried out for freedom. In the time of Jesus the great longing was for deliverance from the might of Rome, and this was probably in the minds of the Jews when they greeted Jesus on Palm Sunday with the words: 'Hosanna' (meaning 'our God saves')! Blessed is he who comes in the name of the Lord!' No doubt many saw Jesus as the long-awaited deliverer of Israel in a political sense. Jesus rejected this interpretation because it was too narrow. He had come to set people free from everything that dehumanized them and kept them away from God.

■ **Revolution.** Jesus came preaching 'repentance' and 'the kingdom of God'. 'Repentance' means 'turning around' or turning right away from yourself to head in a completely new direction. Jesus' call was, therefore, radical. He called his first disciples away from their houses, jobs and families. When Jesus said to Zacchaeus, 'Today salvation has come to your house', he did not mean an insipid change of lifestyle. He meant revolution.

Jesus still calls people to turn away from themselves to a lifelong discipleship in following a Lord who demands obedience and faithfulness. To say that he is 'Lord' means, in fact that I am now his slave and live to please him. Christians are, therefore, 'turned-around people'. They are always undergoing conversion as they seek to follow their Lord Jesus, or, in other words, they are always entering more fully into their 'salvation'.

■ **Wholeness.** The word 'to save' in the New Testament can also mean 'to heal'. So when people asked Jesus to heal them, they were actually crying out: 'Lord, I want to be made whole.' This is at the very heart of salvation. God is not only interested in our souls, he also wants us whole in body, mind and spirit—fully human, as we were created to be.

Today many churches are rediscovering a healing ministry and praying positively for mental and bodily wholeness. But we have to recognize that even the most spectacular of modern 'healings' fall far short of the mighty works that marked the ministry of Jesus. It is important to bear in mind three things when we engage in the work of healing today. First, Jesus' healings were signs of the kingdom, to show that God has broken into this world through the work of Jesus. Modern healings cannot be signs in quite this unique way. Secondly, we must never separate medical from spiritual healing. Medicine and hospital care are part of God's plan for our wholeness. Thirdly, a balanced understanding of the ministry of healing will bear in mind that salvation is never complete in this life. It looks forward to the future when God will usher in his kingdom and take up his reign. In the meantime we live in a fallen world in which sin, sickness and death are always present. Applying these three great pictures to life today, we can see that 'salvation' should operate on many different levels of human experience. We get a warped idea if we limit it to just one area of life.

Salvation applies to our spiritual lives. It is deeply personal. When Jesus died and rose again, this great deliverance opened for us a new way with God. Many images of this are used in the New Testament: a person is 'born again', made a new being, made free, 'justified', or put right with God. All these rich descriptions reveal the deep changes that take place in the life of the Christian. According to the New Testament this salvation must be allowed to flood every area of my life through the work of the Holy Spirit so that I become a 'whole' person with a transformed mind and heart. This spiritual encounter with the living God is a revolution and should lead to 'turned-around' people.

But salvation applies to social and political life as well. Jesus preached a kingdom which was concerned with the poor, the oppressed and the despised. The good news of the gospel cannot be limited just to the individual or pushed into a future world. The Christian church striving for justice is preaching 'salvation'. The gospel cannot live happily with aspects of life which bind or grind down people made in God's image.

Salvation, then, affects the whole of life. It comes from a great God whose love desires our total wholeness and complete freedom. It comes to us through Jesus, whose name means 'he who saves'.

References

Genesis 3:15	Zechariah 12:10
Genesis 12:1–3	Zechariah 13:1
Genesis 15:6	Matthew 25:31–46
Exodus 12:3–7	Mark 2:5–11
Exodus 14:10–31	Luke 4:16–21
Exodus 18:10	Luke 15:4–32
Exodus 24:6–8	Luke 18:9–14
Leviticus 16:6–22	Luke 18:35–43
Deuteronomy 6:21–23	Luke 19:1–10
Isaiah 51:1–6	John 3:1–17
Isaiah 52:13—53:12	John 4:10–14
Isaiah 55:1–7	John 4:42
Isaiah 61:1–3	John 5:24
Jeremiah 31:31–36	John 6:69
Ezekiel 36:24–30	John 9:35–39
Zechariah 9:9	John 10:10

John 10:27–29
John 17:3
Acts 2:38
Acts 3:13–19
Acts 4:12
Acts 9:3–19
Acts 10:43
Acts 16:22–34
Romans 1:16–17
Romans 3:21–26
Romans 5:1–10
Romans 8:1–4
Romans 10:4–9
1 Corinthians 1:18–25
1 Corinthians 1:30
2 Corinthians 6:2
Galatians 2:20
Galatians 3:13
Galatians 5:1
Ephesians 1:3–14
Ephesians 2:8–10
Philippians 3:4–11

Colossians 1:3–5
Colossians 1:13–23
1 Thessalonians 1:10
1 Timothy 1:15
1 Timothy 2:3–5
1 Timothy 4:10
2 Timothy 1:9–10
Titus 3:4–7
Hebrews 2:3–4
Hebrews 2:9–10
Hebrews 9:23–28
1 Peter 1:3–9
1 Peter 1:18–23
1 Peter 2:2–4
1 Peter 2:21–25
1 Peter 3:18–22
1 John 3:1–8
1 John 3:16
1 John 4:9–10
Revelation 7:9–11
Revelation 12:10–11

Sexuality

'If it's fun, stop it.' Many people assume that this is the kind of thing the Bible says about sex. In fact, what it teaches about this aspect of our humanity is positive, perceptive and profoundly realistic.

- **Sexuality is part of our wholeness.** It is in the union of male and female that the 'one flesh' is to be found. God created humankind 'in his own image', but the image consists of 'male and female taken together' not in either to the exclusion of the other. So Paul grasps the liberating truth that the man's body belongs to the woman and the woman's body to the man. The image of God can be expressed through such a partnership and co-operation with another.

- **The act of sex is also a great mystery.** It is one of the most profound ways of knowing another person. Indeed to 'know' is a way of speaking of sexual intercourse. The love of God for Israel is pictured as a marriage. The church is the bride of Christ. Paul argues that you cannot join your body to that of a prostitute without damaging the intimate relationship which the Christian has with Christ. Sex ought never to be seen as a purely physical release. It always has profound effects on our personalities.

- **Erotic love is one of God's gracious gifts to humanity.** The Song of Songs is a hymn in praise of erotic love. It is not, as some Christians have tried to argue, primarily an allegory of God's love for the soul. The song rejoices in sexuality without shame or guilt, in a way which, at times, has been too uninhibited for the church's taste. But Christians ought not to be more 'pure' or 'spiritual' than God himself!

- **Along with this high view of sex goes a realistic understanding of its dangerous power.** Sex is always on the point of claiming godlike power over us and reducing us to slavery. This was literally so in some of the pagan cults of Bible times which depersonalized people through cult prostitution. And it is so today in the pornography industry. But Jesus alone is Lord, not the gods and goddesses of sex.

The Bible's teaching on the single state is entirely in keeping with this. Sexual experience is a grace but it is not the only way to wholeness. People may choose to remain unmarried with no personal loss (and indeed there may be gain to themselves and their service of Christ). The incarnation shows that we do not need to be sexually active to find perfect love, maturity and fulfilment. Jesus was not less 'whole' because he never married.

It is because of the intimate connexion between sex and personality that the Bible hedges the act with so many rules. Sexuality must be expressed in its proper setting—that of husband and wife within marriage. Because sex is so close to the divine and to the demonic, so beautiful yet so dangerous, it must be as carefully insulated as any radioactive material. Hence the prohibitions on sexual acts that deviate from the 'marriage' model. Such acts are condemned as sin.

Yet Jesus offered the sexual sinner not rejection, but love, forgiveness and acceptance. The Samaritan woman, the adulteress and the prostitutes were called to turn from their sin and follow him.

References
Genesis 2:24
Proverbs 5:18–19
Songs 1:1
Matthew 5:28
1 Corinthians 6:18–19
1 Corinthians 7:3–5
1 Thessalonians 4:3–6

Sin

'Sin,' declared G.K. Chesterton, 'is the most demonstrable of all Christian doctrines.' He meant that we do not need to prove the doctrine of original sin—the evidence is all around us.

The Bible teaches about sin on two different levels: original sin and individual sin.

■ **Original sin** means that when Adam and Eve fell, their act of disobedience affected the whole human race. Of course there is disagreement about just how to understand the story at the beginning of Genesis. Is it describing the fall of a real couple called Adam and Eve? Or is it rather a great poetic drama about every person's sin and guilt before God? Either way the story of Adam and Eve is a profound account of humanity's greatest tragedy—our separation from a good and holy God.

The essence of sin is brought out clearly and is made up of two parts, unbelief and pride. First of all, God's word is denied. The tempter questions, 'Has God said?' God's clear command is brushed aside through the voice of doubt. Then comes the second element in sin—pride: 'When you eat (of the fruit of that tree) you will be like God . . .' Here, then, is the irony of human revolt against God. We want to break free of God and his restrictions. But we end up falling into a real bondage, one which binds our wills, our hearts and our minds.

■ **Individual sin** is the working out of this pattern in the lives of us all, in our own unbelief and pride. So we find ourselves daily living the tragedy of sin, wanting to be better people but failing to live up to our good intentions. First we say: 'It is so difficult to believe in God.' But what we may mean is: 'I don't want to obey God.' Again we say: 'I don't want to be a slave to God: I want to be free to be myself.' But we are by nature worshippers. Either we worship God or we worship false gods. Today's false gods include money, sex, prosperity and power. We extend their influence by creating pseudo-faiths such as Communism, totalitarianism and nationalism.

Such, then, are the chains of sin. They bind so tight that no one can break free by himself or herself. As Jesus himself pointed out, sin is not external to us so that it can be washed away; it arises from our hearts and minds. And Paul voiced the agony of many a human heart: 'What a wretched man I am! Who will rescue me from this body of death?'

Paul, of course, answers his own question firmly and triumphantly—Jesus Christ can and will rescue us. The death of Jesus is the only place where we can find forgiveness for our sin and strength to overcome it. Only the cross can free us from the power of evil.

It is easy to forget that Christ's battle against sin, the world and the devil still continues, and that we are on the front line fighting with him in the power of the cross. We live in a sin-shot world, its beauty and goodness distorted by sin and sometimes made very ugly. Political and social structures too often display sin's cancerous presence. This fact will make the mature Christian into a realist. He or she will never disregard the existence of evil: it will never stop spoiling the best human beings can do. But also the Christian will never allow sin the last word. Jesus Christ has ultimately conquered sin.

References

Genesis 3:1–7	*Daniel 9:16*
Genesis 4:7	*Micah 1:5*
Genesis 6:5–7	*Matthew 1:21*
Exodus 32:21–30	*Matthew 3:6*
Leviticus 4:3	*Matthew 26:28*
Leviticus 4:13	*Mark 1:4*
Leviticus 4:27	*Mark 2:5–7*
Leviticus 5:1–6	*Mark 7:14–23*
1 Kings 8:34	*John 1:29*
1 Kings 15:30	*John 3:16–21*
2 Chronicles 25:4	*Acts 2:38*
2 Chronicles 28:10	*Romans 3:23–25*
Nehemiah 1:6	*Romans 5:12–13*
Psalms 32:1–5	*Romans 6:1–6*
Psalms 51:5–9	*Romans 8:2–3*
Psalms 103:10	*Galatians 1:4*
Proverbs 10:12	*Galatians 2:17–21*
Proverbs 14:34	*Titus 3:11*
Isaiah 1:16–18	*Hebrews 1:3*
Isaiah 38:17	*Hebrews 7:27*
Isaiah 53:10–12	*Hebrews 10:2*
Jeremiah 5:23	*1 Peter 2:22–24*
Jeremiah 5:25	*1 Peter 3:18*
Jeremiah 17:9–10	*1 John 1:7–10*
Ezekiel 3:20	*1 John 3:8*

Spiritual Gifts

The first gift the Christian receives is the gift of the Holy Spirit. He comes to every Christian who opens his or her life to Jesus Christ. He works in our lives, deepening our love for Jesus, and honing our abilities and gifts in his service.

The clearest teaching about the gifts given by the Holy Spirit is found in 1 Corinthians 12, though there are also lists in Romans 12, Ephesians 4, and 1 Peter 4. The church of Corinth had a problem, one stemming from their very success. To their great joy they found that their faith actually worked! Things started to happen. There were those who discovered that they had gifts of healing, prophecy, teaching, miracle-working, tongues-speaking, leadership and so on. So great was the Spirit's generosity that his 'anointing' came on many in the fellowship. But instead of these wonderful experiences leading to greater service for Christ and deeper humility, those who received gifts used them to boost themselves, with the result that selfishness, pride and envy began to split the fellowship open. Paul has to remind them strongly that gifts are given by God—Father, Son and Spirit—and they do not originate from us. And they are to be used for one another, strengthening the limbs and organs in the single body of Christ—the church.

Paul makes no tidy classification of the gifts. But for the sake of convenience they can be separated into two kinds:

■ **Speaking gifts.** Among other gifts of speech, Paul mentions teaching, speaking in tongues and prophecy, which are gifts fit to be used in the congregation. 'Tongues' is a gift which has perplexed many. It seems to be a special language given to individuals for praise, worship and strengthening. Sometimes it bubbles forth in ecstatic utterances. Paul does not deprecate the gift but he does deplore people using it for their own sake. He therefore instructs that when it is used in the congregation it must be interpreted. 'Prophecy' is not another form of preaching but, more probably, a special message from God about the spiritual needs of the congregation.

■ **Action gifts.** Paul mentions a number of gifts which are also channels of the Spirit's power but where the emphasis falls on what is done rather than on what is said: healing, miracle-working, helping others and even administration—a much neglected gift.

It would be unwise to expect the experience of the Corinthians to be reproduced in exactly the same form today. 'The Spirit blows where he wills,' and refuses to be confined to what we expect. Yet still he gives gifts which match our needs today.

It is just as important for us as for the Corinthians to heed the controls that Paul set around the use of the gifts in the congregation.

First, they were to be used to build up others. The purpose of spiritual gifts is service. Paul rebukes those 'speakers-in-tongues' whose enthusiasm was hindering the church. We, too, should be cautious of any gift which appears to divide the congregation or exalt the user. We will want to ask: Does this gift build up the life of our church?

Next comes the principle of love. The gifts will pass away when their work is done, but love lasts for ever. What is more, Paul argues, without love to guide and control, spiritual gifts have no more value than the noise of a clanging gong. Alongside his teaching about spiritual gifts, Paul sets a most wonderful passage on the nature of Christian love. Some have suggested that it is modelled on the person and work of Jesus Christ, in whom we find that perfect balance of giftedness and sacrificial love.

And another essential control in the use of gifts is that of order. Paul does not want to freeze out any genuine gift; rather, he wants them to flourish within an ordered spiritual quietness in the fellowship. Speaking in tongues, prophecy and other expressions of the Spirit's activity are allowed in worship, but Paul brings them under sensible control so that all may benefit.

And what about our own experience? Our situation may be the opposite of that of the church at Corinth. Instead of the Spirit working in profusion there may be deadness, dull order instead of spontaneity, apathy instead of eager expectancy. But the Holy Spirit never gives up on the church, and we should never cease to love, pray and hope that God's gifts may flourish in abundance where we are.

References

Exodus 31:1–5
Judges 6:34
Judges 14:6
1 Samuel 16:6
Isaiah 11:2
Joel 2:28
Haggai 1:14
Matthew 25:14–30
Luke 11:13
Acts 2:17
Acts 8:17–21
Romans 12:3–8
1 Corinthians 12:1–13
1 Corinthians 12:27–30
1 Corinthians 14:14–16
Ephesians 1:17
Ephesians 4:11–12
Ephesians 4:30
2 Timothy 1:7
1 Peter 4:10–11

The State

'You would have no power at all over me if it were not given you from above.' On trial for his life and in the presence of the representative of the most powerful state on earth, Jesus sets the whole issue of government and authority in perspective. 'The authorities that exist have been established by God,' wrote the apostle Paul, but real power belongs to God alone.

God, then, has higher power and authority than any state. How does this truth affect us as we live under the authority of governments which range, today as in Bible days, from the benevolent to the oppressive?

- **The Bible teaches that every state will be called to account by God.** It was his laws which defined Israel's existence and ruled her national life. This meant that the nation could be attacked by the prophets whenever she fell short of her calling.

But God is not a local deity. States which knew next to nothing about his Law were condemned for war atrocities—not against Israel or Judah, but against other heathen nations. There could hardly be a more dramatic illustration of the truth that power is delegated by the God of the whole earth. Similarly, God is prepared to use foreign states and rulers for his own purpose, for punishing his people or for liberating them. Always, however, the state is subject to God's power. The taunt songs against Nineveh and Babylon are some of the most terrifying pieces of literature in the Old Testament.

- **Christians are to have respect for government.** In the New Testament, the state still exercises power by God's permission and, for the most part, exercises it responsibly. Paul is impressed by a framework of law and order which allows right to be rewarded and wrong punished. The author of Acts is careful to point out how the Roman authorities were just, and sympathetic to the Christian cause. Peter argues, 'Who is going to harm you if you are eager to do good?' And so the Christians are told to be subject to the state, to respect and pray for its leaders, pay its taxes and make use of its amenities in the service of the gospel. Jesus did not accept the way of violent resistance and even suggested that there were many duties which were owed to Caesar (by which he meant state authority).

- **And yet, because they are 'a colony of heaven', Christians' primary loyalty is to God alone.** With a cool realism the Bible perceives that power corrupts and that any state can start to demand what belongs exclusively to God. Rulers can strut and posture as if they were divine; they can oppress the innocent, crush the weak, stifle the voice of protest and persecute the church. It was a king misnamed 'the Great' who slaughtered the children of Bethlehem, and 'the rulers of this age' who crucified the Lord of glory. At such a terrible time Christians are called to obey God rather than men, to bear witness to their faith, to endure to the end and, if necessary, seal their witness with their blood.

This is not the end of the matter, however. The New Testament contains its own taunt song, in the Book of Revelation, written when the Roman state had begun a cruel persecution of the Christians. The writer sees a terrible vision of the fall of the latter-day Babylon. The powers of the evil state are crushed in the end. Jesus alone is King of kings and Lord of lords.

References

Nehemiah 2:1–8	Acts 17:26
Isaiah 10:5–6	Acts 19:35–41
Isaiah 45:1–8	Romans 13:1–7
Jeremiah 29:7	Philippians 3:20
Daniel 7:23–27	Colossians 2:15
Nahum 3:16–19	1 Timothy 2:1–4
Mark 12:13–17	1 Peter 2:13–17
John 19:10–11	Revelation 11:15
Acts 5:27–29	Revelation 18:1–24

Suffering

'Suffering is the greatest barrier that stops people believing in a loving heavenly Father.' Those who have suffered or have watched others suffer understand this fully. Job's wife could come out with nothing better than, 'Curse God and die.' Job himself grieved that he was ever born and longed 'for a death that will not come'. There can be few who have not asked, 'Why doesn't God do something?'

Although the Bible does not give a direct, intellectual answer to the question of suffering, yet it is possible to draw out some of its insights. First, some suffering comes because human beings have free wills. God has given to humanity a delegated freedom. Adam and Eve may choose either to till the garden or to take of the forbidden fruit. The rulers of this world are free to 'crucify the Lord of glory'. In the story, the prodigal son is free to squander his inheritance in a far country. This is a real freedom. And some kinds of suffering— from war, for instance, or from injustice—are the result of human abuse of this freedom to choose.

The second insight, perhaps more difficult to understand, is that this world is a fallen world. There are some mysterious verses in Paul's letter to the Romans where the apostle suggests that the creation is 'frustrated', 'in bondage to decay'. Sin affects the created world. 'Thorns and briars' grow in the 'garden of the Lord'. It is just possible to see from this how some pain, suffering, disease or natural disaster might be explained. The creation is no longer as it should be; it is somehow spoiled through sin.

Thirdly, we ought not to soften the biblical truth that, in a moral universe, suffering is sometimes the result of sin. This world is a stable world, regular and predictable. It is this which makes real choices possible. But its very regularity means that the fire which warms may also burn and that a sinful life may carry its own retribution within it.

All this is on a mental level, and so of little comfort to those who are actually suffering or watching others suffer. For them the Bible has a different word, which speaks to our faith.

■ **Christ has died, so he understands our pain.** It is easy to forget that at the heart of Christianity is a crucified God. God does not watch his suffering world with detachment. He comes into people's pain; agonizes and bleeds with them. This is the way he has chosen to repair the damage—by working patiently and painfully inside the problem.

■ **Christ is risen, so no one suffers alone.** If Jesus is alive then something good can be brought out of suffering. Even for Jesus there were some things that could only be learned through suffering. Paul discovered that God's grace was enough for him only through being tormented by a thorn in the flesh. Christians are called to believe, sometimes in the teeth of the evidence, that God can transform every situation.

■ **Christ will come again, so suffering cannot be the last word.** One day the universe will be redeemed, the lame leap, the dumb sing. The New Testament ends with the vision of a day when 'God will wipe every tear from their eyes' and 'there will be no more death or mourning or crying or pain'.

References

Job 1:1
Psalms 66:10–12
Isaiah 50:6–8
Isaiah 53:1–12
Lamentations 3:22–58
Mark 8:34–35
Mark 13:5–13
Mark 14:32–36
John 19:1–30
Romans 8:22–23
2 Corinthians 1:3–9

2 Corinthians 11:23–28
2 Corinthians 12:7–10
Philippians 1:29
Colossians 1:24
1 Timothy 2:3
Hebrews 5:8
Hebrews 12:2–11
1 Peter 1:6–7
1 Peter 2:18–25
Revelation 21:4

War and Peace

Did you know that at this present moment at least twenty wars are being fought around the world? Peace seems to be the exception, not war. In spite of our many achievements, humankind cannot find the answer to conflict. We may be able to split the atom but we do not know how to bring together bitterly divided people.

The Christian approach to war and peace is found in the character of God. The Bible describes him as the 'God of peace'. But it also calls him a 'Warrior'. How do we reconcile these two apparent opposites?

The answer is found when we identify the enemy with which God is at war—all forms of injustice, wrongdoing and sin. Instead of keeping himself immune from conflict, God is deeply immersed in battle against the forces of evil. The ministry of Jesus illustrates this. In his works he was in conflict with the various disorders which imprison people; in his words he battled with sin, especially the hypocrisy and practical godlessness of religious people. The final showdown came in his death when he met the full fury of evil and 'made peace through the blood of his cross'. His first words to his disciples after his resurrection were 'Peace be with you', signalling that his victory had brought harmony and reconciliation between God and humankind.

What does this imply for Christians today?

■ **We are involved in God's war.** Followers of Christ are part of God's army fighting against all that opposes his rule. There will only ever be real peace when sin is defeated—sin in human relationships, sin in social life and sin in political structures. Just as Jesus was not slow to speak out against all that oppressed people, so his followers should not be afraid to oppose sin in whatever guise it comes.

■ **We are peacemakers.** The Christian fights best when he or she announces peace, not war. And to drive home this point, Jesus gave the radical teaching that when we are struck on one cheek we should offer the other to the smiter! By this he meant that a positive approach to peace, which was certainly not cowardice or passive submission, was ten times better than violence.

■ **We use the weapons of peace**, as Jesus did: clear teaching which confronts hypocrisy and wrongdoing, a willingness to speak to our 'enemies' and address them with love, understanding and respect; a desire to negotiate rather than drive people away. The Old Testament prophesied that one day only 'peace-weapons' will remain, when swords are beaten into ploughshares.

■ **Violence will always be the last resort.** Christians are divided over the question whether violence is ever justified. There are those who say that Christians should be pacifists, and this tradition is long and honourable. However, I am convinced that when evil comes in its starkest forms which will not listen to the voice of reason, which refuse to negotiate, and which trample down the innocent and defenceless, then there may be cause for citizens to defend themselves and the values which they believe in passionately. This argument is usually called the 'Just War' theory. It asserts that war is only ever justified when four conditions are met. The cause must be just; war must be absolutely the last resort, when all other avenues to avoid conflict have failed; conflict must not involve noncombatants; war should be limited in its scope, avoiding unnecessary loss of life and destruction. It is a large question whether these last two conditions can ever be met in modern, especially nuclear, warfare.

But the Christian's primary commitment is, of course, to peace, and it should be our earnest desire to play a full part in God's battle against the visible and invisible forces which tear this planet apart. The good news is that God is going to have the last word. Sin, death and evil will be defeated and God's reign of peace in all its fulness will one day be a reality. That's worth working for!

References

Exodus 15:3
Deuteronomy 1:41
1 Samuel 17:33
2 Samuel 1:27
2 Samuel 22:35
Psalms 85:10
Psalms 122:6
Psalms 147:14
Ecclesiastes 9:18
Isaiah 2:1–4
Isaiah 9:6–7
Isaiah 32:17
Isaiah 48:22
Isaiah 57:19

Isaiah 66:12
Jeremiah 6:4
Ezekiel 34:25
Malachi 2:6
Matthew 24:6–8
Luke 1:79
Luke 2:14
Luke 19:42
Romans 3:17
Romans 15:33
Ephesians 2:14–17
Ephesians 6:15
Hebrews 7:2
Revelation 6:4

Work and Rest

For some people a job is no more than a nasty interruption of their social life; they cannot wait for Friday night. The Bible's view of work will seem peculiar to them, for the Bible approves of work. God himself is a worker. In the beginning God made the heavens and the earth and he takes pleasure in what he has made. And Jesus spent a good proportion of his life working as a carpenter.

Working, then, is part of what it means to be made in God's image; God works and he gives us the privilege of working. If this is the true perspective on work, then certain important things follow:

■ **It is through our work that we can glorify God.** 'Whatever your hand finds to do, do it with all your might.' 'Do everything in the name of the Lord Jesus.'

■ **Work is also one way in which we can co-operate with God in his rule over creation.** The earliest picture of the relationship between God and humanity is Adam and Eve in a garden—an image of God's life-giving power ('I give you ... every seed-bearing plant') coupled with human responsibility ('till the ground ... subdue the earth'). It is a partnership. God does not do it all himself, nor can we act as if we own the place. Stewardship is the key idea. A steward is in total charge of a project, but he knows that one day he will be called to give an account of how he has discharged his responsibilities.

■ **Our work plays its part in fulfilling our humanity.** It is not good for someone to be idle, and unemployment can be a very reducing experience. The Bible has a high regard for skilled craftsmen, the sort of people who use their talents to make music or build and beautify the temple. 'There is nothing better for a man than to enjoy his work,' says the writer of Ecclesiastes.

■ **And work, of course, is a way of serving others.** 'Work,' writes the apostle Paul, 'so that you may have something to share with those in need.'

This is the ideal. However, the Bible is nothing if not realistic. Work is not always fulfilling and deeply satisfying. Like everything else it has become contaminated by human sin. This is expressed vividly in the Adam and Eve story as God's curse on the ground. What should be joyful labour becomes painful drudgery and toil. So work, like many of God's good gifts, can become a means of exploiting people or even enslaving them. It can be perverted into a way of satisfying greed or hunger for power. In the end something which was meant to fulfil our humanity can degenerate into trudging round a soul-destroying treadmill. And those who have no paid work can find themselves devalued by society.

Work was not the whole story even from the very beginning, however. In a profound insight, the creation story pictures God resting from his labours on the seventh day. Life is meant to have a rhythm of work and rest, of creation and re-creation. So we are given the sabbath. Far from preventing people enjoying themselves, the sabbath was to ensure that people *did* enjoy themselves. It was a day of joy and delight. Even the animals and the soil were given a holiday.

People were not created slaves. It is right that we should serve God in our work but we should also enjoy him in our worship. God did not make people to wander in a wilderness of restlessness. It is good to work hard, but it is also good to discover a still point for our lives by taking time out to rest in God. Only then do we live out the truth to which the rhythm of work and sabbath points.

References

Exodus 20:8–11

Exodus 23:10–12

Exodus 31:1–11

Deuteronomy 16:8

1 Kings 17:13–14

Ecclesiastes 3:22

Ecclesiastes 5:18–20

Ephesians 4:28

Colossians 3:23–24

2 Thessalonians 3:6–13

Hebrews 3:11

Hebrews 4:3–10

Worship

To worship means 'to give God honour' and acknowledge his worth. When we worship, then, we are more or less saying to God: 'Thank you for all you have done for us and given us. Help us to put you first in our daily lives.'

The first Christians were Jews and used to worshipping the God of all creation. But so great was the impact of Jesus Christ on their lives that he turned upside down their understanding of worship; he himself became the centre of their worship along with the Father and the Spirit. Prayer was offered in the name of Jesus and hymns sung in his honour. For example, the famous description of Christ in Paul's letter to the Philippians was almost certainly an early Christian hymn and one well known to Paul's readers. At their baptism, Christians declared 'Jesus is Lord' and so made clear the centrality of Jesus in worship.

The focal point of worship in the New Testament is the Lord's Supper, the thanksgiving meal (eucharist). (See further *Breaking Bread*.)

Worship, then, is our response to what God has done and continues to do. But we must work out in our own culture just how worship is to be carried out, applying principles of New Testament insight.

■ **Is worship to be formal or informal?**
The church of the New Testament had no developed forms of ministry or worship. To judge from Paul's first letter to the Corinthian church, worship was largely improvised with a great deal of freedom of expression and with a vivid awareness of the presence of the Spirit in power. Paul's letter shows that he was not altogether happy with complete spontaneity which, instead of leading to real 'Spirit freedom', resulted in bondage for many. He gently suggests some controls so that all the Christians might feel equally at home.

The Bible gives no norms for worship, which varied according to place and culture. And so surely we should be extremely careful about expressing judgments as to whether any particular style of worship is 'right' or 'wrong'. In our own day some prefer their worship to be offered with full and rich ceremonial—with choirs, processions, vestments and other ritual forms. Others, however, like it plain, with lots of participation, hearty singing and, perhaps, the raising of hands in adoration. Both styles are correct according to the needs of the worshippers, realizing that temperament and culture are important factors to be considered. Some cultures will want it 'high and hazy', other cultures 'low and lazy'. What is important is that our worship should be relevant to the congregation and its culture—otherwise it will not be authentic.

■ **What importance have buildings?**
Christianity began as a non-religious type of faith. Because Jesus had brought a complete salvation and opened the door to the Father, Christians had no need for the temple, a sacrificing priesthood or even religious buildings! Because the first Christians did not conform to contemporary religious ideas they were called 'atheists'! It is a sad irony today that people outside the church identify a congregation by a building rather than by a people.

Now buildings clearly help. To have a base, a home which the family may adapt to express a living faith and where others can be brought in is nothing but gain. But buildings can also become hindrances. We may end up caring more for the building than the gospel and more for our traditions than the Lord of the traditions. We are called not to be museum tenders but a people willing to share our faith in a living Lord.

■ **What makes living worship?** Just as there are no hard and fast laws about the structure of worship, so there are no laws as to what must be included. Certain elements, however, stand out in New Testament church life and demand attention. The first Christians worshipped with grateful and joyful hearts. No one could accuse them of dullness! Paul writes: 'Sing psalms, hymns and sacred songs; sing to God with thanksgiving in your hearts.' Should not joy and praise be a fixed feature in our worship too?

Then again, receiving instruction in the faith appears to have been another important ingredient. This would account for the emphasis placed on teachers and prophets in the early church. Their role was to build up the congregation through their ministry. So today, a church which neglects instruction and sound learning will produce immature and weak Christians. Another element would have been prayers of intercession and confession.

But without any question, the pinnacle of praise and adoration would have been when the New Testament Christians broke bread together and celebrated their 'eucharist'. Let us note, finally, a refreshingly relaxed and unfussed air about the New Testament approach to worship. It was their response in love to Jesus, and love cannot be bound with rules and regulations.

References

Genesis 12:1–9	Matthew 2:2
Genesis 28:10–17	Matthew 2:8
Exodus 3:1–6	Matthew 2:11
Exodus 4:31	Matthew 4:9–10
Exodus 40:16–33	Matthew 28:16–17
Deuteronomy 29:25–26	Mark 5:6
Joshua 5:14	Luke 2:13–14
1 Samuel 1:3	John 4:20–24
1 Kings 18:20–39	John 9:38
1 Chronicles 16:7–42	John 17:1–5
1 Chronicles 29:20	Acts 2:43–47
Nehemiah 8:6	Acts 16:25
Psalms 15:1–5	Acts 17:23
Psalms 48:1–3	Philippians 3:3
Psalms 66:4	Colossians 3:16
Psalms 95:1–7	Revelation 4:8–11
Jeremiah 26:2	Revelation 22:8–9
Zechariah 14:16	

Index